Paul Stapfer

Shakespeare and Classical Antiquity

Greek and Latin Antiquity as Presented in Shakespeare's Plays

Paul Stapfer

Shakespeare and Classical Antiquity
Greek and Latin Antiquity as Presented in Shakespeare's Plays

ISBN/EAN: 9783337274627

Printed in Europe, USA, Canada, Australia, Japan

Cover: Foto ©Thomas Meinert / pixelio.de

More available books at **www.hansebooks.com**

SHAKESPEARE

AND

CLASSICAL ANTIQUITY

GREEK AND LATIN ANTIQUITY AS PRESENTED

IN SHAKESPEARE'S PLAYS

(CROWNED BY THE FRENCH ACADEMY)

BY

PAUL STAPFER

PROFESSOR AT THE FACULTÉ DES LETTRES OF GRENOBLE

TRANSLATED FROM THE FRENCH BY

EMILY J. CAREY

LONDON

C. KEGAN PAUL & CO., 1, PATERNOSTER SQUARE

1880

TRANSLATOR'S PREFACE.

———◆◇◆———

A FEW words to explain why it has been thought well to add, to the already overwhelming number of Shakespeare studies, this translation of the first part of M. Stapfer's "Shakespeare et l'Antiquité," seem not uncalled for in these days, when Shakespeare criticism has already reached such huge proportions as to cause its very name to be received with a half weary, half impatient sigh.

We have heard a good deal lately of German commentators on Shakespeare, but no word has for a long time come to us from France—that land peculiarly famed for literary skill and for acute and delicate criticism; and, therefore, to hear what one of the first French literary critics of the day has to say concerning our great English poet can hardly fail to be of great interest and value.

Moreover, the subject of M. Stapfer's book—not Shakespeare, but Greek and Roman antiquity as represented in Shakespeare's plays—invests it with a special character, and offers many fresh and suggestive points of view; the comparative smallness of the framework admitting also of a more minute and thorough mode of treatment than would otherwise be possible.

That his book should contain any facts or details possessing the charms of novelty for English readers is scarcely likely—the facts of a man's history offer but little scope for invention,—but the point of importance with the literary critic is the use to which the facts are put, and his chief concern with otherwise trivial and time-worn details is to make them full of fresh interest and life for us, by ordering and manipulating them so as to bring the truths they serve to illustrate, or to suggest, into clear and unmistakeable prominence. Unless they float, as it were, upon a sea of thought, in the midst of fresh and invigorating breezes, among the currents and tides of conflicting opinions and ideas, they are altogether vapid and useless to him.

For those readers who only care for discussion of some obscure passage or obsolete word, there will, I fear, be nothing but disappointment in store; the aim of the book is of a purely literary character, and it offers no information of an etymological or philological nature. But though this may render it valueless to one class of readers, it enables it, I trust, to appeal the more surely to those by whom literature—in contradistinction to science, history, and to all books written entirely for the sake of imparting information, without the devotion of any special care to the manner in which the information is given—is prized as one of the most precious forms of art.

It is no easy task to translate a book in which so great a part is played by the style of the author, the charm of which, with all its lightness, point, and grace, it must be vain to hope to render in a translation. I have endeavoured, as far as might be, to convey some slight notion of it, and although the echoes of the original sound can, at best, be only few and faint, I hope the impression may somehow make itself felt that the book in its original form aims at being a work of art.

The work to which M. Stapfer has given the title of " Shakespeare et l'Antiquité," consists of two distinct and independent parts. The first part—" Greek and Latin Antiquity as presented in Shakespeare's Plays "—

which forms the subject of the present volume, is simply, as M. Stapfer says in his preface, a study of one aspect of Shakespeare's work and genius, which necessitates an examination of only seven of his plays.   The second part—"Shakespeare and the Greek Tragedians " *—embraces a wider horizon.   It is a general history of the changes undergone by dramatic art, comparing, in a series of essays, ancient tragedy with modern tragedy; it is a work in which Shakespeare is, rightly speaking, the centre, rather than the precise and actual subject. M. Stapfer continues, "There yet remained to be done for comedy what had been done for tragedy : 'Shakespeare and the Greek Tragedians' might naturally be expected to be followed by 'Shakespeare and Aristophanes,' but a comparison drawn between these two poets hardly offers sufficiently fertile grounds to justify such a title; and I have therefore preferred that of 'Molière, Shakespeare, et la Critique Allemande,' which appears as a separate work at the end of 'Shakespeare et l'Antiquité.' "

It only remains for me to add, that wherever I have in any way deviated from the text, whether by the omission or by the insertion of a few words here and there—which, however, has very seldom been the case,— it has been with the full knowledge and sanction of the author.

EMILY J. CAREY.

* This second part has already been published in Paris; its future appearance in English depends upon various circumstances.

CONTENTS.

SHAKESPEARE

AND

CLASSICAL ANTIQUITY.

INTRODUCTORY.

SHAKESPEARE is justly considered to be the most perfect
representative of the modern or romantic Drama as
distinguished from ancient or classical tragedy on the
one hand, and from neo-classic tragedy on the other; but
the question arises how he came to give this character
to his plays—whether it was from indifference or from
choice. The point to be considered is whether he simply
followed the traditions handed down to him, without
any knowledge of classical antiquity, and with no
classical books or even imitations of classical authors
within his reach; or whether, on the contrary, his
learning gave him access to the originals, and whether
classical imitations and lectures on the doctrines of Greek
and Latin authors were familiar to him. In order
thoroughly to answer the question whether it was with
full knowledge of the subject and well-considered determination that he struck out into new paths of his

B

own, it will be necessary to inquire how far England participated in the great European movement of the Renaissance, and what the average level of classical learning was in Shakespeare's time. We shall also have especially to examine into the state of the Drama, with regard to plays written in imitation of Greek and Latin writers, and to learn whether classical theories were expounded and commended by professors of the poetic art. An attempt must further be made, by means of such authentic information as we possess of Shakespeare's life, and above all, by the help of the indications his works themselves furnish us with, to measure the extent of his literary knowledge, and in some sort to form his library anew, to follow him into the circles where he might hear classical works discussed, and penetrate into his solitude when deep in the perusal of his favourite authors;—but here we are treading simply on conjecture, and returning to more solid ground, must endeavour, wherever it is possible to discover any trace or expression of it, to sound his real feeling with regard to the ancients and their modern partisans.

In the multiform and varied world of his plays, Shakespeare introduces many of the names and personages belonging to antiquity—a subject which occupied his attention from the beginning of his literary activity, and indeed especially at the beginning, as is shown by his descriptive poems of "Venus and Adonis," and "Lucrece," which, at least in their title and motive, are respectively Greek and Latin, and belong, as do also the sonnets, to the Italian school of poetry, the influence of which was so widely felt in the sixteenth century. And, in fact, the first dramas attributed to him are so laden with classical reminiscences and traditions of the schools, that we should have to look upon Shakespeare as rather over-cumbered with learning, not to say pedantic, if they are to be accepted as his work and his only.

From the dawn of Shakespeare's poetical career to the close, classical antiquity is more or less present in all his works, either in a direct quotation or in a mere coincidence which recalls some well-known passage, here by some expression or allusion, and there by a proper name. In the "Midsummer Night's Dream," for instance, we meet with Theseus, Duke of Athens; in the "Tempest" the fantastic spirits are called Iris, Ceres, and Juno; King Lear is a descendant of Æneas; Cymbeline belongs to the same dynasty, and makes war upon the Romans, who march against him under a general named Caius Lucius. But details such as these are insufficient to stamp the plays in which they occur with the seal of antiquity, and only the following dramas can really be said to be *classical:* the "Comedy of Errors," the story of which is furnished by the "Menæchmi" of Plautus; "Troilus and Cressida," in which the personages are those of Homer in the "Iliad;" "Timon of Athens;" "Coriolanus;" "Julius Cæsar;" and "Antony and Cleopatra."

But even these six plays bear but a very doubtful resemblance in character and tone to ancient classical works, and bring us face to face with the question as to how Shakespeare obtained his knowledge of classical subjects, whether he did so straight from ancient authors —either in their own tongue or in translations,—or rather, through mediæval traditions, or even perhaps from those handed down by the stage.

Of the different plays to be examined, bearing this question in mind, the first in date, though not in importance, is the "Comedy of Errors," which charming as it is to read, must be regarded more in the light of a recreation than of a study. It has comparatively little to teach us with regard to Shakespeare's relations with antiquity, but it may afford an opportunity of re-reading the "Menæchmi," and of comparing the works of Rotrou and of Regnard with that of Shakespeare. No play, on the contrary, is more important than "Troilus and Cressida," in which Shakespeare treats the actual subject of the "Iliad," and represents the very world of Homer; but so fancifully is it done, with so much hardihood and irreverence, that it has more greatly scandalized his severe judges, and driven his enthusiastic devotees to talk wilder nonsense than any other of his works. The offence consists in his having made his play a parody of Homer's heroic world, to the delight of the detractors of Homer, if there still be any such, but a matter of amazement and grief to those whose religious admiration of the great romantic poet has not rendered them unfaithful to the cultus of the classics. It is worth while to read the sublime explanation evolved by the German critic, Ulrici, in his attempt to reconcile the gods, and to satisfy his own mind, which was evidently divided and troubled between his adoration of both Homer and Shakespeare: it is a curious specimen of transcendental criticism.

"The great Shakespeare with his deep insight," says Ulrici, "certainly did not mistake the beneficent effect that an ever-increasing intercourse with the culture of antiquity had already produced, and would continue to produce on the Christianized spirit of Europe. But he saw the danger of an unguarded admiration for classical antiquity, the religion and morals of those who admire it unreservedly, being inevitably doomed to the lowest depths of decadence, and such was the destiny of the eighteenth century to the eyes of the attentive observer. Inspired by his prophetic spirit, which penetrated with equal clearness of vision the obscurity of centuries to come and the clouds hanging over the most remote ages of the past, Shakespeare wrote this profoundly significant satire of the heroic world of Homer. It was not his intention to degrade the lofty, or to lessen the glory of the great, still less to attack Homer and heroic poetry in general, but he wished to give a solemn warning to those who might be tempted to exaggerate the value of the ancients and to worship them as idols."

Thus according to the German critic, "Troilus and Cressida" would be a sort of prophetic protest in the name of religion and morality against the abuse one day to be made of the masters of antiquity. A French translator of Shakespeare, M. François Victor Hugo, also seems to consider this singular play in the light of a prophecy. "Shakespeare," writes the son of Victor Hugo, " wished to deprive classic types of a prestige which was becoming dangerous to the liberty of art. He wished to prevent the narrow and illiberal spirit of criticism which would impose an idolatrous worship of the past upon the future, and to protest beforehand against a literary reaction of which he foresaw the excess." But such explanations as these betray, not only far too superstitious a mode of regarding genius, but also a remarkable want of the sense of history and of reality. Shakespeare's sympathy with the Trojans and his scanty love for the Greeks was simply the outcome of a Latin tradition which was cherished all through the Middle Ages, and was still rife in the sixteenth century. When the Barbarians overthrew the Roman Empire, the sight of the colossal power which they had upset made an immense impression on their imagination. The conquerors set themselves to imitate the vanquished, whom they wished to resemble in every way, and made a point of honour of possessing a genealogy in common with them,—and as a belief which was sanctioned not only by poetry but also by history, attributed the origin of Rome to the Trojans, the Barbarians also ambitiously laid claim to the Trojans as their forefathers. We see the different peoples of Europe celebrating some prince of the family of Hector as their ancestor—the Franks taking Francus, the Normans Antenor, the Bretons Brut or Brito. These legends which flourished all through the Middle Ages were held at the dawn of the Renaissance in still higher honour than ever; in 1572 they inspired the *Franciade* of Ronsard, and when Shakespeare wrote " Troilus and Cressida " they still lingered in the memory of his contemporaries. In making Hector act a glorious part, and Achilles an infamous one, Shakespeare was but following a national tradition; and though his humorous fancy led him to make merry with the Greeks, he had no intention of writing a caricature of the Iliad. No poet was ever of a less revolutionary or aggressive spirit; the basis of his humour is an unchanging serenity, and he remains floating in the pure regions of art high above all our literary disputes—content to create and disdaining all combat.

"Timon of Athens" also claims a place among Shakespeare's Greek plays, in virtue of the place in which the scene is laid, and of the names of its personages. We shall have occasion further on to inquire how much of it he may have borrowed either directly from Plutarch and Lucian, both of whom speak of Timon, or from contemporary playwrights, by whom the same subject had been treated. Nothing, indeed, could be less Greek in spirit than many of the details in this play, as also the whole part of Alcibiades, and above all, the hero's exaggerated and gloomy misanthropy which belongs by right only to a northern type of character. But the want of authenticity in some parts of it, and the extreme uncertainty as to the text, make it a difficult matter to judge of this play. The finest of Shakespeare's dramas taken from antiquity are his Roman tragedies, for the composition of which the only source he had was Plutarch's "Lives." But the medium through which he became acquainted with the Greek historian has been a debated point. M. Philarète Chasles counts four intermediate steps: in 1603, an Italian, named Florio, who knew several languages, translated the essays of Montaigne into English. Shakespeare read this translation, and taking a great fancy to Montaigne, was struck by the admiration he expressed for Plutarch and Amyot. An English translation of Plutarch's "Lives," by Sir Thomas North, taken not from the Greek, but from the French of Amyot, had been published twenty years before, but Shakespeare would appear not to have noticed it until his attention was drawn to Plutarch by Montaigne's Essays. Then he read it, and in the space of three or four years there appeared successively "Julius Cæsar," "Coriolanus," and "Antony and Cleopatra." This ingenious theory, built up by M. Philarète Chasles, is unfortunately not supported by facts. "Julius Cæsar" was written before the famous year 1603, which figures in the imagination of the too-inventive writer just quoted, as a sort of climacteric date in Shakespeare's history. There is no doubt that Shakespeare knew of Montaigne's works, as he has introduced several passages from the Essays into his plays, particularly into the "Tempest," but that this acquaintance exercised any great influence upon him, and directed his thoughts into an entirely new channel, is a most gratuitous supposition. It would therefore be hazardous to say that Plutarch was revealed to Shakespeare by Montaigne; one thing, however, is certain, and that is, that it was only through Amyot, or rather through his English translator, Sir Thomas North, that Shakespeare became acquainted with Plutarch. The proof of this is easy and amusing. In comparing the texts, we find the poet following the translator so closely as to borrow from him not only whole passages and various little peculiarities— an indulgence in epithets, and a certain redundancy of expression, characteristic of good old Amyot—but also even his errors and mistranslations.

It would be an entertaining study to compare Shakespeare's Roman tragedies with the corresponding "Lives" of Plutarch. Very interesting would it be to note the exact reproductions, and still more curious, to observe how the poet's art transformed the accounts of the historian into a drama; and above all, nothing could be more fruitful of instruction than to see how he discarded his model whenever the claims of poetry demanded a departure from strict historical truth. But this necessity seldom arose, and in almost every instance Shakespeare was able to follow his guide with scrupulous fidelity, without treachery to the higher rights of poetry; he, who in general treated the source of his materials with sovereign independence, showing the most surprising humility and submission to Plutarch. The secret of this is to be found in the poetical imagination of the Greek historian, who was more desirous of moral than of historical truth, and who set himself to write not *history* but *biography*, so that Plutarch himself did more than half of the necessary transformation of history into poetry. But however it may be with Plutarch's poetical qualities and Shakespeare's conformity with him in this particular case, the general proposition is none the less true, that a poet is not an historian, and that his mission is other than to write an historical work. Poetic or ideal truth is of a different nature and of a higher order than historical fact. We shall see more than once, further on, how it corrects the prosaic element in history, all that has to be said resolving itself into a commentary on the well-known passage in Aristotle's Poetics—"Poetry is a more philosophical and a more excellent thing than History, for Poetry is conversant with the Universal, History with the Particular."

But if a poet is not an historian, still less is he a bookworm. Shakespeare's plays are full of anachronisms and departures from local and temporary truth, which pedantic and shallow critics delight in pointing out and reproaching him with. We must make some allowance for this line of criticism, and acknowledge certain anachronisms to be outrageous, but the distinction here between what is and what is not permissible is very delicate, and perhaps there is no other point in æsthetics on which it is more difficult to lay down positive rules. Generally speaking, it is right to say not only that little inaccuracies of time and place are merely venial faults, but also that they necessarily result from the essential conditions of art itself, and that every drama derived from ancient history, which is the creation of a poet, and not a slavish copy by a mere man of learning, may fearlessly violate temporary and local characteristics and present huge anachronisms. "Shakespeare," says Goethe, "turns his Romans into Englishman, *and he does right*, for otherwise his nation would not have understood him." With Ben Jonson the case was different; he endeavoured with all the scrupulously exact details furnished by a careful and minute learning to put true Romans on the stage, and ended by writing two tragedies which can only be understood and relished by men of learning, and are quite without interest for the general public. But note the miracle performed by genius:—while Ben Jonson scrupulously preserves the outward covering, the soul escapes him, and his Romans have nothing Roman about them but their costume; but Shakespeare, the creator of souls, makes truer Romans at heart than Ben Jonson does, just because the Englishmen around him, whom we are told he took for his models, have traits of character in common with the citizens of the ancient Republic, and the populace of London is the living image of the populace of Rome, and because what he paints is eternal humanity. Such in rapid outlines are the principal questions that have here to be examined in regard to Shakespeare's classical plays. As of these plays there is only half a dozen, it is a tolerably wide study in a small compass, and this new mode of approaching the genius of the great poet would, if there were any need, make the subject fresh and new, only I venture to think that Shakespeare, under whatever aspects he may be studied, will always possess as fresh an interest as on the day that criticism first laid hands upon him.

The study of Shakespeare, far from being stale or from having been worn threadbare, is always new, not only in the sense in which it is true of every great genius by virtue of the unfathomable depths of his thought, but also from circumstances peculiar to his case. Though born in a period on which the full light of history is shed, scarcely anything is known either of his life or character. The ascertained facts of his history are so " few and far between," that, in order to make a coherent whole, his commentators are driven to fill up the shadowy outlines with conjectures. They ransack his works in hopes of finding some revelation of his personal character, and interrogate his sonnets, which are full of obscurity; but though one commentator is followed by another no two commentaries are alike. They turn to his plays and say, "Hamlet is Shakespeare," and they also see certain features of his disposition in the melancholy of Jaques, the misanthropy of Timon, and the grave sadness of Vincentio; until a new interpreter arises and says, " You are all wrong. Henry V., hiding practical good sense and a love of action under the mask of madcap jollity, is the real Shakespeare." Nothing is more hazardous than such a mode of proceeding, which tends unconsciously to despoil Shakespeare of his highest glory; forgetting, in fact, that dramatic art is essentially impersonal, and that if Shakespeare is the greatest of dramatic poets it is owing to the infinite variety of characters which he created, as if in play, in more lavish profusion than any other writer, while he floats above them with the quiet smile of a creator standing aloof from his work—so much aloof, in fact, that he would seem not to have troubled himself about it. One would almost say he took up the profession of a poet simply to make his fortune, and this end being attained, he retired from the stage in the full flow of life and talent, and spent the rest of his days in the country, in the enjoyment of the ease and comfort he had secured, without even taking the trouble to publish his works. And yet it can hardly be said that he felt no anxiety about his literary reputation, for he carefully edited and re-edited his poems and sonnets; neither can it be said that he was ignorant of his greatness as a dramatic poet, for the admiration bestowed by his contemporaries spoke plainly enough on this point; nor, finally, can it be said that dramatic works had no existence outside the theatre, and that their fortune was inseparably linked with scenic representation, for Ben Jonson not only published his plays but also found readers, and the drama-loving public was so eager to read Shakespeare's, that eighteen of them were printed off in great haste, and very incorrectly, as works published without the consent and concurrence of the author stand a good chance of being.

Thus Shakespeare himself is an enigma to begin with, to which, as to all insoluble enigmas, a different explanation is given by every new guesser.

Passing from his personal history to his works, and in the first place to criticism of the text, we find the same uncertainty reigning everywhere. Whether it was that he did not deign to take any trouble about his fame, or that time was wanting to carry out his intentions, or from any other reason that we are pleased to imagine, the fact remains that Shakespeare, as has already been said, did not himself collect and publish his plays. The first complete edition appeared in 1623, seven years after his death, in a folio volume, which, as it swarms with printers' mistakes, unintelligible passages, false lines, wrong punctuation, and errors and absurdities of every kind, cannot be appealed to as the true text, and can only serve as the basis for conjecture. A glance may here be thrown over some of the latest conjectures concerning what are called his doubtful plays, for besides numerous doubtful passages, there are whole plays of which the authenticity is anything but clearly established.

Critical studies of his works are published by the *New Shakspere Society,* which, it may be remarked in passing, has adopted, in the absence of unanimity among critics as to the right mode of spelling the celebrated name it bears, one that has hitherto not been generally in use, so that Shakespeare's very name is uncertain. Many conjectures about disputed points are put forth by the society, but often what is suggested by one member is disputed and contradicted by another: for example, Rev. F. G. Fleay thinks that "Titus Andronicus"—a horrible drama attributed to Shakespeare, at all events in part—should be entirely taken off the list of his works, while Mr. Wheatley protests against this view, and brings forward external proofs which have often done service before in the discussion, and also breaks new ground in producing internal evidence, pointing out all the lines of this atrocious tragedy, which seem to him undoubtedly to bear the mark of the master's hand.

Another doubtful play is "Timon of Athens," the incoherencies and inconsistencies of which appear to point to a want of unity in the workmanship; besides which, several scenes are pronounced by competent judges to be baldly and tamely written in a prosaic style quite unlike that of Shakespeare. A duality in its composition is generally admitted, but till now it was usually supposed that Shakespeare rehandled a play already in existence as an acting piece, and introduced new scenes into it. A member of the New Shakspere Society ingeniously reverses this hypothesis, and takes the original portion, the nucleus of the play, to be of Shakespeare's authorship, but believes that it afterwards received amplification at the hands of a clumsy workman. As to the reason of this unfortunate amplification the conjecture advanced by the critic is most original. The printers of the folio edition of 1623, in consequence of some mistake in their measurements, found themselves short of thirty pages, needed to make up the volume. In this necessity they must have taken "Timon of Athens," which was the last play remaining to be printed, and have put it into the hands of some dramaturge, charging him to fill it up to the required length. It may be well to add that the author of this conjecture, justly frightened at his own audacity, owns himself that it is bold even to impudence.

The same reversal of opinion has taken place with regard to "Pericles," the third doubtful play. It is now suggested that Shakespeare, instead of touching up and finishing an earlier play, wrote the first sketch of it, composed only of the history of Marina; and to this view Tennyson lends the support of the great authority that belongs to him as a poet. These details sufficiently show how fresh and endless an interest there still is in the critical study of the text of Shakespeare.

And much the same uncertainty exists with regard to the chronological order of his plays, a point which used to be looked upon as settled. The question has been again thrown open by a new set of arguments deduced from the changes in the structure of his verse at successive periods of his life. It has been remarked, for instance, that his verses in his youth, when he showed a predilection for rhyme, move with a caution and timidity which they afterwards shook off. In proportion to the ripening of his talent, his versification became ampler and more free, and between his first plays and his last there are differences analogous to those between "Les Orientales" of Victor Hugo and his "Légende des Siècles." Dryden, deeming the drama of "Pericles" unworthy of Shakespeare's genius, regarded it as a work rehandled by him in his youthful days, an opinion in which all critics followed suit, until now, when its original portion, the romance of Marina, is ranked amongst his latest productions. The "Midsummer Night's Dream," which is classed by M. Philarète Chasles, in his "Etude sur Shakespeare," among his latest works, is now, on the strength of internal evidence which is further corroborated by external testimony dating from 1598, carried back to his very earliest. We have had Malone's chronology and Dr. Johnson's, then that of Payne Collier, which is now replaced by that of the New Shakspere Society,—can we be quite sure that this will be the last?

With respect to all matters of erudition therefore, the subject of Shakespeare may still well be called new, and it now remains to show that it is fresh and fruitful also as regards literary and æsthetic criticism.

It is not here intended to trace the history of the reputation in which Shakespeare was held in the seventeenth and eighteenth centuries, or to repeat the often-quoted judgments of the critics of those days either in France or England, but merely to indicate the standpoint of the older criticism clearly and distinctly, and to single out the idea underlying the whole dispute and held alike by those who attacked and those who defended him. Both friends and enemies saw in Shakespeare a poet innocent of all rules of art, hardly conscious of what he did, a pure child of Nature, a sublime monster destitute of taste and judgment, comparable, according to Coleridge's figure of speech, to the "inspired idiots so much venerated in the East, uttering amid the strangest follies the sublimest truths," or to a sort of grand Lama to whom the most superstitious reverence is paid but who possesses no authority nor real influence.

That Shakespeare was "a huge dunghill" was disputed by no one, the debated question simply turning on the point of the greater or smaller value of the treasure lying buried in it, Voltaire professing to find only "a few pearls" where admiring critics discovered myriads.

Mrs. Montagu defended Shakespeare against the attacks made upon him by Voltaire, but she placed herself so precisely in the same point of view that he did, that there is no essential difference between the attack and the defence. "We confess," writes Charles Knight, "we have more sympathy with Voltaire's earnest attack upon Shakespeare than with Mrs. Montagu's maudlin defence."

"Our author," in fact writes Mrs. Montagu, "by following too minutely the chronicles of the times, has embarrassed his dramas with too great a number of persons and events. The hurly-burly of these plays recommended them to a rude illiterate audience who, as he says, loved a noise of targets. His poverty and the low condition of the stage (which at that time was not frequented by persons of rank) obliged him to this complaisance; and unfortunately he had not been tutored by any rules of art, or informed by acquaintance with just and regular dramas."

She quotes a speech of Lear's, and says: "Thus it is that Shakespeare redeems the nonsense, the indecorums, the irregularities of his plays." "Let us not forget," she says, finally, as if to conclude and sum up all her defence, "that these pieces were played in a miserable inn, before an unlettered audience, scarcely emerged out of barbarism." Barbarous but full of admirable beauties, such is the view formerly taken by critics of all nations, and it would be too bold to assert that this mode of looking at Shakespeare has ever really been abandoned in France. Diderot, who was' of an enthusiastic temperament, expressed the highest degree of admiration ever attained by Frenchmen for Shakespeare, in a passage too daring to be quoted verbally, in which he draws a magnificent comparison between Shakespeare and the statue of St. Christopher of Notre Dame, which, though rough and rudely sculptured, is so colossal that all the great French poets, with their heads held never so high, could pass between his legs.

Nearly a hundred years after Voltaire, M. Villemain, in his "Essai littéraire sur Shakespeare," of which a new edition appeared in 1839, while he is lavish in expressions of the most lively admiration, yet writes that the other dramas of the Elizabethan Period were *extravagant and barbarous like Shakespeare's*, only without his genius; and that what is chiefly admirable in him is that the chaos of his plays is lighted up with such brilliant flashes of lightning. And such has always been at bottom M. Villemain's opinion of Shakespeare. In 1856, in an article in the *Journal des Savants*, he contrasts the merits of Ben Jonson's "Catalina" with the "sublime touches scattered here and there" in "Julius Cæsar" and "Coriolanus." "Sublime touches scattered here and there," "lightning-flashes through chaos," such expressions we may be sure mark the highest tide to which M. Villemain's opinion of Shakespeare ever rose.* Even Victor Hugo, in his "William Shakespeare"—a book abounding in strange paradoxes, but filled with an imaginative insight deep and far reaching, clothed in all the glowing splendour that the author has taught us to expect at his hands,—is still in reality of the old way of thinking, only the expression is singularly full of animation and youth.

"Shakespeare's drama moves with a kind of wild rhythm. His head swims, and this dizziness he imparts to us. . . . His own vastness makes him shudder and communicates to him huge and mysterious oscillations. Wild and intoxicated, says Voltaire. So be it. Wild as the virgin forest, drunken as the rolling sea!"

M. Taine writes of Shakespeare with all his accustomed brilliancy and talent, but not without his wonted prejudices, for his chief enjoyment undeniably consists in

---

* M. Villemain goes so far as to explain by Shakespeare's contact with Ben Jonson, Chapman, Decker, and other *classical* writers of the day, "many things of profound art that he introduced into his composition and style!"

bringing to light the blind and unconscious powers of the man, whose predominant faculty appears to him to be "an impassioned imagination untrammelled either by reason or by morals."

And, to give one more instance of the same way of regarding Shakespeare, at M. Mézière's reception at the Académie Française in 1875, M. Rousset, after speaking of Shakespeare, wished to turn to Goethe, and effected his transition from the poet by instinct to the deliberate artist, in these words :—

"In his excellent study of Shakespeare, M. Guizot calls upon us to admire, amongst the original beauties of the poet, his unaffected ignorance of the marvellous riches that he scatters with an open hand. Could a compliment of the same nature be paid to Goethe ?"

The modern idea that Shakespeare also was an artist made its appearance in England about 1815, introduced from Germany by the translation of William Schlegel's "Lectures on Dramatic Art and Literature."

"To me," said Schlegel, " he appears a profound artist, and not a blind and wildly luxuriant genius. . . . Even in such poets as are usually given out as careless pupils of nature, devoid of art or school discipline, I have always found, on a nearer consideration of the works of real excellence they may have produced, even a high cultivation of the mental powers, practice in art, and views both worthy in themselves and maturely considered. . . . The world of spirits and nature have laid all their treasures at Shakespeare's feet: in strength a demigod, in profundity of view a prophet, in all-seeing wisdom a guardian spirit of a higher order, he lowers himself to mortals as if unconscious of his superiority, and is as open and unassuming as a child." *

Schlegel sounded the first note, and ever since, both in Germany and England, a chorus of unanimous and uninterrupted praises has been sung, in which not only the genius of Shakespeare, as in former criticism and in that of the French school especially, was taken as the theme, but also his profound knowledge and immense intellect.

---

* John Black's translation. Lecture 23rd.

Coleridge* maintains with the impassioned pertinacity that bespeaks a favourite theory worked out by himself, that Shakespeare's judgment equalled his genius. He refused to see any faults in his plays, and when it was impossible to close his eyes to their presence (for he was as candid as he was clear-sighted) he would lay the blame on the dimness of his sight rather than throw doubt on Shakespeare's infallibility. " I cherish the hope," he writes of an apparent defect in " Coriolanus," " that I am mistaken, and that becoming wiser, I shall discover some profound excellence in that in which I now appear to detect an imperfection." (" Notes and Lectures upon Shakespeare.")

To justify all the faults of which Shakespeare had been accused by former critics was the rule followed by the new criticism, and in the accomplishment of its task it has shown no lack of wide and elevated thought, nor of delicate analysis, even to subtlety. Only a small number of English writers, of a Latin rather than a Teutonic turn of mind, amongst whom may be mentioned Hallam and Macaulay, have shown any reserve in their admiration.

In Germany, æsthetic criticism of Shakespeare has made astounding progress since Schlegel's time. This expression must not be taken more ironically than is really intended. I have a profound admiration for German æsthetics, and am far from forgetting that a German professor, Gervinus, is the author of the greatest book ever written on Shakespeare. German æsthetics tower far above anything of the kind produced in England or France, and are unmatched in boldness and originality, but it is the fate of much that is original and daring to split upon the rock of extravagance.

---

* Coleridge's lectures were given in 1811 and 1812; the question whether he or Schlegel gave the initiative to the revolution in Shakesperian criticism is a debated one.

Every German interpreter has taken Shakespeare's works as the text for a philosophical commentary; but it is not precisely on that account that they are to be blamed, as such a mode of proceeding must freely be allowed if we admit, with Plato, Hegel, and all the great metaphysicians in art and poetry, that the Beautiful is but one form of the True. But the paradoxical idea of the new commentators is to consider Shakespeare a philosopher as much as a poet, and to exalt him as a worker upon the profoundest principles, fully aware of the depth of his own convictions. Yet they might have learned from Goethe himself that a poet is not exactly the same thing as a philosopher. It irritated him to be asked what idea he wished to embody in "Faust." "What do I know?" he answered. "How can I say? I have received impressions and pictures upon my soul. . . . 'Faust' is a wild, mad work." If "Faust" is a wild, mad work, it is possible that "Hamlet" may not be a strictly logical production. In making a philosopher of Shakespeare, German critics have lent him as many different doctrines as there are philosophical systems in Germany, and as M. Mézière well says, "except the unanimous affirmation of the divinity of Shakespeare, I see nothing but contradictions in the opinions expressed by the priests of the new cultus."

Criticism having reached this point of exaggeration, a reaction has become inevitable. It needs no prophet to foretell it,—the movement has already begun—naturally not in England, nor in France, where the admiration for Shakespeare has always been below rather than above what it should be, but as we should expect, in Germany. Symptoms of reaction made themselves apparent in Kreyssig's lectures, and it openly declares itself in Gustave Rümelin's very curious work, recently published at Stuttgard. In it he again opens the much-contested question of Shakespeare's literary merits, which since the eighteenth century had either been left alone or languidly acquiesced in, and goes over every detail from beginning to end, bringing forward a few new arguments and a good many old ones. He does not fail to recognize the poet's genius, with regard to the creation of characters, but he criticises his art and accuses him of not having sufficiently matured the conception or condensed the plot of his plays, and of having too often borrowed the canvas just as he found it in the old tales and chronicles which fell into his hands, " satisfied with adorning it with flashes of wit and wisdom, deep thoughts and brilliant metaphors, as one fastens little wax-tapers on to a Christmas-tree."

It is evident, therefore, that the last word has not yet been said by æsthetic criticism on this subject, that nothing is fixed or definite, and consequently its interest is still new and full of life. Not only do individual opinions vary, but a change takes place in the general point of view ; and criticism, swayed by wide oscillations, swings back to its former position. I know of nothing analogous to this constant renewal, this ebb and flow, in the course of the literary reputation of any other prince of modern poetry. There is none that has been discussed, commented on, deified and called into question again as Shakespeare has been. Schlegel, it is true, attacked Molière, but his criticism, dictated by national prejudice, was of little æsthetic value and awoke no echo. The verdict already passed on nearly every matter affecting the greatest literary genius of France is sufficiently established to render it difficult when speaking of him to say anything but commonplaces. Molière is no longer on his trial, and all that remains to be done is to develop the judgment held by all the world concerning him. But with Shakespeare no such disadvantage—or resource—exists, and there being no universally accepted opinion, it becomes absolutely necessary to exercise the right of private judgment and to choose a side of one's own. How, for instance, are we to reconcile opinions so flatly contradictory as M. Taine's admiration for Shakespeare's impassioned imagination freed from the shackles of reason and morality, and that of M. Mézière, who, like Ulrici and Gervinus, is more and more struck by the reason and moral significance of Shakespeare's plays as his knowledge of them increases, and finally that of M. Philarète Chasles, who defines him as a sceptic, akin to Montaigne, a calm and often cruel observer ?

When desirous of studying Molière we have only to take up his works and read them—nothing could be simpler, —merely being careful, if we happen to be gifted with taste, to choose a good edition with a clear pleasant type, and unobscured by any explanatory footnotes. But with respect to Shakespeare it is far from being such an easy matter, and the labour acknowledged on all sides to be requisite for the task shows that even in England it is no ordinary enterprise. Hallam, complaining of the extreme obscurity of Shakespeare's diction, says—

" His style is full of new words and new senses, . . . it is impossible to deny that innumerable lines were not more intelligible in his time than they are at present. . . . Can we justify the very numerous passages which yield to no interpretation, knots which are never unloosed, which conjecture does but cut, or even those which, if they may at last be understood, keep the attention in perplexity till the first emotion has passed away? We learn Shakespeare, in fact, as we learn a language, or as we read a difficult passage in Greek with the eye glancing on the commentary."

Mr. Furnivall, the founder of the New Shakspere Society, in a prospectus written in 1874, has carefully drawn up a list of books useful and profitable to the student of Shakespeare. At the end of these bibliographical notices, he gives the following charming and genial piece of advice: "Get up a party of ten or twelve men and four or six women to read the plays in succession at one another's houses, or elsewhere, once a fortnight, and discuss each for half an hour after each reading." Round this cosy little arrangement with its prescribed numbers there floats a delicate mystical aroma which seems to suggest a sort of meeting of the faithful for the worship of Shakespeare.

There is no danger of making a religion of Shakespeare in France. We shall approach the work of the greatest poet of England and of modern Europe with deep respect, but without holding him to be infallible, and if we see some breach in his genius or blemish in his art, we shall not necessarily think like Coleridge that our sight deceives us, and that the apparent imperfection must perforce conceal a hidden excellence. The limits we have chosen have this advantage—that as they do not attempt to embrace every side of his immense genius, we are the better enabled to give a definite character to our study, more instructive than the vague generalities of a universal and superficial admiration. But before beginning our investigation of Greek and Latin antiquity as found in Shakespeare's works, a few words must be said about the Renaissance of letters in England.

CHAPTER I.

CLASSICAL ANTECEDENTS AND EXAMPLES.

WARTON, the historian of English poetry, tells us that it was about the year 1490 that the classics began to be read in England. In the reign of Henry VIII., in 1520, a play by Plautus was acted before the court, and there is reason to believe that the representation was in Latin, as it was given in honour of four French hostages left in England for the performance of the treaty relating to the surrender of Tournay, and no English translation of so early a date is known of any of the plays of Plautus. Before 1530 mention is made of a translation intended for representation of Terence's " Andria." *

" In the latter end of the same king's raigne " (Henry VIII.), writes Puttenham, an author of the sixteenth century, " sprŏg vp a new companie of courtly makers, of whom Sir Thomas Wyat, the elder, and Henry, Earle of Surrey, were the two chieftains, who, having trauelled into Italie, and there tasted the sweete and stately measures and stile of the Italian Poesie, as novices newly crept out of the schooles of Dante, Ariosto, and Petrarch, they greatly pollished our rude and homely mañer of vulgar Poesie from that it had bene before, and for that cause may iustly be sayd the first reformers of our English meetre and stile."

The literary movement was, however, interrupted for a time by the political and religious dissensions which

---

* See Payne Collier's " Hist. Dram. Eng. Poetry," Vol. I.

troubled the reigns of Edward VI. and Mary Tudor; less rapid and vigorous than on the continent, the Renaissance only again resumed its course under Elizabeth, and hardly completed itself until the end of her reign. The dramatic poetry of the Middle Ages had a longer life in England than on the other side of the Channel; miracle-plays continued to be acted until the year 1598, and the first year of the seventeenth century saw the Queen present at a representation of a morality, entitled, "The Contention between Liberality and Prodigality," in which, under the features of Liberality, Elizabeth might recognize her own portrait. This little fact deserves to be noted for the significance of its teaching; Elizabeth made profession of a wise eclecticism in literature, and while she was friendly to the classical renaissance, she also consented to patronize with her presence the representation of a play belonging to the gothic art of mediæval times. She had the tact— so rare in royal lovers of literature—not to side with either of the different schools that divided the camp of letters, presenting a marked contrast in this respect to the despotic spirit in which Richelieu bestowed his protection upon literature.

Let us picture to ourselves for a moment the learned court of Elizabeth, beginning with the Queen who was one of the best educated persons of her time. And here it is not enough to repeat the words of Roger Ascham, that the Queen read "more Greek in a day than some prebendary of the Church doth read Latin in a whole week," this praise being not only vague but equivocal, for a prebendary has all sorts of occupations which may prevent him from devoting many hours a week to reading Latin, and we must endeavour to fathom the depth of Elizabeth's knowledge with greater precision. Nathan Drake tells us that she wrote a commentary on Plato, translated two orations of Isocrates, a play of Euripides, a treatise by Xenophon and another by Plutarch—so much for her Greek: and as for Latin, she translated the "Jugurtha" of Sallust, Horace's "Art of Poetry," the "Consolation of Philosophy," by Boethius, a long chorus from Seneca's "Hercules Œtæus," and also an epistle by Seneca and another by Cicero. She could write in Latin, as her many Latin letters testify. In English she could handle verse as easily as prose ; and, finally, she spoke five languages with such facility that she could apostrophize the ambassador of France in French, the envoy of Venice in Italian, the imperial nuncio in German, the Spanish *attaché* in Castilian, and the representative of Poland in Latin.*

Hallam, a scrupulously exact historian, relates that "an address was delivered in Greek verses to Elizabeth at Cambridge, in 1564, to which she returned thanks in the same language." ("Introduction to the Literature of Europe," Vol. II., p. 34.)

Elizabeth was not the only learned woman of her times, and there is more than one name worthy of a place beside hers: Lady Jane Grey; the daughters of Sir Anthony Cooke, Lady Cecil, Lady Russell, and Lady Killigrew, who was celebrated, says Craik, "not only for her Latin and Greek, but even for her Hebrew erudition" ("Manual of English Literature"), and various others. In Shakespeare's comedy of the "Taming of the Shrew," it may be noted that one of the suitors of the fair Bianca sends her " a small packet of Greek and Latin books."

Without speaking of men of learning by profession, there were many gentlemen, courtiers, statesmen, military and naval officers, who had a remarkable amount of knowledge: as, for instance, the illustrious sailor, Sir Walter Raleigh ; Thomas Sackville, the author of several works highly important in the literary history of the

---

* François Victor Hugo, Vol. VI., p. 40, of his translation of Shakespeare.

sixteenth century, and particularly of a tragedy of which mention will be made further on; the Earls of Oxford and of Pembroke; and the intimate friend of Shakespeare, the Earl of Southampton.

The following picture of society towards the end of Elizabeth's reign has been left us by Harrison :—

"This further is not to be omitted, to the singular commendation of both sorts and sexes of our courtiers here in England, that there are verie few of them, which have not the use and skill of sundrie speeches. . . . And to saie how many gentlewomen aud ladies there are, that beside sound knowledge of the Greek and Latin toongs are thereto no less skilfull in the Spanish, Italian, and French, or in some of them, it resteth not in me."

And speaking further on of the court, he says—

"The stranger that entereth into the Court of England upon the sudden, shall rather imagine himself to come into some publike schoole of the universities where manie give ear to one that readeth, than into a prince's palace."

The taste for classical antiquity which reigned in Elizabeth's court was strongly tinged with a quaint pedantry, of which Warton in his " History of English Poetry " gives some amusing details :—

"When she paid a visit at the house of any of her nobility, at entering the hall she was saluted by the Penates, and conducted to her privy-chamber by Mercury. . . . In the afternoon, when she condescended to walk in the garden, the lake was covered with Tritons and Nereids ; the pages of the family were converted into wood-nymphs, who peeped from every bower, and the footmen gambolled over the lawns in the figure of Satyrs. . . . When her Majesty hunted in the park, she was met by Diana, who, pronouncing our royal prude to be the brightest paragon of unspotted chastity, invited her to groves free from the intrusions of Actæon. . . . When she rode through the streets of Norwich, Cupid, at the command of the mayor and aldermen, advancing from a group of gods who had left Olympus to grace the procession, gave her a golden arrow, which under the influence of such irresistible charms was sure to wound the most obdurate heart. ' A gift,' says honest Holinshed, ' which her Majesty, now verging to her fiftieth year, received very thankfullie.' "

Furniture, tapestry, everything, even down to cooking, bore the seal of this rage for mythology.

".Even the pastry-cooks," again writes Warton, "were expert mythologists. At dinner, select transformations of Ovid's metamorphoses were exhibited in confectionery; and the splendid icing of an immense historic plum-cake was embossed with a delicious basso-relievo of the destruction of Troy."

But it must not be supposed that the learning in which Elizabeth and her court rejoiced, can be taken as a fair sample of the amount of education possessed by society at large; and Hallam, who distrusts all exaggeration, does well to warn us against the ordinary mistake of considering the knowledge acquired by a few celebrated persons—celebrated just because they are exceptions—as the common lot of all. Still it would be wrong to look upon the court as an absolutely unique and isolated phenomenon; it became the model that all classes of society set themselves, more or less successfully, to imitate, and it exercised a potent influence on the formation of taste and the general tone of society.

In England, as well as on the continent, knowledge in the sixteenth century was an aristocratic possession— a natural consequence of the rarity and high price of books,—but as editions of Greek and Latin authors grew more numerous, knowledge also gradually became an element in the general life of the nation. The first writers of the drama properly so-called were not all noblemen like Thomas Sackville, Lord Buckhurst, but were most of them sons of artisans or peasants; Marlowe, the greatest of them all, was the son of a shoemaker. The first thing that strikes one with surprise is the amount of their learning, and to find that nearly all of them were classical scholars, and men who had received a university education.* But their parents could only

---

* Craik's "Compendious Hist. Eng. Lit." Vol. I.

have secured such teaching for them at the price of great self-sacrifice, and the contrast between their brilliant education and the obscure condition from which they sprang, testifies to the wide-spread love of learning, and to the great wish of the people to be as well taught as the upper classes.

Nathan Drake, the author of a voluminous work on "Shakespeare and his Times," relates that the editor of Saint Chrysostom's works, Rev. John Boys, during his fellowship of St. John's College, Cambridge, voluntarily gave a Greek lecture every morning in his own room at four o'clock, which was regularly attended by nearly all the fellows of his college,—a fact equalling the renowned ardour for work exhibited by Budœas, or the enthusiasm for learning with which Ronsard and Baïf were devoured during their years of study at Coqueret.

A list must here be given of the principal editions and translations of classical authors published in England before 1616, the year of Shakespeare's death; the task is a somewhat dry one, but we must needs know what sources of classical antiquity were open to him.

With the exception of some important translations of Seneca's tragedies, to which I shall return later on, English translators in the sixteenth century seem at first to have turned their attention to the Greek and Roman historians sooner (in both senses of the word) than to the poets. Between the years 1550 and 1616 all the great historians of Greece and Rome were rendered accessible to English readers, either wholly or in part : from the Greek they had the first two books of Herodotus, Thucydides, a great part of Polybius, Diodorus Siculus, Appian,[*]

---

[*] This translation of Appian which appeared in 1578 must be especially noted. Plutarch was the great, and it may be said the only source from which Shakespeare drew for his Roman tragedies; still, the famous speech of Antony in Julius Cæsar curiously resembles in some points the one that Appian puts into his mouth in the same circumstances.

Josephus, Ælian, Herodian, and Plutarch's "Lives," translated by Sir Thomas North in 1579 from the French of Amyot; and from the Latin, Livy, Florus, Sallust, Suetonius, Tacitus, Cæsar, Justin, Quintus Curtius, Eutropius and Marcellinus.*

A translation of the "Menæchmi" of Plautus appeared in 1595, with no other information as to its author than two initial letters "W. W." The "Iliad" was published in Greek in 1591, "The Knights" of Aristophanes in 1593, and Chapman's celebrated translation of Homer, or more accurately speaking, the translation of seven books of the "Iliad" and of the description of Achilles' shield, in 1598. Chapman completed the work in 1611.

To the Greek versions already mentioned may be added that of Lycophron, the obscure and enigmatical author of "Cassandra," who, in the strange confusion of taste that prevailed everywhere in the sixteenth century, when equal veneration was paid to all relics of antiquity, had the good fortune to be taken for a great poet, and to be ranked by some beside Homer and Pindar.

Merely for the sake of completing the list, I further mention the appearance in Greek of six homilies of St. Chrysostom, the first book of Herodotus, fifteen orations of Demosthenes, one oration of Lysias, a treatise by Plutarch and three orations of Isocrates.

As to editions of Latin authors the list is too long for enumeration, and moreover it is so full and complete that it would be useless to give it. The Latin writers were far more read than the Greek, and it was Seneca and not Sophocles who was taken as the great model of dramatic literature in the sixteenth, and even in the seventeenth century. No other writer of antiquity had perhaps so great an influence as he had, and the importance of the part he played in the constitution of the neo-classic

---

* List given by Nathan Drake.

drama in England as well as on the continent can hardly be overrated. For the harmonious and graceful art of Sophocles a more mellowed and cultured taste is required, and it is easy to understand how the sixteenth century, in all the effervescence of its youthful imagination, was more open to the charms of the pomp and splendour of Seneca.*

Much as Ben Jonson, who was the most deeply versed in classical literature of all the poets of the time, might preach in favour of the imitation of ancient models, he himself followed as little as anybody the great Greek masters.

"From this example," says Schlegel, "we see the influence which the prevailing tone of an age, and the course already pursued in any art, necessarily have upon even the most independent minds." † Between the years 1559 and 1566, translations into English of all Seneca's tragedies appeared in succession. During this time mention is only once made of a Greek tragedy, and this was hardly a translation, but rather a very free imitation of the "Phœnissæ" of Euripides, from which Gascoigne with two fellow-helpers made up a play entitled "Jocasta."

In 1581 (when Shakespeare was seventeen years of age) a complete edition of Seneca's tragedies appeared in English, composed of all the preceding translations.

In speaking of the defects of mediæval poetry, M. Littré makes a very good observation on the imperative necessity of modern art seeking instruction from that of the ancients.

"Greek and Latin antiquity," he says, "amassed treasures of style without which no finished work could present itself for the future in

---

* Senecam nullo Græcorum majestate inferiorem existimo, cultu vero ac nitore, etiam Euripide majorem. Inventiones sane illorum sunt: at majestas carminis sonus, spiritus, ipsius.—"Poetique," by J. C. Scaliger, Book VI., Chap. VI.

† "Dramatic Art and Literature," Lecture XXVII.

the regions of ideal beauty. Antique art is both a model and a stepping-stone for modern art, and this model and this stepping-stone were wholly wanting to the *trouvères*."

The English play-wrights of the sixteenth century were almost as ignorant as the *trouvères*, of Greek art, but with Latin works they were well acquainted, and it is something to say that they read and admired Plautus, Terence, and Seneca.

From the time that this partial knowledge of the classics began to spread in England a sensible improvement may be remarked in its dramatic art. In the reign of Edward VI. or of Mary—the exact date is not known —a comedy was written entitled "Jack Juggler," in imitation of Plautus, the author expressly stating in his prologue that he took for his model the *first* comedy of the Latin poet—viz. "Amphitryon." We see in it a new Sosie under the name of Jenkin, and a new Mercury under the name of Jack, who, after having taken the reform and appearance of Jenkin, tries to pursuade him that he is not himself but some one else; the reasons given only succeed in bringing conviction home to Jenkin's mind when they are corroborated, according to custom, by the peremptory arguments of blows.

In the prologue to "Ralph Roister Doister," a comedy written about the same time, the author, Nicholas Udall, head master of Eton and afterwards of Westminster School, refers by name to Plautus and Terence, of whom he claims to be a follower.

The oldest dramatic work extant in England, in which personages borrowed from classical legends appear on the scene, is a burlesque interlude entitled "Thersites," which was acted in 1537, though not printed until somewhere between 1560 and 1563. It is an absurd play and without any literary merit, but it possesses a certain historical interest. I only pause for an instant over it, with the view of enlivening this dry enumeration of names and dates with a few burlesque quotations.

The title page sets forth the purport of the piece in these words: "Thys enterlude folowynge dothe declare how that the greatest boesters are not the greatest doers." Thersites, at his entrance on the stage, says that he has just returned from the siege of Troy, while at the same time he speaks of King Arthur and the Knights of the Round Table, and expresses his resolution to walk through London in spite of all opposition from the civic authorities. Having lost his armour at the siege of Troy he applies to Vulcan for a new suit; he asks for *a sallet*, by which he means a helmet, but which Vulcan persists in understanding as a salad, thus giving rise, says Collier, to "a colloquy of equivoque, the oldest on our stage."

> "*Thersites.* I meane a sallet with whiche men do fyght.
> *Vulcan.* It is a small tastinge of a man's might
> That he shoulde for any matter
> Fyght with a few herbes in a platter.
> No greate laude shoulde folowe that victorye.
> *Ther.* Goddes passion, Vulcan, where is thy wit and memory?
> I wolde have a sallet made of stele.
> *Vul.* Whye, Syr, in youre stomacke longe you shall it fole,
> For stele is harde for to digest."

These jokes are poor enough, and have no other merit than that of showing us the art of punning in its earliest and most ingenuous infancy, in what has wittily been termed its *hieratic* age.

Thersites finally gets his armour, and donning it he cries:—

> "I wyll neyther spare nor for heate nor for colde,
> Where art thou, King Arthur, and the knightes of the round table?"

The entrance of a soldier on the scene twice puts the braggadocio to flight, who in order to run faster on the second occasion throws away both club and sword. Collier further adds that, in the course of the play,—

"Telemachus, a child troubled with worms, arrives with a letter from Ulysses to the mother of Thersites, soliciting a remedy; for the cure of Telemachus a charm is subsequently given, but it is difficult now to understand the humour of this part of the piece, which perhaps had some temporary application." *

At the beginning of Elizabeth's reign we meet with several plays with classical subjects: "Cambyses," "a lamentable tragedy," runs its title page, "mixed full of pleasant mirth;" "Appius and Virginia," an allegorical rather than an historical piece, and much in the style of the old Moralities. Conscience, Justice and Rumour are personified, and employ themselves chiefly in punishing Appius and in consoling Virginius. Virginia and her mother go to church, and Virginius, like a sound orthodox believer, explains the creation of man and woman in full conformity with the second chapter of the Book of Genesis. Mention is also made of an historical play called "Julius Cæsar," which was acted before the court in 1561 or 1562, and is "the earliest instance," says Collier, "of a subject from the Roman history being brought upon the stage."

The 18th January, 1562, is an important date in the history of the English stage. On that day, two years before Shakespeare was born, took place the representation before the Queen, at Whitehall, of a tragedy which marked the opening of a new era. This was the tragedy of "Gorboduc," or "Ferrex and Porrex," written by Thomas Sackville, who has been already mentioned among the nobles of Elizabeth's court distinguished for their learning. Sackville studied some time both at Oxford and Cambridge, at which latter university he took his Master's degree. Protector of letters, writer of sonnets, author

---

* "Hist. Dram. Poetry," Vol. II.

of the Induction, or poetical preface, to the "Mirror for
Magistrates," he distinguished himself later on as a statesman, and after the death of Burleigh was made Lord
Treasurer. He was created Lord Buckhurst by Elizabeth,
and Earl of Dorset by James I. "Gorboduc," in which
Sackville is said to have had the assistance of Thomas
Norton, is the first regular tragedy that ever appeared
on the English stage. It is written in the style that the
growing love for antiquity had brought into fashion, but
we must remember that the word antiquity here implies
only that of Latin origin, and especially the tragedies of
Seneca.

Like its classical models, the tragedy of "Gorboduc"
makes most of the action take place behind the scenes,
supplies its place with narrative speeches, and winds up
each act with a chorus; it is grave and serious from
beginning to end, Sackville, unlike the author of Cambyses, being careful not to mix his "lamentable tragedy,"
with a little "pleasant mirth." It shares the qualities,
both good and bad, that belong to all the plays of the same
kind : it is well written but it is tiresome, the speeches are
eloquent but long and sententious, the characters talk too
much and do too little, and the high-sounding maxims
they pour forth have nothing to do with the plot of the
play. There is nothing living or individual in its characters. But if it is devoid of passion this is due to no
lack of murders, slaughter, and massacres, for the author,
while not allowing himself to shed one drop of blood upon
the stage, conscientiously performs his duty as a tragic
poet and kills off all his characters one after another. In
one important point Sackville departed from his classical
models, for the unities of time and place are not observed
by him, and we shall see further on what regrets his
licence in this particular caused Sir Philip Sidney, who
otherwise was a great admirer of "Gorboduc."

As we advance in Elizabeth's reign, plays with

classical subjects increase and multiply, and it becomes more and more impossible to enumerate them all. In the space of twelve years eighteen of such dramas were acted before the Queen, amongst which we find "Orestes," "Iphigenia," "Ajax and Ulysses," "Narcissus," "Alcmæon," "Quintus Fabius," "Mutius Scævola," and "Perseus and Andromeda."

In 1584, George Peele, one of Shakespeare's companions at the Blackfriars theatre, wrote a play entitled "The Arraignment of Paris." It was written for the court, and contains an extravagant compliment to the Queen. The actual text is unknown to me, but Collier states that it was the same as one addressed by Udall, fifty years before, to Anne Boleyn on her entrance into London after her marriage, when a dramatic pageant took place, in which the judgment of Paris was represented. Five persons appear on the scene, Mercury, Paris, Juno, Pallas, and Venus, and speak as follows :—

"*Mercury.* Juppiter, this aple unto thee hath sent,
Commanding in this cause to geve true judgoment.
   Paris. Juppiter a straunge office hath geven me,
To judge whiche is fairest of these ladies three.
   Juno. All riches and kingdomes bee at my behest:
Give me the aple, aud thou shalt have the best.
   Pallus. Adjuge it to me, and for a kingdome
I shall geve the incomparable wisdome.
   Venus. Preferre me, and I shall rewarde thee, Paris,
With the fairest ladie that on the erthe is.
   Paris. I should broke Juppiter's high commaundement,
If I should for mede or rewarde geve judgement.
Therefore, ladie Venus, before both these twain,
Your beautie moche exceding, by my sentence
Shall win and have this aple. Yet, to bee plain,
Here is the fouerthe ladie, now iu presence,
Moste worthie to have it of due congruence,
As pereless in riches, wit and beautie,
Which are but sundrie qualities in you three.
But for hir worthyness, this aple of gold
Is too symple a reward a thousand fold."

There was nothing ridiculous in such a compliment addressed to Anne Boleyn in all the freshness of her youth and beauty, but bearing in mind that it was served up again for Elizabeth, who had never been handsome and was then fifty-one years old, and that flattery thus thickly laid on was a sure means of pleasing her, we can but wonder where the limits to human illusion and feminine vanity are to be found.

In 1586, or soon afterwards, Thomas Lodge wrote a tragedy called "The Wounds of Civil War," founded upon Plutarch's lives of Marius and Scylla. And here it would be necessary, if it were my intention to present a complete picture of dramatic art in the Elizabethan period, to give a prominent place to two very considerable authors, John Lyly and Christopher Marlowe. Lyly was the celebrated author of a new style of writing called Euphuism, from the title of his principal work "Euphues," a prose romance full of quaint affectation and extravagant conceits. Euphuism was in England pretty much what, either a little earlier or later, *gongorism* was in Spain, *marinism* in Italy, and *l'esprit précieux* in France. But it is not from this point of view that Lyly here chiefly concerns us, and we must turn to his dramatic works, of all of which, with one exception, the subjects are taken from classical antiquity, such as "Galathea," "Endymion," "Midas," "Alexander and Campaspe," etc. In the last-mentioned one, all the witty anecdotes and sayings that have been handed down from antiquity of Alexander and Diogenes are collected and put together, as in a mosaic.

One remark may be made in passing, about Lyly and his school. Like the poets of the *Pleiad* in France, these followers of the classics had the most thorough aristocratic contempt for the vulgar and the tastes of the vulgar. The line from Horace, "Odi profanum vulgus et arceo," was their motto. They looked upon poetry, and even the stage, as an art of delicate refinement and graceful luxury, intended to delight, not the people, but a small and elect circle of dainty admirers. But unless the dramatic poet be in close communion with the large and mighty heart of humanity, the stage necessarily loses the character of a popular institution, and becomes the amusement merely of a small group of learned persons, great lords and courtiers. Very different is Marlowe, in spite of all his learning. His passionate and powerful dramas of "Tamburlaine," "Edward II.," and the "Jew of Malta," stand out in marked contrast to classical tendencies in literature; but neither these nor his masterpiece, "Dr. Faustus," must here receive more than a parenthetical notice, and the only one of his works that claims mention at our hands is "Dido, Queen of Carthage," which he wrote in conjunction with the poet Nash. It does not rank among his best plays, though it contains many poetical passages; there is much that is glaring and extravagant in it, which Shakespeare may possibly have intended to parody in "Hamlet" (Act II., Sc. 2)—*possibly*, because there is reason to doubt, in the first place, whether there is any connection between the lines that Hamlet bids the player recite and those of Marlowe, and also whether Hamlet's real intention was as ironical as is taken for granted by French translators of Shakespeare.

In 1594, Thomas Kyd, who owes his celebrity, however, to other works, published the tragedy of "Cornelia," a translation from the French of Garnier, who closely imitated Seneca and Lucian. Towards the close of the sixteenth century there were three purely and exclusively classical poets: Daniel, who complained of the barbarism of the time, and blamed the "idle fictions" and "gross follies" of the romantic drama, and, in order to show how things ought to be done, wrote his "Cleopatra" and "Philotus;" the Countess of Pembroke, sister to Sir

Philip Sidney, who translated Garnier's tragedy of
"Anthony;" and Brandon, the author of "Virtuous
Octavia." All these plays are sufficiently tedious, possessed of even less interest than "Gorboduc" while
sharing in all its faults. Brandon, when he wishes to
say that it is evening, deems it necessary to use a
periphrasis of four lines long. The following remarks
on Daniel's tragedy of "Cleopatra" are borrowed from a
critic who has had the courage to read it:—

"In order that the unities of time and place may be respected,
Cleopatra appears only during the last hours of her life; even at the
moment of her deepest suffering, she never dares to utter a moan, from
fear of failing in tragic dignity, and she dilates upon her sorrow
instead of expressing it. She dies behind the scenes, and her death
is related by a messenger in a most rhetorical style, with a lavish
profusion of periphrases and ornamental details." [*]

We have now come to Ben Jonson, who, by virtue
of his great talents and strongly marked individuality,
sums up the whole classical school in England at the
close of the sixteenth century. He is a man over whom
it is scarcely permissible to throw a rapid and hasty
glance as over the other contemporaries of Shakespeare,
and to abstain from any attempt to estimate his true
value is preferable to judging him inadequately.

It is enough therefore for the present simply to recall
him as the author of "Sejanus" and "Catilina," tragedies
full of classical allusions and entirely inspired by the
spirit and the letter of antiquity, and to mention that
Shakespeare acted a part in "Sejanus" when it appeared
on the stage in 1603.

And here the examination into the classical tastes,
knowledge, and studies in England in the sixteenth
century may be interrupted, to point out a conclusion
that further researches will only confirm.

At the time of Shakespeare's death in 1616, the

---

[*] Mézières, "Prédécesseurs et Contemporains de Shakespeare," p. 56.

Greco-Latin renaissance, a little slower and more tardy than in France, had gone through all the natural phases of its development. When Shakespeare, born in 1564, entered upon his literary career about the year 1590, the lovers of classical literature were gradually forming a school, of which every day the followers became more numerous. To the end of his life, works written in imitation of the ancients never ceased multiplying around him, so that if he deviated from the steps of Sackville and Jonson it was because it was his wish and intention to do so. In the preference he has given to a different form of drama must be seen the voluntary choice of a clear-sighted intelligence, not the impulse of a blind and unreflecting instinct. It is time to leave off representing Shakespeare as a sort of rude, uncultivated genius, richly dowered by nature alone ; no fatal necessity of race, or time, or circumstances determined his decision, and he went on his way, of his own free choice, with perfect knowledge and conviction. It was quite open to him, had he thought good, to have founded the neo-classic drama in England, just as Corneille, when he first conceived the idea of "The Cid," might, with the help of a little audacity, have founded the romantic drama in France.

CHAPTER II.

CLASSICAL PRECEPTS ENFORCED BY SIR PHILIP SIDNEY.

HAVING noticed in the preceding chapter the classical examples given by Elizabethan writers that Shakespeare may have seen, we must now consider the rules and precepts he is likely to have heard.

In the middle of the sixteenth century, Whetstone, in his dedication to "Promos and Cassandra," from which play Shakespeare derived the story of his "Measure for Measure," complains of the neglect of the unities, saying :—

> " The Englishman in this quality is most vain, indiscreet, and out of order. He first grounds his work on impossibilities ; then in three hours runs he through the world ; marries, gets children, makes children men, men to conquer kingdoms, murder monsters, and bringeth Gods from Heaven and fetcheth devils from Hell."

There are many famous passages in the prologues of that great disciple of the ancients, Ben Jonson, in which he attacks the barbarisms of the stage, and makes his profession of purely classical doctrines. In the prologue to "Every Man in his Humour," he laughs at the poets who in one and the same play—

> " Make a child, now swaddled, to proceed
> Man, and then shoot up in one beard, and weed,
> Past three score years : or with three rusty swords,
> And help of some few foot-and-half-foot words,

Fight over York and Lancaster's long jars
And in the tiring-house bring wounds, to scars.
He rather prays, you will be pleased to see
One such to-day, as other plays should be.
Where neither *chorus* wafts you o'er the seas ;
Nor creaking throne comes down, the boys to please ;
Nor nimble squib is seen to make afear'd
The gentlewomen."

But a series of detached quotations, which could be lengthened out indefinitely, would soon become wearisome ; the complete analysis of a single work presents far greater attractions, and none could better suit the purpose than the elegant and too-little known treatise of Sir Philip Sidney, entitled " An Apologie for Poetrie." ᐧ

It not unfrequently happens in the history of literature, that in consequence of a few partial and mutilated quotations, an author acquires a reputation quite other than he deserves. Such, for instance, is the case in France with Joachim du Bellay, who is set down as a rash and confused writer,* because all French manuals of literature, in speaking of his " Defence and Illustration of the French Language," confine themselves to quoting the last page, in which he exhorts French poets, in a somewhat fantastic and emphatic style, to storm and pillage ancient Greece and Rome, and they are not careful to note that this conclusion oversteps the general import of the book, and would give an erroneous notion of it if taken as the true summary of its doctrines. Much the same thing has befallen Sir Philip Sidney. The only pages of his " Apologie for Poetrie " generally quoted, are those in which he laughs at the playwrights of his time for violating the unities of time and place. The drawback to this isolated quotation is that it gives the perfectly false notion of Sir

---

* Mr. Pater, in his exquisite study of Joachim du Bellay (" Studies of the History of the Renaissance "), has made it impossible for such a reproach to be cast upon English readers.

Philip Sidney that he was a narrow-minded pedant, whereas, in reality, there was nowhere to be found a more liberal and delicately cultured mind than his. His criticism was founded upon the noblest philosophy of art, and amongst the numerous treatises on poetry, which form an entire and very curious branch of literature in the sixteenth century, that of Sir Philip Sidney is in every respect the most remarkable. In addition to the learning of a Scaliger, and the enthusiasm of a Ronsard, he possessed a quality that both these men were lacking in, which, for want of a better word, I must call an *atticism*, or, more strictly speaking, an *urbanity*, taking care to retain the especial meaning of a graceful and witty raillery, which is contained in the Latin word but not to the same degree in the Greek.

Ronsard was just a little lumbering in his ardent flights, and Scaliger was a born pedant, but Sidney was the polished man of the world, and by an exception tolerably rare amongst the scholars of his day, he appears to have been as familiar with Greek literature as with that of Rome; but with him all this weight of learning was wholly graceful and full of a living interest, for Sidney was a true *humanist*. And, indeed, speaking generally, there is nothing perhaps more exquisite in literature than the writings of an occasional and spontaneous character, of men gifted with knowledge and talent by whom literature is not followed as a trade.

Sir Philip Sidney, born in 1554, was pre-eminently an accomplished courtier and a man of brilliant deeds: "courtier, ambassador, poet, romancist and soldier," he stands forth as the very flower of knighthood, and, as his contemporary, Sir Robert Naunton, says of him, "was a noble and matchlesse gentleman."

> " He grew up fast in goodnesse and in grace,
>   And doubly fair wox both in mynd and face.

Which daily more and more he did augment,
With gentle usuage and demeanure myld:
That all men's hearts with secret ravishment
He stole away, and weetingly beguyld."

It does not appear that he published any of his works during his short and brilliant career, which came to an end in 1586, when he was mortally wounded at the battle of Zutphen: but he was the enthusiastic votary of every kind of culture, and had received an education deeply imbued with the humanistic spirit of the Renaissance.

One of his school-fellows, Fulke Greville, testifies of him that even as a child he had a gravity beyond his years, combined with a rare sweetness and charm. He travelled over Europe, and was in Paris during the massacre of St. Bartholomew. At Frankfort he made the acquaintance of the learned Hubert Languet, with whom he kept up a correspondence in Latin, and on his return to the court of Elizabeth, was sent by her, at the age of twenty-two, as ambassador to the Emperor Rudolf II. In 1580, when a temporary disgrace with Elizabeth led him to withdraw for a while from the court and from the cares of public life, he wrote his famous pastoral, the "Arcadia." The following year he wrote his "Defence of Poetry," which remained un-published till fourteen years afterwards, when, in 1595, it appeared under the title of "'An Apologie for Poetrie,' written by the right noble, virtuous, and learned Sir Philip Sidney, Knight. *Odi profanum vulgus, et arceo.*" The "Defence," or "Apology of Poetry," was written as an answer to the libel against poetry and the drama by Stephen Gosson, who had actually had the infatuation to dedicate his works to Sidney. A strange choice, truly, of a patron! "Such follie is it," writes Spenser, on this subject, "not to regarde aforehande the inclination and qualitie of him to whom we dedicate oure bookes." Sir

Philip Sidney had a chance of being elected King of Poland, only Elizabeth would not hear of "the jewel of her times" accepting the crown. He was appointed to the Governorship of Flushing, and during the war with Flanders he was wounded at the battle of Zutphen, and died at the age of thirty-two. In the anecdote which everybody knows, a noble action is recorded of him. As he lay mortally wounded and parched with thirst he called for water, but when they brought it to him, Sidney, seeing a soldier carried along, even more grievously wounded than himself, and who cast longing looks at the water, handed it to him, saying, "Thy necessity is yet greater than mine."

The "Apology for Poetry" is written in a style not unlike that of Montaigne, full of imagery and quaint conceits, more exuberant than correct, and more daring than accurate; but though to the colder and more severe and timid taste of modern times, it may not seem free from a certain affectation, its delicate fancies and old-world aroma give it a peculiar charm.

"To all them," says Sidney, "that professing learning inveigh against Poetry, may justly be objected, that they go very near to ungratefulness, to seek to deface that, which in the noblest nations and languages that are known, hath been the very first light-giver to ignorance, and first Nurse, whose milk by little and little enabled them to feed afterwards of tougher knowledges."

Here, inspired by Horace, he proceeds to quote on the part of Greece, Musæus, Homer, Hesiod, Linus, Amphion, and Orpheus, whose lyre charmed both beasts and stones, that is to say, "stony and beastly people;" on the part of ancient Italy, Ennius, and Livius Andronicus; for modern Italy, Dante, Boccaccio, and Petrarch; and for England, Gower and Chaucer. He reminds his readers that the earliest philosophers were poets, and that Thales, Empedocles, Parmenides, Pythagoras, and Phocylides, threw their cosmogonies, or their systems of morals, into verse.

Sidney is mistaken in some of his examples; Petrarch especially has nothing primitive about him—the whole character of his poetry heralds the approach of what is called the "modern spirit,"—but his general criticism is none the less true and searching. In every nation literature made its first appearance in poetry. Either because in the absence of writing, verse was considered the surest aid to memory, or rather, because it is the form which every idea that struggles to express itself and to live instinctively chooses to extend its influence beyond the circle of every-day concerns, and to prolong its life beyond the bounds of our earthly existence, there has always been at first a period of creative activity in the human mind, during which prose literature did not as yet exist, and verse was the only mode of expression men knew for thoughts that raised themselves above the ordinary conditions and pre-occupations of life. As there was nothing written in prose, poetry could not form a separate and distinct branch of literature, but included everything; it was *encyclopædic*, and held itself aloof from neither natural science, philosophy, morals, nor politics. As long as this primitive age lasts, poetry, as Sidney well says, is the teacher of the people. No moment in the history of a nation's literature is more important than that in which poetry ceases to be an encyclopædia, and distinguishes and separates itself from learning in general, and, becomes an art cultivated for its own sake, while, as a consequence of the same process of evolution, the appearance of prose literature occurs. No treatise on poetry could begin with reflections of a higher order than these, and in thus starting with them, Sir Philip Sidney gives evidence of his rare distinction of mind.

"And truly even Plato," he continues, "whosoever well considereth, shall find, that in the body of his work, though the inside and strength were philosophy, the skin, as it were, and beauty, depended most of

Poetry. . . . Besides, his poetical describing the circumstances of their meetings, as the well ordering of a banquet, the delicacy of a walk, with enterlacing mere tales, as *Giges'* ring, and others, which who knoweth not to be flowers of poetry, did never walk into Apollo's garden."

Like many great minds of the sixteenth century Sidney was a Platonist. The sentence of his master, which has been a stumbling-block to many devout followers, in which the philosopher banishes poets from the ideal Republic, threw him, as will be seen further on, into a momentary embarrassment, but by a very simple explanation he succeeded in reconciling the homage he paid to poetry, with the respect he everywhere displayed for the teaching of Plato.

"And even historiographers," continues Sidney, " (although their lips sound of things done, and verity be written in their foreheads) have been glad to borrow both fashion and perchance weight of poets. So Herodotus entituled his history by the name of the Nine Muses : and both he and all the rest that followed him, either stole or usurped of poetry their passionate describing of passions, the many particularities of battles, which no man could affirm ; or if that be denied me, long orations put in the mouths of great kings and captains, which it is certain they never pronounced."

This criticism or remark of Sidney's applies more especially to historians of the old school, who made no more scruple about fabricating fine speeches for their heroes than if they had been the authors of a tragedy, and it is far less applicable to history as understood and written in the present day. It has not, however, lost all its truth, seeing that an historian, unless he reduces history to a bald statement of documents and authorities, is obliged to introduce some kind of arrangement, to submit to the rules of literary, and even, to a certain extent, to those of dramatic composition. From this moment, history ceases to be a mere simple representation of reality, and as Sidney maintains, borrows somewhat from the poet's art; of which, being thus beholden to it, it would ill become it to speak evil.

In reading the works of authors more or less forgotten and comparatively little known like Sidney, we are surprised at nearly every step, and a little disconcerted, at meeting with ideas generally supposed to be peculiar to modern writers, and at seeing how true the words are with which La Bruyère begins his book: "Everything has been said." What we call a new idea is most often one already old, but which the penetrative touch of genius has endowed with a new strength and precision, or to which an ingenious writer has succeeded in giving the piquancy of a paradox. More than one idea, expressed moreover with rare ability, in the "Apology for Poetry" strikes the mind as new when met with in the conversations of Goethe or Hegel's course of æsthetics. Amongst the number is the truth, too original ever to have become commonplace, but which in Sidney's generation was still further from being a truism than in our own, that the products of art are superior to those of nature.

"Nature," writes Sidney, "never set forth the earth in so rich tapestry, as divers poets have done, neither with pleasant rivers, fruitful trees, sweet-smelling flowers, nor whatsoever else may make the too much loved earth more lovely. Her world is brazen, the poets only deliver a golden; but let those things alone and go to man, for whom as the other things are, so it seemeth in him her uttermost cunning is employed, and know whether she have brought forth so true a lover as Theagenes, so constant a friend as Pylades, so valiant a man as Orlando, so right a prince as Xenophon's Cyrus, so excellent a man every way as Virgil's Æneas."

The preference given by Sidney to art over nature recalls to mind several passages in Goethe's conversations recorded by Eckermann, especially the one in which, standing before a landscape of Rubens, he exclaims :—

"So fine a picture has never been seen in nature, any more than a landscape by Poussin or by Claude Lorraine, for which, although they look very natural to us, we should search in vain in actual reality."

And another passage in which, speaking of the sculptures of the Parthenon, he says :—

"There are masterpieces in which the Greeks have not only equalled but excelled nature. The English, who are the best judges in the world, of horses, admit that there are two antique heads of horses so absolutely perfect in form that no race in existence offers anything to equal them : and when such works astonish us we are not to think that the sculptors had more perfect models to work from, but rather that through the progress of time and of art they had arrived at bestowing upon nature an ideal perfection, which their own minds had conceived."

We all know the objection, or rather the indignant protest, that uncritical and shallow minds never fail to raise against this theory : to rank the works of art higher than those of nature is, they say, to put the power of man above that of God ; it is impious and blasphemous. This objection was foreseen and forestalled by Sidney, and his answer is full of sense and wisdom :—

"Neither let it be deemed too saucy a comparison to balance the highest point of man's wit with the efficacy of nature ; but rather give right honour to the heavenly Maker of that maker : who having made man to His own likeness, set him beyond and over all the works of that second nature, which in nothing he showeth so much as in poetry, when with the force of a Divine breath he bringeth things forth far surpassing her doings."

Hegel, in refuting the same objection, has not expressed himself with greater insight and elevation of thought than Sidney :—

"The high place that belongs to works of art," says the great philosopher, "is contested by a prejudice of the vulgar. Nature and its products, it is said, are the works of God, of His wisdom and goodness, while the monuments of art are only the performances of men. This involves the mistake of believing that God neither works in man nor through man, and that the circle of His activity is circumscribed by external nature. So erroneous an opinion must never be admitted for an instant if we wish to form a true idea of art. Far from being true, it is in the contrary proposition that the right view must be sought —that God derives more honour and glory from the products of the human mind than from those of nature; for not only is there a Divine essence in man, but the Divinity manifests itself in him far more sublimely than in nature. God is Spirit, and consequently His truest instrument and medium is man."

An idealistic nature like Sidney's would naturally consider poetry independent of versification, and define it by qualities he felt to be more important than those of metre and rhyme.

"It is not rhyming and versing that maketh a poet, no more than a long gown maketh an advocate." If poets have chosen verse "as their fittest raiment," it is because the dignity of their subject leads them to distinguish their language from all other modes of discourse, "not speaking words as they chanceably fall from the mouth," but "there have been many most excellent poets, that never versified, and now swarm many versifiers that need never answer to the name of poets." The "Cyropedia" of Xenophon is not in verse but is a perfect heroic poem. For poetry is truly a *creation*, and that in a more absolute sense than any other of the arts, which have their matter given them to form and fashion: in painting (here I paraphrase Sidney rather than transcribe him) the idea is incorporated in form and colour; in music the sentiment is identified with sound, to say nothing of sculpture and architecture, arts too visibly material to require mention. But the poet spins his own web, and has to give form only to the conceptions of his own imagination; "for him," says Hegel, "even words are only an accessory, they are mere signs and simply a means of transmission of thought, and the mind is brought face to face only with itself." A poet, "lifted up with the vigour of his own invention," can not only create a world better than nature but also new forms "such as never were in nature, as the Heroes, Cyclops, Chimeras, Furies, and such like, freely ranging only within the zodiac of his own wit." Sidney gives the Greek etymology of the word poet,

E

and makes several comments upon it; he evidently has in his mind, although he does not quote it, the passage of Plato in the "Banquet." "Poetry is complex and manifold, and all creation or passage of non-being into being, is poetry or making, and the processes of all art are creative, and the masters of arts are all poets."

The essence of poetry thus being defined, Sidney proceeds to show its practical value and merit, and here the moral and platonic tendencies of his soaring mind especially reveal themselves. To refine the mind, to enrich the memory, to sharpen the judgment, to enlarge the domain of thought, constitutes the ordinary notion of education; but "the final end is to lead and draw us to as high a perfection as our degenerate souls, made worse by their clayey lodgings, can be capable of." Therefore the art that best serves this end "has the most just title to be prince over all the rest." And he proceeds to show how, in this, poetry outsteps all other competitors, and is of greater moral efficacy than philosophy or history.

He then personifies Philosophy and History, between whom a brilliant and animated discussion ensues, touching their respective value as teachers of mankind; the conclusion finally arrived at is that the one gives the precept and the other gives the example. But philosophy is obscure and cold and misty, and its teaching is so general and abstract that "happy is that man who may understand it, and more happy he that can apply what he doth understand."

History is wanting in the Ideal, it clings to crude facts, and to that which is,—not to principles and to that which should be; the examples that she boasts of producing are not always good to imitate, and convey a less wholesome teaching than the precepts of philosophy. But the poet, the peerless poet (Sidney never mentions the poet or poetry that takes the heart captive without giving vent to his affectionate admiration in some enthusiastic epithet) weds precept to example, and while philosophy confines itself to telling us that such and such things should be done, the poet gives us a perfect picture of it in the conduct of his characters; and thus where philosophy can only bestow "a wordish description," which has no very powerful effect upon the mind, the poet everywhere sheds life.

"Tully," says Sidney, "taketh much pains to make us know the force, love of our country hath in us. Let us but hear old Anchises speaking in the midst of Troy's flames, or see Ulysses, in the fulness of Calypso's delights, bewail his absence from barren and beggarly Ithaca. Anger, the Stoics say, was a short madness; let but Sophocles bring you Ajax on a stage, killing and whipping sheep and oxen, thinking them the army of Greeks, and tell me if you have not a more familiar insight into anger than finding in the schoolmen its genus and difference. See whether wisdom and temperance in Ulysses and Diomedes, valour in Achilles, friendship in Nisus and Euryalus, even to an ignorant man carry not an apparent shining; and contrarily, the remorse of conscience in Œdipus, the soon-repenting pride of Agamemnon, the self-devouring cruelty in his father Atreus, the violence of ambition in the two Theban brothers, the sour-sweetness of revenge in Medæa, and to fall lower, the Terentian Gnatho, and our Chaucer's Pandar, so expressed that we now use their names to signify their trades."

The fable related by Menenius Agrippa, that of the prophet Nathan, the parables of the Gospels, and a thousand examples taken from antiquity sacred and profane, are brought forward by Sidney in his desire to show that poetry is the "most excellent workman " in teaching virtue, and he bestows upon the poet the ingenious appellation of the "popular philosopher."

There is, according to him, more to be learned from the "feigned" Cyrus of Xenophon than from the real Cyrus of Justin, from the imaginary Æneas of Virgil than from the actual Æneas of Dares of Phrygia. History is too often illogical and unjust, "for see we not valiant Miltiades rot in his fetters? The just Phocion and the accomplished Socrates put to death like traitors? The cruel Severus live prosperously? The excellent Severus miserably murdered? Sylla and Marius dying in their beds. Pompey and Cicero slain then when they would have thought exile a happiness?"

Poetry has none of these iniquities; if it makes Ulysses undergo storms and other rude trials, it is simply with the intent of giving scope to his patience and magnanimity, "to make them shine the more in the near-following prosperity; and of the contrary part, if evil men come to the stage they ever go out so manacled, as they little animate folks to follow them."

Sidney mentions four objections commonly raised against poetry, and refutes them one after the other. The discussion is not of equal interest throughout, but nothing could be more witty than his answer to the second objection, that poets are liars :—

"Of all writers under the sun, the poet is the least liar: and though he would, as a poet can scarcely be a liar, the astronomer with his cousin the geometrician, can hardly escape, when they take upon them to measure the height of the stars. How often, think you, do the physicians lie when they aver things, good for sicknesses, which after-wards send Charon a great number of souls drowned in a potion before they came to his ferry. And no less of the rest which take upon them to affirm. Now, for the poet he nothing affirms and therefore never lieth. For, as I take it, to lie is to affirm that to be true which is false. So as the other artists, and especially the historian, affirming many things, can in the cloudy knowledge of mankind, hardly escape from many lies. But the poet, as I said before, never affirmeth. . . . He citeth not authorities of other histories, but, even for his entry, calleth the sweet Muses to inspire into him a good invention: in troth, not labouring to tell you what is, or is not, but what should or should not be: and therefore, though he recount things not true, yet because he telleth them not for true, he lieth not, without we will say, that Nathan lied in his speech to David. Which, as a wicked man durst scarce say, so think I, none so simple would say that Æsop lied in the tales of his beasts: for who thinks that Æsop writ it for actually true, were well worthy to have his name chronicled among the beasts he writeth of."

With regard to the sentence in which Plato banished

poets out of his Republic, the platonist Sidney gets out of
the difficulty by saying that Plato here found fault with
the poets of his time who "filled the world with wrong
opinions of the Gods, making light tales of that unspotted essence," and that it was the abuse of poetry and
not the real thing that he wished to banish, and he adds
that to get at Plato's real opinion about poetry, we
have but to read his beautiful dialogue called "Ion," "in
which he giveth high and rightly divine commendation
to poetry."

The last pages of the treatise are dedicated to the
examination of the then existing condition of English
poetry, which, according to Sidney, was one of little
brilliancy. Other nations put England to shame, and
preceding ages, agitated as they were and disturbed by
war, had nevertheless produced greater poets than those
of his own peaceful times. "Now that an over-faint
quietness should seem to strew the house for poets, they
are almost in as good reputation as the mountebanks at
Venice."

Although this severity on Sidney's part shows that
he was not altogether free from the prejudice that occasionally prevents the most sane and liberal minds from
rendering justice to their own period, it can nevertheless in a great measure be justified, for it must be remembered that at the time when he was writing nothing
was known of Shakespeare, and Spenser had not, as
yet, added his "Faerie Queen" to the treasures of the
world.

Looking back to earlier poets, Sidney pronounces
Chaucer to have done excellently well in his poem of
"Troilus and Cressida," which, he says, no succeeding
age has equalled; he also gives praise, however, though
not unreservedly, to more modern productions, such as
Sackville's "Mirrour for Magistrates," the Lyrics of the
Earl of Surrey, and the "Shepherd's Calendar."

We arrive finally at the criticism of the stage :

"Our tragedies and comedies (not without cause cried against), observing rules neither of honest civility, nor of skilfull poetry, excepting 'Gorboduc,' which, notwithstanding as it is full of stately speeches and well-sounding phrases, climbing to the height of Seneca's style, and as full of notable morality, which it doth most delightfully teach ; and so obtain the very end of Poesie ; yet, in troth, it is very defectious in the circumstances, which grieveth me, because it might not remain as an exact model of all tragedies. For it is faulty both in place and time, the true necessary companions of all corporeal actions. For where the stage should always represent but one place, and the uttermost time pre-supposed in it should be, both by Aristotle's precept and common reason, but one day : there is both many days and many places inartificially imagined. But if it be so in 'Gorboduc,' how much more in all the rest? Where you shall have Asia of the one side, and Affrick of the other, and so many other under-kingdoms, that the player when he cometh in must ever begin with telling where he is : or else the tale will not be conceived. Now ye shall have three ladies walk to gather flowers, and then we must believe the stage to be a garden. By and by, we hear news of shipwreck in the same place, and then we are to blame if we accept it not for a rock. Upon the back of that comes out a hideous monster, with fire and smoke, and then the miserable beholders are bound to take it for a cave. While, in the mean time, two armies fly in, represented with four swords and bucklers, and then what hard heart will not receive it for a pitched field? Now, of time they are much more liberal, for ordinary it is that two young princes fall in love. After many traverces, she is got with child, delivered of a fair boy ; he is lost, groweth a man, falls in love and is ready to get another child, and all this in two hours space. . . . But some will say, how then shall we set forth a story which containeth both many places and many times? And do they not know that a tragedy is tied to the laws of poetry and not of history? not bound to follow the story, but, having liberty either to feign a quite new matter, or to frame the history to the most tragical conveniency. Again, many things may be told which cannot be showed, if they know the difference betwixt reporting and representing. As, for example, I may speak, though I am here, of Peru, and in speech digress from that to the description of Calicut ; and so was the manner the ancients took, by some Nuncius, to recount things done in former time or other place. . . . I have a story of young Polidorus, delivered for safety's sake, with great riches, by his father Priam to Polymnestor, king of

Thrace, in the Trojan war-time. He, after some years, hearing the overthrow of Priam, for to make the treasure his own, murdereth the child: the body of the child is taken up by Hecuba; she the same day findeth a slight to be revenged most cruelly of the tyrant: where, now, would one of our tragedy writers begin but with the delivery of the child? Then should he sail over into Thrace, and so spend, I know not how many years, and travel numbers of places. But where doth Euripides? Even with the finding of the body, leaving the rest to be told by the spirit of Polidorus. . . . But besides these gross absurdities, how all their plays be neither right tragedies nor right comedies: mingling kings and clowns; so as neither the admiration and commiseration, nor the right sportfulness is by their mongrel tragi-comedy obtained . . . which, like an unmannerly daughter showing a bad education, causeth her mother Poetry's honour to be called in question."

This is the famous passage by which critics have been led to represent Sir Philip Sidney as no better than a sort of pedagogue of retrogade and routine-loving disposition, who set himself up to make laws against the independence and splendid audacity of genius. But this is a strange and most unjust mistake to fall into, as those who reproach Sidney for his opinions with regard to the drama, judge them by the light of Shakespeare's plays, which had not as yet appeared. And surely Sidney cannot be accused of having misunderstood the rules of modern tragedy because the greatest dramatic genius the world had ever seen since Æschylus, afterwards reared in front of the Greek drama, a rival drama, widely different in every respect. If he could have anticipated the genius of Shakespeare, he would have been as great as Shakespeare himself; and if we carry ourselves back to the epoch in which he lived, we shall see how natural and right his opinions were, and that the astonishing thing is, not that Sidney said what he did say, but that Shakespeare should have done what he has done. Sidney lived in the full light of the truth as possessed by his own day,—in harmony with the sixteenth century, he thought like it and with it,

participating in all the passions and enthusiasm of the
Renaissance. To suggest that in 1581 we should all
have been of his way of thinking, implies no hint of
discourtesy or disrespect to our dignity, and, on the
contrary, it admits that we should have been men of
ability and education, on a level with the general spirit
of the age: on a level, is saying too little,—Sir Philip
Sidney represents the very flower of the intellect and
of the society of the times in which he lived. As an
author of imaginative works, his renown was equal to
that of the greatest poets amongst his contemporaries,
and in criticism and theories of art he rose high above
all his countrymen, Bacon only excepted; and it is not
too much to say that we must pass over an interval of
nearly two hundred years, before we can find any
philosophical writers, in this particular order of æsthetic
and literary reflections, of sufficient originality to be
compared to him.

Such were the doctrines sanctioned and enforced by
learning, by good sense and talent, when Shakespeare
began his career as a dramatist, and we may expect to
find that like all young writers of the future, he followed
the teaching of the best masters of the time, until he, in
his turn, became a master. And thus it was indeed that
he began, during that first tentative period when youth
gropes its way and imitates its forerunners; and so he
might have continued had he been an ordinary man of
talent, but the inspirations and promptings of genius are
infinitely different from the counsels of mere wisdom,
as Shakespeare brilliantly proved by breaking away
from the example given by such a man as Sir Philip
Sidney.

CHAPTER III.

SHAKESPEARE AND THE UNITIES.

SHAKESPEARE came up to London in 1586, when he was between twenty-two and twenty-three years of age, and here he lived for about twenty-five years, mixing in good society as well as that of the stage. His friends in the world of fashion were the highly educated men of Elizabeth's court, and great lords, all partisans of the classical revival, and of the imitation of the ancients: his companions at the theatre were scholars, graduates of either Oxford or Cambridge, so that he must assuredly have been well informed as to the doctrines of the neo-classic school, and was, doubtless, warmly urged on all sides to follow its precepts and examples. He frequented the Mermaid tavern where the famous club, said to have been founded by Sir Walter Raleigh, was held, where Ben Jonson, Beaumont, Fletcher, Donne, Selden, Chapman, and many others all met. In a letter to Ben Jonson, Beaumont says—

> " What things have we seen
> Done at the Mermaid ! heard words that have been
> So nimble, and so full of subtile flame,
> As if that every one from whence they came
> Had meant to put his whole wit in a jest."

Here Shakespeare had literary discussions with Ben Jonson, or rather, listened to Ben Jonson's dissertations, smiled, put in a word here and there, and eluded the

grasp of his powerful adversary with the graceful tact
of a man of the world, who feels that in such encounters
where nothing is absolutely false, nor absolutely true,
all weighty and impassioned persistence would be out of
place. On one side, were force, ardour, and serious convictions; on the other, the careless, easy attitude of the
true artist, indifferent to theories because he found it
infinitely more amusing to create than to teach, and
because he knew well that in being a poet and not a
professor he had chosen the better part. Thomas Fuller
has left us a sketch (of which, however, the materials
must have been furnished by others, as he himself was
not born till 1608) of these brilliant tournaments at the
Mermaid, where, after supping, Shakespeare and Ben
Jonson distinguished themselves in such different ways,
and he has very skilfully characterized the tempers of
the two speakers.

"Many were the wit-combats betwixt Shakespeare and Ben
Jonson; which two I behold like a Spanish great galleon and an
English man-of-war: Master Jonson, like the former, was built far
higher in learning; solid, but slow in his performances. Shakespeare,
with the English man-of-war, lesser in bulk but lighter in sailing,
could turn with all tides, tack about, and take advantage of all winds
by the quickness of his wit and invention."

Neither this passage, whatever its interest may be,
nor the significant epithet of 'gentle poet' bestowed by
his contemporaries upon Shakespeare, would authorize
us, in our dearth of information as to biographical details,
to consider him as exempt from all harshness, all pedantic
dogmatism, and as entirely given up to a creative activity,
if a general examination of his works did not finally lead
us to the same conclusion. Running through them from
this point of view, we shall, however, everywhere see
his utter indifference with regard to the literary doctrines
which were so fiercely debated in his time, and have continued to be so in all times since.

In "Hamlet," for instance, there is a sentence in which mention is made of the *Unities* and so-called regular plays. Polonius announces the arrival of the actors to the Prince :—

"The actors are come hither, my lord, . . . the best actors in the world, either for tragedy, comedy, history, pastoral, pastorical-comical, historical-pastoral, tragical-historical, tragical-comical-historical-pastoral, scene individable, or poem unlimited : Seneca cannot be too heavy, nor Plautus too light. For the law of writ, and the liberty, these are the only men."

This farrago of nonsense is uttered by a pompous and foolish old person, and the poet's intention is evidently ironical, but his irony is not specially levelled at the plays in which the rules are strictly observed; it has a wider and more general scope, and is aimed at the pedantic luxury of divisions and sub-divisions. Divested of its ironical clothing, the author's real feeling is that it matters little whether dramatic works observe the rules or not, and whether they respect the unities of time and place or violate them ; it is by no such outward and superficial characteristics that the worth or mediocrity of a play is to be measured, and whether it is good or bad depends upon deeper causes.

A more explicit passage is to be found in " A Winter's Tale." This play is divided into two distinct parts, separated by an interval of sixteen years. The princess who is born in the first part is married in the second, the scene is laid sometimes in Sicily, sometimes in Bohemia; there is therefore a flagrant infraction of the unities of time and place. Of this Shakespeare is quite aware, but without being in the least disturbed by it. The first part is comprised of the first three acts, the second part of the last two ; at the opening of the fourth act, Time, filling the office of chorus, or rather of the prologue, presents himself in person before the audience and makes the following frank declaration :—

> "I, that please some, try all,—both joy and terror
> Of good and bad,—that make and unfold error,—
> Now take upon me, in the name of Time,
> To use my wings. Impute it not a crime
> To me, or my swift passage, that I slide
> O'er sixteen years, and leave the growth untried
> Of that wide gap; since it is in my power
> To o'erthrow law, and in one self-born hour
> To plant and o'erwhelm custom. Let me pass
> The same I am, ere ancient'st order was,
> Or what is now received: I witness to
> The times that brought them in: so shall I do
> To the freshest things now reigning; and make stale
> The glistering of this present, as my tale
> Now seems to it. Your patience this allowing,
> I turn my glass; and give my scene such growing,
> As you had slept between."

It would be impossible to speak in a quieter and prouder tone than this, and nothing is more striking in Time's speech than its dignified calmness and serenity. To some critics these words seem to wear an accent of revolt and protestation, but what a pitiful mistake! Shakespeare never troubled himself about the legislators of Parnassus, or even did them the honour of recognizing their existence. He is far above all our paltry wranglings, and from the philosophical point of view to which he rises, a space of sixteen years is of no longer duration than an interval of twenty-four hours, both alike are nothing in the devouring flight of time.

The historical drama of "Henry V." also offers a chorus at the beginning of each act, which in five prologues, most poetically conceived and expressed, invites the spectators to leap in thought over both time and space and to supply by the power of imagination all that was wanting in the representation.

The first prologue says:—

> "O for a muse of fire that would ascend
> The brightest heaven of invention!

A kingdom for a stage, princes to act,
And monarchs to behold the swelling scene !
Then should the warlike Harry, like himself,
Assume the port of Mars ; and, at his heels,
Leash'd in like hounds, should famine, sword, and fire,
Crouch for employment.   But pardon, gentles all,
The flat unraisèd spirit, that hath dared
On this unworthy scaffold to bring forth
So great an object : can this cockpit hold
The vasty fields of France ? or may we cram
Within this wooden O * the very casques
That did affright the air at Agincourt ?
O, pardon ! since a crooked figure may
Attest, in little place, a million ;
And let us, ciphers to this great accompt,
On your imaginary forces work :
Suppose within the girdle of these walls
Are now confined two mighty monarchies,
Whose high upreared and abutting fronts
The perilous narrow ocean parts asunder.
Piece out our imperfections with your thoughts :
Into a thousand parts divide one man,
And make imaginary puissance :
Think, when we talk of horses, that you see them
Printing their proud hoofs i' the receiving earth :
For 'tis your thoughts that now must deck our kings,
Carry them here and there ; jumping o'er times,
Turning the accomplishment of many years
Into an hour-glass ; for the which supply,
Admit me Chorus to this history ;
Who, prologue-like, your humble patience pray
Gently to hear, kindly to judge our play."

The second prologue is explanatory of the action, and praises the people of England, in whose breasts the warlike spirit is awakened :—

" The French advised by good intelligence
Of this most dreadful preparation,
Shake in their fear ; and with pale policy
Seek to divert the English purposes.

---

* An allusion to the circular or oval form of the Globe Theatre, where the first representation of " Henry V." took place.

> O England! model to thy inward greatness,
> Like little body with a mighty heart,
> What might'st thou do, that houour would thee do,
> Were all thy children kind and natural!"

But there are traitors who, won over by French gold,
have plotted "conspiracy with fearful France." The
Chorus goes on to announce that as soon as the King has
set out from London, the scene will be transported to
Southampton.

> "And thence to France shall we convey you safe,
> And bring you back, charming the narrow seas
> To give you gentle pass. . . .
> But, till the King come forth, and not till then,
> Unto Southampton do we shift our scene."

The third prologue again appeals to the imagination
of the audience, but although the idea is the same as in
the two quoted above, we cannot refrain from giving it
here on account of the beauty of its expression, which
makes it rank as the most poetical of the five prologues.

> "Thus with imagined wing our swift scene flies,
> In motion of no less celerity
> Than that of thought. Suppose that you have seen
> The well-appointed king at Hampton pier
> Embark his royalty; and his brave fleet
> With silken streamers the young Phœbus fanning.
> Play with your fancies; and in them behold,
> Upon the hempen tackle ship-boys climbing;
> Hear the shrill whistle which doth order give
> To sounds confused: behold the threaden sails,
> Borne with the invisible and creeping wind,
> Draw the huge bottoms through the furrow'd sea,
> Breasting the lofty surge: O, do but think
> You stand upon the rivage, and behold
> A city on the inconstant billows dancing;
> For so appears this fleet majestical,
> Holding due course to Harfleur. Follow, follow!
> Grapple your minds to sternage of this navy;
> And leave your England, as dead midnight still,
> Guarded with grandsires, babies, aud old women,

> Either past, or not arrived to, pith and puissance;
> For who is he, whose chin is but enriched
> With one appearing hair, that will not follow
> These culled and choice-drawn cavaliers to France?
> Work, work your thoughts, and therein see a siege:
> Behold the ordnance on their carriages,
> With fatal mouths gaping on girded Harfleur.
> Suppose, the ambassador from the French comes back;
> Tells Harry, that the king doth offer him
> Katharine, his daughter; and with her, to dowry,
> Some petty and unprofitable dukedoms.
> The offer likes not; and the nimble gunner
> With linstock now the devilish cannon touches,
> And down goes all before them. Still be kind,
> And eke out our performance with your mind."

At the beginning of the fourth act the chorus begs assistance in representing the shades of night. The two armies are encamped in front of each other: on one side are the French "proud of their numbers and secure in soul, the confident and over-lusty French," playing at dice; and on the other side, the English, seated by their watch-fires, "inly ruminate the morning's danger." Meanwhile King Henry, the hero dear to Shakespeare, goes from "watch to watch, from tent to tent," visiting and cheering his captains and soldiers, "bids them good-morrow with a modest smile, and calls them brothers, friends, and countrymen," and at the sight of his "cheerful semblance and sweet majesty" each heart, however wearied, plucks up fresh courage.

The prologue ends as usual in asking indulgence for all defects in the representation, which it begs may be filled up by the spectators' imagination.

> "And so our scene must to the battle fly;
> Where (O for pity!) we shall much disgrace—
> With four or five most vile and ragged foils,
> Right ill-disposed in brawl ridiculous—
> The name of Agincourt. Yet, sit and see;
> Minding true things by what their mockeries be."

The fifth and last prologue renews the usual excuses and exhortations. King Henry is victorious and has to be borne away in thought to Calais, and thence "athwart the sea" to England, where he lands and proceeds to London, where he makes his solemn entry.

> "But now behold,
> In the quick forge and working-house of thought,
> How London doth pour out her citizens!
> The mayor and all his brethren, in best sort,—
> Like to the senators of the antique Rome,
> With the plebeians swarming at their heels,—
> Go forth and fetch their conquering Cæsar in."

In "Pericles," also, the chorus beseeches the public to picture to themselves the ship of the Prince of Tyre tossed about on the waves. Like Time in "A Winter's Tale," Gower, the Chorus in "Pericles," says (Act IV., Sc. 4)—

> "Thus time we waste, and longest leagues make short,
> Sail seas in cockles, have, and wish but for't,
> Making (to take your imagination)
> From bourn to bourn, region to region.
> By you being pardoned, we commit no crime
> To use one language, in each several clime
> Where our scenes seem to live."

It is evident at a glance that Shakespeare's choruses have nothing in common with those of Greek tragedies, neither do they present the least likeness to the choruses in Seneca, or to Lord Buckhurst's imitations of Seneca, in his tragedy of "Gorboduc."

In Seneca the chorus is simply and entirely declamatory, and appears on the scene, only to utter rhetorical amplifications of well-known mythological tales, or of moral truisms: to relate the labours of Hercules, or to describe the return of Aurora, to deplore the inconstancy of men or to extol the joyous repose of a life free from ambition. And so, too, the author of "Gorboduc."

"The chorus of this tragedy consists of four ancient and sage men of Britain, who regularly close every act, the last excepted, with an ode in long-lined stanzas, drawing back the attention of the audience to the substance of what has just passed, and illustrating it by re-capitulatory moral reflections and poetical or historical allusions." *

Shakespeare's choruses, on the contrary, confine themselves to explaining the action, and to supplementing by their commentaries the inadequacy of the representation, or to narrating what the poet necessarily made take place behind the scenes; they fulfil in fact the office of prologues, which would be a much fitter name for them.

Whether chorus or prologue, the fragments quoted above from "Henry V." contain interesting revelations of the material poverty of the stage in the days of Shakespeare. There were then no shifting scenes or movable decorations, and a board was hung up, stating in large letters in what place the scene lay. As Sir Philip Sidney has already told us :—

"You shall have Asia of the one side and Africa of the other, and so many other under-kingdoms, that the player, when he cometh in, must ever begin with telling where he is, or else the tale will not be conceived. Now ye shall have three ladies walk to gather flowers, and then we must believe the stage to be a garden."

This poverty of theatrical furniture would raise a smile on the part of our authors of the present day, who, aided by the stage manager, show themselves such adepts in the movement of the most complicated machinery; but it was in reality favourable to art. Experience and reason agree in showing that it is in the face of feeble material help that the poetical resources unfolded by genius are greatest. When it depends solely and entirely upon the poet to create the illusion, and to take the hearts of his audience captive, his talent must evidently be more keenly stimulated than when he partly relies upon the ingenuity and the purse of the manager. So clearly is this the case, as hardly to admit

* Warton's " History of English Poetry."

of any divergence of opinion theoretically; and if in
the present day managers of theatres expend enormous
sums in putting plays upon the stage, they do so simply
in order to satisfy the false taste of the public, and please
the eye at the expense of the mind; but the defence
of truer principles has never been wanting, and the
French dramatic critic of the day, M. Francisque Sarcey,
actively keeps up the campaign of common sense.*

The historian of the English stage, Payne Collier,
truly says :—

"It is a fortunate circumstance for the poetry of our old plays
that painted movable scenery was then unknown; the imagination
of the auditor only was appealed to, and we owe to the absence of
painted canvas many of the finest descriptive passages in Shakespeare.
The introduction of scenery gives the date to the commencement
of the decline of our dramatic poetry." ("History of Dramatic
Poetry," Vol. III.)

Hallam, in commenting on this remark, enforces it
in his usual clear and incisive style :—

"Even in this age," he writes, "the prodigality of our theatre
in its peculiar boast, scene-painting, can hardly keep pace with the
creative powers of Shakespeare. It is well that he did not live when
a manager was to estimate his descriptions by the cost of realizing
them on canvas, or we might never have stood with Lear on the
cliffs of Dover, or amidst the palaces of Venice with Shylock and
Antonio. The scene is perpetually changed in our old drama precisely
because it was not changed at all." (Hallam's "Literature of Europe,"
Vol. III., Chap. 6.)

Kreyssig ventures further, and in speaking of "Antony
and Cleopatra," he rejoices not only at the want of
scenery which obliged the poet to concentrate in the

---

* The Greeks, it is true, required a magnificent setting to their
dramatic representations, but these, it must be remembered, were great
religious fêtes, given once a year with great solemnity. And, moreover,
the splendour of the scene was always of an ideal and conventional
character, quite the reverse of the material and realistic display now
aimed at.

Queen of Egypt all the fascination she exercised upon every one within her reach, but also at the then usual custom of the part being played by a young boy. Under such barren conditions as these, the only possible seductive charms were those of poetry, unaided by the powerful natural ally to be found in the throat and shapely shoulders of a beautiful *prima donna.*[*] The most elegant turn given to the subject is by an American commentator of Shakespeare, Rev. H. N. Hudson. As a shepherd of souls he is desirous of making his literary criticism subserve a moral or religious purpose, and says—

"It is to the poverty of the old stage that we owe in part the immense riches of the Shakespearian Drama, since it was thereby put to the necessity of making up for the defect of sensuous impression by working on the rational, moral, and imaginative forces of the audience. And undoubtedly the modern way of glutting the senses with a profusion of showy and varied dress and scenery, has struck, as it must always strike, a dead palsy on the legitimate processes of Gothic art. . . . So that here we have a forcible illustration of what is often found true, that men cannot get along because there is nothing to hinder them. For in respect of the moral and imaginative powers it may be justly affirmed that we are often assisted most when *not* assisted, and that the right way of helping us on is by leaving us unhelped. That the soul may find and use her wings, nothing is so good as the being left where there is little for the feet to get hold of and rest upon."[†]

In those days of youthful strength and simplicity, the imagination of the people was as active as that of the poet. As yet unsurfeited with scenic splendours—of which the sensuous pomp dazzles the eye, but blunts the powers of the mind, and makes them languid and exacting,—the pleasures of illusion, to which both nations and individuals in their childhood are so keenly sensitive, could be provided for them at small material cost.

---

[*] "Vorlesungen über Shakespeare," Vol. I., p. 448.

[†] "Shakespeare: his Life, Art, and Characters," Vol. I., p. 160.

" The greater the imagination and freshness of mind possessed by a people," says M. Vitet,* " the less do.they require a regular system of imitative decorations in their theatres. Look at children ! They *make believe* all they wish for, and change everything just as they like ; bestriding a stick they are on horseback, with a stick on their shoulder they are soldiers ; and so it is with nations, when they are young their eyes are tractable and obliging enough to show them all they wish."

M. Taine, in speaking of the old English drama, says—

" Recall your own youth. For my part, the greatest emotion I ever felt in a theatre was excited by a wandering company of four actresses, who acted vaudevilles and melodramas on a sort of platform at the further end of a *café* : it is true I was only eleven years old. In the same way, the English theatre was at that time filled with young and fresh minds, ready to feel, as the poet to dare, everything."

The famous Wall and Moonshine in " Pyramis and Thisbe " are illustrations that will at once occur to the mind of every reader, and as Theseus, Duke of Athens, philosophically remarks of that primitive play, " The best in this kind are but shadows ; and the worst are no worse, if imagination amend them " (" Midsummer Night's Dream," Act V., Sc. 1).

In order to know the real nature of Shakespeare's feelings, with regard to the rules which the upholders of a poetic art supposed to be derived from the ancients endeavoured to impose upon the modern drama, it is highly important to notice that they are observed in two or three of his plays. The " Tempest," for instance, is a very regular play, written in conformity with the law of the unities of time and place : the action is comprised within the space of three hours, and the storm which wrecks the vessel in the first scene, occurs in sight of the island in which the rest of the play takes place. " Richard II." and " Macbeth " are entirely serious plays, from which the comic element is

---

* " Études sur l'Art et le Théâtre Antiques."

excluded, and in which nothing occurs to break in upon their prevailing gravity of tone.* From this it has been concluded that Shakespeare allowed himself, not indeed to be convinced, but to be roused into trying his hand at the game, and that he wished, without making any retractation, to show his opponents, by means of a few specimens, that he, too, was quite capable of composing tragedies according to strict rules. In support of this conjecture, the sort of affectation with which in the "Tempest" the different personages carefully mark the time, is brought forward. But this is not a very satisfactory explanation of the presence of two or three regular dramas amongst Shakespeare's plays, and it is, I think, a truer way of looking at the matter to say that Shakespeare had no feeling whatever of hostility to classical doctrines, but was absolutely indifferent with regard to them. In France, poets may constantly have been seen occupying themselves with Boileau for the purpose of refuting him; the very opposition is, in its way, an act of homage to him, recognizing, if not his authority, at all events his importance, and shows that though the dictum of the master is not submitted to, it is still deemed deserving of consideration, since it is thought worth while to contradict it. The disdain with which Shakespeare treats the Boileaus of his time is of a very different order; he never thinks of them at all, and he puts their precepts into practice at need, or, as is generally the case, leaves them unfulfilled, with equally small concern as to whether he pleases or displeases them. A romanticist of the present century would deem himself disgraced if such a mischance as writing a tragedy in accordance with the classical rules were to befall him, but such accidents happened with Shake-

---

* With the exception in "Macbeth" of the porter's scene, which some critics take to be an interpolation.

speare, just because he cared about the rules not at all.
His one thought was the treatment necessarily required
by the subject, and if the subject invited it, he would
pay due attention to the unities, as in the " Tempest," or
would write tragedies without any admixture of comedy,
like " Macbeth " and " Richard II. ; " for an artist such as
he was, was not the man to spoil his work for the
pleasure of teasing Sir Philip Sidney, or of enraging Ben
Jonson.

Of all men, Shakespeare is the least *doctrinaire* ; the
idealistic, revolutionary, theory-loving order of mind is
the direct opposite of his. He is a practical, prudent
Englishman, desirous of progress, but preferring it without violent shocks and changes, and very conservative
in his tastes. With the instinct of a practical man of
business, prompt to detect from what quarter the wind
of success is likely to blow, he thoroughly grasped the
fact that the time for classical simplicity was irrevocably
passed, and that for a modern spectator, and especially
for an Englishman—that barbarian of the North, with a
taste so little Athenian,—more highly spiced entertain-
ments were needed. He accordingly put before his
comtemporaries and countrymen, plays suited to their
tastes, and while Daniel's " Cleopatra " and Brandon's
" Virtuous Octavia," were acted to empty benches, or
had even not life enough to drag themselves on to the
stage, Shakespeare, combining a keen eye to business
with consummate knowledge of his art, had the satisfaction
of seeing crowds flock to his plays, and at the same time
of adding considerably to his little fortune. This less
ideal side of his character must not be lost sight of,
which made him a practical man as well as a poet : he
invariably looked to the result, to the substantial benefit
as well as the poetical use to be made of the materials
he employed, and without entangling himself in theories
or systems he went straight to the *fact*.

To regard him as the founder of a school, or merely as a man capable of writing a neatly turned preface to his works, would be to make the greatest possible mistake concerning him. It is true, that if we wish to gather up the æsthetic ideas scattered throughout his works, we shall find a few here and there, beginning with Hamlet's famous speech to the players, but they are rare, and their whole interest and meaning may be summed up in the advice given to different artists, to painters as well as to poets, and to poets as well as to actors, to follow nature. This intellectual modesty is undoubtedly the cause of the error so long believed in, of the unconscious nature of Shakespeare's art. The truth is, that he hides himself behind his works with an unparalleled self-abnegation, which makes them well-nigh resemble the impersonal productions of primæval poetry, and which, within certain limits, would go far to justify a comparison between his genius and that of Homer. There are some readers, of a tender disposition, who feel the need of taking to their hearts the authors of their favourite books, and to such gentle souls, Shakespeare offers no satisfaction. We admire and respect him, we contemplate his impassible objectivity with astonishment mingled with awe, we may find both pleasure and profit in living in familiar intercourse with him, turning over the pages of his masterpieces with "a daily and nightly hand," as Du Bellay says of Horace; but we do not *love* him. In order to love a poet it is necessary to see the man in him, and this we do not do in Shakespeare; his personal qualities, and above all, a few defects, some weaknesses in secret harmony with our own nature are necessary to endear him to us, and the irritating problem of an impenetrable personality must not be presented to us, as in Shakespeare, in every page. Schiller, in his " Naïve und sentimentalische dichtung," honestly confesses that at first he felt repelled by

Shakespeare, and required some time to familiarize himself with his imposing, rather than lovable, genius.

" Accustomed, from my own knowledge of modern poets, first of all
to seek the poet in his works, to meet *his* heart, to reflect *with him*
upon the matters treated of, and in short to look for the object in the
subject, I felt it to be intolerable that Shakespeare should never let
himself come within my grasp, and that I could nowhere get speech of
him. I had studied him and given him my utmost respect for many
years before I learnt how to love him personally. I was incapable
then of understanding Nature at first hand. And the same thing
also happened to me with Homer, with whom I made acquaintance
later on."

The indifference shown by Shakespeare towards all
doctrines, and the practical character of his creative
powers, are cardinal features of his genius to which we
shall have to return in speaking of his political and
religious sentiments. As regards classical antiquity, he
had no literary passion for it of any kind, he was neither
its foe nor its friend, and regarded it merely as a vast
storehouse of materials for his art. Of such storehouses
he had two or three; antiquity, the Middle Ages, national
history; and borrowing largely, sometimes from one
and sometimes from another, he calmly and cheerfully
built up his own edifice.

CHAPTER IV.

THE question as to whether Molière was able to read Aristophanes, Terence and Plautus, in the original, would hardly be likely to excite a very lively interest in the mind of any Frenchman. Molière is held to be a great comic poet by his countrymen, and it may be doubted whether, if they were shown that over and above that he was also a good Greek and Latin scholar, it would greatly add to their estimation of him, or if it were proved that classical authors were only known to him through translations whether their admiration for the author of the " Misanthrope " would suffer any diminution. But in England people think and feel otherwise, and the question regarding Shakespeare's knowledge of Greek and Latin, would appear to be of vast importance in their eyes, to judge from the extraordinary eagerness with which it has generally been discussed. The combatants in this strange dispute are even more curious than the debated point itself, for—admitting for an instant the truth of the most unfavourable conclusions with regard to Shakespeare's classical learning—it is difficult to understand how such an avowal could be harmful to his glory, and that, on the contrary, it should not rather redound to his credit, and redouble our wonder and admiration for the wealth and penetrative power of a genius able, by itself alone, to furnish so many marvellous beauties that have hitherto been, to a certain extent, attributed to study and to the imitation of others. But though the controverted point has no intrinsic importance, the controversy itself is both amusing and instructive.

Great value is attached by the English, who are at heart an aristocratic people, to the distinctions inherited by noble birth and to those gained at the universities; the greatest recommendation a man can have is a title of nobility, the next is a university degree. While a democratic Frenchman, in spite of the small amount of personal merit or renown he may possess, affects as a matter of good taste to conceal his title or degree, an Englishman always proclaims and displays them; dukes and earls, those even whose talents and real worth have made them justly famous, are as exacting on this point as the obscurest of country squires; the Bachelor of Arts with his honours fresh upon him is not more careful to write after his name the initials of the degree he has just taken than are Oxford and Cambridge professors of long standing. Influenced by this national prejudice in favour of birth or, in default of that, of the certificate in due official form of a university education as a passport to a position in society, it would almost seem as if Englishmen had been a little ashamed of this poor William Shakespeare, who not only was no lord or earl, like Lord Buckhurst, but was not even a graduate of either of the universities, as Marlowe, Greene, Peele, Lyly, Lodge, Gascoigne, Richard Edwards, and, in short, as nearly all the other dramatic authors of his time were; and also as if they held it necessary for the honour of England to show that he might have been at any rate a Bachelor of Arts.

Another reason for the passionate interest with which English critics have fought over this point may be found in their evident predilection, when dealing with poets, for adding a few more units, whether great or small, to the sum of clearly ascertained biographical facts: it matters not that the discovery should be insignificant to the last degree—that it is a fact is all-sufficient. And an excellent opportunity for research of a precise and not too abstract nature, and for questions of small facts, is afforded in the measurement of the exact amount of Shakespeare's classical learning. The subject opens a fine field for erudition. Æsthetics, taste, feeling, philosophy and thought are quite unnecessary here, and all that is wanted is to ferret out and scrape together and pile up higher and higher, mountains of notes, proceeding after the manner of rats—

> " Qui, les livres rongeants
> Se font savants jùsques aux dents."

This is where the tribe mentioned by Voltaire in his " Temple of Taste " shines forth, Baldus, Scioppius, Lexicocrassus, Scriblerius, " a swarm of commentators who restored passages and compiled huge volumes about some word they did not understand."

> "Là j'aperçus les Daciers, les Saumaises,
> Gens hérissés de savantes fadaises,
> Le teint jauni, les yeux rouges et secs,
> Le dos courbé sous un tas d'auteurs grecs,
> Tout noircis d'encre et coiffés de poussière.
> Je leur criai de loin par la portière :
> ' N'allez vous pas dans le Temple du Goût
> Vous décrasser ? Nous, messieurs ? point du tout,
> Ce n'est pas là, grace au ciel, notre étude ;
> Le goût n'est rien ; nous avons l'habitude
> De rédiger au long de point. en point
> Ce qu'on pensa ; mais nous ne pensons point.' "

The family of Lexicocrassus is by no means confined to England ; in the present day æsthetics are everywhere supplanted by erudition, and criticism conceived as a work of art and of thought is stigmatized with the withering name of dilettanteism, by grammarians who pride themselves on possessing neither style nor ideas; while the easy-going public accepts an auctioneer's catalogue as literature. Careful research in France has recently procured for us an inventory of Molière's library, plate-chest and carpeting; and truly a knowledge of a poet's stock of household goods is not without its interest—as, for instance, to know that Malherbe's rooms were very shabbily furnished, and that, as Racine says, he had only seven or eight rush-bottomed chairs; and that Victor Hugo surrounds himself with sumptuous and artistic pieces of furniture, is not a matter of indifference to a philosophical thinker, but only on condition of his penetrating through the given facts to the general idea expressed by them, and not remaining absorbed in the contemplation of a pair of tongs, three frying-pans and a couple of chafing-dishes.

It is in this philosophical spirit that I wish to approach the task of making out the inventory of Shakespeare's intellectual furniture in the way of learning, endeavouring to extract from the mass of dry details some ideas of general interest, and taking especial care to avoid falling into the weakness of imagining that the *genius loci* can suffer either increase or diminution of glory from the riches or poverty of the house he dwells in.

It is necessary first of all to get rid of a most senseless but common confusion which has too often prevailed in the discussion touching the amount of Shakespeare's knowledge, by which the knowledge of languages has been and still is continually confounded with learning strictly so called. Yet they are assuredly two very different things. A knowledge of languages is a key wherewith to unlock the treasures of learning, but it is not learning itself. There are persons who think the key so curious that they pass their whole life in examining it, without once using it to open anything whatever,—of such are grammarians. But it is better to get into literature by a false key or by any other means, no matter what, than to rest contented with studying the ingenious mechanism of the right key; it is better to read translations of Homer and the Greek tragedians than to be satisfied with being well up in our Greek conjugations and syntax. Few men have been as learned as Goethe; few men have imbibed the Hellenic spirit and have understood it as he did, yet Goethe did not know Greek. / Did Shakespeare know Greek, and did he know Latin? The whole question has been reduced to these pedantic limits, and no higher idea has been conceived of the education of a poet. While some have denied him all knowledge of classical languages, others have exaggerated his acquaintance with them, —both assertions, in spite of their contradictory nature, affording equal satisfaction to the vanity of critics; for a pedant can make as much capital by exposing the ignorance of a man of genius, as he can by the opportunity afforded him by the learning possessed by the author under review, to display his own erudition.

The origin of the debate is to be found in a line written by Ben Jonson, in an enthusiastic epistle "to the memory of his beloved William Shakespeare," in which he exclaims that the great poet England had just lost outweighed all antiquity, though he knew "small Latin and less Greek." This line has occasioned as much wrangling and hairsplitting as any text in Perseus or Lycophron; for what, it has been asked, does Ben Jonson mean by "small Latin"? In the estimation of a mighty classical scholar like himself, a very respectable knowledge of Latin might rank as a small matter. And then, it was further remarked, he does not say "no Greek" although his metre would have perfectly allowed of his doing so, but "less Greek." Therefore—oh joy!—Shakespeare did know a little Greek.

"Du Grec, ô ciel! du grec! il sait du grec, ma sœur!
    Ah, ma nièce, du grec! du grec, quelle douceur!"

And finally, in spite of the sincerely affectionate tone
of Ben Jonson's epistle, it has been hinted that the
"small Latin and less Greek" might have been dictated
by secret jealousy; and since then it has dropped out of
account.

In the eighteenth century Warburton and divers other
learned commentators, finding curious points of resemblance between Shakespeare and Sophocles, Euripides,
Lucian, etc., had no hesitation in concluding that he had
both read and copied the Greek writers. It was in 1767
that Dr. Farmer's famous essay on the learning of Shakespeare appeared.

In comparing the text of Shakespeare's Roman
tragedies with Sir Thomas North's English translation
of Plutarch's "Lives" from the French of Amyot, Farmer
showed that Shakespeare had borrowed entirely from
that translation,—that he had copied many phrases and
even whole pages from it without taking any pains to
verify its accuracy by the slightest examination of the
original text, as he everywhere follows the English
version blindfold, even to its errors and mistranslations.
For example, in the third act of "Antony and Cleopatra,"
Octavius, speaking of the illustrious lovers, says—

> " Unto her
> He gave the 'stablishment of Egypt; made her
> Of lower Syria, Cyprus, *Lydia*,
> Absolute Queen."

Lydia is a mistake for Lybia, of which Plutarch speaks,
but the mistake is made both by Amyot and by North.
Again, in the fourth act, Octavius, when challenged by
Antony whom he had just defeated, answers—

> " My messenger
> He hath whipt with rods; dares me to personal combat,
> Cæsar to Antony. Let th' old ruffian know
> I have many other ways to die; meantime,
> Laugh at his challenge."

"I have many other ways to die" is a mistranslation;
Plutarch says not "I have" but "he has," that is, that
Antony has many other ways to die. His sentence,
translated word for word, runs thus: "After this, Antony
sent to defy Cæsar to single combat, and received for
answer that he might find other means of ending his life."
Amyot cannot be said to be in fault here, he translates
it: "And another time Antony sent to challenge Cæsar
to single combat. Cæsar sent him word that he had many
other ways of dying than that;" but Shakespeare was
misled by the ambiguous use of the word *he*, which is
also found in the English version by North, "Cæsar
answered that he had many other ways to die than so."

Shakespeare's Timon composes the following epitaph
for his tomb:—

"Here lies a wretched corse, of wretched soul bereft:
Seek not my name; a plague consume you wicked caitiffs left!
Here lie I Timon; who, alive, all living men did hate:
Pass by, and curse thy fill; but pass and stay not here thy gait."

This epitaph is taken word for word (one word only
being changed) from Sir Thomas North, who here thinks
it well to follow Amyot's example of turning the lines
into verse. Shakespeare's version, or that which is
attributed to him, for "Timon of Athens" is full of
incoherencies and doubtful passages, — presents the
strange anomaly of uniting in one, two perfectly distinct
epitaphs, distinguished as such by North and by Amyot,
as well as by Plutarch: one is by Timon himself, the
other by the poet Callimachus. It is absurd to say,
"Seek not my name," and two lines further on, "Here
lie I Timon." In North the passage is, "On the tomb
was written this epitaph:—

"Here lies a wretched corse of wretched soul bereft,
 Seek not my name; a plague consume you wicked wretches left."

It is reported that Timon himself when he lived made

this epitaph; for that which is commonly rehearsed was not his, but made by the poet Callimachus :—

> " Here lie I Timon, who alive all living men did hate:
> Pass by and curse thy fill, but pass and stay not here thy gait."

Turning to "Julius Cæsar," we find Antony (Act III. Sc. 2) saying, when reading Cæsar's will to the people :—

> "Moreover, he hath left you all his walks,
> His private arbours, and new-planted orchards,
> On *this* side Tiber."

" On this side Tiber," writes Shakespeare. Plutarch wrote περαν τοῦ ποταμοῦ, " *across* the Tiber," but Shakespeare was misled by North, who had been misled by Amyot.

> "He bequeathed," says North, "unto every citizen of Rome twenty-five drachmas a man, and he left his gardens and arbours unto the people, which he had on *this* side of the river of Tyber."

But the most striking instances of Shakespeare borrowing from North occur in " Coriolanus," where, in the hero's speech to Aufidius, demanding his hospitality and alliance, and in that of Volumnia to her son, in which she beseeches him not to war upon Rome,* Shakespeare has done little more, says Dr. Farmer, than throw the very words of North into blank verse.

The best and most conclusive part of Dr. Farmer's essay is his demonstration of the third-handedness of Shakespeare's knowledge of Plutarch, but it contains also several other curious little revelations; as, for example, that concerning the plagiarism from Anacreon that commentators have been pleased to detect in the following passage from " Timon of Athens " (Act IV., Sc. 3) :—

> " The sun's a thief, and with his great attraction
> Robs the vast sea. The moon's an arrant thief,
> And her pale fire she snatches from the sun.

---

* " Should we be silent and not speak, etc."—Act V., Sc. 3.

> The sea's a thief, whose liquid surge resolves
> The moon into salt tears.   The earth's a thief,
> That feeds and breeds by a composture stol'n
> From general excrement : each thing's a thief."

Dr. Farmer shows that, even supposing it impossible for Shakespeare, "who was generally able to think for himself," to have originated it, it cannot be quoted as a proof of his knowledge of Greek, seeing that Anacreon's ode had been translated several times into Latin, French, and English, before the end of the sixteenth century, notably by Ronsard in his drinking song :—

> " La terre les eaux va buvant ;
> L'arbre la boit par la racine ;
> La mer salie boit le vent,
> Et le soleil boit la marine.
> Le soliel est bu de la lune ;
> Tout boit, soit en haut ou en bas ;
> Suivant cette règle commune,
> Pourquoi donc ne boirions nous pas ? "

It was not only in the case of Greek authors that Shakespeare gladly availed himself of translations, for, as Farmer shows, in many instances where it would have been easy for him to consult the Latin originals he preferred having recourse to English translations, as is the case, for example, with Prospero's address to his attendant spirits in the " Tempest."

> " Ye elves of hills, of standing lakes, and groves,"

which Warburton took to be copied from Ovid, but which a comparison of texts clearly proves to be borrowed not from the Latin poet but from the English translation by Arthur Golding in 1567.

Farmer makes some very sensible remarks on the subject of Shakespeare's frequent allusions to classical fables and memories.   To infer from these allusions that Shakespeare had read Ovid, Virgil, and Homer, at any rate in English, and had himself drunk at the fountain-

G

head of Greek and Latin antiquity, is a quite uncalled-for conclusion. The literature of the Middle Ages and of the Renaissance had popularized all the legends of antiquity, and turned them into current coin long before translations of Greek authors were in people's hands. To quote an example, Shakespeare, in the "Midsummer Night's Dream," happens to mention Dido, and thereupon commentators carefully point out that there was no translation of Virgil's "Æneid" in Shakespeare's time. But what does that matter? "The fate of Dido had been sung very early by Gower, Chaucer, and Lydgate; Marlowe had even already introduced her to the stage."

Another passage in the "Midsummer Night's Dream" shows that Shakespeare knew of the distinction made by Ovid between Cupid's two sets of arrows, some of them being pointed with lead, and others with gold; and again the question arises whether he derived this directly from Ovid, in either Latin or English. He may possibly have done so, but still such a conclusion is perfectly unnecessary, as "Cupid's arrows appear with their characteristic differences in Surrey, in Sidney, in Spenser, and in every sonneteer of the Elizabethan period." Later on, Voltaire, when he in his turn inherited the tradition, thus describes them in the first scene of "Nanine":—

> " Je vous l'ai dit, l'amour a deux carquois :
> L'un est rempli de ces traits tout de flamme
> Dont la douceur porte la paix dans l'âme,
> Qui rend plus purs nos goûts, nos sentiments,
> Nos soins plus vifs, nos plaisirs plus touchants ;
> L'autre n'est plein que de flèches cruelles,
> Qui, répandant les soupçons, les querelles,
> Rebutent l'âme, etc."

The conclusions that Dr. Farmer draws are, however, exaggerated, and overstep his premisses; he is of opinion that he has proved that Shakespeare knew neither Greek nor Latin, but in reality he has only shown that the poet made use of translations from both languages as much as possible, and besides this, that independently of any translations, much of his classical knowledge may have been culled from the literature of the Middle Ages and of the Renaissance.

In criticising Shakespeare's attainments, Dr. Farmer fell into the egregious folly of speaking in a strain of impertinent conceit; it is as if the little man—for little he must assuredly have been—was eaten up with vanity, and was bursting to show that he knew more of Greek and Latin than Shakespeare did.

Of the same order of research and of the same spirit was another equally famous work that appeared in the eighteenth century—" Illustrations of Shakespeare," containing an essay " On the Anachronisms and some other Incongruities of Shakspere," by Francis Douce. In this big book, bristling with erudition but devoid of talent, and very foolish and irreverent towards Shakespeare, the poet's historical and geographical blunders are pointed out with pedantic and ponderous care, and without the least understanding of the subject; but an inquiry into Shakespeare's anachronisms, and the further criticism of Douce's book, must be reserved for another chapter.

When Shakespeare was looked upon as an "intoxicated savage," his literary learning was, naturally enough, held in small esteem, and rated lower than it really deserved; but when a complete revolution in opinion was introduced by Schlegel and Coleridge, who proclaimed that he must no longer be regarded as a mere child of nature, but as a wise and enlightened artist knowing perfectly what he was about, people fell into the opposite extreme, and entertained the most extravagant notions as to the extent and depth of his acquirements. Our own century has discovered that Shakespeare

knew everything, like Dr. Pancrace, in Molière's comedy
of the "Mariage Forcé," "fables, mythology and history,
grammar, poetry, rhetoric, dialectics and sophistry; mathe-
matics, arithmetic, optics, oneiro-criticism and physics."
A legal system, a treatise on mental maladies, a complete
guide-book to country life, lessons on ornithology, ento-
mology, and botany have all been extracted from his
works; while from the propriety with which he uses
technical terms appertaining to military matters, to
hunting and to jurisprudence, it has been concluded that
he must have been a soldier, a poacher, and a lawyer.
Several of his titles to the professorship of universal
knowledge have escaped my memory, but those already
mentioned make up a tolerably long list, in which
Shakespeare figures as a doctor, a lawyer, an agriculturist,
a zoologist, a botanist, a hunter and a soldier.

A complete ethnological system has also been discovered in his works by Mr. O'Connell, the author of
a "New Exegesis of Shakespeare," published in 1859,
according to whom "that which constitutes the novel and
peculiar greatness of Shakespeare, is that being the first
to rise to a wider and, at the same time, deeper contemplation of human nature, he has depicted, not only
individuals and families, but has also sketched the
character of the principal European races. While
Æschylus and the ancient drama limited the sphere of
action to the family, the founder of the modern drama
carried it further, and included larger groups in conformity with the general progress made in the knowledge
of men and of nature. What Asia Minor and Hellas
were to the Athenians, Europe, in its vast extent, was
to the English people in the days of the Renaissance.
The subjects of the Æschylean drama were the house of
Pelopides and that of Labdacides; those of Shakespeare
were the Germanic, Italian, and Celtic races: in this
system, Iago represents the character of the Italian,

Hamlet the Teutonic, and Macbeth the Celtic race." * It was this exaggerated notion of Shakespeare's learning and philosophy which also gave rise to the famous paradox, brought forward from time to time by some lunatic, that Shakespeare never existed, and that his name was only a fictitious one, adopted by the most learned and philosophical thinker of the time, Francis Bacon !

To rehabilitate Shakespeare as a Latin scholar was a task that lay very close to the hearts of his commentators, and they entered upon it with such eagerness and simplicity, that the disinterested observer feels quite bewildered, and tries in vain to decide which of the two sides is the more ridiculous—the one which Shakespeare's presumed ignorance rendered vainglorious of its own learning, or the other which thought the poet's glory would be enhanced by showing that he might have carried off a prize for Latin verse. As a sample of the extremely acrimonious language in which those of Coleridge's school speak of " the detractors of Shakespeare's learning," may be quoted the passage in which Knight, the well-known editor and critic of Shakespeare, expresses his appreciation of Dr. Farmer's essay :—

" He wrote an essay on the learning of Shakespeare which has not one passage of solid criticism from the first page to the last, and if the name and the works of Shakespeare were to perish, and one copy could be miraculously preserved, the only inference from the book would be, that William Shakespeare was a very obscure and ignorant man whom some misjudging admirers had been desirous to exalt into an ephemeral reputation, and that Richard Farmer was a very distinguished and learned man who had stripped the mask off the pretender."

That such a passage should ever have been written is almost inconceivable, not on account of the hard measure dealt out to Dr. Farmer, but because of the singular notion implied in it, that if Dr. Farmer were right in

---

* Littré, " Littérature et Histoire."

alleging Shakespeare's ignorance of languages, the poet would be a mere pretender to the crown of fame. For my part, I am most willing to grant Shakespeare's acquaintance with Greek and Latin, not so much for the honour of the poet, as to gratify Mr. Knight, since he takes the matter so much to heart; I believe, and will give my reasons for believing further on, that Shakespeare at all events knew Latin,—only, in truth, the strange arguments with which this view has sometimes been upheld makes one doubt whether it can possibly be the truer one.

In the second part of "Hamlet," Polonius, in introducing the players to the Prince, praises their skill, and says, that for them, "Seneca cannot be too heavy, nor Plautus too light;" that simply is, as the German critic Delius justly remarks, "They can act with facility both the comic Plautus and the tragic Seneca." There is no hidden subtlety of meaning in the two adjectives, *heavy* and *light*. But Knight discovers in them an admirably profound and concise definition of the talent of Seneca and of Plautus.

"In 'Hamlet,'" he says, "Shakespeare gives in a word the characteristics of two ancient dramatists; his criticism is decisive as to his familiarity with the originals, 'Seneca cannot be too heavy, nor Plautus too light.'"

In the "Comedy of Errors" (Act V., Sc. 1), a servant rushes in, crying—

"O mistress, mistress, shift and save yourself!
My master and his man are both broke loose,
Beaten the maids a-row, and bound the doctor,
Whose beard they have singed off with brands of fire;
And ever as it blazed they threw on him
Great pails of puddled mire to quench the hair."

This, it appears, is an imitation of Virgil, for in the twelfth book of the "Æneid" (lines 298, and following), we read :—

" Corinæus took a lighted brand from the altar, and at the moment when Ebusus was about to strike him he threw it in his face, the flames surrounded him, and his huge beard caught fire and burnt with a great smell of burning."

Thus, whenever the incident of a beard maliciously set on fire occurs in literature, we must go back to Virgil as its source; as, for instance, in "Tristram Shandy," where Sterne shows us Susannah setting fire with her candle to Dr. Slop's wig (Vol. VI., Ch. III.), who, in a passion, flings in her face the cataplasm that had been prepared for little Tristram. Again, the passage in which Shakespeare, in " As You Like It," has described the death of a stag, and "the big, round tears coursing one another down his innocent nose " (Act II., Sc. 1), must presumably be derived from the seventh book of the "Æneid ;"—and yet, is it not possible that so great a poacher might have seen such a sight for himself?

But when we find Knight placing a passage in which Shakespeare puts the eulogy of blows into Dromio's mouth, side by side with one in which Cicero celebrates the praises of learning, we begin to think that we are dreaming, and rub our eyes and read the paragraph over again :—

"' When I am cold he heats me with beating; when I am warm he cools me with beating; I am waked with it when I sleep; raised with it when I sit; driven out of doors with it when I go from home; welcomed home with it when I return ' (' Comedy of Errors,' Act IV., Sc. 4.): ' Literature,' says Cicero,' is the exercise of youth and the charm of old age; adorning fortune, it also offers in adversity a refuge and a consolation; the delight of the domestic hearth, easily enjoyed everywhere, it bears us company at night, travelling, and in the country.' " *

As to Greek authors, Knight hardly ventures to affirm positively that Shakespeare read them in the

---

* Hæc studia adolescentiam agunt, senectutem oblectant secundas res ornant, adversis perfugium ac solatium præbent, delectant domi, non impediunt foris, pernoctant nobiscum, peregrinantur, rusticantur.

original, but he evidently wishes to intimate as much to his readers. When comparing Shakespeare's misanthrope with that of Lucian, he complacently passes in review the numberless points of resemblance between them, and significantly observes that no translation of Lucian had appeared in Shakespeare's time ; as, however, the subject of Timon the Misanthrope was popular before then, and had even appeared on the stage, Knight is obliged to admit that Shakespeare may have known it in its principal details without having had recourse to the original in Greek.

In the historical drama of " Henry V." (Act I., Sc. 2) we read :—

> " While that the armed hand doth fight abroad,
> The advised head defends itself at home ;
> For argument, through high, and low, and lower,
> Put into parts, doth keep in one concent ;
> Congreeing in a full and natural close,
> Like music."

Then, after a very poetical comparison of the "work of honey-bees " to a well-governed state, there follows a series of similes, all tending to set forth the truth that—

> " So may a thousand actions, once afoot,
> End in one purpose, and be all well borne
> Without defeat."

The same idea is met with in Plato's " Republic," as well as in a fragment, preserved by Augustine, of Cicero's long-lost treatise, " De Republica." *   Knight, in his

---

* Theobald was the first of Shakespeare's commentators to whom it occurred to quote this passage, which runs as follows : " Ut in fidibus ac tibiis atque cantu ipso ac vocibus, concentus est quidam tenendus ex distinctis sonis, quem immutatum ac discrepantem aures eruditæ ferre non possunt, isque concentus ex dissimillimarum vocum moderatione concors tamen efficitur et congruens : sic ex summis et infimis et mediis interjectis ordinibus, ut sonis, moderata ratione civitas consensu dissimillimarum concinit, et quæ harmonia a musicis dicitur in cantu, ea est in civitate concordia, arctissimum atque optimum omni in republica vinculum incolumitatis : quæ sine justitia nullo pacto esse potest."

edition of Shakespeare, gives the following note on this subject :—

" The words of Cicero, to which the lines of Shakespeare have so close a resemblance, form part of a fragment of that portion of his lost treatise ' De Republica ' which is presented to us only in the writings of St. Augustin. The first question therefore is, Had Shakespeare read the fragment in St. Augustin ? But Cicero's ' De Republica ' was, as far as we know, an adaptation of Plato's ' Republic,' the sentence we have quoted is almost literally to be found in Plato ; and what is still more curious, the lines of Shakespeare are more deeply imbued with the Platonic philosophy than the passage of Cicero. . . . They develope unquestionably the great Platonic doctrine of the Tri-unity of the three principles in man, with the idea of a state. The particular passage in Plato's ' Republic ' to which we refer is in Book IV., and may be thus rendered : ' It is not alone wisdom and strength which make a state simply wise and strong, but it (order), like that harmony called the diapason, is diffused throughout the whole state, making both the weakest and the strongest, and the middling people concent the same melody.' Again, ' the harmonic power of political justice is the same as that musical concent which connects the three chords, the octave, the bass and the fifth.' There was no translation of Plato in Shakespeare's time except a single dialogue by Spenser."

In a question of this kind, in which, to whatever side we may incline, it is impossible to lay claim to absolute certainty, it is well to keep within the bounds of a prudent and modest reserve ; but one rule that always holds good is from among the various explanations of a fact to choose out the simplest.

What has here to be accounted for is the presence in Shakespeare's works of a passage which is imbued with the spirit of platonism, and is so beautifully expressed, and so full of an antique wisdom and philosophy that it might have been written by Plato himself. It must, in the first place, be remembered that the comparison of a well-ordered government to a concert in which every instrument plays its part, or to a bee-hive, has long since become a commonplace in literature. Ever since it was set in circulation by Plato and Cicero in their respective treatises on the "Republic," there has probably been no ancient philosopher or poet from whose writings some analogous simile could not be quoted. In the time of the Renaissance Plato was held in the highest favour by English poets; as Coleridge tells us, " the star of serenest brilliance in the glorious constellation of Elizabeth's court, our England's Sir Philip Sidney, held high converse with Spenser on the idea of supersensual beauty." Lyly, the author of " Euphues," borrowed the name of his hero from Plato's "Republic," and his romance teems with comparisons between human governments and those presented to us in nature, especially in the case of bees. The tedious length of his exemplification places it far below the poetry of Shakespeare's passage, and makes it infinitely less worthy to be compared to the antique model, but it is precisely in such cases as this that we catch a glimpse of genius at work in one of its most marvellous operations, by virtue of which, diving through all the prolixity and exaggeration that a whole host of imitators have lost themselves in, it re-discovers an ancient conception, and makes it live again in all its first freshness and truth : for there is a brotherhood among all great minds, and Shakespeare happening to meet with the enfeebled expression of what had once been a thought of Plato's, was able to re-think it, almost back to its original form. A most striking example of this power of resurrection, which is the birthright of genius, is afforded in the character of Cressida, as will be seen further on. In all probability Shakespeare knew nothing of the poem of the obscure Norman trouvère who first conceived the idea of the brilliant coquette, but amidst all the more or less clumsy alterations made by numberless imitators of Benoit de Sainte-More, he has grasped the essential features of her character with sure and unerring hand.

Amongst the many minor points of resemblance in details to the texts of classical antiquity, so abundantly offered by Shakespeare's plays, those which touch upon philosophy possess the greatest chance of being interesting, as in them we may hope to meet not only with words, but with at least a few reflected rays of thought. Professor Nebler, of the University of Berne, has dedicated one chapter of his book on Shakespeare (Aufsätze über Shakespeare ") to pointing out 'all the passages in which Shakespeare alludes to the name or ideas of an ancient philosopher, and from his pages I have culled the following sentences, adding those I have gathered from my own reading of Shakespeare.

Nothing could well be more poetical than the opening of the fifth act of the " Merchant of Venice." Jessica and Lorenzo are sitting one summer's night in Portia's garden, singing the eternal hymn of love, while the exquisite grace and charm of the duet is enhanced by the classical reminiscences more or less vague and inaccurate, which mingle with their strains :—

> "*Lor.* The moon shines bright :—in such a night as this,
> When the sweet wind did gently kiss the trees,
> And they did make no noise,—in such a night,
> Troilus, methinks, mounted the Trojan walls,
> And sighed his soul toward the Grecian tents,
> Where Cressid lay that night.*
> *Jes.*   In such a night
> Did Thisbe fearfully o'ertrip the dew ;
> And saw the lion's shadow ere himself,
> And ran dismayed away.
> *Lor.*   In such a night
> Stood Dido with a willow in her hand †
> Upon the wild sea-banks, and waft her love
> To come again to Carthage.
> *Jes.*   In such a night
> Medea gather'd the enchanted herbs
> That did renew old Æson.

---

* A recollection of Chaucer.

† Steevens notes this passage as a proof out of many that Shakespeare was no reader of the classics.

> *Lor.* . . . . Look how the floor of heaven
> Is thick inlaid with patines of .bright gold,
> There's not the smallest orb which thou behold'st
> But in his motion like an angel sings ;
> Still quiring to the young-eyed cherubins :
> Such harmony is in immortal souls.
> But whilst this muddy vesture of decay
> Doth grossly close it in, we cannot hear it."

The idea of the music of the spheres belongs primarily to the philosophy or rather to the poetry of Plato ; and the same thought is finely expressed by Cicero in the fragment known under the title of "The Dream of Scipio." In "Antony and Cleopatra," Cleopatra, bewailing Antony's death, compares his voice to the " tunèd spheres " (Act V., Sc. 2) ; and in " Twelfth Night " Olivia pays the same compliment to the page in disguise, with whom she is in love. Pericles, prince of Tyre, in his ecstasy at finding his daughter Marina, suddenly hears sounds of music unheard by the others, which he calls the music of the spheres.

The name of Aristotle occurs in the first scene of the " Taming of the Shrew," but there is a more curious mention of him in " Troilus and Cressida," Act II., Sc. 2. In the council held by Priam, Troilus and Paris with the unreflective impetuosity of youth vote for the continuation of the war ; but Hector, no less calm and prudent than brave, maintains that it would be right as well as politic to restore the wife of Menelaus to her lawful husband, and reproves his two scatter-brained brothers, saying—

> " Paris and Troilus, you have both said well ;
> And on the cause and question now in hand
> Have glozed,—but superficially ; not much
> Unlike young men, whom Aristotle thought
> Unfit to hear moral philosophy."

For Hector to speak of Aristotle is an amusing ana-chronism, but it is difficult to decide whether Shakespeare fell into it intentionally or through inadvertence, the humorous licence which runs through the whole play lending probability to the former suggestion; just as Goethe, it may be remembered, has been pleased to put the name of Luther into the mouth of Faust. It would be as idle to conclude, as Gervinus does, on the strength of Hector's speech, that Shakespeare had read Aristotle's "Ethics," as it would be to imagine that every poet of the present day who alludes to a tenet of the Cartesian philosophy or of eclecticism or of positivism has necessarily read the works of Des Cartes, of Cousin, or of Auguste Comte. In his "De Augmentis," Bacon quotes Aristotle's same opinion of young men, and strangely enough makes precisely the same mistake that Shakespeare does; it being politics, not moral philosophy, for which the Greek philosopher deemed young men unfit.

Pythagoras is several times mentioned in Shakespeare, and always with some ironical allusion to his doctrine of the transmigration of souls. The lively Gratiano, in the "Merchant of Venice," tells Shylock that he must have been a wolf in a former existence (Act IV., Sc. 1); Rosalind, in "As You Like It," has a confused recollection of having once been an Irish rat (Act III., Sc. 2); and in "Twelfth Night," the clown, when mocking and jeering at Malvolio, advises him not to kill a woodcock lest he should thereby dislodge the soul of his grandmother (Act IV., Sc. 2). The authority of Pythagoras is invoked by name in each of these three passages.

Shakespeare alludes to Heraclitus, though without mentioning his name, in Act I., Sc. 2, of the "Merchant of. Venice," in which Portia says of one of her suitors, the melancholy and morose County Palatine, that when he grows old he will become like the weeping philosopher.

Epicurus is only treated as the voluptuous materialist of common tradition, and is thus presented in "Antony and Cleopatra" (Act II., Sc. 1); in "King Lear" (Act I.,

Sc. 4); in "Macbeth" (Act V., Sc. 3) and in the "Merry Wives of Windsor" (Act II., Sc. 2).

The only mention of Socrates occurs in the "Taming of the Shrew," where, as may readily be guessed, it is not as the philosopher but as the husband that he is alluded to : Petruchio replies to his friend's report of Katharine's shrewish disposition, "Be she as curst and shrewd as Socrates' Xantippe she moves me not." (Act I., Sc. 2.)

Shakespeare, it may be noted, is fond of laughing at philosophers, which indeed is not only allowable but is in fact a highly philosophical proceeding ; for if, as Pascal says, "to laugh at philosophy is really to philosophize," to laugh at philosophers is still more so.   In "Much Ado about Nothing" (Act V., Sc. 1), Leonato observes that—

> "There was never yet philosopher
> That could endure the toothache patiently ;
> However they have writ the style of gods,
> And made a push at chance and sufferance."

In "King John," Constance, after the loss of her son Arthur, says to Cardinal Pandulph (Act III., Sc. 4)—

> "I am not mad ;—I would to heaven I were !
> For then 'tis like I should forget myself ;
> O, if I could, what grief should I forget !—
> Preach some philosophy to make me mad."

And King Lear calls Edgar, who is counterfeiting madness, his *philosopher.*

But Shakespeare especially makes fun of the truisms philosophers are wont to deal in—commonplace truths which noodles admire as profound thoughts and to which the seven wise men of Greece are so greatly indebted for their fame.   Touchstone, in "As you like it," deals continually in sentences in imitation of the seven sages ; as, for instance, when he gravely says to William the simple countryman, who opens his eyes wide at hearing such fine words (Act V., Sc. 1)—

"I do now remember a saying: 'The fool doth think he is wise, but the wise man knows himself to be a fool.' The heathen philosopher, when he had a desire to eat a grape, would open his lips when he put it into his mouth; meaning thereby, that grapes were meant to eat and lips to open."

Sir Hugh Evans, in the "Merry Wives of Windsor," thinks with equal truth that lips are a part of the mouth, an opinion which he says he shares with many philosophers. Falstaff displays no less wisdom when, in acting the part of King Henry, he thus addresses his royal son :—

"There is a thing Harry which thou hast often heard of, and it is known to many in our land by the name of pitch; this pitch, *as ancient writers do report*, doth defile; so doth the company thou keepest." ("King Henry IV.," Pt. I., Act. II., Sc. 4.)

Any learned scholar who took a delight in what I confess seems to me the barren and ungrateful task of pointing out all the passages in Shakespeare capable of serving as a text, or pretext, for classical quotations, would have to distinguish three separate classes : first, the passages borrowed directly from ancient authors ; second, those borrowed indirectly; third, mere coincidences. The distinction is not always easy to make; as, for instance, when Ophelia is buried, Laertes takes last leave of her in the touching and poetic words :—

> "Lay her i' the earth ;
> And from her fair and unpolluted flesh
> May violets spring !"   (Act V., Sc. 1.)

And in Persius we find—

> "Non nunc e manibus istis,
> Non nunc e tumulo fortunataque favilla
> Nascentur violæ ? "

Did Shakespeare borrow this, or is it a mere coincidence ?

Polonius says of Hamlet's madness, that "Though this be madness, yet there is method in it :" upon which a

commentator remarks that this is precisely Horace's line—
"Insanire paret certa ratione modoque." Yet I think that
without Horace's line, Polonius's speech would be just as
it is. Again, when Hamlet speaks of "the undiscovered
country from whose bourn no traveller returns," it is
natural to recall the fine lines of Catullus :—

> "Qui nunc it per iter tenebricosum,
> Illuc, unde negant redire quemquam."

But there is not the slightest necessity to thrust in a
remark that no English translation of Catullus had yet
appeared; surely the imagination of both poets may
have met here.

Sleep, as an image of death, is a well-known idea,
and appears under various forms—in "Macbeth," "this
downy sleep, death's counterfeit;" in "Cymbeline,"
"Sleep, the ape of death," and in the "Midsummer
Night's Dream," "Death counterfeiting sleep;" but a
critic must have but a poor opinion of Shakespeare's
imagination to suppose the comparison was suggested to
him by a passage translated by Marlowe from Ovid.

Coriolanus says, " I shall be loved when I am lacked "
(Act IV., Sc. 1), and the same thought occurs in Antony
and Cleopatra :—

> "The ebb'd man, ne'er loved till ne'er worth love,
> Comes dear'd by being lacked;"

in connection with which is quoted Horace's line—

> "Extinctus amabitur idem;"

and to this there is no objection, but we ought also to
note the old proverb: "When people are missed then
they are mourned."

In the "Two Gentlemen of Verona," when Proteus
tells Silvia that Valentine is dead, she answers :—

> "In his grave
> Assure thyself my love is buried."
>
> (Act IV., Sc. 2.)

As Dido affirms, in like manner, that Sicheus has borne her love with him into the tomb :—

> "Ille habeat secum servetque sepulchro,"

we are left to decide whether Shakespeare obtained Silvia's answer from Virgil, or from the natural feeling of the heart.

In the "Tempest," Miranda says to Ferdinand (Act. III., Sc. 1)—

> "I am your wife, if you will marry me ;
> If not I'll die your maid ; to be your fellow
> You may deny me ; but I'll be your servant,
> Whether you will or no."

This is so completely the natural language of passion, while at the same time the five exquisite lines of Catullus * rush so irresistibly into the mind, that it is very embarrassing to decide whether we have here a coincidence or a case of borrowing.

The same thing occurs in the passage in the "Comedy of Errors," in which Adriana says to Antipholus :—

> "Come, I will fasten on this sleeve of thine :
> Thou art an elm, my husband, I, a vine ;
> Whose weakness, married to thy stronger state,
> Makes me with thy strength to communicate."
>
> (Act II., Sc. 2.)

Shakespeare may very well have imitated Catullus :—

> "Lenta, qui, velut assitas
> Vitis implicat arbores,
> Implicabitur in tuum
> Complexum ; "

but in Beaumont's and Fletcher's "Elder Brother," the

---

* "Si tibi non cordi fuerant connubia nostra
Attamen in vestras potuisti ducere sedes
Quæ tibi jucundo famularer serva labore,
Candida permulcens liquidis vestigia lymphis
Purpureave tuum consternens veste cubilo."

H

scholar, Charles, says to his servant, "Marry thyself to understanding, Andrew" (Act II., Sc. 4); and in the "Femmes Savantes," Armande says to Henriette, in exactly the same spirit and in almost the same terms, "Marry yourself to philosophy, my sister," without Molière having imitated Beaumont and Fletcher.

But the quotation of classical authors would only form the easier portion of the task of drawing up a list of all the passages in Shakespeare in which some reminiscence of antiquity is evoked, for it would be requisite to show by what means the poet came to know them, whether it was from contemporaneous literature, or through translations, or from the originals. For instance, in "Troilus and Cressida," we read—

> "For to be wise and love
> Exceeds man's might; that dwells with gods above."

This thought is first met with in Publius Syrus, a Latin author of the first century before Christ, and accordingly, commentators began by saying, that Shakespeare had translated a passage direct from Publius Syrus. But later on, the discovery was made by some learned bookworm, of an English translation of Publius Syrus, by Taverner, published in 1553, at the end of a little. duodecimo volume called the "Distichs of Cato;" and it then seemed more natural to suppose that it was through this translation that Shakespeare had acquired his knowledge of Publius Syrus. This is not all, however, for another learned bookworm found the same thought in Marston's play of "The Dutch Courtezan" (1605), and in Spenser's "Shepheardes Calender;" from this time the third explanation was adopted, more likely to be true than either of the two others, that Shakespeare had simply borrowed the passage of Publius Syrus from the current literature of the day. Examples of this sort are innumerable, *ab uno disce omnes.* However great a reader of ancient authors Shakespeare may have been, it will be readily admitted on all hands that the writers of his own time and country were those he knew best; and not the faintest shadow of disparagement is thrown over his fame by our agreeing with Dr. Farmer, that he was more familiar with translations than with the originals. In the "Taming of the Shrew," for instance, we read—

> "Young budding virgin, fair and fresh and sweet,
> Whither away·; or where is thy abode?
> Happy the parents of so fair a child;
> Happier the man, whom favourable stars
> Allot thee for his lovely bedfellow!"

The first thought of this salutation belongs to Homer; from whom it was borrowed by Ovid; Golding translated Ovid, and Shakespeare knew and imitated Golding, as is admitted, not only by Steevens, but even by Delius. It matters little whether a translation intervened or not,—the perfume of antiquity clings none the less to Shakespeare's passage, and it could not be more Homeric if he had transcribed it straight from the Odyssey.

There are, however, lines which, to all appearances, were translated, or imitated, from the classics by Shakespeare himself. In the "Comedy of Errors," Ægeon begins the account of his tragic history with these words :—

> "A heavier task could not have been imposed
> Than I to speak my griefs unspeakable."

This beginning resembles too closely the even then familiar and well-known "Infandum regina jubes renovare dolorem," to leave room for any doubt as to its having been directly borrowed. Further on, when speaking of the storm in which his ship perished Ægeon describes the obscured light of heaven, and how everything—

> "Did but convey into our fearful minds
> A doubtful warrant of immediate death."

Virgil's line :—

> " Præsentemque viris intentant omnia mortem,"

is here very closely followed.

In the "Tempest" (Act IV., Sc. 1), we read—

> " Highest queen of state,
> Great Juno comes ; I know her by her gait,"

which is evidently a recollection of the " Incedo Regina."
In the "Taming of the Shrew," Petruchio, after having
said of Katharine, " Be she as curst and shrewd as
Socrates' Xantippe," adds, " Were she as rough as are
the swelling Adriatic seas," which is a close translation
of the "Improbo iracundior Adria," in Horace's well-
known ode to Lydia, " Donec gratus eram."

Shakespeare frequently introduces Latin words and
phrases into his text; as, for instance, in the last-named
comedy, he quotes two lines from Ovid,* and a line from
Terence,† which last line does not indeed exactly tally
with the text of the Latin author, and which it has
been proved Shakespeare took from Lilly's Latin
Grammar ; but he could have taken it with equal ease
from Terence.   He heads his poem of "Venus and
Adonis" with a Latin epigraph, and we may rest
assured that, to a nature as free from every kind of
pedantry and pretence as his was, it would have been
utterly repugnant to affect a knowledge he did not
really possess.   Shakespeare, we need not doubt, knew
Latin as well as any man of his time ; and in his time
the educated portion of the public knew it better than
they do now.

At Stratford-on-Avon, where Shakespeare was born,

---

* " Hac ibat Simois, hic est Sigeia tellus,
    Hic steterat Priami regia celsa senis."

(Act. III., Sc. 1.)

† " Redime te captum, quam queas, minimo."

(Act I., Sc. 1.)

there was a free grammar school, which could be entered under the three conditions of residing in the town ; being seven years old ; and knowing how to read. Little William Shakespeare was sent by his father to the school, probably in 1571, when he had attained the age of seven, and knew how to read. The school hours were decidedly long—from daybreak to dark in winter, from six in the morning to six at night in the summer, excepting intervals for meals and recreation. Here Latin was certainly taught, and perhaps—but this is not equally certain—Greek, French, and Italian. Terence, Virgil, Cicero, Sallust and Cæsar were the principal authors read by the boys, while they learned the rules of grammar from Lilly, Donatus, or Valla. Various traditions, all agreeing on one point, relate that about 1578, that is, after about seven years of schooling, Shakespeare was removed from the school before having finished his regular course of study. His father seems at this time to have been undergoing a crisis in his pecuniary affairs, and as the family was both numerous and poor, it is hardly likely that young Shakespeare found time after leaving school to continue his studies. Added to which, he married at the age of eighteen, and by the time he was twenty-one found himself the father of a son and two daughters, and under such circumstances his hours of studious leisure must necessarily have been few. He became an actor, although as his sonnets show, not without some suffering to his pride from the humiliations attaching to the position ; he touched up old plays and was ready to turn his hand to anything for which he could get paid, and thus earn a livelihood. In short, the beginning of his dramatic career was rude enough, and left him no time for any occupation of which the aim was other than present and practical utility, none consequently for the patient and thorough study which alone deserves the name. He absorbed knowledge from a thousand channels with ravenous

activity, not to keep it and meditate upon it, but in order
to give out again immediately whatever he had learned.
As money came in, immunity from want came with it;
yet even when no longer under the burden of necessity,
Shakespeare's reading preserved to the end of his life the
hasty character that it had at the beginning; his materials
were never slowly accumulated, and carefully stored up
in the memory for some grand monumental edifice in the
future, but were eagerly seized upon with a view to
immediate use. It was on this account that he fastened
upon North's translation of Plutarch, a translation at
secondhand, taken from the French of Amyot, and consequently doubly liable to inaccuracies, without troubling
himself in' the least as to what they would think of it at
Chæronea. Capable of building up a palace out of such
stones as it furnished him with, he cared little as to the
intrinsic value of the raw material;—the work of transformation was no secret to him. And in the same way,
it was not on account of an insufficient knowledge of
Latin that he preferred to use the English translation of
Ovid's "Metamorphoses" rather than the original, but
because he read English more quickly, and less time was
lost.

Seven years at school are enough to enable a lad to
read easy passages in Latin fluently and to puzzle out
the harder bits. In the sixteenth century Latin was still
almost a living language; the world was only just emerg-
ing from the Middle Ages when it had been constantly
spoken, and many men of letters and of learning continued
to write it. It was in fact an ordinary element in the
education of both men and women, and there is no
shadow of reason for refusing it to Shakespeare. In all
probability the "Menæchmi" of Plautus was read by him
in the original, no English translation having appeared
till some years after the "Comedy of Errors." The
various conjectures as to the means by which Shakespeare

could have known the old comedian all proceed upon the
unfounded assumption of Shakespeare's incapacity, in case
of need, to get through a Latin play by himself.

Gervinus, on the other hand, affirms that Shakespeare
was deeply versed in Seneca and Plautus, which is saying
a good deal. It is extremely probable that he should
have read, either in Latin or more likely still in English,
all Seneca's plays, so well known and greatly admired as
they then were, and also several of Plautus's, but Gervinus speaks of an intimate familiarity, which is not an
assertion that should have been advanced without proof.
I know of no instance in which Shakespeare has copied
Plautus except in the " Comedy of Errors," and not even
that has been completely demonstrated to be directly
borrowed. In Act V., Sc. 4, of "Cymbeline," Jupiter,
seated on an eagle, descends amidst thunder and lightning
and pronounces his decrees in the same antique metre
that Heywood and Studley had employed in their translation of Seneca : such is the only proof given by Gervinus of Shakespeare's thorough acquaintance with the
Latin tragedian. Warburton took the line in " Antony
and Cleopatra " (Act IV., Sc. 10)—

" Let me lodge Lichas on the horns o' the moon,"

to be imitated from Seneca's " Hercules," but Steevens
deems it more likely to have been borrowed from Book
IX. of the " Metamorphoses." Gervinus adds :—

" If Shakespeare had had occasion at any time to name his ideal,
and to denote the highest examples of dramatic art which lay before
him, he would have named none but Plautus and Seneca."

In spite of this purely gratuitous assertion, the conclusion
arrived at in our preceding chapter must be repeated and
maintained : that Shakespeare's feelings towards classical
antiquity were those of complete indifference, that he
considered it only as a rich mine of wealth, in which
light it stood on exactly the same footing in his regard

as the legends of the Middle Ages, and the traditions of
English history.

Hallam, who advances no opinion lightly, notices the
occurrence of numerous Latinisms in Shakespeare's works,
" phrases, unintelligible and improper, except in the sense
of their primitive roots," such as, " Things base and vile,
holding no *quantity*," for value; rivers that have " over-
born. their *continents*," the " continente ripa" of Horace;
"*compact* of imagination;" "something of great *constancy*,"
for consistency; "sweet Pyramis *translated* there," " the
law of Athens, which by no means we may extenuate : "
" expressions which it is not very likely that one, who
did not understand their proper meaning, would have
introduced into poetry." Hallam's remark is repeated by
Gervinus; and Mr. S. Neil, the author of a very careful
critical biography of Shakespeare, has no hesitation in
saying that the poet's language is strongly tinged with
Latinisms.

With regard to Greek, we may boldly affirm that he
did not know it. Even admitting that he may have
learned the declensions and verbs at school, such knowledge would have been quite insufficient to enable him to
read a Greek author in the original. Every one knows
that Greek is not learned at school, and Hallam declares
that if in the sixteenth century men were better versed
in Latin than they are now, the case was different with
Greek. The extent of Shakespeare's knowledge of it
may therefore fairly be measured by that of a school-boy
of the present time, whose studies have been broken off
unfinished, the result being the most absolute ignorance.
But there was no occasion for Knight to make apologies
for the great poet on this account—he is not singular in
his ignorance, and even Schiller and Goethe, as their
correspondence attests, read Homer, Aristotle, and the
tragedians in translations.

In discussing the question of Shakespeare's learning,

it must never be left out of sight, that poets are possessed of an instrument which is not in the hand of every student—the instrument of genius.

"Great artists," M. Taine has well said, "have no need to learn,—they guess. I have seen such an one, by means of a suit of armour, a costume, or a collection of old furniture, penetrate more deeply into the spirit of the Middle Ages than three savants put together. They rebuild, naturally and surely, in the same way that they build up, by virtue of an inspiration that lends wings to reasoning."

If we take the word "learning" in its large and liberal sense, and no longer reduce the question to a miserable pedantic wrangling over his more or less of Greek and Latin, then, of all men that ever lived, Shakespeare is one of the most learned.

"Armed with indefatigable curiosity, he was an incessant reader," writes Philarète Chasles, "and made himself acquainted with all the current literature of the day: Harrington's translation of Ariosto, Amyot's and North's translations of Plutarch, Fairfax's Tasso, and Florio's translation of Montaigne, were in his hands as soon as published. He read the travels of Sir Walter Raleigh, and a translation of those of Hakluyt, and of the 'Week,' by Du Bartas. Stories, histories, plays, chronicles, theological works, amorous sonnets, everything printed in the sixteenth century, everything that fell into his hands, all was devoured by him, and his plays form a complete encyclopædia of his times."

Rabelais, too, he knew, a recollection of whom is found in two of his comedies.* And what an open door into classical antiquity he possessed in Montaigne's essays! Besides these, Pliny's "Natural History" was another book in his library; in "Antony and Cleopatra" (Act III. Sc. 7), there is a learned dissertation on the Nile, and in "Troilus and Cressida" (Act V., Sc. 3), Troilus reproaches

---

* In "As You Like It" (Act III., Sc. 2), Rosalind says to Celia, "Answer me in one word;" to which Celia answers, "You must borrow me Gargantua's mouth first, 'tis a word too great for any mouth of this age's size." In "Love's Labour's Lost," the schoolmaster's name is Holofernes.

Hector for his clemency towards the vanquished, which he says, "better fits a lion than a man,"—a notion belonging to Pliny the Elder, who observes that "the lion alone of all wild beasts is gentle to those that humble themselves before him, and will not touch any such upon their submission, but spareth what creature soever lieth prostrate before him."

Like all men of real learning, Shakespeare was fully conscious of his ignorance. The greatest stores of knowledge that any man has ever possessed are as nothing in comparison with the infinite number of things of which he is ignorant. A dark night lies all around us, and the more brightly our little torch burns, the better are we able to gauge the depth of blackness. In one of his sonnets (LXXVIII.), the image chosen by Shakespeare to describe an immense abyss is the distance that separates learning from his "rude ignorance," and elsewhere he says that ignorance is the malediction of God, and that learning is the very wing that bears us up to heaven.

Pope's reflection on this subject is very acute, in which he suggests that Shakespeare's ignorance was exaggerated for the sake of opposition and of symmetry, to form a sharper contrast with the vast learning of Ben Jonson. There is, perhaps, no more pernicious source of error in criticism than this mania for contrasting celebrated comtemporaries in hard and fast lines;— because Shakespeare is full of fancy, Ben Jonson is set down as having none; and because Corneille writes with a masculine vigour, Racine, in spite of his "Athalie" and "Britannicus," is said to be characterized by a feminine tenderness. And after all, it is childish to discuss the amount of learning possessed by an author who has taught the whole world, and from whom statesmen declare they have drawn their first notions of politics and of history.

CHAPTER V.

SHAKESPEARE'S ANACHRONISMS.

AN anachronism, according to the definition given by Bossuet, is the error that consists in a confusion of times, or, in other words, a mistake in chronology. An anachronism in dress, language, or manners, consists in attributing to one age the dress, expressions, or customs, which belongs to another age; and, besides this, in poetry and painting, any fault with regard to the peculiar features, the essential characteristics of the subject, is also an anachronism, as accuracy in chronology and in local colour—truth of time and of place—are closely and inevitably united.

There are many anachronisms to be found in Shakespeare's plays, which have been laboriously pointed out by Francis Douce, but his work, "Illustrations of Shakespeare," written chiefly in the cavilling spirit of a mere pedant, enters into none of those higher considerations that the subject admits of. It will be shown further on, how the question of anachronisms in the drama touches a very lofty æsthetic problem, but it will be necessary first to follow in the steps of Douce, and to give, if not a complete, at all events, an adequate enumeration of Shakespeare's anachronisms.

To begin with the plays taken from classical antiquity, and with "Timon of Athens" in the first place:

to introduce into the age and place in which Alcibiades
lived, two personages belonging to domestic life in feudal
times, a page and a fool, both of whom were unknown
to the ancients, is a glaring error as regards chronology
and local colour. The guests at Timon's banquet sit
upon stools, instead of reclining upon couches, as the
Greeks did, and one of the characters speaks of the use
of paper. "In a Roman drama," writes Douce, "it might
have passed, but we have no evidence that the Greeks
used the papyrus plant at this early period."

In "Troilus and Cressida," the great anachronism consists in the presence of the manners and customs of
mediæval chivalry, at the siege of Troy. The heroes,
armed from head to foot, with closed helmets on their
heads, are mounted on war horses, instead of fighting in
chariots as in the "Iliad:" judges of the lists; crests,
devices, gauntlets, gorgets; love, ladies, honour and fidelity,
all the vocabulary and all the customs of chivalry are to be
found in this play; and when Æneas brings the challenge
from Hector to the Greeks, he bears himself precisely in
the manner of a herald-at-arms at a tournament. Agamemnon and old Nestor himself speak much in the same
style; and Pandarus, when he wishes to be figurative,
borrows metaphors from falconry. Besides this fundamental anachronism in manners and habits, there are
several little oversights in the details of the speeches
which are amusing enough, such as the mention of
Aristotle by Hector; of Milo of Crotona by Ulysses;
of Friday and Sunday by Pandarus, while the Trojan
cookery seems not to be a whit behind the culinary art
in England.

In the "Comedy of Errors," where the scene is laid
in ancient Ephesus, we meet with ducats, marks, guilders,
and an abbess. Allusion is made to Henry IV., of
France, and there is also express mention of America
and of various kingdoms of modern Europe. We hear

the striking of a clock, and are shown a rapier and Turkish tapestry. And for yet further anachronisms we have Satan, sorcerers from Lapland, and even Noah and Adam, and in one place Antipholus is pleased to style himself a Christian.

In " Julius Cæsar " also, a clock strikes three ; Cicero speaks in Greek to the people of Rome, and a tribune scolds the small artisans, the cobblers and the carpenters, etc., for walking " upon a labouring day without the signs of their profession." But under these superficial anachronisms of furniture, dress and costumes, Goethe, who, however, is far from intending it as a matter of reproach, points out one of far greater psychological importance ; namely, that Shakespeare has made Englishmen of his Romans. In "Antony and Cleopatra," Antony uses terms borrowed from the language of cards ; he talks of the knave and the queen, of hearts and trumps, like any whist-player. In " Coriolanus," the hero wipes his bleeding brow with a " mailed hand," ladies fling their gloves, scarves, and handkerchiefs upon him as he passes ; mention is made of theatres,* and of drums ; and Alexander, Cato, Galen, and Censorinus, are prematurely named, as also graves in the " holy churchyard."

In " Pericles," we are presented with a pudding and with pistols. In " Titus Andronicus," we meet with a child sent to Adam the Moor, to be baptized, a clown who invokes God and St. Stephen, and the son of a Roman Emperor accused of twenty evil deeds worthy of a *papist*. To finish with Shakespeare's sins against chronology and topography, against truth of time and of place, the most notorious in the rest of his plays are these : " A Winter's Tale " turns Bohemia into a maritime kingdom, and Julio Romano, the great artist, into a contemporary of the Delphic Oracle. In " A Midsummer

---

* There were no theatres in Rome until two centuries later.

Night's Dream," Theseus, Duke of Athens, sends a young
girl into a nunnery, and greets his friends with—

> " Good morrow, friends !   Saint Valentine is past ; "

mention is also made of guns.   The historical drama
of " Henry V. " shows us the Turks already masters of
Constantinople, though the city only fell into their
hands thirty years after the death of that king.   In
" Henry VI." the name of Machiavelli is twice introduced, and the art of printing mentioned before its time.
In " King Lear," we hear of Turks, holy water, Nero,
Bedlam, etc.; and, finally, Hamlet studied in the University of Wittenberg.

Such are the principal anachronisms in Shakespeare,
and it now remains to decide what we are to think
of them.   It is easy and not unnatural, to look upon
them as faults, as unimportant as they are evident, and
to attribute them to Shakespeare's ignorance ; and those
who consider that this ignorance, far from being peculiar
to him, was shared in by the greater part of his contemporaries, and that in his day, people generally were
not so well informed as they are in our own, will deal
gently and indulgently with his anachronisms.   They
would go no further than this in their correction of
Douce's criticism, and remain at heart pretty much of
his opinion.   But in reality it is a far more complicated
question, and one that involves a very delicate æsthetical
problem.

At the first superficial glance thrown over the history
of literature, it would appear that anachronisms in art
diminish in exact proportion to the general progress
of learning.   It was at the most brilliant period of
historical studies, when the past was brought back and
made to live again before the eyes of men, by the powerful imagination of such writers as Michelet and Augustin
Thierry, that the romantic drama prided itself upon the

rendering of local colour to a degree undreamed of by classical tragedy, in times when history was less well known; and that poets were pre-eminently ambitious of bestowing scrupulously exact and historical costumes and manners upon their dramatic personages. On the other hand, the further we penetrate into the ages of ignorance, the more we see the drama, and all poetry and art in general, failing in accuracy with regard to historical characteristics and any sort of notion of chronology.

In Shakespeare's time, anachronisms still abounded on the stage, although they were beginning to be less startling and numerous, and the marked improvement made by the seventeenth century in this respect already began to make itself felt. It may help to extenuate Shakespeare's geographical and historical blunders, and to place them in their true perspective, if we notice briefly some of those of his contemporaries.

Beaumont and Fletcher, who, having received a university education, may be presumed to have been greater scholars than Shakespeare, had no scruples about committing anachronisms. The "Humorous Lieutenant," says M. Mézières, is the title of a tragi-comedy, which deals with the successors of Alexander, and of which the heroes are Antigonus and Demetrius. They speak in it of a colonel commanding a regiment, and citizens in the heart of Asia telling tales in the "old chimney corner." In "Thierry and Theodoret," the soldiers of Brunehaut are armed with muskets. In "Rollo, Duke of Normandy," Norman pirates quote historical and mythological names, as if fresh from Oxford, and appear to be as familiar with Venus, Dædalus, and Vulcan, as with the deities of Scandinavia. In "Bonduca," one of the finest tragedies of the time, we see the Roman soldiers busy eating pudding. In the "Two Noble Kinsmen," the scene is laid in Greece, at the court of Theseus, who

had already been made Duke of Athens by Shakespeare.
We here find a farcical schoolmaster, who talks Latin
before the siege of Troy, and heroes who speak the same
language of mediæval chivalry that they do in Chaucer's
" Knight's Tale," and in the Greco-roman romance from
which the play is taken.   Theseus surprises Palamon
and Arcite fighting by themselves in the midst of a
forest, and interrupts their duel, saying—

> " What ignorant and mad malicious traitors
> Are you, that, 'gainst the tenor of my laws,
> Are making battle, thus like knights appointed,
> Without my leave, and officers of arms ? "

And immediately afterwards he invites them to a
tournament.

The poet, Robert Greene, a Master of Arts of the
University of Cambridge, made Bohemia an island, just
as Shakespeare made it bordering on the sea in " A
Winter's Tale."   A translator of Plautus, and a good
Latin scholar, deemed it his duty to turn into English
the list of viands at the entertainment ordered by
Menæchmus; and in the same play introduced constables
and excisemen, as well as potatoes and claret.   The
" Arcadia," of Sir Philip Sidney, classical scholar as he
was, is full of anachronisms; and, lastly, even Ben
Jonson, of all poets of the time the most deeply
steeped in learning, forgot himself so far as to observe,
in describing the character of obsequious clients, in
" Sejanus " (Act I., Sc. 1), that they observe their patron
" as his watch observes his clock."

Anachronisms occur with still greater frequency in
earlier playwrights, and are even more absurd.   In a
drama written by Thomas Lodge, about the year 1586,
called the " Wounds of the Civil War," we are introduced
to a Gaul in the time of Marius, who swears by Jesus
and by God's blood, while Marius himself swears by Our
Lady.   In a play, entitled " Appius and Virginia," written

in the beginning of Elizabeth's reign, Virginia goes to church with her mother, and Appius expounds to his family the creation of man and woman, in full conformity with the Book of Genesis.

Anachronisms increase both in abundance and in amusing simplicity the further we go back into early English literature. In Lydgate, Amphiaraus is a bishop, and we read of guns being used at the siege of Troy; Hector is buried in the Cathedral before the High Altar, and priests say masses, and pray for his soul.* Chaucer makes Calchas a bishop, and the Palladium a holy relic, while Cressida reads the "Lives of the Saints."

It need scarcely be said that anachronisms are not peculiar to early English literature, and are easily to be found in that of France, Germany, and Italy. Ronsard, notwithstanding his great erudition and classical tastes, seems to have confused the "Iliad" with the romances of Arthur and of Launcelot; and the heroic ages of Greece with those of chivalry, when he spoke in his preface to the "Franciade," of "the Trojan and Greek knights, so long absent from their wives, children, and homes." Hans Sach, an old German poet of the sixteenth century, represents God the Father, Adam and Eve, and the Patriarchs like regular Nuremburg citizens; and, as Hegel observes, "God the Father gives religious instruction to the children of Adam in the very tone and style of the schoolmasters of the day; he teaches them the Catechism, the Ten Commandments, and the Lord's Prayer." In Boccaccio's poem of "Filostrato," Troilus, who is usually attired in the hunting dress of a mediæval prince, with a hawk upon his wrist, proposes to enter the Greek camp disguised as a pilgrim.

As we trace the literature of the Middle Ages to its

---

* Alexander Büchner, "Les Troyens en Angleterre," in the "Mémoires de l'Académie des Sciences, Arts et Belles Lettres de Caen" (1868).

earliest period, in the thirteenth, twelfth, and eleventh centuries, anachronisms are incessantly to be met with, poetry no longer offering even a shadow of historical truth.   An illuminated manuscript of Heinrich von Weldecke, a German epic poet, at the end of the twelfth century, sets forth the heroes of the poem as dressed in the prevailing fashion of the author's day, and gives a picture of Æneas playing at chess.

In the " Æneas " of Benoît de Sainte-More, the Latin Prince Turnus is made a marquis, and the banner of Æneas floats on the castle of Montauban which is attacked by the High Constable.   Our ancestors had, in the words of Schlegel, " a powerful consciousness of the universal validity and the solid permanency of their own manner of being, an undoubting conviction that it has always so been, and will ever continue so to be in the world." *
M. Joly, author of a work on "The Metamorphoses undergone by Homer and the Greco-Latin epic in the Middle Ages," remarks with much acuteness that the classical subjects chosen by Benoît de Sainte-More, the " Romance of Æneas " and the " Romance of Troy," were easily relished by the people whose very ignorance here stood them in good stead.

" The Middle Ages have no idea of chronology," he writes, " as is characteristic of a people in its infancy ; all they can do is to distinguish between *yesterday* and *days of old*.   The Arab not only cares little for historical dates, but even lets the days go by uncounted,— time is nothing to him.   Even the peasant has no notion of different degrees of antiquity, and only knows that a thing is ' very old.'   In fact, in his mind there are no dates but two, the present and the past, and all past ages are to him equally remote and mingle in the same nebulous distance.   For this reason the Middle Ages never trouble themselves to distinguish between pagan antiquity and Jewish or Christian antiquity ; they mix up altogether the Bible and Paganism, the East, Rome, and Greece ; and only know the *ancients*.   Turn over

---

* Translation by John Black of Schlegel's " Dramatic Art and Literature," Lecture XXI.

the leaves of the most learned man of his day, John of Salisbury; his works are a vast encyclopædia, a whole library of historical details borrowed indifferently from all times and all nations; but for him it is simply the history of the ancients—and not of the ancients only, but also of ancestors, ' majores nostri ' as a Roman senator would have said. John of Salisbury appropriates the Latin authors and speaks of ' noster Terentius.' This explains at once why the heroes of Greek and Roman history bécame as popular as those of the *Chansons de Geste*. They were all ancestors, only some had lived a little longer ago than others. The difference of time was vaguely felt, but without having any importance attached to it." *

Only one example need be given of this naïveté (as ignorance is poetically termed), which led the Middle Ages to confound sacred antiquity with profane, Homer with Scripture, and Greece and Rome with the East. In the " Roman de Troie," when Diomedes conducts Cressida to her tent, the poet thinks it right to inform us that this tent had belonged to Pharaoh who was drowned in the Red Sea.

> " Diomedes tant la conduit
> Qu'il descendi al paveillon,
> Qui fut al riche Pharaon
> Cil qui noia en la mer Roge."

Anachronisms in the drama, in poetry, and in art generally, are therefore, apparently, in an inverse ratio to the progress of learning; innumerable in times of ignorance, but becoming rarer in proportion to·the spread of historical knowledge. Such at least is the conclusion to which we are led by the first superficial glance thrown over the history of literature. For my part, I freely and willingly admit that there are anachronisms due to pure ignorance or carelessness, positive though slight and venial mistakes that might easily have been avoided by a little more knowledge or attention. It is evident, for instance, that Shakespeare would have done better in not

---

* " Benoit de Sainte-More et le Roman de Troie, ou les Metamorphoses d'Homère et de l'Épopée Greco-Latine au moyen âge," by A. Joly, Vol. II.

giving clocks to the Romans and rapiers to the Greeks, and in not putting the name of Aristotle into Hector's mouth, or that of Milo of Crotona into a speech of Ulysses. But there are anachronisms in Shakespeare that go deeper than these, anachronisms in manners, such as transforming Romans into Englishmen, if Goethe's remark is true, and Trojan heroes into mediæval knights; and that such as these are to be looked upon as wrong and as inevitably to be swept away by the onward march of learning may be very greatly questioned.

The difficulty by which the artist (speaking chiefly though not exclusively of the dramatic poet) finds himself confronted, is that he is compelled, for the sake of poetry, to seek his subject in a world far removed either by time or space from his own, while at the same time, if he wishes to interest his audience, he must necessarily paint a picture in which his countrymen and contemporaries can recognize a likeness to themselves. He is forced to go far afield for his subject, because the spectacle offered by the ordinary world around him is devoid of poetry; comedy alone being capable of dealing with the prosaic realities of every-day life. It was during that most prosaic period of the literary history of France, the eighteenth century, that the drama of domestic middle-class life began to flourish. To eloquence, to pathos, to moral truth it may justly lay claim, but by its very definition it negatives all thought of poetry. It proceeds upon the ridiculous assumption that only the real and the actual, or in other words the prosaic, should be admitted on the stage, as if the theatre was not a necessarily and essentially conventional place, and as if it would be worth while to pay the price of a box or of a stall, and appear in evening attire, in a brilliantly lighted scene, amongst beautiful and gaily dressed women, merely to see and hear the sights and sounds of every-day life!

If we look at the two great periods of dramatic poetry in France, the seventeenth century and the year 1830, and also examine the times in Germany and England when it reached its highest point of excellence, it will be seen that romantic and classical tragedy, Victor Hugo and Racine, German tragedy and English, Schiller, Goethe and Shakespeare, all alike borrow the subjects of their masterpieces from past ages or far-off countries. The reason is very simple. Liberty is an imperative necessity for the poet's imagination which is miserably cramped and straightened by the vulgarities of the present, and by its paltry and circumstantial details; and so, travelling forth in search of the Ideal, it plunges into the boundless and vague regions of centuries more or less forgotten, or of countries that are little known, and there at last it meets with the untrammelled generalities suited to poetical representations.*

But on the other hand, the poet is the true child of his age. Every great work of art bears so clearly and deeply the impress of the time when it was created, that the products of literary and artistic genius may be ranked among the most valuable and authentic historical documents. The contradiction inherent to the very nature of the poetic drama, the anachronism that lies at its very

---

* Racine, in his preface to "Bajazet," has some excellent remarks on this matter: "In truth, I would never advise an author to choose so modern a plot as this for the subject of a tragedy, had it happened in the country in which his tragedy was to be acted, nor to place upon the stage heroes whom the greater part of the audience had known. Tragic personages require to be looked at in a different light from that in which we generally regard those whom we have seen near. It may be said that heroes receive respect in proportion to their distance from us: *major e longinquo reverentia.* Remoteness of country may in some sort make up for too close proximity in time; for people make little difference between what, if I may so say, is a thousand years or a thousand miles off. And it is for this reason that Turks, for instance, however modern they may be, yet always have a certain dignity on the stage."

root, is that while its subject is necessarily ancient or foreign, its spirit must be modern and national.

This contradiction must beyond all question be fully accepted and allowed in art, and the wish to suppress it should never for an instant be entertained; all such inconsistencies, for there are many others, far from being injurious, are the very secret of life and of beauty, and all that happens when an artist or a critic of sound judgment, but more matter-of-fact than subtle or acute, condemns or suppresses them, is that the delicate plant of art perishes for the sake of logic under his well-meaning but clumsy hands.

Ben Jonson is an example of the error into which a dramatic poet falls, when, in order to avoid this fundamental anachronism, he abstracts himself from all surrounding realities, and shuts himself up with jealous knowledge in the period and place whence he has taken his subject. The tragedies of "Sejanus" and of "Catalina" are prodigies of accurate and patient learning. Ben Jonson applied himself with minute care to the task of not introducing a single speech of which the text or model could not be found in some classical author; continual footnotes send the reader to corresponding passages in Tacitus, Suetonius, Juvenal, and Pliny, etc., to assure him that the poet has written nothing by inspiration, and has indulged in no random flights of imagination, nor allowed himself a single word or gesture unauthorized by antiquity. But the result of this painful and conscientious learning is two remarkable, but perfectly cold works, which are extremely entertaining to antiquarians but without the slightest interest for the people. Yet it is for the people, for the hard-working clerk, who only reads his newspaper, and for "poor Laforest,* who

---

* The name of Molière's servant, to whom it is said he read his plays. (See Alfred de Musset's "Namouna.")

could not read at all," that the dramatic poet writes, not for the members of learned academies. As Hegel says in his lectures on Æsthetics :—

" Works of art should not be composed so as to be objects of study and a matter of learning. They ought to make themselves immediately understood and appreciated without all the paraphernalia of knowledge, for art is not destined for a small privileged class composed of scholars and erudite persons, but for the whole nation. . . . A work of art should be clear, easily apprehended by all of us, men of our own time and nation, without demanding any great learning. In a word, it should make us feel at home, and not bring us face to face with a foreign and unintelligible world."

It is from having failed to recognize this great principle, that the author of " Sejanus " and of " Catalina " has laid himself open to the judgment pronounced upon him by M. Mézières—a judgment admitting of no appeal, because, while criticising the faults that strike him, he assigns a due place to praise :—

" In his two tragedies, Ben Jonson remains what he was in his comedies—a learned man and a vigorous writer, rather than a dramatic poet. . . . He treats certain parts with singular force, but his great erudition lies upon him like a burden. . . . He fancied that by an abundance of exact details, he could reproduce the physiognomy of a past epoch, and never perceived that the life and action of the drama lay crushed beneath their weight. The same error prevented him, when composing his tragedies, from placing himself sufficiently on a modern standpoint, and he never properly took into account the public he was about to address, but wrote as if his audience were composed of Romans of the first or second century, A.D. . . . He concerned himself about questions which may have been interesting to the contemporaries of Catalina and of Sejanus, but which failed to excite the faintest interest in Englishmen of the seventeenth century."

A short digression on the present state of literature in France, or rather on one of its aspects, may here be allowed, for it would seem that archæological versifiers after the manner of Ben Jonson have risen up, and have attempted an enterprise not unlike his, although made in another sphere of art than that of the drama.

A taste for exotic curiosities brought to light by learned research, the natural exhaustion of the great lyrical vein, after the outburst of masterpieces by the great French poets of this century, and a mistaken application of the formula of art for art's sake, have given birth to a school of versifiers called Parnassians, on account of their having withdrawn from the world to the summits of Mount Parnassus. There, raised above all local and temporary influences, they compose admirable verses, written under no condition of time or place, and dated from eternity. But their poetry labours under one little drawback—that of making the reader yawn, and of being wearisome beyond all expression. The cardinal doctrine of their creed makes it a duty to flee from giving expression to anything so common as the immediate interests of the day, the general feelings and spirit of the hour, lest art should be vulgarized by contact with the present; but this failure, on their part, to recognize that Art has no exclusive affinity with the past, and that all ages are equal in her sight, inevitably suggests a doubt with regard to their possession of adequate poetic power to mould even their favourite subjects, chosen from the earliest traditions or remotest lands, into true works of art. The Parnassians ransack Turkey, China, Norway, Morocco, or Japan, in search of fit subjects for their pictures; and when they have displayed an undoubted talent for the picturesque, an undeniable attention to local colour, and a great facility of versification, they believe themselves to have produced a work of poetry. But this is a mistake, for the Turkey of the Turks, the China of the Chinese, belong to the regions of knowledge, and not to those of poetry. The sentiments expressed by the Turks, in common with the Greeks and Romans that Racine placed upon the stage, were French and modern sentiments, and this very thing that to superficial criticism appears a ridiculous error, is in fact an essential law of art. Whether a poet sing of past or of present, one thing is certain, that it is his clear duty to interest his readers, and if he cannot or will not do this, the just and logical consequence is that he will not be read. A great poet not only reveals beauties hitherto invisible, but is also the spokesman of humanity, gathering up and condensing the vague murmurs he hears around him, and giving high and clear expression to the inarticulate instincts of the people.

In the eighteenth century, through ignorance of history and excessive national vanity, French poetry and criticism fell into the opposite error to that committed by Ben Jonson and all archæological versifiers. Voltaire, whose name sums up all the art and philosophy of his times, was led by his blind admiration for the age of Louis XIV. to represent what was only a passing phase of thought, of feeling, and of writing, as an absolute and universal type of beauty. The great poets of Louis XIV.'s time had, in obedience to the canons of art, committed their own particular anachronism, and had brought upon the stage Greeks and Romans penetrated with the spirit of the seventeenth century : and this, indeed, was well ; but it was likewise natural and right that a fresh anachronism should take the place of the former one, and finally, in its own turn, be superseded by another ; for although poets borrow their subjects from the great treasures open to them all, poetry is the flexible expression of a changing and fleeting society. But this was not understood by Voltaire, whose admiration for the age of Louis XIV. was so excessive, that he considered its style a model for all times and for all places, and by a strange aberration of the poetic and historical sense, he found fault with the heroes of Æschylus, of Sophocles, and of Euripides, with the supernatural personages of Milton, and with the men and women of Shakespeare, for not speaking like Racine's lords and ladies ; that is, like the

court of Louis XIV. All that departed from this model
was regarded as barbarous and in bad taste; and to give
a French colouring to ancient and foreign authors was
considered an indispensable improvement,—such was the
blindness of an infatuated nation on the morrow of its
greatest literary epoch.

This lasted until the awakening of historical criticism, and the spread of foreign literature culminated in
the great poetical revolution of 1830, when ridicule
was let loose upon the Frenchified Greeks of Racine,
and much noise was made about local colour, and men
boasted of committing no more anachronisms. But here
they strangely deceived themselves; for in reasserting the
right of dramatic art to be the expression of an existing society, instead of being that of one that had long
ceased to exist, they simply inaugurated a new anachronism. They shook off, and with good reason, the yoke
of an artificial and obsolete type, but they did no more
than this, and the Romantic revolution may be defined,
with a certain amount of truth, as the " emancipation of
the natural anachronisms of art." Under the dazzling
variety of their scrupulously historical costumes, the
personages of the new drama once more became and
remained Frenchmen of the day. Hernani and Ruy
Blas are not Spaniards, but the young men of 1830, with
their imaginations heated by Byron and Châteaubriand.
But far from this being a blemish, the admission of such
anachronisms is in fact the only condition upon which
true poetry can thrive at all. The vital principle of
the drama is the soul and spirit of the age, history
being but the framework and outward form; local and
temporary characteristics are therefore only of secondary
importance, and are not so much the business of the
poet as of some archæological friend and of the stage-
manager. But then, in all fairness, these gentlemen of
the Romantic School must give over laughing at the

anachronisms of Racine; and the ineptitude of Douce's remarks, when he banters Shakespeare for having turned his Greek and Romans into Englishmen of the sixteenth century, must be fully recognized. As M. Taine forcibly says :—

> " Racine has been blamed for having given portraits of Louis XIV.'s courtiers under ancient names, but this is precisely wherein his real merit lies. The stage always represents contemporary manners ; the mythological heroes of Euripides are orators and philosophers like the young Athenians of his day ; when Shakespeare wished to paint Cæsar, Brutus, Ajax, and Thersites, he depicted men of the sixteenth century, and all the young men in Victor Hugo's plays are sons of the people, brooding and ripe for revolt, descendants of Réné and Childe Harold. An artist copies but what he sees, and can copy nothing else; distance and historical perspective only help him to endow the facts with poetry."

This natural and essential anachronism in art, consisting in the necessity under which a poet lies of taking his subject from distant countries or from past times, and in the obligation, on the other hand, of representing the spirit of contemporaneous and national life, it would be folly to attempt to destroy ; but there are two methods of lessening its effect and of preventing it from offering too rude a shock. One of them is open to all men of talent, but the other is the secret of genius alone.

The first method consists in the writer choosing his subject from the early history of his own country, by which means the unavoidable anachronism in time is not further complicated by that of place, and even the incongruity of time is softened and mitigated in those countries where the traditional national character has been preserved. This was the case with the tragedies of Æschylus, of Sophocles, and of Euripides in Greece, with the romances of the Cid in Spain, and with the historical plays of Shakespeare in England. No such instance, or none at least of equal importance, can be produced in France, but this perhaps is not much to be regretted. In

France the revolutions of public opinion have been so great, and the thread of national tradition has been so often interrupted, that it would be exceedingly difficult for French poets, when introducing heroes of their own history, to unite the spirit of former ages with that of the new.

Those critics who are shocked to meet with the language and manners of the court of Louis XIV., in Achilles and Agamemnon, would be at least equally shocked to meet with them in the contemporaries of Charlemagne, Philip Augustus or Saint Louis.

But art is not condemned to the exclusive treatment of national subjects. Full liberty must be allowed to the poet to choose his own dwelling-place wherever his imagination may be pleased to alight; and one means invariably remains to him of resolving all anachronisms into a wider harmony, but it is the secret and very miracle of genius. It consists in painting that which is *everlastingly human*, in all the characters borrowed from whatsoever scrap of history, or fragment of the human race. And in this way they become matters of interest, not only at the time and at the place at which they first appear, but for all time and for all places: Ben Jonson affords interest to a few learned men of his own epoch and of ours, but Shakespeare interests all Englishmen of his own day and all men of every century.

I cannot entirely agree with M. Taine in the clever and amusing passage with which he closes his study of Racine :—

"If I had the pleasure of being a duke, and the honour of being a millionaire, I should endeavour to collect a small group of persons of noble birth and high-bred manners; and I would shake every branch of my genealogical tree in hopes of dislodging some oracular old relation, who in the solitude of the provinces had preserved a courtly politeness and old-world dignity, and I would beg of him to honour me with his counsels. I should decorate some lofty hall with sculptured panels, and high looking-glasses of a slightly greenish hue, and I should beg of my guests to make it their pleasure to represent the manners of their ancestors. I should be careful not to swathe their limbs in linen nor to let their pointed elbows appear, in vain attempt to imitate the nudity of Greek statues. I would have nothing to do with such miserable travesties of Greek plays as Lekain, and after him Talma, imposed upon the stage, and I would propose that they should dress themselves up like the courtiers of Louis XIV., only increasing the magnificence of their embroideries and gewgaws, accepting at most, from time to time, a semi-antique helmet, which they would hide under a large cavalier-like plume of feathers. I should entreat the ladies as a favour to speak just in their usual manner, with all their smiles and witticisms, and airs and graces, and to make believe they really were at court. Then, for the first time, I should see the stage of Racine, and at last think 1 understood it."

"*And at last think I understood it.*" If Racine is only intelligible under the conditions here laid down by M. Taine, he has only succeeded in depicting society in the time of Louis XIV., and not mankind in general. But for my part, I believe that Racine possessed genius, and that he too, in common with all poets of genius, painted universal humanity, so that it is still possible, even without having recourse to any aged relative, to understand and admire his plays.

Douce concludes his sentence of condemnation on Shakespeare's anachronisms with these words: "The stage should be a true and perfect mirror of history and manners." But the stage is not the mirror of history, but of nature, as Hamlet teaches the players, and should reflect the present, not the past. Goethe remarks with great insight—

"Properly speaking there are no historical personages in poetry; only, when a poet wishes to represent the moral world he has conceived, he does certain individuals he meets with in history the honour of borrowing their names for the beings he has created."

"History," says Dumas, with picturesque abruptness, " is the peg on which I hang my drama." *

---

* In looking through this chapter preparatory to its publication in this volume, I perceived that I had omitted to indicate the limits, which are, however, easily recognized, within which the plea for anachronisms in art must be confined. Antique personages and modern sentiments are easily admissible, but it is scarcely possible to tolerate a mixture of antique and modern sentiments in the same personage. Barbarous customs, such as that of human sacrifices, are irreconcilable with the courteous manners and polished language of the heroes of Racine's "Iphigénie," the delicate refinements of the love-plot in "Andromaque" agree but awkwardly with a state of civilization iu which it was possible for the conqueror of Hector to reduce his royal spouse to the condition of a slave. The author of the German "Iphigenia," with his great perception and great art, knew how to avoid this kind of anachronism. The exquisite beauty of Goethe's masterpiece consists in so perfect a moral harmony that, in the part of the heroine at least, not the slightest incongruity of this sort appears, any more than in the Roman tragedies of Shakespeare, in which the asperity of the Roman nature and the roughness of the English nature coalesce.

CHAPTER VI.

VENUS AND ADONIS. LUCRECE.

THE interest attached to the beginning of Shakespeare's career is due rather to the modest and tranquil regularity with which his genius developed itself, than to the production of any brilliant and striking work. Classical antiquity and its most direct heir, the Renaissance in Italy, were then the two great schools of art and taste, and it was in imitation of these that Shakespeare's first efforts were made.

Far from shutting himself up from others and from choosing an isolated point to start from, he sought support from the motor forces around him, whether at court or amongst literary celebrities. The company of actors of which he became a member on his arrival in London was the first in importance, on account of the distinguished patronage with which it was honoured, it being composed of the Lord Chamberlain's men, who somewhere about 1583 had received the title of the Queen's players, and whose leader, James Burbadge, built the Blackfriars and Globe theatres. Elizabeth distinguished the Blackfriars company with her favour more than that of any other actors, and it continued to receive the royal patronage of James I., who it is said wrote with his own hand a letter to Shakespeare, thanking him for the flattering allusion to his person in "Macbeth." Without insisting upon this

tradition, which appears to be apocryphal,* we may accept
as true the general fact of which it is the legendary
expression; that Shakespeare as actor and as poet had
entered, as might naturally be expected, into relations
with the eloquent and lettered society that took delight
in the theatre and especially favoured the company to
which he belonged. The tastes of this society are well
known : enamoured of classical antiquity and the Italian
Renaissance, "they swore but by the ancients or their
imitators." Shakespeare's chief friends amongst the
aristocracy were the Earl of Essex, and, above all, the
Earl of Southampton, to whom he dedicated the poems
of " Venus and Adonis " and " Lucrece."

Shakespeare followed the fashion of the day, and
like every one else imitated other writers,—imitating not
only Virgil or Petrarch, but also contemporary English
poets, after the manner of all beginners; not disdaining
to borrow the three stanzas and concluding couplet for
the form of his sonnets from Daniel, the author of " Cleopatra," the very same who blamed the " idle fictions "
and " gross follies " of the romantic drama.

Some critics think that Shakespeare had travelled
into Italy,† and it is certain that many of his stage
comrades had visited that fair land, " the empire of the
sun, the mistress of the world, and the cradle of letters,"
as Corinne calls it, and that their enthusiastic memories
of their sojourn there were not without influence on
the imagination of the young poet.

Classical reminiscences of every kind occur too
frequently, as we have already seen, throughout Shake-

---

* Payne Collier (I. 370) and Hallam ("Lit. of Europe," III. 320) call
into question the authenticity of the anecdote related by Malone.

† See on the subject a dissertation, written with much learning and
moderation, in the "Essays" of Karl Elze. The conclusion arrived at by the
author, is that Shakespeare did travel in Italy, but he places no credence
in the other journeys, to Scotland and elsewhere, attributed to him.

speare's plays for there to be any reasonable hope of
bringing to an end the work of patience, rather than
of intelligence, of pointing them all out. They especially
superabound in his earlier works; "Henry VI.," "Titus
Andronicus," the first acts of "Pericles," "Love's Labour 's
Lost," "The Taming of the Shrew," "The Comedy of
Errors," and two or three others are profusely adorned,
sometimes even to excess, with classical allusions and
quotations. This lavish use of Latin erudition clearly
betrays the young author, eager to throw open all the
stores of his mind, and anxious to please the reigning
taste of the day. And for the same reason he turned to
Italian models. From Ariosto's comedy of "I Suppositi,"
translated into English by the poet, George Gascoigne,
in 1566, he borrowed part of the subject of "The
Taming of the Shrew," in which the love-plot is developed in true Italian fashion, and old Gremio, who
makes himself ridiculous by courting young Bianca, is a
true *Pantaloon*. Such also, in the "Comedy of Errors,"
is Pinch, combining the functions of a schoolmaster, a
conjuror, and a doctor :—

> "A hungry lean-faced villain,
> A mere anatomy, a mountebank,
> A thread-bare juggler, and a fortune-teller;
> A needy, hollow-eyed, sharp-looking wretch,
> A living dead man." (Act V., Sc. 1.)

And the case is the same with all the distinctive
features of the Italian school, its quaint conceits and
play upon words, which, like the flowers of classical
learning, show themselves more or less in all of Shakespeare's plays, but are especially numerous in those
of his youth. A specimen may be given from the
"Comedy of Errors," in which Luciana, when spoken to
of love, exclaims :—

> "What, are you mad, that you do reason so?
> *Ant.* Not mad, but mated; how, I do not know.

K

Luc. It is a fault that springeth from your eye.
Ant. For gazing on your beams, fair sun, being by.
Luc. Gaze where you should, and that will clear your sight.
Ant. As good to wink, sweet love, as look on night. . . .
Mine eye's clear eye, my dear heart's dearer heart;
My food, my fortune, and my sweet hope's aim,
My sole earth's heaven, and my heaven's claim."

The language of Mercutio in "Romeo and Juliet," another of Shakespeare's earlier plays, is a continual display of fireworks. The comedy of "Love's Labour's Lost" turns entirely upon witty affectations and the love of "a mint of phrases." If, as has been alleged, Shakespeare intended it as a satire upon Euphuism, the satire, it must be confessed, is of the gentlest description, and one in which he shows himself singularly guilty of the very mania at which his shafts are aimed; he enjoys it, he delights in it, and revels in it to his heart's content; "*indulget genio suo.*"

Shakespeare never indeed completely freed himself from the spirit of the Italian style; the glittering and artificial play upon words occurs far more frequently than could be wished, until we reach the period of his full maturity of genius, beginning with "Julius Cæsar," and ending with "Cymbeline" or the "Tempest;" but it is especially in the outset of his career, in his comedies, that its factitious lustre is most dazzling. The young people in his plays speak a language of their own; and as in order to match the subject its description should be brilliant, I here borrow the pen of M. Taine.

"They are full of animation," writes the historian of English literature, "their heads are filled to overflowing, and they amuse themselves, like nervous and enthusiastic artists of the present day, in the seclusion of their own studios. They speak, not to convince nor to be understood, but in order to satisfy their exuberant imagination, and to give an outlet to the mental sap with which they are running over. They play with words, twisting and turning them in and out of every kind of shape, and delight in new and sudden perspectives and in violent contrasts, which they strike out one after another in rapid and endless succession. They heap flower upon flower, and glitter upon glitter; they are captivated by everything that is brilliant, and their language is embroidered with gold and lacework like their coats."

Shakespeare's first products, however, were not comedies, but two descriptive poems,—"Venus and Adonis," and "Lucrece." Greek and Latin respectively in title and subject as these two poems are, as well as by virtue of various details and several passages in imitation either of Virgil or of Ovid, yet in spirit they are wholly Italian. Their defects are those with which it is usual to reproach Italian literature at that period of its history when, the subject-matter beginning to fail, it fell into excessive refinements and subtleties of form. Shakespeare's sonnets are no less penetrated with the Italian spirit of Petrarch and the Petrarchists. His poems and sonnets, as Gervinus has well remarked—

"place him among the number of those clients of the nobles, those scholars trained in a foreign school, those lyric and epic poets at whose head stands Edmund Spenser. If we possessed nothing from Shakespeare but these poems, we should rank him among the Draytons, Spensers, and Daniels, and not a doubt would have arisen over the nobility and dignity of his school and education." (Page 43.)

"Venus and Adonis" appeared in 1593, and "Lucrece" in 1594, when the Earl of Southampton, to whom they were dedicated, was about twenty years of age, but they were probably written several years before they were published. They are full of the exuberance of youth, under the form of a flood of passion and of poetry in the first, and of rhetoric and of prolixity in the second.

In "Venus and Adonis," the subject is the sensual passion of a woman and the cold disdain of a boy; in "Lucrece," the sensual passion of a man and the purity of a woman. The symmetry is complete, but the difference in the merit of the two poems is considerable. It has been said that Shakespeare wrote "Lucrece" in

expiation of his sin in writing " Venus and Adonis," and
if the theory of this very unlikely repentance on his part
were admissible, it might furnish a psychological explanation of the mediocrity of the second poem ; inspiration had departed, leaving nothing in its place but an
honest wish to accomplish a pious task, which is not
at all the same thing.   In a similar manner, it occurred
to Lamartine, after having written the sublime lines of
his " Désespoir," that his ode was not quite orthodox,
and accordingly he set himself to compose in cold blood
the fine, but comparatively feeble, stanzas in which he
imagines an answer from " La Providence à l'Homme."

There are two diametrically opposite views taken of
" Venus and Adonis."   According to one view,—which is
that in which I share,—it is a work full of passion.
Everything in this poem " betrays," writes Gervinus,
" that it was written in the first passion of youth."
The German critic, whilst acknowledging that Shakespeare has even exceeded the redundant rhetoric of the
Italian school, adds that his poem was distinguished
amongst the many elaborate imaginative works then
produced by English and Italian writers by its sincerity
and truth of feeling.   " In treating this subject," he
says again, " Shakespeare appears a Crœsus in poetic
ideas, thoughts and images, a master and victor in the
matter of love, a giant in passion and sensual power."
This is also the opinion of M. Taine, whom " Venus and
Adonis " has inspired with a page as warm and glowing
as the subject itself.

But a different view is held by three important
English critics—Hazlitt, Coleridge, and Professor Dowden.
Hazlitt says, " The two poems of ' Venus and Adonis,'
and of ' Tarquin and Lucrece,' appear to us like a couple
of ice-houses.   They are about as hard, as glittering, and as
cold."   " Shakespeare writes in this poem," says Coleridge,
" as if he were of another planet, charming you to gaze

on the movements of Venus and Adonis as you would on the twinkling dances of two vernal butterflies." And lastly, Professor Dowden says : " In holding the subject before his imagination, Shakespeare is perfectly cool and collected . . . he remains unimpassioned—intent wholly upon getting down the right colours and lines upon his canvas."*

It is a matter of individual impression. The feeling of English readers, especially of those who have tact and judgment, undoubtedly possesses great weight; nevertheless, I cannot refrain from thinking that the coldness of " Lucrece," which is in truth a freezing poem, has reacted disastrously on " Venus and Adonis."

Perhaps there may also have been a little over-anxiety to recognize the central quality of Shakespeare's dramatic talent, in his descriptive poems, the calm strength, and height of irony by virtue of which he remained distinct and separate from all the various passions he depicted ; for in point of fact his two first poems evince remarkably little dramatic power, and it is this absence of almost every indication of the direction that his genius was afterwards to take, that is the most extraordinary thing about them. If their authenticity were not thoroughly well attested, it would probably never have occurred to anybody to attribute them to Shakespeare.

" Venus and Adonis " brims over with poetry—erotic, lyrical, elegiac, and descriptive,—but of dramatic poetry there is none. In a passage imitated from Ovid,† Venus, alarmed at the risks that Adonis runs in his passion for boar-hunting, entreats him, if he needs must hunt, to pursue instead inoffensive animals, like the hare or fox or roe, and she gives a description of a hunted hare, suffi-

---

* " Shakespeare : His Mind and Art," p. 50.
† " Metamorphoses," Book 10, lines 587 and following.

ciently out of place, dramatically speaking, but full of
the most exquisite poetry :—

> " And when thou hast on foot the purblind hare,
>   Mark the poor wretch, to overshoot his troubles,
>   How he outruns the wind, and with what care
>   He cranks and crosses, with a thousand doubles:
>   The many musits through the which he goes
>   Are like a labyrinth to amaze his foes.

*   *   *   *   *   *   *

> " By this, poor Wat, far off upon a hill,
>   Stands ou his hinder legs with listening ear,
>   To hearken if his foes pursue him still ;
>   Anon their loud alarums he doth hear ;
>   And now his grief may be comparèd well
>   To one sore sick that hears the passing bell.

> " Then shalt thou see the dew-bedabbled wretch
>   Turn, and return, indenting with the way ;
>   Each envious briar his weary legs doth scratch,
>   Each shadow makes him stop, each murmur stay."

Passages of this kind, full of the fresh scents and sounds
of the country, lend great colouring to the supposition
that "Venus and Adonis" was written before Shakespeare left Stratford ; moreover, in his dedication to the
Earl of Southampton, he calls it "the first heir of my
invention." With the same careful touch that he paints
the hunted hare, he also describes the courser of Adonis,
of which he gives a description of quite technical
accuracy. Professor Dowden here calls upon us to notice
the attention which Shakespeare bestowed upon the outward world. His studies of landscapes and of animals,
though of minor importance, are preludes to his great
study of mankind. With his eye fixed upon reality, he
was cautiously feeling his way, each day discovering
some new aspect of nature until he grasped the whole
of it. It was by this slow but sure progress that he
became a great master—very different in this respect
from those idealistic poets, who, wishing to astonish

mankind with some splendid audacity, construct the world *à priori* instead of studying it, and never lay hold of it otherwise than partially and superficially.

Shakespeare has been reproached with having debased and degraded the mythological riches of his subject in not presenting Venus as a goddess instead of as a mere beautiful amorous wanton; but the reproach is singularly wanting in perception, for it is precisely this that gives life to his picture. While rejecting the cold mythological verbiage of the Renaissance, he has kept the material and voluptuous spirit of its paganism, and produced this admirable picture of a woman, which has justly been compared to a painting by Titian for richness and depth of colour.

But side by side with passages of real beauty in "Venus and Adonis" we find many far-fetched conceits, which could only suit the taste of the admirers of "Euphues;" after the death of Adonis, for example, Venus makes a funeral oration, and says :—

> " But when Adonis lived, sun and sharp air
>   Lurk'd like two thieves to rob him of his fair.

> " And therefore would he put his bonnet on,
>   Under whose brim the gaudy sun would peep;
>   The wind would blow it off, and, being gone,
>   Play with his locks; then would Adonis weep:
>   And straight, in pity of his tender years,
>   They both would strive who first should dry his tears.

> " To see his face the lion walk'd along
>   Behind some hedge, because he would not fear him;
>   To recreate himself, when he hath sung,
>   The tiger would be tame, and gently hear him;
>   If he had spoke the wolf would leave his prey,
>   And never fright the silly lamb that day.

> *   *   *   *   *   *

> " But this foul, grim, and urchin-snouted boar,
>   Whose downward eye still looketh for a grave,

> Ne'er saw the beauteous livery that he wore:
> Witness the entertainment that he gave;
>   If he did see his face, why then I know
>   He thought to kiss him, and hath kill'd him so."

This too-caressing boar who killed Adonis with a kiss had not been *seen* out hunting as the hare had; and the yet young and inexperienced poet mingled the fresh beauties of a sketch drawn from nature with the flat and insipid commonplaces of an artificial fancy. In many places in his poem, and notably in the description of the boar, Shakespeare followed Ovid, invariably adding, however, great amplification in the shape of long paraphrases. Those who think that it touches Shakespeare's honour to show that he was a good scholar as well as a great poet, will be grieved to learn that instead of having had recourse to the original work in Latin, he made use of Golding's translation, as becomes evident from a comparison of the texts. The principal charm of the poem, it may be added, lies in the dexterity of the workmanship and the music of its sounds.

Like "Venus and Adonis" the poem of "Lucrece" has its source in antiquity. The story of Lucretia is told by Ovid in his "Fasti," and is also to be found in Dionysius of Halicarnassus, in Livy, in Dion Cassius, and in Diodorus of Sicily. A translation of Ovid's "Fasti" into English verse appeared before the year 1570. But without going back to the ancients, Shakespeare may very well have known the story through popular tradition: all through the Middle Ages Lucretia was continually quoted as an illustrious example of conjugal fidelity, and a little indication that Shakespeare derived the story from Gothic sources would seem to be afforded by his making his Romans *knights*. Lucrece, before stabbing herself, says to her husband's friends—

>   " You, fair lords,
> Shall plight your honourable faiths to me,

> With swift pursuit to venge this wrong of mine;
> For 'tis a meritorious fair design
>   To chase injustice with revengeful arms:
>   Knights, by their oaths, should right poor ladies' harms."

And the poet proceeds:—

> " At this request, with noble disposition
>   Each present lord began to promise aid,
>   As bound in knighthood to her imposition."

The legend of Lucrece is found in Chaucer, and English literature in the sixteenth century had produced several poems on the same subject prior to Shakespeare's; the two best-known ballads are "The Touching Complaint of Lucretia" and "The Death of Lucrece."

The poem consists of two hundred and sixty-five stanzas of seven lines each, so that Shakespeare takes eighteen hundred and fifty-five lines to relate a history that Ovid, who is not generally looked upon as a concise writer, tells in one hundred and forty lines. Nor is its length the sole defect of "Lucrece," for it is also marred by an exaggerated indulgence in the style then so much in vogue in Italy, which Shakespeare himself, later on, characterized as—

> " Taffata phrases, silken terms precise,
>   Three-piled hyperboles, spruce affection,
>   Figures pedantical."

Take, as an example of these fantastic graces, the lines in which the poet describes Lucrece asleep:—

> " Her lily hand her rosy cheek lies under,
>   Cozening the pillow of a lawful kiss;
>   Who therefore angry, seems to part in sunder,
>   Swelling on either side to want his bliss."

Here we have a jealous pillow, of a fiercer temperament, apparently, than that of the wild boar in love with Adonis. But the most striking point of all in "Lucrece"

is the way in which the author of this tedious poem
so long drawn out, everywhere avoids the slightest
approach to dramatic action and movement: it would
be impossible to be less of a forerunner of "Macbeth"
and of "Othello." The only passage that has been discovered in which anything of the great dramatic psycho-
logy of Shakespeare's plays reveals itself, is that in
which Lucrece, overwhelmed with shame, after a night
of wild despair, calls a young groom, and giving him
the letter she has written to recall her husband, charges
him to hasten with it to Collatinus in the camp. Bashful and timid, the young man blushes as he stands before
her; but Lucrece, full of her own thoughts, imagines
that it is on account of her dishonour, and remains confused and trembling before the groom whom her own
presence abashes.*

Rhetoric, or the art of speaking much and saying
little, occupies a large place in the poem of "Lucrece:"
to make so slight a subject fill so large a frame it was
necessary to piece it out with a prolixity capable of
extending its story indefinitely, and the narrative is interrupted by reflections at every step. Before his crime,
Tarquin continues for fifty-six lines "justly to control
his thoughts unjust;" and after the crime, Lucrece gives
vent in two hundred and seventy-three lines to her
complaints against Tarquin, and against Night, Time,
and Opportunity. She bethinks herself of—

> "A piece
> Of skilful painting, made for Priam's Troy;
> Before the which is drawn the power of Greece,
> For Helen's rape the city to destroy."

This gives the poet a fine opportunity to describe the
picture, to recall the story of "perjured Sinon" as told
by Virgil, and to compare the fate that menaced the

---

* Guizot.

family of the Tarquins, in vengeance of Lucretia's wrongs, with the miseries that befell the family of Priam for the sake of Helen.

A very appropriate epigraph for a critical study of the poem could be furnished by two of its passages: in the midst of her interminable soliloquy Lucrece exclaims:

> " Out idle words, servants to shallow fools!
> Unprofitable sounds, weak arbitrators!
> Busy yourselves in skill-contending schools,
> Debate where leisure serves with dull debaters."

But she maunders on none the less, ingenuously adding—

> " This helpless smoke of words doth me no right."

Further on, when she writes to Collatine to beseech him to return home, the poet represents her as criticising the letter herself:

> " This is too curious-good, this blunt and ill:
> Much like a press of people at a door,
> Throng her inventions, which shall be before."

Shakespeare's first achievements in literature were, it is evident, not those of a revolutionary innovator or of a leader of a school. He began almost timidly: classical subjects and the Italian style being the taste of the day, he took classical subjects and moulded them in the Italian fashion. As Gervinus remarks, young writers with a great future before them are seldom tempted by the search after novelty; they simply follow the most natural way, and put themselves to school under some contemporary master and work out their apprenticeship under him. The ambition of breaking away from existing landmarks and of taking the world by storm with some unprecedented performance is a temptation chiefly to youthful minds that are more infatuated with themselves than really fertile, and that possessed but of one idea are eager to express it in their own way,—the idea once expressed, they do nothing all the rest of their life but turn it complacently round and round.

The process of Shakespeare's development was gradual and unmarked by any violent shocks, unfolding itself through practice, experience, and reflection. Not one of his works is suggestive of a defiant temper, nor of a spirit of system or paradox. The movement by which he disengaged himself from the false classicality of the Renaissance, in order to give an increasingly large and independent character to his poetry, was not the sudden revolt of an emancipated slave throwing off the yoke, but was simply a series of progressive stages. Starting with imitation of the ancients, by degrees, as he ceased to imitate them, he came to be their equal. The firmness with which he followed the promptings of his genius reveals a strength all the more astonishing when we remember that the admiration of his contemporaries was especially excited by the class of poetry that he subsequently felt impelled to abandon. None of his works had more success or were more praised in his own times than his two descriptive poems. They passed through six editions in thirteen years. Meres, in his "Wit's Treasury" (1598), said, "As the soule of Euphorbus was thought to live in Pythagoras, so the sweete wittie soule of Ovid lives in mellifluous and hony-tongued Shakespeare; witnes his 'Venus and Adonis,' his 'Lucrece,' and his sugred sonnets;" and Gustave Rümelin, in his "Shakespeare Studien," quotes an opinion, purporting to be that of Thomas Nash—though all attempts to discover the passage in any of his works have proved unavailing,—which declares Shakespeare's poems had gained him a reputation as a poet which his dramatic works only served to damage, and that if he had but confined himself to writing in the Italian style he might have become even a greater poet than Daniel, the first poet of the age.

CHAPTER VII.

THE COMEDY OF ERRORS.

THE " Comedy of Errors " is based upon the "Menæchmi" of Plautus. As the whole scene is laid in Ephesus, and the plot is comprised within the space of one day, the unities of time and place are strictly observed.

It is proved by a concurrence of evidence both external and internal to be one of Shakespeare's youthful plays : in the first place, it must necessarily be anterior to 1598, as mention is made of it in that year by Meres in his "Wit's Treasury." Besides this, rhymed lines are of frequent occurrence in it, and rhyme is a characteristic of all Shakespeare's earlier productions; added to which, it contains many lines in doggrel verse, such as the concluding couplet :—

> " We came into the world like brother and brother,
>   And now let's go hand in hand, not one before another ; "

which resemble those of M. Tibaudier in " La Comtesse D'Escarbagnas : "—

> " Vous devriez, vous contentant d'être Comtesse,
>   Vous dépouiller en ma faveur d'une peau de tigresse."

Doggrel verse was very frequently employed in comic literature before Shakespeare, and we meet with it in several of his earlier comedies, such as " Love's Labour 's Lost," and " The Taming of the Shrew," but it soon disappeared from his plays. And finally, a more precise date of the composition of the piece is furnished by a pun in Act III., Sc. 2, where Dromio, in his description of a fat kitchen-wench, " no longer from head to foot than from hip to hip, and spherical like a globe," in whom he could find out countries, says of France that it is " In her forehead, armed and reverted, making war against her *heir,*" in allusion to the civil wars of France, when the " Ligue " was fighting against the legitimate heir to the throne, Henry IV. The " Comedy of Errors " was there-fore written not later than either before or in the year 1594, when Paris submitted and Henry's coronation took place.

This question of date has its importance. An English translation by W. Warner of the " Menæchmi " of Plautus existed in Shakespeare's time, but it was not published before 1595. On account of Shakespeare having used translations whenever he could, many persons have con-cluded that he was incapable of doing without them if need were, and that therefore he must have read the English translation in manuscript; and they moreover recall that on New Year's Eve in 1576–77, a comedy was acted at Hampton Court, entitled, " The Historie of Error." This piece is no longer extant, but it was possibly founded on the "Menæchmi," and Shakespeare may have taken the idea of his play from it; but these are only con-jectures, and to those who think—and their opinion seems to me to be right—that Shakespeare could very well have read Plautus's comedy in Latin, there is nothing embar-rassing in the date of publication of Warner's translation.

In whatever manner Shakespeare became acquainted with Plautus's play, it is at all events certain that the classical source of the " Comedy of Errors " is the " Me-næchmi." An excellent analysis of this play has been given by M. François Victor Hugo, which I here borrow: A merchant of Syracuse had had twin sons. These children, perfectly alike in height, size and face, had been

separated ever since they were seven years old. One,
whom his father had taken to the games at Tarentum,
had been stolen in the crowd and taken to Epidamnus
by a rich citizen, who before dying had adopted him,
made him his heir, and married him to a rich wife in his
city. The other had remained in his native country
with his grandfather, who called him Menæchmus, after
the child that was lost, and after having attained to years
of manhood he had set out to search for his brother: he
travelled all over the known world in vain, his twin-
brother was nowhere to be found. At last a propitious
wind blew his sail to the very place where this wished-
for brother lived; and at this point the play opens.

We are at Epidamnus, before the house of Menæchmus
the citizen, where Peniculus the parasite comes to ask
for alms. Just as Peniculus is about to knock at the
door, Menæchmus comes out of the house railing at his
wife for always expecting him to give an account of his
doings. This uncourteous husband determines as a fit
revenge to go and dine with the courtesan Erotium, and to
present her with a splendid mantle taken surreptitiously
from his wife's wardrobe. Peniculus, having overheard
this secret resolve, craftily offers to accompany him, and
Menæchmus, afraid of being exposed, is obliged to invite
him, and accordingly he and his troublesome self-con-
stituted companion go off together to Erotium; she
receives them very well, accepts the handsome present,
and only stipulates for time to provide a good dinner.
While the cook Cylindrus makes his preparations, Menæchmus proceeds to the forum, where his presence is
required for some important affair, accompanied by the
parasite Peniculus, who follows him like a shadow; and so
ends the first act.

Interrupting the analysis for a moment, a comparison
may here be made between the Latin play and Rotrou's
translation of it into French verse, which is in the main

sufficiently faithful, but which contains a few alterations made to suit the manners of his century. With him, Erotium becomes a *précieuse*, full of affectation and conceit, a prude of the school of Mademoiselle de Scudéry, who proclaims that " at her altars none but the most purified vows are offered up," nor does her lover fail to call her cruel and inhuman.

> " Je tiens votre amitié pour un rare bonheur
> Pourvu qu'elle demeure aux termes de l'honneur,
> Que mon honnêteté ne soit point offensée,
> Et qu'un but vertueux borne votre pensée."

The Menæchmus of Rotrou instead of a robe offers a diamond pin for the hair as a present to the fair Erotium.

> " Ce poinçon qui vous est dédié
> Aura l'heur de servir à ce poil délié ;
> Et je m'estimerai le plus heureux du monde
> De le voir tous les jours sous cette tresse blonde,
> Et tous les jours touché par ces divines mains
> A qui le ciel permet d'enchaîner tant d'humains."

Erotium takes it at once, modestly replying—

> "Quoiqu' indigne, monsieur, d'un present de la sorte,
> Puisque vous l'ordonnez, il faut que je le porte."

But to return to Plautus. The second act introduces the other Menæchmus of Syracuse, who has just landed at Epidamnus, accompanied by his slave Messenio. Menæchmus declares that he will go on seeking for his brother until he meets some person " who can say that he knows that he is really dead ; after that I shall never take any trouble in seeking further. But otherwise, I shall never, while I am alive, desist; I know how dear he is to my heart." * Menæchmus and Messenio meet Cylindrus the cook, and the series of *errors* begins. Erotium, supposing him to be her Menæchmus, invites the traveller to the feast she has prepared. The new arrival

---

* Riley's translation.

eats his brother's dinner with an excellent appetite, and when he leaves Erotium takes with him the stolen mantle, under the pretext of effecting some change in the embroidery to prevent it being recognized. As he leaves the house he knocks up against Peniculus, who heaps invectives upon him and accuses him of having sneaked away in the crowd in order to dine alone with Erotium. Menæchmus of Syracuse tries in vain to justify himself, protesting that he does not even know Peniculus; the parasite only sees an offensive irony in his protestations of innocence, and enraged with spite flies to the wife of Menæchmus of Epidamnus to inform her of the theft of her mantle. "By my troth, never shall any one prevail upon me not to tell your wife the whole matter now, just as it happened. I'll take care that you shan't have devoured the dinner unpunished."

The wife comes to the place that Menæchmus the traveller had only just left, and meets her husband on his way to Erotium; she reproaches him with his theft, and gives him clearly to understand that he shall not enter the house until he brings the mantle back. Alarmed and confused, Menæchmus sheepishly presents himself before Erotium, and beseeches her to return the stolen goods to him. Erotium, who has given the mantle to the other Menæchmus, looks upon his request as a mockery, and shuts her door upon the hapless joker. In the fifth and last act, Menæchmus of Syracuse passes in front of his brother's house, wearing the stolen mantle. His sister-in law comes out to meet him, and rates him soundly for his shameful behaviour. To the recriminations of this woman whom he does not know, the traveller retorts in equally uncomplimentary language. Violent altercation ensues, and the wife at length sends for her father.

This old father is a man who knows how to live peaceably with his neighbours, and preaches patience

L

to his daughter, with arguments full of practical worldly wisdom. When she exclaims, trembling with passion—

"He's in love with a courtesan here close by," he judiciously answers, "He is exceedingly wise. . . . If he has done wrong in anything, be sure I shall censure him. But since he keeps you provided for and well clothed, and finds you amply in female servants and provisions, 'tis better, Madam, to entertain kindly feelings."

Menæchmus of Syracuse is, of course, completely mystified, and understands nothing of all that the wife and her father say to him. They begin to think that he has gone crazy, and with great presence of mind Menæchmus accepts the position, which seems to him to present the surest means of escaping from their clutches; he therefore enacts the part of a madman, and gesticulates and screams and storms about, terrifying the old man and his daughter, who run off in search of a doctor. The man of medicine arrives, but in place of the wrong husband, who had managed to escape, he finds the real one, and a very funny scene ensues. Menæchmus of Epidamnus, pressed with questions by the doctor, tries to send him about his business. "Why don't you ask whether I am wont to eat dark bread, or purple, or yellow? Or whether I am wont to eat birds with scales. or fish with wings?" By degrees he becomes exasperated, and then the doctor, convinced of his madness, orders him to be carried off to the doctor's house. Four men seize him, to the utter amazement of the unlucky wretch, who exclaims, "What do you want? What do you seek? Why do you stand around me? Whither are you dragging me? I am undone! I entreat your assistance, citizens, men of Epidamnus: come and help me!" Just at this critical moment, Messenio, the slave of the other Menæchmus, appears on the scene, and thinking he sees his master in trouble, falls upon the four men, disperses them, and sets Menæchmus of Epidamnus free, to whose stupefaction he adds the finishing stroke, by begging for his liberty in return for the good services he has just rendered. With this touching scene, Plautus closes the series of errors. Menæchmus of Syracuse returns in search of Messenio, and at length finds himself face to face with Menæchmus of Epidamnus. The twins question each other, give explanations, recognize each other and embrace. Menæchmus of Syracuse is so overjoyed, that he sets Messenio free; Menæchmus of Epidamnus is so happy, that he swears never to leave his brother again, and in order to depart with the greater celerity he sells by auction all his possessions, his slaves, his furniture, his farms, his house, *and* his wife !

Such is the Latin comedy: it is full of fun and amusement which never flag; but when set by the side of Shakespeare's, we are struck by the harshness of its manners, and by a certain rigidity and dryness in the working out of the plot. Menæchmus of Epidamnus is a brutal husband, who robs his wife; Menæchmus of Syracuse, when invited by mistake for his brother by Erotium, is withheld by no delicacy of feeling from profiting by the occasion; Erotium, indeed, deserves to be treated with no more ceremony than she receives, but we shall see a little further on, what a poetic charm is thrown round Shakespeare's comedy by his women-characters, and with what tenderness and grace, love expresses itself in a similar situation. Plautus is by no means liberal in his treatment of his personages, whose characters are strictly limited to the essential feature necessary to explain their line of conduct; this leading motive once indicated, he endows them with no other sentiments whatever, such as would be required to make them in any way complete and lifelike. To brotherly love, for instance, he gives full and adequate expression, but he reduces all the complexity of human nature to this one emotion, which stands out from all other good qualities in isolated relief. The same poverty is evinced in the development of the plot: one and undivided, according to classical rules, the Latin comedy proceeds towards the final end, true to the teaching to be given later on by Horace, without losing itself in any sinuous byways of fancy.

Shakespeare's comedy is, to begin with, richer and more varied in incident than that of Plautus, and is possessed of an extra couple of twins, slaves to the two brothers. In thus adding to the comical character of the plot, Shakespeare clearly announces his intention of not keeping within the bounds of probability: nature might once in a way produce two men exactly alike, but that those two men should be attended by two slaves equally resembling each other, is too ingenious an arrangement not to be a sport of the imagination rather than a freak of nature. We are in the kingdom of frolic and fun, and the poet is free at starting to imagine what things he pleases, however extraordinary; his only obligation being to make them acceptable by weaving them into a merry and amusing play. The imbroglio resulting from these four likenesses of each other must necessarily be singularly complicated, and however great the dexterity of the author may be, it is to be feared that the attention necessary to follow all the windings of such a labyrinth must prove a little fatiguing. It is difficult to see how the " Comedy of Errors " can be satisfactorily performed on the stage; of two things one, as Hazlitt has remarked: either the resemblance of the twins must be exact, in which case the recognition of them would be as embarrassing to the audience as to the characters in the play; or else there must be some difference between them, and this would render the spectators unable to acquiesce in the mistakes of those who confound them. The difficulty was evaded in a very simple and happy manner by Regnard, who, like Plautus, presented only one pair of twin-brothers on the stage,—Valentine puts a mark on the hat of his master, Menæchmus, and says that will serve as a beacon :—

> " Pour ne nous plus tromper regardons ce signal
> Il doit, dans l'embarras, nous servir de fanal."

The slaves present a repetition, not only of the likeness that exists between their masters, but also of their sentiments and actions, to which they form a sort of parody. This species of symmetry appears to have been a favourite with Shakespeare in his youthful days, rather than in his maturity; it is not of frequent occurrence in his works as it is in those of Molière, where the passion of Cleanthis for Mercury forms a burlesque counterpart to Jupiter's love for Alcmena; and where Covielle and Nicole, Gros-René and Marinette, are caricatures of the lovers in the " Bourgeois Gentilhomme," and the " Dépit Amoureux." Every French critic has drawn attention to the similarity of the scene in which the cook, wife to Dromio of Ephesus, thrusts her importunate affections upon Dromio of Syracuse, whom she takes to be her husband, to the scene between Cleanthis and Mercury in "Amphitryon;" and it is also noticeable that Shakespeare's scene is not acted but narrated, and is none the less vivid for it: just as in the " Taming of the Shrew," the account given of " such a mad marriage as never was before " is brim-full of animation and life, and poetically speaking, is worth a hundred times more than the actual sight of the thing. The peculiar excellence of dramatic talent consists in its power of depicting events and objects in such vivid colours that they can be seen by the mind's eye without the aid of physical sight; and the reproach, made by certain disciples of the romantic school, against classical tragedies and comedies, such as Molière's " Ecole des Femmes," for instance, that the action is sacrificed to the narrative, is based only upon a low and material view of art.

The "Comedy of Errors" not only surpasses the "Menæchmi" in the greater complexity of its plot, its greater variety of incident, but also in its more generous treatment of human nature. Not that elaborately wrought-out characters are to be sought in it; for this, it must be remembered, is Shakespeare's most absolutely comic, and almost farcical play, and in this particular class of work he never handled the incisive tool of an engraver, like Molière,—his pencil runs galloping over the canvas with a light fantastic touch; and this play is, moreover, one of his most youthful performances. But already he shows touches of fine discrimination; thus Antipholus of Syracuse is not like his brother, Antipholus of Ephesus, in every point of his character. His is a more delicate nature, and is rendered more interesting by a tinge of melancholy and reverie. In speaking of his slave, he calls him (Act I., Sc. 2)—

> " A trusty villain, sir, that very oft
> When I am dull with care and melancholy,
> Lightens my humour with his merry jokes."

And when the merchant says, as he leaves him, " Sir, I commend you to your own content," Antipholus remarks—

> " He that commends me to my own content,
> Commends me to the thing I cannot get.
> I to the world am like a drop of water,
> That in the ocean seeks another drop;
> Who, falling there to find his fellow forth,
> Unseen, inquisitive, confounds himself."

When Antipholus of Syracuse is lead by a series of "errors" into his brother's house, where he sees Luciana, the charming young sister of the wife of Antipholus of Ephesus, he immediately, in the midst of his mystification, feels himself struck by a sudden love for her; the manneristic and romantic style in which he expresses his passion is most assuredly as little antique in tone, as little like old Plautus, as anything in all of Shakespeare's plays (Act III., Sc. 2):—

> " Sweet mistress (what your name is else, I know not,
>   Nor by what wonder you do hit of mine),
> Less, in your knowledge, and your grace, you show not,
>   Than our earth's wonder ; more than earth, divine.
> Teach me, dear creature, how to think and speak ;
>   Lay open to my earthy-gross conceit,
> Smothered in errors, feeble, shallow, weak,
>   The folded meaning of your words' deceit.
> Against my soul's pure truth why labour you,
>   To make it wander in an unknown field ?
> Are you a god ? would you create me new ?
>   Transform me then, and to your power I'll yield.
> But if that I am I, then well I know,
>   Your weeping sister is no wife of mine,
> Nor to her bed no homage do I owe ;
>   Far more, far more, to you do I decline.
> O train me not, sweet mermaid, with thy note,
>   To drown me in thy sister flood of tears ;
> Sing, siren, for thyself, and I will dote :
>   Spread o'er the silver waves thy golden hairs,
> And as a bed I'll take thee, and there lie ;
>   And in that glorious supposition, think
> He gains by death, that hath such means to die :—
>   Let love, being light, be drowned if she sink ! "

His dreamy and impressionable disposition, however, does not prevent him from occasionally beating his slave a little, when he suspects him of mystifying him, but he is not hard or brutal at heart. Even the reprimands he gives to Dromio have in them a touch of poetry, and in forbidding him to jest when he himself is sad he makes use of the fanciful image—

> "When the sun shines let foolish gnats make sport,
>   But creep in crannies when he hides his beams."

Antipholus of Ephesus is cast in a commoner mould ; he is not, however, devoid of all sense of delicacy and honour, and is far removed from the coarseness of moral fibre shown by the husband in the "Menæchmi," who begins by purloining his wife's mantle. On the contrary, his first laudable intention is to present his wife with a gold chain, which he has just bought for her. It is only when, on wishing to enter his house with some of his friends, he finds the door shut against him, and a stranger occupying his place, that he changes the destination of his gift.

> " I know a wench of excellent discourse,
>   Pretty and witty : wild, and yet too, gentle ;—
>   There will we dine : this woman that I mean,
>   My wife (but, I protest without desert)
>   Hath oftentimes upbraided me withal ;
>   To her will we to dinner . . .
>   That chain will I bestow
>   (Be it for nothing but to spite my wife)
>   Upon mine hostess there."

Antipholus is greatly exasperated with his wife, not, it must be admitted, without some reason. He even sends to buy a rope's end, which he intends using with good effect " among his wife and her confederates," but as this conjugal quarrel is the result of only a misunderstanding it must inevitably end in a reconciliation. We are quite willing, if necessary, to take his word for it that he in no way deserves the reproaches addressed to him by his wife, whose one fault seems to be an over-jealous love of him, and whose wifely tenderness expresses itself in language of the purest poetry (Act II., Sc. 2)—

> "Thou art an elm, my husband ; I, a vine,
>   Whose weakness, married to thy stronger state,
>   Makes me with thy strength to communicate :
>   If ought possess thee from me, it is dross ;
>   Usurping ivy, briar, or idle moss."

Shakespeare draws no sharp contrast therefore between the characters of the two brothers, but simply indicates certain delicate shades of difference, as nature demanded, the physical resemblance of the twins requiring a not too great difference in their moral natures.

But besides the greater intricacy of plot and the fuller handling of his characters, Shakespeare has also enriched his comedy by the addition of a serious element, which is full of a noble and tragic gravity. No art is displayed in the setting forth of the "Menæchmi," which merely begins with a prologue according to classical usage; but the "Comedy of Errors" opens grandly with two majestic forces—the state and paternal love.

Ephesus and Syracuse being at enmity with each other, every Syracusan that sets foot within the rival town is condemned by law to death. An old man from Syracuse has just landed at Ephesus, at the peril of his life, and is brought before the Duke. It is Ægeon, the father of the twin brothers, and in the fine and pathetic speech he makes before the Duke, he relates how years ago, returning home to Syracuse from Epidamnus with his wife and new-born twins, their ship was wrecked in a storm; his wife and one of the babes being taken up by fishermen of Corinth, and he and the other child by a ship from Epidamnus. His remaining son, when eighteen years of age, implored him to let him go in search of his brother :—

> "Whom whilst I laboured of a love to see,
> I hazarded the loss of whom I loved.
> Five summers have I spent in farthest Greece,
> Roaming clean through the bounds of Asia,
> And, coasting homeward, came to Ephesus:
> Hopeless to find, yet loth to leave unsought,
> Or that, or any place that harbours men.
> But here must end the story of my life;
> And happy were I in my timely death,
> Could all my travels warrant me they live."

This mortal enmity between two towns, this appearance of a Syracusan before the Duke of Ephesus, this old man sentenced to death, and his touching narrative, make up an opening unsurpassed by any in the annals of the stage. But what shall be said of Shake-

speare's prodigality in setting so slight a sketch in so
rich a frame, and in bestowing this magnificent overture
upon a piece of fun and buffoonery ?

When Ægeon, failing to make up the necessary sum
of money for his ransom, is on his way to be beheaded,
and recognizes Antipholus of Ephesus whom he sees, as
his son, while his son protests he does not know him,
the pathetic note of the father's grief reaches its highest
pitch.

> "Not know my voice! O time's extremity!
> Hast thou so crack'd and splitted my poor tongue,
> In seven short years, that here my only son
> Knows not my feeble key of untuned cares?"

The opportune arrival of Antipholus of Syracuse
unravels the mystery and brings the comedy to a happy
conclusion; but the serious and tragic background is
nobly conceived, and adds greatly to the charm of the
play.   The comic notion of a series of errors arising from
a similarity between twins evidently tickled Shakespeare's fancy, and we find him repeating it in "Twelfth
Night," in which a brother and a sister closely resemble
each other.   The same subject has been treated in Germany from the earliest times; in Italy even oftener than
elsewhere, and in France Regnard wrote a comedy under
the same name as that of Plautus, in which the treatment
however is wholly different.

The chief point of interest in the "Ménechmes" of
Regnard, as far as concerns the comparative study of
literature, is the degeneration which fraternal affection
and all the higher feelings in general of human nature
undergo in the world of rogues and sharpers from which
Molière's successors drew their favourite heroes.   The
Knight Ménechme is nothing but a rascally adventurer,
who makes arrangements with his valet to dupe his
brother, a sort of rough and stupid Pourceaugnac.
The scene is laid in Paris, where the two brothers have

just arrived unknown to each other. The valet goes
to the custom-house to get his master's portmanteau,
and returns with another one, bearing the name of
Ménechme. Although it is not his portmanteau, his
master, as it has his name on it, forces the lock and
opens it, and finds within it a letter to his brother,
written by a notary in Paris, who summons him to come
and receive sixty thousand crowns left to him by his
uncle's will, and to espouse the fair lady Isabelle. The
twin-brothers having been separated from childhood, and
neither having heard the other spoken of since, had completely forgotten each other, and each supposed the other
to be dead. The knight now learns from the notary's
letter not only that his brother is alive, but also that he
is about to inherit a tidy little fortune, and to make a
most desirable marriage. From this moment the thought
of cheating his brother out of his sixty thousand crowns
and of his destined bride, takes possession of him and completely absorbs his mind. For the execution of his plans
he relies upon the assistance of his valet, and still more
upon the likeness to his brother, bestowed upon him by
nature. He repairs in the first place to the notary, and
receives the sixty thousand crowns, and then flies to
Isabelle's house, where he gets himself accepted by the
young lady and her father. The two knaves, the master
and his valet, play all manner of tricks upon the other
luckless Ménechme, and in one scene the valet even goes
so far as to make the poor foolish fellow pay his brother's
debts as his own. At the close of the play, when the
recognition takes place, the knight, with hypocritical
tears, throws himself on his brother's neck, exclaiming :—

"My brother is that you? O what a welcome sight!
Can I believe my eyes, that I have this delight?"

And Ménechme, all in a maze, answers to this embrace :

"My brother, in truth . . . My joy can't be said . . .
Still I certainly always made sure you were dead."

CHAPTER VIII.

TROILUS AND CRESSIDA. ANALYSIS OF THE PLAY.

AMONGST all the allusions to classical antiquity that occur so constantly in Shakespeare's works, and more especially in his earlier plays, none are more frequent than those relating to the Trojan war. In the poem of "Lucrèce," we have seen the much-wronged wife of Collatinus contemplating a picture of the destruction of Troy, with many sad applications to her own case. In "Henry VI." the messenger who relates the death of the Duke of York to his sons, compares him to Hector holding the Greeks at bay (Pt. III., Act II., Sc. 1); and Henry VI. himself says to Warwick, "Farewell, my Hector, and my Troy's true hope" (Pt. III., Act IV., Sc. 8).

Mention is also made, in the same play, of Helen and Menelaus, of Priam, Nestor, Ulysses, and Sinon; and in "Much Ado about Nothing," Benedict is declared to be as valiant "as Hector" (Act II., Sc. 2). Similar instances may be found in Shakespeare's later plays, as in "Antony and Cleopatra," where Antony, congratulating his companions-in-arms after their victory, says to them, "You have shown all Hectors" (Act IV., Sc. 8); and in "Coriolanus," when Volumina blames Virgilia, who trembles lest her husband should be wounded (Act. I. Sc. 3):—

" Away, you fool ! it more becomes a man
Than gilt his trophy : the breasts of Hecuba,
When she did suckle Hector, look'd not lovelier
Than Hector's forehead when it spit forth blood
At Grecian swords' contending."

And further on, Aufidius hurls defiance at Coriolanus
in these words (Act I., Sc. 8) :—

" Wert thou the Hector
That was the whip of your bragg'd progeny,
Thou should'st not scape me here."

/ But it would be useless to multiply quotations.   The
point of special import and significance is that Shakespeare *always* shows a predilection for the Trojans, while
the Greeks find but little favour in his sight.

This undoubted bias on his part exhibits itself in
an especially lively manner, and has its widest scope,
in " Troilus and Cressida."   There are far grander works
amongst Shakespeare's plays, but there is none more
curious,—there is none that affords more matter for
reflection and commentary in the realms, not only of
learning and of history, but also of æsthetics, than does
" Troilus and Cressida."   Questions that we must endeavour to answer crowd upon us, touching the legendary
accounts of the two lovers; the origin of Shakespeare's
sympathy with the Trojans and with Hector, and of
his grudge against Achilles and the Greeks ; and touching the immediate sources of his knowledge, as well as
the consideration of the real worth and value of this
caricature of epic poetry, with respect to which the most
conflicting judgments have been pronounced, it being
declared on the one side to be the least deserving of
Shakespeare's productions, while it is admired on the
other side as one of his most brilliant masterpieces.   But
we must, in the first place, turn to the play itself.

Its personages are those which all accounts of the
Trojan war have made familiar to us : Priam, Hector,

Paris, Æneas, Antenor, Calchas, Agamemnon, Achilles,
Ulysses, Nestor, Ajax, Diomedes, Patroclus, Thersites,
Helen, Andromache, Cassandra, etc.; besides these, there
are two persons who, in Homer, have only a shadowy
existence—Troilus, son of Priam, and Cressida, daughter
to Calchas. All that we learn from Homer concerning
Troilus is that he fought mounted in a chariot, as was
the case with many another of his heroes. In the 24th
Book of the "Iliad," Priam laments the death of his son,
saying—

> "Oh, woe is me,
> Who have begotten sons, in all the land
> The best and bravest; now remains not one;
> Mestor and Troilus, *dauntless charioteer*,
> And Hector, who a god 'mid men appeared:
> All these hath Mars cut off."

This mention of his death, and the epithet of little significance added to his name, represents all the information
concerning him given us by Homer. As to Cressida,
daughter to Calchas, who is called Chryseyde by Chaucer,
and Brisaida by Boccaccio, the Homeric origin of her
name may be sought either in Chryseis, daughter to
Chryses, a priest of Apollo, or in Briseis, the loved and
lovely captive of Achilles; but her story has nothing
in common with that of either Briseis or Chryseis.
Shakespeare's Calchas bears very little resemblance to
the character in Homer, and is a Trojan priest who has
sided with the Greeks, and is in the Greek camp while
his daughter remains at Troy with her uncle Pandarus,
who plays an important part in the piece.*

The prologue, which is thought by several critics
not to have been written by Shakespeare, relates the
story of the Trojan war, and announces the writer's

---

* There are two personages named Pandarus in Homer, and one in
Virgil, but their name is all they have in common with the character
in Shakespeare.

intention of leaping over the first part, and beginning
in the midst of the course of events.

The opening scene is laid in Troy, in front of Priam's
palace. Troilus and Pandarus enter, and Troilus at once
makes Pandarus the confidant of his love for Cressida.
Pandarus adds fuel to the fire by singing praises to her
beauty and her wit ; Troilus interrupts him with—

> " O Pandarus ! I tell thee, Pandarus,—
> When I do tell thee, there my hopes lie drown'd,
> Reply not in how many fathoms deep
> They lie indrench'd."

In Troilus we see all the fervent love and trust of a
first youthful passion. His impetuosity and innocence
of heart make him believe the uncle and the niece to be
a thousand times more stern, more difficult to be persuaded and to be won, than they are in reality.

> " O gods, how do you plague me !
> I cannot come to Cressid but by Pandar ;
> And he's as tetchy to be woo'd to woo,
> As she is stubborn-chaste against all suit."

But Pandarus is no more " tetchy " than Cressida is
" stubborn-chaste." The worthy man pretends to hold
back, but it is merely in order to be further pressed, and
he only declares he will neither meddle nor make in
the matter for the sake of increasing his importance,
and of making the value of his services doubly felt.

In the second scene, he begins to open his batteries
upon Cressida. As he enters, she is talking with her
servant about Hector, who had started before sunrise
for the field of battle. Pandarus immediately joins in
the conversation, but only to bring forward the name of
Troilus, whom he praises at every turn for his courage
and wit and . beauty. Cressida answers with a running
fire of taunts and epigrams. It might be concluded that
she was perfectly indifferent towards Troilus, if it were
not that, from the first moment of her entrance, her

excessive levity of tone, at times outrunning the limits
of decorum, and the suspicious compliancy of her mind
excite doubts, but too well founded, as to the truth and
honesty of her words and character.   While the uncle
and niece thus bandy words together, a retreat is sounded,
and the Trojan army returns.

"Hark! they are coming from the field: shall we stand up here,
and see them, as they pass toward Ilium? good niece, do; sweet
niece Cressida."

Pandarus points out the different heroes to his niece,
impatiently wondering, as each goes by, where Troilus
is.   At last Cressida asks—

"What sneaking fellow comes yonder?"

"*Pan.* Where? yonder? that's Deiphobus;—'tis Troilus! there's
a man, niece!—Hem!—Brave Troilus! the prince of chivalry! . . .
O brave Troilus!—look well upon him, niece; look you how his
sword is bloodied, and his helm more hacked than Hector's; and how
he looks, and how he goes!—O admirable youth! he ne'er saw three
and twenty. Go thy way, Troilus, go thy way; had I a sister were a
grace, or a daughter a goddess, he should take his choice. O admirable
man! Paris?—Paris is dirt to him; and, I warrant, Helen, to change,
would give money to boot." *

When Cressida is left alone, she further enlightens
us as to her character by an edifying soliloquy, in which
she gives a short but substantial statement of principles.

"But more in Troilus thousandfold I see
    Than in the glass of Pandar's praise may be;
    Yet hold I off. Women are angels, wooing:
    Things won are done, joy's soul lies in the doing:
    That she belov'd knows nought that knows not this,—
    Men prize the thing ungain'd more than it is:
    That she was never yet that ever knew
    Love got so sweet, as when desire did sue:

---

* A scene striking in its analogy to this is to be found in the "Phœnissæ"
of Euripides, in which Antigone watches the field of battle from one of
the terraces of the palace, and au old servitor tells her the names of all
the chiefs of the enemy's army.

Therefore this maxim out of love I teach,—
Achievement is command; ungain'd, beseech:
Then, though my heart's content firm love doth bear,
Nothing of that shall from mine eyes appear."

/The third scene transports us to the camp of the Greeks, before Agamemnon's tent, where the chiefs are met in deliberation. It would be puzzling to say exactly what they are talking about, or what the precise subject of their conference consists in. They talk much but say little; in fact, all through the play the speeches of the Greeks are characterized by the possession of more words than meaning. Their language is ludicrously bombastic and verbose, and the poet evidently intended to ridicule them. This irony, no doubt, plays round all, but he certainly shows a greater respect for the Trojans, who have not only more sense, but are also more courageous, and act a comparatively nobler part both in words and deeds.

Agamemnon inquires of his companions what grief has set the jaundice on their cheeks—is it because after a seven years' siege Troy walls still stand? Nestor is the next to open his mouth, and with a lavish profusion of metaphors says nothing. Then Ulysses takes his turn. He begins by addressing extravagant compliments to the two preceding orators, and is himself outrageously verbose and diffuse; it is, however, possible to gather one fact from his lengthy discourse, that fact being that discipline has grown lax, that all authority has disappeared, and that each man in the army does as seems best in his own eyes, instead of obeying the orders of his superior. "Troy in our weakness lives, not in her strength." Finally, leaving generalities to come to more definite accusations, Ulysses complains of the conduct of Achilles, who —

" Having his ear full of his airy fame,
Grows dainty of his worth, and in his tent
Lies mocking our designs,"

M

while Patroclus keeps him in roars of laughter at his imitation of the different chiefs.

The conference is interrupted by the sound of a trumpet, and Agamemnon asks Menelaus to look and see what it means. "From Troy," announces Menelaus. Æneas enters with a message from Troy, and salutes Agamemnon with an address couched in such ridiculously high-flown terms, that even the haughty " king of men," "the high and mighty Agamemnon," hesitates about accepting it as serious. Æneas is the bearer of· a challenge from Hector 'to all the Grecian Princes, which he delivers in true chivalrous style, after the mode of mediæval heroes. His challenge for the morrow is accepted, and Agamemnon then conducts Æneas to his tent to entertain him worthily.

Ulysses and Nestor remain talking over the matter, and agree that the challenge "relates in purpose only to Achilles," who is the only Greek fit to cope with Hector. But on no account must he be allowed to fight—for either he will conquer or be conquered ; if he should be conquered his shame would be theirs, if he should conquer, his glory would be his own, and would only add to his overweening insolence. Ulysses therefore suggests that a lottery should be held, when it could be easily contrived that " blockish Ajax draw the sort to fight with Hector."

> " Hit or miss,
> Our project's life this shape of sense assumes,—
> Ajax employ'd, plucks down Achilles' plumes."

And with this little plot on the part of Ulysses and Nestor, the first act comes to an end.

The second act introduces a personage who might be said to fulfil the function of Chorus in the play, if it were not that the vileness and meanness of his nature render him quite unworthy of so dignified an employment as giving voice and expression to the sentiments of the collective conscience of humanity, concerning men and things. Like the Thersites of Homer, Shakespeare's Thersites is a reviler, but it is no longer only upon Achilles, Ulysses, and Agamemnon that he spits forth his venom,—he reviles the whole world, and his foul-mouthed insults, infinitely grosser than those of the Thersites of the "Iliad," are of greater depth and of far wider significance. The causes of the Trojan war are summed up by him, in the coarsest terms, as being a dishonoured husband and a guilty wife; and in the innermost heart of each hero of the war, both Greek and Trojan, the only ruling passion that he recognizes is that of lust, with which he reproaches them in torrents of gross and obscene words unfit for handling. A tolerably accurate notion of the part played by Thersites may be obtained by considering him as a sort of court fool. Like the fools and jesters of old, he dresses up truth in so strange a garb that it is scarcely recognizable; like them also, he possesses wit, sets a high value upon it, is wholly occupied in finding it both in himself and in others. The reason of his contempt for Ajax is, that he "has not so much wit as will stop the eye of Helen's needle," and Achilles is in much the same predicament, having but "little, little, less than little wit; which will not deliver a fly from a spider without drawing the massy irons and cutting the web." (Act II., Sc. 3.)

This decided taste that Thersites has for wit leads him to pass a comparatively favourable judgment upon Nestor and Ulysses, the only warriors for whom he appears to entertain the faintest spark of respect, as their wit, unlike that of Achilles, lies not in their sinews. "There's Ulysses and old Nestor,—whose wit was mouldy ere your grandsires had nails on their toes,—yoke you like draught oxen, and make you plough up the war." Rail as he will, the company of Thersites is put up with on account of the amusement he affords, and because he

has an evil tongue and serves as a convenient butt for
any one who feels an itching desire to insult and beat
some one else, a further distinguishing feature possessed
by him in common with court fools.

The scene now changes to Priam's palace at Troy,
where the old King is holding council with four of his
sons. The question is whether Helen should be given up
to the Greeks in order to obtain peace. The character of
Hector is very nobly drawn in this scene; his courage is
well-known, but he here shows himself as prudent and
as politic as he is brave, and his sense of justice and
honour is peculiarly clear and high. He advises that
Helen should be sent back to Menelaus, her lawful husband, and Helenus the priest is of the same opinion.
But Paris and Troilus, who both have strong personal
reasons for desiring the continuation of the war, get hot
and angry, and strenuously inveigh against the dictates
of good sense and morality, and they finally succeed in
making their warlike advice prevail. As we shall see
further on, in mediæval romances Hector's character was
always distinguished by a certain modesty, a courteous
deference to the opinions of others; and it is interesting
to note how well this salient point in his nature has been
preserved by Shakespeare.

The apparition of Cassandra, the raving prophetess, in
the midst of their deliberations, forms a short and
splendid episode.

> " *Cas.* [*Within.*] Cry, Trojans, cry !
> *Pri.*   What noise ? what shriek is this ?
> *Tro.* 'Tis our mad sister, I do know her voice.
> *Cas.* [*Within.*] Cry, Trojans !
> *Hect.* It is Cassandra.
>
> *Enter* CASSANDRA, *raving.*
>
> *Cas.* Cry, Trojans, cry ! lend me ten thousand eyes,
> And I will fill them with prophetic tears.

*   *   *   *   *

Cry, Trojans, cry ! practise your eyes with tears !
Troy must not be, nor goodly Ilion stand ;
Our firebrand brother, Paris, burns us all.
Cry, Trojans, cry ! a Helen, and a woe :
Cry, cry ! Troy burns, or else let Helen go."

But Cassandra's destiny is never to be believed, and she prophesies in vain. The passion of Troilus and Paris gains the day over the larger wisdom of Hector, and precipitates Troy upon its ruin.

A grand and serious beauty pervades the whole scene, but in returning to the Greek camp we again fall into comedy.

Agamemnon thinks it high time for Achilles to leave off his airs and graces, and comes to his tent determined to see him. Patroclus, however, brings back an ironically polite message from Achilles, who had retired within his tent, to the effect that he is sick and that he regrets that it is impossible for him to receive his illustrious visitor. The blockish Ajax gives vent to his astonishment at the pride exhibited by Achilles :—

" *Ajax.* What is he more than another ? . . . . Do you not think he thinks himself a better man than I am ?

Agam. No question.

Ajax. Will you subscribe his thought, and say he is ?

Agam. No, noble Ajax ; you are as strong, as valiant, as wise, no less noble, much more gentle, and altogether more tractable.

Ajax. Why should a man be proud ? How doth pride grow ? I know not what pride is."

This is the very moment for inflaming Ajax's vanity, and for heaping compliments upon him proportionate to the egregious folly of the man. Ulysses and Nestor seize the opportunity, and nothing could be more amusing than the manner in which they vie with each other in showering pretty speeches upon him so as to lead him in the way they wish him to go,—it would be impossible to express praise in a tone of more witty raillery.

The third act brings Troilus and Cressida again on the

scene. The officious Pandarus has contrived—without
any very great effort being necessary—to bring the two
lovers together. It is this delusion on his part as to his
services being quite indispensable that renders his part
so comical. He fusses about, and pants and perspires,
and gives himself a great deal of very needless trouble.
Cressida, as we have seen, is already won, and what
appears like hesitation on her part is only the wily trick
of a finished coquette, that none but the eyes of so simple
a lover as poor Troilus could mistake for the expression
of a shy and startled modesty.

Troilus is the first to enter, and lingers in the orchard,
lost in expectation of the joy that awaits him. Pandarus
soon appears bringing Cressida with him, and after
joking Troilus for his silence and confusion, he leaves the
two lovers alone together. The scene that follows is
exquisitely painted ; not only have we the delicious
poetry softly murmured by two lovers, but there is not a
single word set down at random, every word is a feature
and each feature is a stroke of the brush. The wicked
little flirt provoking him by an ambiguous expression to
kiss her, and then protesting in the most innocent manner
that he had quite misunderstood her, puts the finishing
touch to her own portrait.

Solemn oaths of fidelity and love then pass between
them, to which Pandarus, who has returned, acts as witness. The *happiness* of the lovers is complete, as a
French writer has with some levity expressed it, forgetful of Shakespeare's wise sonnet in which he says possession does not ensure delight.

> " Enjoy'd no sooner but despisèd straight,
> Past reason hunted : and no sooner had,
> Past reason hated, as a swallowed bait
> On purpose laid to make the taker mad. . . .
> A bliss in proof,—and proved a very woe.
> Before, a joy proposed ; behind, a dream :
> All this the world well knows ; yet none knows well
> To shun the heaven that leads men to this hell."

A terrible blow is about to fall upon the lovers : Calchas the Trojan priest who has gone over to the Greeks, and is the father of Cressida, begs of Agamemnon in recompense for the sacrifice he has made in abandoning Troy and all his possessions there, and in incurring the name of traitor from his countrymen, to obtain the restoration of his daughter from the Trojans, for which a good opportunity has just presented itself in the capture by the Greeks of the noble Antenor,—let him be given back to the Trojans in exchange for Cressida. This. request strikes Agamemnon as just and reasonable, and he instructs Diomedes ˙to take back Antenor and to return with Cressida, and not to omit putting on his best clothes as befits the occasion, and at the same time, to—

> " Bring word if Hector will to-morrow
> Be answered in his challenge : Ajax is ready."

Then follows the comical scene when by Ulysses's advice, in order to rouse Achilles from his lethargy by wounding his vanity, Agamemnon and all the princes walk in procession past his tent without taking any notice of him, or only giving him a cold and distant greeting. Achilles by no means relishes the joke, and tries to discover what it all means from Ulysses, who takes the opportunity of treating him to a long psychological and ethical dissertation on the fickleness of fortune, interspersed with illustrations drawn from the case of Ajax.

> " Now shall we see to-morrow,
> An act that very chance doth throw upon him,
> Ajax renowned. . . .
> Then marvel not, thou great and complete man,
> That all the Greeks begin to worship Ajax ;
> *Since things in motion sooner catch the eye,*
> *Than what not stirs.* The cry went once on thee,
> And still it might, and yet it may again,
> If thou wouldst not entomb thyself alive."

We see in this scene that the reason of the inaction

displayed by Achilles is very different from that given in the first book of the "Iliad:" he is in love with Polyxena, Priam's daughter, and holds secret communications with the enemy; everything, in fact, that can serve to lower this hero of Homer's and to render him ridiculous and contemptible, is complacently presented to us by Shakespeare in this play, and further on - we shall even see him fall into the meanest deeds of cowardice and treachery.

The words let drop by Ulysses rankle in his mind, and the thought of Ajax probably returning with honour and glory from his combat with Hector, begins decidedly to torment him; it is, however, too late now to prevent it. A singular idea occurs to him.

> "Go call Thersites hither, sweet Patroclus ;
> I'll send the fool to Ajax, and desire him
> To invite the Trojan lords after the combat,
> To see us here unarm'd : I have a woman's longing,
> An appetite that I am sick withal,
> To see great Hector in his weeds of peace ;
> To talk with him, and to behold his visage,
> Even to my full of view."

In the fourth act Diomedes accomplishes his mission of conducting Antenor to Troy, and of receiving Cressida in exchange. The lovers separate with infinite sorrow and protestation on both sides; sad presentiments are felt by Troilus, who warns Cressida against the seductive charms of "the Grecian youths." For himself, he cannot sing or dance, or make fine speeches, or play at subtle games, he has only a true and faithful heart :—

> "Fear not my truth ; the moral of my wit
> Is—*plain and true,*—there's all the reach of it."

He gives Cressida a sleeve, as a love-token, and she gives him a glove.

We next see Cressida's arrival at the Greek camp, when all the chiefs in turn salute her with a kiss—a

tribute to her charms which she gaily accepts, dealing
out witty retorts, and even jesting in light and lively
terms at the expense of poor Menelaus. " A woman of
quick sense," remarks Nestor, as she withdraws with
Diomedes to her father's tent, but Ulysses has seen through
her at a glance and answers severely :—

> " Fie, fie upon her !
> There's a language in her eye, her cheek, her lip,
> Nay, her foot speaks ; her wanton spirits look out
> At every joint and motive of her body."

The combat between Hector and Ajax takes place,
but is soon interrupted by Hector on account of the relationship that exists between Ajax and himself, through
Hesione, mother to Ajax and aunt to Hector. A cessa-
tion of arms ensues, and the cousins tenderly embrace
each other, after which Hector visits the Greek chiefs in
their tents. The interview with Achilles is of a ferocious
character, but the ferocity is on the side of the Greek,
not of the Trojan.

> " *Ach.* Tell me, you heavens, in what part of his body
> Shall I destroy him ? whether there, or there, or there ?
> That I may give the local wound a name ;
> And make distinct the very breach whereout
> Hector's great spirit flew : answer me, heavens ! "

We now come to the fifth act. The baseness of Achilles
now manifests itself in a fresh direction : just as he was
about to bestir himself after his long inaction and at
last take up arms again, he receives a letter from Hecuba,
and a gift from her daughter—

> " Both taxing me, and gaging me to keep
> An oath that I have sworn. I will not break it.
> Fall, Greeks ; fail fame ; honour, or go, or stay ;
> My major vow lies here, this I'll obey."

But let us turn to watch what is going on in front of
Calchas's tent, in which Cressida is, and where some one
has arrived upon " important business, the tide whereof

is now." This is none other than Diomedes, who is
secretly followed in the darkness of the night by Ulysses
and Troilus. They are unseen witnesses of his interview
with Cressida and of all her alluring wiles, and finally
see her give him the sleeve Troilus had given to her. It
is unnecessary to say that at this juncture the poor
deceived lover swears to kill Diomedes. As soon as
Cressida has retired into the tent, he bursts out into
bitter complaints, in which the note of inextinguishable
love still makes itself heard through all the storms of
indignation and rage.

> " Was Cressid here ? . . .
>   This she ? no, this is Diomed's Cressida ;
>   If beauty have a soul, this is not she. . . .
>   Cressid is mine, tied with the bonds of heaven.
>   Hark, Greek : as much as I do Cressid love,
>   So much by weight hate I her Diomed :
>   That sleeve is mine that he'll bear in his helm ;
>   Were it a casque composed by Vulcan's skill,
>   My sword should bite it. . . .
>   O Cressid ! O false Cressid ! false, false, false !
>   Let all untruths stand by thy stained name,
>   And they'll seem glorious."

Meanwhile, in the palace at Troy, Hector is arming himself for battle, in spite of the prayers and entreaties of
Andromache whose dreams have filled her with gloomy
forebodings. In vain too, always in vain, does Cassandra
join her prophetic warnings to the supplications of his
wife ; Hector listens to neither, but on Troilus entering,
armed and ready to follow him, he counsels him to stay
at home.

> " Unarm thee, go ; and doubt thou not, brave boy,
>   I'll stand to-day, for thee, and me, and Troy,"—

language doubly generous on the part of the hero
who in the Council Chamber had advocated peace in
opposition to the harebrained youths who clamoured for
war. But Hector's advice is of no avail : Troilus has too

raging a thirst for vengeance and for blood, and the two brothers depart for the field of battle.

The attack begins. Groups of fighting soldiers pass in succession across the stage, as is customary in the scenes of Shakespeare's historical dramas, and which must produce so peculiar an effect when acted. Hector kills Patroclus, whose death rouses Achilles, and he swears to avenge his friend. But the utter baseness of his vengeance is the very point in this tragi-comic parody most calculated to scandalize the classical admirers of the "Iliad."

In an encounter earlier in the day with Achilles, Hector, seeing him overcome with fatigue, proposes, with all the courtesy of a Roland or an Oliver of mediæval times, that their combat should be postponed until he has rested and recovered his strength; and Achilles, though with a very bad grace, avails himself of the offer. Towards evening, Hector says:—

> "Now is my day's work done : I'll take good breath :
> Rest, sword : thou hast thy fill of blood and death,"

at the same time, taking off his helmet and hanging his shield behind him. At this moment, Achilles arrives with his Myrmidons, and seeing Hector unarmed, rushes upon him, crying:—

> "Strike, fellows, strike ; this is the man I seek,"

and Hector falls dead. "Come," adds Achilles,—

> "Tie his body to my horse's tail ;
> Along the field I will the Trojan trail."

In the Trojan camp the news causes the deepest consternation and grief.

> "*Tro.* Hector is slain.
> *All.* Hector ? The gods forbid ! . . .
> *Tro.* . . . Hector is gone !
> Who shall tell Priam so, or Hecuba ?
> Let him that will a screech-owl aye be called,
> Go in to Troy, and say there—*Hector's dead.*"

As Troilus is going out, Pandarus enters from the other
side and tries to stop him, but Troilus will not listen :—

> " Hence, broker lackey ! ignomy and shame,
>   Pursue thy life and live aye with thy name."

Troilus goes off, and with a cynical epilogue from
Pandarus, the scene closes.

CHAPTER IX.

TROILUS AND CRESSIDA: THE STORY OF THE TWO LOVERS.*

BESIDES the passage already quoted from the twenty-fourth book of the "Iliad," in which mention is made of Troilus, only to say that he fought in a chariot and that he was dead, we may fairly expect to find other traditions concerning him in the literature of antiquity. Sophocles wrote a tragedy called "Troilus," which is unfortunately lost, four lines of it only being preserved. Ancient commentators of Homer relate how the fate of Troy was bound up with that of Troilus, and how the town would be taken if the child died before attaining his twentieth year; they further tell us that Troilus was killed by Achilles in the temple of Apollo, and they discuss the question whether his death took place before or after the time at which the "Iliad" opens. Horace, Virgil, Ausonius, Seneca the tragedian, Apollodorus, Lycophron, Quintus of Smyrna, and other poets or grammarians of Greco-Latin antiquity, speak of Troilus,

---

* Works used in the composition of this chapter: "Introduction de MM. L. Moland et C. d'Héricault aux Nouvelles françaises en prose du XIVᵉ. siècle." "Le Roman de Benoît de Sainte-More et le Roman de Troie, ou les Métamorphoses d'Homère et de l'épopée gréco-latine au Moyen âge," par A. Joly. "Die Sage von Trojanischen Kriege in dem Bearbeitungen des Mittel Alters und ihren antiken Quellen," von Dr. Hermann Dunger.

but they add nothing to our knowledge of his history,
and content themselves with repeating, with more or
less detail, that he was young, and that he met his death
at the hands of Achilles; it will be sufficient here to
quote the passage from Quintus Smyrnæus, who is
generally supposed to have lived in the fourth century,
A.D.

" Within the sacred walls of Troy, Hecuba brought Troilus into the
world, but he remained not long to be an honour to her, for the rude
lance and prowess of Achilles deprived him of his life. . . . As in a
flowery garden, beside a stream, the sharp scythe comes in search of
the yet green ear of corn or of the poppy, and mows them down or
ever their fruit be ripened, cutting them off before they come to sweet
maturity, not leaving them till the harvest: the smooth steel taking
away all hope of the offshoots that the gentle dews had promised in
the fulness of time; so did Achilles slay the son of Priam, the god-
like Troilus in the flower of his youth, ere he had known the joy of
clasping a bride within his arms, and still occupied himself with boyish
games. Thus did the Fatal Sister cut the thread just at the time when
he was approaching the joyous years of manhood, when the body is full
of strength, and the blood of audacity."

With regard to Cressida, Cryseyde, Brisaida, Briséida,
the Homeric origin of her name, as has already been
remarked, may be sought either in Chryseis, the daughter
of Chryses, a priest of Apollo, or in Briseis, the "beauteous
prize " of Achilles. At the opening of the " Iliad," Chryses
comes to ransom his daughter, who has fallen to the lot
of Agamemnon after a victorious attack of the Greeks.
Agamemnon refuses to accept the proffered ransom, and
Apollo, to avenge his priest, smites the Grecian army
with a plague. Calchas, encouraged by Achilles, declares
that the plague will only cease when Chryseis is given
back to her father, and Agamemnon, sorely wounded in
his pride, sees himself obliged to restore his fair portion
of the booty; but he revenges himself upon Achilles,
whom he hates as the instigator of the oracles pronounced by Calchas, by demanding Briseis from him in
return.

Those who prize accuracy in even the insignificant details of research, will have the satisfaction further on of being able to decide in favour of Briseis, rather than of Chryseis, as the veritable original of Cressida ; but in sooth, it is a matter of little moment, for the story of Shakespeare's coquette is perfectly distinct from that of the two characters in the "Iliad," who remained throughout antiquity as Homer made them from the first.

In the course of the fifth century, or in the beginning of the sixth,—the exact date is not known,—there appeared a book, the importance of which was without parallel in the literary history of the Middle Ages, and even in that of the Renaissance. The history of the destruction of Troy, "Historia de Excidio Trojæ," was written by an impostor, whose real name is unknown, but who presented his work as a translation of the writings of a Phrygian priest named Dares, an eye-witness of the Trojan war, who was supposed to have kept a sort of journal of the siege. A little anterior to this, another journal, written during the siege, had been brought to light under the title of "De Bello Trojano," by another impostor, who gave himself out as Dictys the Cretan, another contemporary of the Trojan war, and companion-in-arms to Idomeneus. The pseudo-Dares and the pseudo-Dictys were the greatest and almost only source of all that the Middle Ages knew, and of all that they repeated, concerning the events related in the "Iliad." Homer was forgotten, and his place usurped by these two authors, and for ten or eleven centuries, no really ancient poet, not even Virgil, exercised a greater influence than they did over the imagination of men.

We shall have occasion to return to the fictitious Dares and the fictitious Dictys in the next chapter, when treating of the legends and traditions of the Trojan war

current in the Middle Ages, and even down to the time
of Shakespeare. In the present chapter we are merely
concerned with the story of Troilus and Cressida, and it
is only necessary to cull from the two apocryphal narra-
tives whatever they may contain relating to the two
lovers. In future, for the sake of brevity, I shall simply
call them Dares and Dictys, without adding any epithet
to their names as a reminder that they were not whom
they pretended to be. It appears that there really had
existed a Dares of Phrygia, a priest of Vulcan, who is
mentioned in the fifth book of the " Iliad," and a Dictys
of Crete, companion-in-arms to Idomeneus, and there is
some reason to believe that they left behind them documents concerning the Trojan war, which Homer afterwards made use of. Ælian states that the writings of
Dares (he makes no mention of Dictys) were extant in
his day (supposed to be about the middle of the third
century of the Christian era), but these writings, which
were lost in the general wreck of classical antiquity, were
certainly not those which made their appearance in the
sixth century.

Troilus is spoken of both by Dares and by Dictys;
we will quote Dictys first :—

" Lycaon was taken prisoner, as was also Troilus, son of Priam ;
Achilles, enraged at not having yet received the answer he was expecting from Priam, ordered him to be strangled. At the news, the
Trojans reflecting on the tender age of Troilus, bewailed his death with
tears and great moaning ; for the youth, scarcely emerged from boy-
hood, was beloved by all for his grace and beauty of form, as well as
for his modesty and truth of heart."

Dares says that—

" Troilus was of good stature and of great comeliness, full of
courage, and of vigour beyond his years, and impatient to distinguish
himself." He adds, " Ulysses and Diomedes said of Troilus; that he
was no less valiant than Hector."

We also learn from him that Achilles could only kill

the brave Troilus by attacking him behind, treacherously. Thus we see Troilus beginning to reveal himself and to grow into a man; he is no longer the stripling of classical antiquity, the tender flower cut off before its time. In a council of war held by Priam, he boldly sides with Paris in favour of action and of continuing the war, contesting the point, as in the second act of Shakespeare's play, with Helenus, who advocates a more timorous policy; he is already a hero, but not as yet in love.

From Dictys we learn nothing of Cressida, but Dares, who has a great fondness for describing his personages, has drawn her portrait for us.

"Briséida," he says (and this would seem to decide the knotty point of Cressida's origin in favour of Briseis, the captive of Achilles), "Briséida was of great beauty, tall and white, with light hair,* eyebrows meeting at their birth, most gracious eyes and well-proportioned body; she was sweet and gentle with modesty of heart, and she was simple and pious."

This description is all that we find said about Briséida in Dares. Nothing is told of her relationship to Calchas, nor of the story of her love and her coquettish ways. She is simply Briseis, the captive of Achilles. We may remark in passing, that Dares is the first writer who represents Calchas the priest as a Trojan gone over to the Greeks in consequence of his prophetic spirit, by which he foreknew the fatal future of Troy.

The real originator of the story of Troilus and Cressida was a Norman *trouvère*, who lived in the latter half of the twelfth century, the *classical* epoch of what may be called the early French Renaissance in the Middle Ages,

---

* In the Middle Ages neither man nor woman was considered handsome if they had not light hair. Shakespeare's Pandarus acknowledges with regret that Cressida's hair was a little darker than Helen's. Shakespeare however in his 127th Sonnet, has rehabilitated the brunette type of beauty.

an epoch when the influence of French literature was paramount in Europe, as again later in the seventeenth and eighteenth centuries,—less perfect indeed than then, but endowed perhaps with greater freshness and fertility of imagination. Unfortunately, the language of those times, more logical and in certain respects better than the French of the present day, has done more than merely grow old, it has become a dead language that Frenchmen themselves can decipher only with trouble and study. History, however, fills up the blank caused by the absence of direct knowledge and true understanding of the spirit of these mediæval works, and teaches us that in the eleventh, twelfth, and thirteenth centuries, French literature took the initiative amongst the countries of Europe; Germany, Italy, Spain, and England borrowing largely from it for a considerable space of time.

"There was a tolerably wide interval," writes Littré, in the preface to his "Dictionnaire de la Langue Française," during which France exercised no literary ascendency over the rest of Europe, but it separates two epochs when this ascendency—a more legitimate one than most, because those who submitted to it did so willingly and of their own choice—was all-powerful: the epoch that takes in the twelfth and thirteenth centuries, and that which begins with the century of Louis XIV. . . . In the earlier period, it was the originality of its creations and the perfect harmony between its conceptions and the then prevailing beliefs and manners that recommended French literature to Europe;—in the riper and more cultured age, it was a certain sustained correctness and its perfect elegance, it was the clearness of intellect, and, a little later on, the boldness of its philosophic speculation, that made so many foreign hands seize upon French books."

The Norman *trouvère,* whose imagination gave birth to the story of Troilus and Cressida was Benoit de Sainte-More, and the history of their love forms an episode in a long epic poem entitled " Le Roman de Troie." M. Joly has published the entire poem of Benoit de Sainte-More, adding a work of considerable size and of the highest interest upon the metamorphoses undergone by Homer and the Greco-Latin epic during the Middle Ages; and to this instructive study I am greatly indebted for much relating to the traditions of the two lovers, and for still more with respect to the legends of Troy.

The materials for the "Roman de Troie" were almost entirely derived from Dares. In a sort of preface to his narrative, Benoit announces that Dares is his guide, and that he intends following him; but that still he will not deny himself the pleasure of inserting here and there, as occasion offers, any pretty little fancy that may occur to him.

> " Le Latin suivrai et la lettre.
> Nulle autre rien n'y voudrai mettre,
> Sinon comme le trouve écrit.
> Je ne dis pas qu'aucun bon dit
> N'y mette, si faire le sai,
> Mais la matière ensuivrai."

The episode of the coquette, Briséida, is one of these pretty little fancies, one of these "bons dits," as he says himself, and forms a welcome interruption to the monotony of a poem of more than thirty thousand lines, in which battle follows battle with wearisome uniformity. For the readers, or rather listeners, in the Middle Ages were full of the childlike and easily satisfied imagination that is one of the most beautiful possessions of early youth, both of individuals and of nations; they never tired of listening to stories, and to stories always the same. Their poets knew nothing of the art of composition, of selecting the essential point of a subject and grouping everything round it as a centre in true perspective, and in proportion to the importance of each detail. They simply followed the whole course of the events themselves, beginning with the very first and ending with the very last. With them every poem was a cycle, and hence arises their tedious length, which we of the present day find so intolerable.

"Generally speaking," writes Sainte-Benne, "the infinite or the. indefinite, anything interminable, is the distinguishing mark of these artless compositions. . . . These people have a passion for details and for length. . . Everything unfolds itself and nothing is knit together."

It is, therefore, an exceptional piece of good fortune to alight in these immense poems upon a comparatively short episode, complete in itself, which can be detached from the rest of the history, just in the same manner that the loves of Troilus and Cressida, in Shakespeare's play, are independent of the rest of the plot and can easily be separated.

The highest place of interest in Benoit's narrative is not occupied by Troilus, of whom the long but insignificant description may be passed over in silence, but the portrait of Briséida calls for closer attention. It is the first sketch of the picture afterwards to be painted by Shakespeare, and what makes it still more remarkable is that it is not only the first sketch, but also the only sketch. The portrait of the young Trojan beauty has been drawn again and again by many different hands, and even by such celebrated poets as Boccaccio and Chaucer ; but the essence of its character has undergone such important alterations that the original outline of the old *trouvère* is the only one amidst all these after-touches that has any true affinity with the type chosen and fixed by Shakespeare.

"She was very comely," says Benoit, "neither too little nor too big ; she was fairer and whiter and more lovely than any flower of the lily, or snow upon the branch, but her eyebrows had the mischance of meeting. She had wide-open beautiful eyes, and *her wit was quick and ready*. She was graceful and of demure countenance. She was well-beloved, and could also herself love well, but *her heart was changeable*. She was of an amorous and simple nature, and in alms-giving very charitable."

"Of quick and ready wit," and "a changeable heart," such are the two interesting and novel details in this description, all the rest of which is simply borrowed from

Dares. Briséida has now become the daughter of Calchas, and her history is the same as that related by Shakespeare. Troilus and Cressida love, and are happy ; but one day Calchas reclaims his daughter, and she is conducted to the Greek camp, where she soon consoles herself with Diomedes for the loss of Troilus. Leaving aside the well-known facts of this little romance, it is to the indications given of her character that attention must here be paid.

Benoit de Sainte-More begins his account at the time when Troilus and Cressida have to part ; but it is very difficult to convey in a modern translation any of the quaint grace of the old French story :— *

"Whoever else may be merry and joyous, Troilus is sorely grieved for the daughter of Calchas, for he loved her with all his heart, and she him. And when the damsel knew that she must depart to the Greek camp, she began to make great lamentations! 'Alas!' said she, ' what sorrow is mine, that I must leave the land where I was born, and all the people among whom I was brought up, and must go amongst a strange folk! Ah, Troilus! my own sweet friend, who hast loved me above all things, and whom I have loved with all my heart; so that I know not how I can live without thee. Ah, King Priam! since it has pleased thee to send me away out of the land where I have had all the good things of life and all its honours, God grant I may not live till day. Come, Death! for that I desire above all things.' Troilus came to her . . . and they wept together bitterly and very tenderly, for they well knew that the next day they would be far apart, the one from the other, and perhaps never again might it chance for them to be even as they would together. . . . And they told the one to the other what great grief and sorrow he caused them who thus divided them. . . . And thus they remained until the coming of day. And when Troilus had left, the damsel made ready to depart, and had all her rich treasures and apparel gathered together, to take with her, and then took leave of many, who were sad at her departure."

Then follows a long description of how Cressida was dressed—a detail not without its psychological interest,

---

* The quotations are taken from a translation into French prose made in the Middle Ages.

for although it is probable that the poet wrote it simply in obedience to the taste of the Middle Ages for interminable enumerations, yet it discloses, unconsciously and instinctively, a feature of the character of the coquette. The absence of conscious intention on the part of a poet, especially in early and primitive times, has never been held by any critic who understood his task aright, as a reason for abstaining from seeking a thousand meanings that the author himself never suspected.*

"The damsel was dressed and apparelled very richly, and wore a mantle that had been made in India with great skill, and with the aid of magic arts. And it was rosy-red and white, and changed its colour many times a day, according to the course of the sun. And a wise poet of India had sent it to Calchas out of great love for him. The fur of the mantle was of great richness and rarity, for it was made of the whole and entire skin, without a seam, of an animal, called dindialos, which inhabits the East. And it was of so many colours, that there is no colour, either in stones or in flowers, that it did not possess. And this animal is caught by a strange kind of people, called Cynocephales, who have heads like unto a dog. . . . The hem of the mantle was made from an animal of great price, that lives by the river of the Earthly Paradise, and it was adorned right richly with precious stones. So seemly and beautiful a mantle was never seen before, and it became her well; and with other garments, also, she was daintily arrayed."

Briséida sets out on her way, and here the simple-hearted poet feels constrained to give us a warning beforehand, of which the consummate art of Shakespeare had no need, and foretells that the little beauty will prove faithless to Troilus. This precaution on his part is certainly somewhat wanting in dexterity of touch, but at all events, with Benoit de Sainte-More, our attention having been first awakened by certain hints in the description of the young girl's character, and by a knowledge of her sensual tastes, and having then been

---

* For the explanation of this paradox, see the beginning of the chapter on Brutus.

duly warned of her future behaviour, we are not taken
by surprise when the catastrophe occurs;—when one is
not a great poet, it may be as well to be fairly logical.
But logic and art are alike wanting in Boccaccio and
Chaucer; with them, Cressida's unfaithfulness bursts
upon the astonished reader like a thunderbolt, without
preparation of any kind, and the writers themselves
loudly express their own surprise. This amazement on
the part of an author at his own narrative bespeaks,
perhaps, still less skilful handling than the naïve precautions and somewhat clumsy transitions of earlier
poets.

"The damsel," sings the trouvère, "is in despair, but her grief
will soon be quieted. Soon she will have forgotten, and her heart be
so changed, that she will remember but little about Troy. Though
now she mourns, joy will return to her, and she will soon have given
her love to one whom she has never yet seen, soon she will be comforted. With women, sorrow lasts but a little while; they weep with
one eye and laugh with the other. The hearts of most of them are
quick to change, and the wisest of them is giddy enough. All that
she has loved for seven years, has she in one day forgotten. Solomon,
he who was so full of wisdom, says in his writings, that the man who
can find a virtuous woman should praise the Lord: to meet beauty and
virtue joined together is a mighty rare thing it seems; a treasure far
above precious stones and vessels of gold."

The coquette, perceiving that she is loved, resolves to
play off all her haughty pranks, as in the soliloquy given
her by Shakespeare, to increase the ardour of her lover
and make her dominion doubly sure.

"The damsel is full of merriment and joy because she has got
him in her net. Fair dames are ever of this nature: if one of them
sees you love her, forthwith she begins to show herself proud and
haughty."

Briséida is received in the Greek camp as she is in
Shakespeare's play.

"Greatly was the damsel praised, and much did the Greeks look
at her—

      'Moult est belle, disent-ils tous.'"

She is admired, not only for her beauty, but also for her sprightliness and wit, and so complete was her success, that ere four days were over she felt quite consoled, and had no longer any "desire or heart to return to the city."

Then Diomedes offers her his heart.

"Among the Greeks came Dyomedes, with great pomp," writes one of the numerous compilers, who during the Middle Ages paraphrased "Le Roman de Troie" into French prose, "and when he saw the beauty of Briseyda he felt such great love for her that he could no more leave her; he drew near and accompanied her, talking and laughing, to her father's tent. On the way Dyomedes opened his heart to her, to which she answered courteously, excusing herself from giving or granting him her love *at that time.*"

This kindly reservation for a future day is to be found mentioned in all the followers of Benoit. In Jacques Milet, Cressida refuses her heart to Troilus, "at least, for the present;" in Raoul le Fèvre, she answers, that she refuses it "for this time."

"Dyomedes had great gladness of heart at this answer, inasmuch as he was not refused altogether. . . . . Breséida acted very wisely in giving him hope without disheartening him over much, so that his love waxed hotter and hotter."

Thus encouraged, Diomedes ventures upon a second assault upon her heart, and this time Briséida answers, according to Raoul le Fèvre, "that she could not hate one who loved her with such good heart;" or, according to another version, "Since he loves me, I should be a poor wretch not to love him in return."

Briefly speaking, the upshot of the siege, of which the progress is narrated step by step, is that she succumbs, justifying her faithlessness by the highly humorous excuse, "I was in mortal anguish at receiving no comfort from Troilus; I should have died outright, had I not sought to console myself."

Good old Benoit de Sainte-More ought no longer to

be forgotten, and it is really high·time that reparation should be made for the injustice he has so long suffered under, literary thieves having substituted their names for his so successfully that the Norman *trouvère* was almost unknown for five or six centuries,* and has only been re-instated in possession of his rights through the efforts of recent research. The Middle Ages felt none of· our scruples relating to literary property, as may easily be understood when the impersonal character of mediæval poetry is taken into consideration; it bore as yet no unmistakable impression of the individuality of the author. And besides this, it is the very nature of children —whether nations or individuals—to enjoy a work of art in the same manner as a work of nature, without troubling themselves as to who made it, without considering that it could not, like Melchizedec, have come into the world without father or mother, and without the thought ever occurring to them that it is interesting as the product of some one mind in particular, and that it is well worth while to inquire whether the signature is of Peter or of Paul. Indifference in this respect was pushed to such lengths, that in the fourteenth century a French writer translating a work of Boccaccio's calmly states that the writing before him is by Petrarch. A plagiarist of the thirteenth century brought out the "Roman de Troie" under his own name, scratching out the name of Benoit wherever it occurs and putting his own in its place, and actually carries his impudence so far as to express his surprise that no one should ever before have related the history of Troy as told by Dares. But the most fortunate of all Benoit's despoilers was the famous Guido Colonna, a Sicilian physician, who a century later than the Norman poet turned the "Roman de Troie" into bad Latin.

---

* Learned authors were however, before the more recent discoveries, at least aware of his existence. He is quoted by Douce.

The success of his spurious performance was immense :
it was translated into Italian, English, Spanish, German,
Saxon, Dutch, Danish, Flemish, Bohemian, and even into
French. The National Library in Paris alone contains
eighteen copies.

"It is Guido's name," remarks M. Joly, "that will be pronounced
for the future whenever the fabulous 'Iliad' of the Middle Ages is
spoken of. He will always pass as the original author and Benoit as
the imitator. Guido is still quoted by learned commentators of Virgil
to whom the very name of Benoit is unknown." *

Guido's edition is not a mere translation. It is easy
to take liberties when pillaging an unnamed author. So
he made no scruples about embellishing, or disfiguring, it.
With him Cressida puts on the passionate character of a
woman of the South. In describing the leave-taking of
the two lovers, our Sicilian writes with more force than
elegance—

"She shed upon her garments such an abundance of tears that
quite a large pool of water might have been wrung out of her gown.
With her nails she tore her charming mouth, separated with her white
skin the golden hair wildly scattered over her shoulders, and as with her
cruel nails she tore her cheeks already flecked with blood, the sight of
it was like lilies torn to pieces mingled with shreds of roses," etc.

The episode of Troilus and Cressida is the most interesting portion of Guido's book. And so Boccaccio felt
when, like all the rest of educated Europe, he too read it,
and he determined to take the story and throw it into a
mould of his own making. And so, in fact, he brought
out under the name of "Filostrato," that is, "the man overthrown by love," an original work differing profoundly
from that of either Guido or Benoit. He was then in
love with "La Fiammetta," whom he has so celebrated,
and it is his own heart that speaks, his own personal
sentiments that find utterance, in "Filostrato," describing

---

* The same thing has befallen the Chronicles of Turpin.

the pleasures he had enjoyed, the pangs of separation he had undergone, all the anguish and torture he himself had known, and adding to the sorrows of absence, the bitterness and desolation of being forsaken. The relative importance of the lovers naturally changes, it is no longer Briséida but Troilus, or in other words Boccaccio, that now occupies the principal place. The whole interest is concentrated on his love, and the character of Briséida grows faint and shadowy. So entirely is it a personal and heartfelt romance, that it makes Troilus meet Briséida for the first time *in church*,—it was thus that Boccaccio first saw the woman he loved, and he has added another touch drawn from his own history, in the transformation of the daughter of Calchas into a young widow.

It is strange that a work so profoundly subjective, lyrical, and impassioned, should not always have been felt to have nothing in common with the subtle and acute observation that distinguishes the art of a dramatic poet or of a writer of romances, and most surprising that any one should so misinterpret its inner significance as to praise it for its rare psychological value as a picture of the human heart. The "Filostrato" is a love-song, and as such may indeed be admirable, but it is no study of character. Take for example the inconsistency shown in that of Cressida; the poet tells us she has always been and still is a most modest lady, and the one above all others who despises the things of love. She resists for a considerable time all the entreaties of her lover, and when at last she yields, nothing could exceed the tenderness, thoroughness, and sincerity of her surrender.

"I beseech you that when I am away from you, you will take no other lady, however fair or sweet; for if I were to know it you may truly believe that I would kill myself like one out of her mind; and I should lament and moan beyond measure, that contrary to all right and reason you had deserted me for another; for you know right well that you are more loved by me than ever man was loved before by woman."

In the Grecian camp she mourns and weeps—

"not to see her sweet love. There is none who if he had seen her in this grief and anguish could have foreborne from shedding tears, so piteous was the sight."

It is difficult to imagine how the writer will manage to make Cressida turn from the love of Troilus to that of Diomedes, but he effects it in the following manner :—

"Her heart was still fixed upon her faithful lover Troilus, but it did not long remain so, for she shortly changed her mind, and abandoned him who loved her so loyally, for a new lover. . . . Her great and faithful devotion was soon changed for another and a newer love."

There is not the least atom of dramatic talent or power shown here, or even the least shadow of reason and likelihood. It is not by the reason, not by the "dry light" of the logical intellect, that the charm of Boccaccio's poem can ever be tasted, but by the heart and soul, by the senses and by all the emotional side of our nature. Troilus, who is of an Italian type of character, without strength or energy, sinks beneath the violence of his passion. "All the strength of his body left him, and so little force was left in his limbs that he could scarcely hold himself up." After he has lost all hope, he speaks of killing himself, but his courage fails him.

"'O evil fortune! why didst thou not take from me my father, or Hector my brother, who is the strength and hope of this present war? Why didst thou not deprive me of my sister Polyxena, or Paris my brother, with beautiful Helen? If only Brisaida had been left to me no other grief would thus afflict me. . . . O my sad soul! why dost thou not flee from this most unhappy body? O wretched craven soul! leave the body and follow Brisaida. Alas! why dost thou linger?'" He falls ill and takes to his bed. "In a few hours his room was filled with gentle-hearted dames and maidens, and with all kinds and sorts of melodious instruments. On one side was Polyxena his sister, fair as an angel, on the other the beautiful Helen, and in front of him were Cassandra, Hecuba, Andromache, and other cousins and relations who were all assembled round him. Each comforted him as best she could,

and tenderly asked him from what pain he suffered. But to all this
he answered nothing, and piteously in his heart remembered Brisaida;
but all the time the sweet melody of sounds soothed him a little."

An excellent picture of soft Italian ways,—the handsome young hero lying languishing of love, his couch surrounded by music and by fair ladies, "who stand round
in a hush and thrill of sympathetic spectatorship!"

In Benoit de Sainte-More, Troilus soon passes from
sorrow to contempt of the faithless one who has forsaken
him, and expresses his disdain with the cold irony of one
whose heart is completely cured of its wound; plunging
into the thick of the battle he cries out to Diomedes to
watch well over Cressida, for her constancy is of short
duration, and she will assuredly deceive him too, in his
turn, and not fail to give him a successor.

Still more complete in Shakespeare, Troilus unites
both phases of feeling—the bitter cry of a wounded heart,
and the energy of a manly resolution. The Troilus of
Benoit de Sainte-More is a Gaul, that of Boccaccio an
Italian, but the Troilus of Shakespeare is a man.

It is in the "Filostrato" that Pandarus first makes
his appearance, but Boccaccio's Pandaro differs, as widely
as night from day, from the Pandarus of Shakespeare
and Chaucer, and the contrast between them brings out
in a very forcible manner the difference of moral nature
in the northern and the southern races. We have already
seen what a sorry part is borne by Pandarus in Shakespeare, and in Chaucer it is even worse. It is evident
that in English eyes the man's trade is a vile one. But
Pandaro has nothing vile about him. "Boccaccio," says
one of his critics, "was too devoted a slave to Love, not to
look upon everything that concerned or could procure
love as sacred and well-nigh venerable." His go-between
is therefore a knight who is himself in love, a faithful,
disinterested, devoted friend, who holds it to be a duty
owed alike to friendship and to chivalry to serve Troilus

in his love affairs, but who expects no recompense in
return.   He does "what one friend should do for another
when he sees him in tribulation."   He is indeed by far
the noblest character in the story.   A stern moralist
would pronounce him to be thoroughly corrupt, but he
must be taken in connection with all the surrounding
circumstances, with the voluptuous land of Italy where
to love is not only a law of nature but also the admitted ·
rule of good society, and where there are no backward or
bashful lovers.   Troilus, sincerely touched by what Pandaro has done for him, offers him quite simply and in
good faith either his sister Polyxena or the beautiful
Helen.

"And that you may know the love I bear you, there is my sister
Polyxena whose beauty is held in higher esteem than all others, and
there is also the beautiful Helen my brother's wife : question your heart
a little to see if neither of these would please it, and then leave me to
settle with the one that would give it most pleasure."

Thus Troilus is ready, out of gratitude, to reverse their
position and to play the part of Pandaro to his friend.
We must be allowed one more quotation to listen to the
consolation offered to the lover by his friend, when
Brisaida has deserted him :—

"You see that the whole city is full of beauteous and gentle ladies,
and I swear to you by the love and loyalty that I bear to you that
there is not one, however proud and cold, who if she were to see you
and know that you loved her would not take pity on you.   Let me do
this thing for you, for I will willingly and gladly do it. . . . A new
love chases away the old love, and your present misery will be chased
away by new pleasure." *

Chaucer's poem of "Troylus and Cryseyde" was
written about the year 1360.   The poet was not in the
same state of feeling as Boccaccio was from whom he
borrowed his story; his heart was free from pain, and

---

* The quotations are taken from a French translation made towards
the end of the fourteenth century.

there is nothing particularly passionate about his Troylus.
Cryseyde is a widow, as in Boccaccio, and even more
obdurate than the Italian Brisaida, and Troylus only succeeds by means of a treacherous plot, in the Lovelace
style of adventure, which he plans in concert with Pandarus. Cryseyde ends by loving him very dearly, which
might well be, but ere long she leaves him and is no
longer faithful to him, and the poet hardly knows what
to make of her treachery. He may well be amazed.
After the prolonged resistance exhibited by this coy
widow, after all the noble sentiments to which she has
given vent, both when she repulsed the advances of
Troylus and also later on when she left him, we are
completely at a loss ʼto understand her conduct with
Diomedes.

One of Chaucer's commentators praises him for having
enabled us to feel a sympathy and liking for Cryseyde,
and blames Shakespeare for not having done as much for
his Cressida. To listen to the animadversions of certain
critics would almost make one believe that the mission
of. art is the representation of virtue rather than of
human nature, and that the finely painted portrait of a
Helen or a Phryne is not a more pleasing sight than a
badly executed portrait of the most worthy wife and
mother. It is a matter of deep regret to Gervinus that
Shakespeare should have given Cressida so light and
fickle a nature, and is one of the reasons why to his
grave and serious mind, this masterpiece of irony is
so disconcerting and unsatisfactory; he remarks with
genuine sorrow that Cressida is a stain in the gallery
of Shakespeare's heroines, who are generally so pure.
Would to heaven that there were many more such
stains in hisˑ plays, and that some of the heroines of
his tragedies, as well as of his comedies, even at the
risk of being less ideal women, were as lively and
lifelike as the brilliant daughter of Calchas! We are

not here concerned with awarding a prize for virtue to
the most deserving woman, but with deciding which
author has best fulfilled the laws of art; and from this
point of view the preference must be given, not to the
most highly moral character, but to the most poetical
execution.   Consistency and truth of character are wanting in Chaucer's poem as in that of Boccaccio's, and it is
the less excusable in Chaucer's case because his work was
of a purely objective and impersonal character, so that he
was master of his subject,—he was not throwing his own
heart and recollections and his own history, upon paper,
as the Italian poet had done.

Benoit de Sainte-More, the old French *trouvère*, in
spite of all his inexperience and his clumsiness, is the
only one to whom the simple and natural idea occurred
of representing Cressida from the very beginning as a
coquette.

Whether Shakespeare knew this poem of Benoit's is
extremely doubtful; but when tradition gave him the
story, which in the course of four hundred years had
undergone so many changes and additions as it passed
from hand to hand, he rediscovered, with the clear and
piercing glance of genius, the original conception, and
putting aside the incomprehensible widow of Boccaccio
and of Chaucer, he again brought to life the young girl
"of quick and ready wit, but whose heart was changeable," of Benoit de Sainte-More.

CHAPTER X

SHAKESPEARE'S play of "Troilus and Cressida" has
excited among critics more absurd and chaotic discussions than perhaps any other of his writing. This
parody of the heroic world of Homer, the irreverent
manner in which the Greeks are treated, has been a
subject of joy with some, of virtuous horror with many,
and of wonder with all. The thought of the stupendous
genius of Shakespeare, who to all his great titles to
glory,—to "Macbeth," "Hamlet," "Othello,"—has added
the singular honour of having anticipated MM. Meilhac
and Halévy in composing "La Belle Hélène," and of
having written in the sixteenth century a libretto for
Offenbach, is quite overwhelming.

M. François Hugo can hardly contain himself for joy,
and glorifies Shakespeare as prospectively raising the
standard of revolt against classical tragedy from which
he wished beforehand to tear its " periwig,"—*beforehand*,
for the best of the matter is, that the periwig had yet to
come, and that Shakespeare's protest has in consequence
all the value of a prophecy. The German critic Ulrici
also regards the play with admiration and awe as a
prophetic warning; not, however, as one made in the
name of art, but in the name of morals and religion,[*]

---

* See Introductory Chapter, p. 4.

O

and Coleridge assumes his most thoughtful and solemn aspect to warn us that we are here standing in front of a great mystery and that no other of Shakespeare's plays is so difficult to explain.

And yet "Troilus and Cressida" is not difficult to explain; bright and joyous as sunlight, it shines with no less clearness, but the explanation is not to be sought for in the future, in conjectures and wild dreams, but in the past and in actual facts; and it is ignorance of these facts, which happen to be but little known, that accounts for. the groping in the dark and for the mistakes made by bewildered criticism.*

As long as the historical and literary traditions in conformity with which Shakespeare wrote his play remain unknown, the ridicule so lavishly poured upon the Greeks, and the marked respect shown for the Trojans, may seem to be a shaft aimed at Homer and all classical writers, and to defy all that we now consider as the rightness and fitness of things; but as soon as we become acquainted with them, the difficulty vanishes and the explanation is complete.

Shakespeare's partiality for the Trojans is in perfect harmony with a Latin tradition which was transmitted by antiquity to the Middle Ages, and from the Middle Ages to the Renaissance. For it was Latin literature, the poetry and history of Rome, it was Virgil—not

---

* I do not desire by means of a few quotations, made for the most part at second hand, to usurp any reputation for recondite research: the greater part of the present chapter may be taken as an epitome of M. Joly's quarto volume, in six hundred and odd pages, on the "Métamorphoses, d'Homère et de l'épopée gréco-latine au Moyen âge" (see preceding chapter). I have also made use of Dr. Hermann Dunger's much shorter but solid and well-written pamphlet on "Die Sage von Trojanischen Kriege in den Bearbeitungen des Mittelalters und ihren antiken Quellen," Leipzic, 1869. I am also indebted to a work by M. Alexandre Büchner on "Les Troyens en Angleterre," published in the "Mémoires de l'Académie des Sciences, Arts, et Belles Lettres de Caen," (1868). My other sources are indicated in footnotes.

Homer or Greece—that constituted the whole classical education of the Middle Ages and the greater part of that of the Renaissance. The aim of the present chapter is to make this quite clear; it is a point which may well claim attention for its own sake, and for the peculiar interest attaching to it, but at the same time it will furnish us with the key to the enigma presented by Troilus and Cressida, and a considerable advance will have been made in our present study when we have become fully aware that whatever classical knowledge is to be met with in Shakespeare's plays formed a portion of the rich legacy bequeathed by Latin antiquity.

Every one knows that the hero of the "Æneid" is a Trojan, the founder of the Roman race and power, *romanæ conditor arcis :* but how completely national the subject of Virgil's poem was, and to what an extent history and poetry here coincided, is a little less well known. "The town of Rome," says Sallust, "was founded and inhabited at first by fugitives from Troy, who wandered from place to place under the leadership of Æneas." And Livy's great work opens with these words :—

"It is a well-ascertained fact, that after the taking of Troy all the rest of the Trojans were put to death, the lives of Æneas and Antenor alone being spared by the Greeks, on account of an ancient rite of hospitality, and because they had always advised that peace should be made and Helen be given back to the Greeks. Later on, after divers accidents, Antenor penetrated as far as the Adriatic Sea. Æneas, exiled from his country by a similar disaster, but destined to lay the foundations of a mightier power, first came into Macedonia . . . then landed on the plains of Laurentum, which he occupied."

The roots of this legend stretched far back into the past. The object of the first treaty of which there is any record between the Romans and the Greek States, was the liberation of the Acharnanians demanded by the Senate from the Ætolians, and this intervention was based upon gratitude towards a people whose ancestors alone among the Greeks had taken no part against *the*

Trojans, the ancestors of the Romans. At various times of its history, Rome showed a real or an affected interest in the little and then obscure town of Ilion; as, for instance, in the great joy manifested by the Scipios at revisiting their ancestral home when they crossed the Hellespont. This belief of the Romans in their Trojan descent outlived the days of the Republic, and under the Empire it again cropped up, and even reappears after the Empire had quitted the Eternal City, and established itself at Byzantium. In the "Novellæ" of Justinian, Æneas is again put forward as the first King of Rome, and the Romans are called his descendants.

Nothing is more striking and noticeable when contemplating the great invasions that took place in the fifth century, than the numerous and varied evidences of the respect and admiration excited in the Barbarians by the colossal power they had overthrown. Rome, even when conquered, still exercised her spell over men's imagination, and the victorious people adopted the language, customs, and religion of the vanquished nation. The chiefs appropriated to themselves some shred of the Roman purple, and Clovis, King of the Franks, was proud to receive the titles of Consul and Patrician, and to bear the outward tokens and ornaments of his new dignity. By degrees, the barbarians came to consider themselves as related to the great Roman people, their "good and loyal cousins," according to the expression of an old chronicler, and the more powerful chiefs amongst them ambitiously dreamed of continuing the Empire. Romans and Northmen thus being cousins, they must of necessity have descended from the same stock, and in this way the Trojan traditions passed from antiquity down to the Middle Ages.

The earliest French chroniclers, whose knowledge was still in a confused and uncertain stage, undertook to connect the history of the origin of France with the legendary history of the origin of Rome. One of them, Frédégaire, writing in the middle of the seventh century, says—

"At this time Priam carried off Helen. . . . It is to him that the origin of the Franks goes back. Priam was their first king. . . . A part of the Trojan people, escaping from captivity, wandered into many regions with their wives and children. They chose for their king a certain Francio, who gave his name to the Franks. Under the guidance of this intrepid chief, they passed over into Europe, and settled themselves between the Rhine, the Danube, and the sea. There Francio died."

This legend was no invention on the part of Frédégaire, for it is of older date than his time: it appears to have been popular before he was born, and—

"at the same time that he wrote, we hear of it receiving the official sanction of the administrative authorities. We also hear of the princes solemnly parading their Trojan origin. . . . In a charter granted by Dagobert, it is stated that the Franks descended from the very noble and very ancient blood of the ruins of Troy, *ex nobilissimo et antiquo Trojanarum reliquiarum sanguine nati.*" *

The princes of the Carlovingian race repeated what had been said by the Merovingians, and Charles the Bald speaks in a charter in precisely the same manner as Dagobert.

In the thirteenth century, the learned monk Vincent de Beauvais, author of the "Speculum Magus," or the "Great Mirror of the World," a species of mediæval encyclopædia, dedicates a special chapter of his immense work to the Trojan origin of the Franks. In the prologue to the "Chroniques Françaises de Saint Denis," we read that "this history begins with the high lineage of the Trojans, from which it has descended in long succession." The historian records the reign of Priam I., who ascended the throne "in Troy the Great, four hundred and four years before Rome was built;" also the flight of Helen

---

* Joly, p. 121.

and the destruction of Troy; and he further gives us this curious etymology of the name of the city of Paris, the primitive name of which had been Lutetia, which means "muddy town" :—

"Marcomir (the son of Priam II., and father to Pharamond, king of the Franks) changed the name of the city, which had been called *Leuthèce*, which is as much as to say, a town full of mud, and gave it the name of Paris, after Paris, the eldest son of Priam, king of Troy, from whom he was lineally descended."

In the fourteenth century, Christine of Pisano, wishing to flatter Louis of Orleans, calls him the *son of Hector*. Again, Nicolas Gilles, an historian in the fifteenth century, writes in his "Annales de France," that "from Dardanus, king of Phrygia, came the Trojans, from whom are descended the French, Venetians, Romans, English, Normans, Turks, and Austrians."

"The fame of King Priam," he also tells us, "is so well known and proclaimed throughout all the lands, that no other mortal man could be found who lived of old that is so well known from the writings of ancient histories as he is." We also learn from him that the Franks bore on their banners, "Gules with a golden pale in the middle, which had been the coat-of-arms of Paris, son of King Priam."

Louis XII., after the battle of Ravenna, took as a motto, *Ultus avos Trojæ.** But here we must pause, for this brings us to the threshold of the Renaissance, and before stepping over it we must throw a glance over other countries.

The Franks were not the only people who claimed to be of Trojan descent. With nearly all the Christian peoples, and kingly or princely families of the West, this alleged origin became the theme at once of historians and of poets, and it even spread beyond the limits of Christendom.

---

* Joly, pp. 528 to 534.

"The Trojan myth penetrated into the most national and popular portion of the epic poetry of Germany, the 'Niebelungen Lied,' in which Hagen, the slayer of Siegfried, possesses a castle of the name of Tronje, and passes as one of the descendants of Priam." *

An echo of the legend comes from still more distant parts of Europe in the mythologies of the extreme North. A Scandinavian account in the thirteenth century makes mention of Antenor and Æneas, and—

"among the Icelandic sagas, preserved in manuscript in the library of Stockholm, there is one, without the name of its author, in thirty-one chapters, entitled 'Trojumanna Saga,' which begins with the expedition of Jason and Hercules into Colchis, and relates the flight of Helen, and the siege and destruction of Troy, in which we find the names of all the heroes who took part in the war." †

The Normans also maintained their descent from the Trojans, choosing Antenor for their ancestor; and in this way, M. Joly concludes, the heroes of the Trojan war came to be meted out amongst the different peoples.

Troilus also was adopted as an ancestor,—by none other than the Turks. As he was brother to Hector, and had a son, Turcus, and as the father of the Franks was Francio, son of Hector, it naturally followed that the French and the Turks were first-cousins. And this community of origin has actually been invoked in the course of the diplomatic relations between the Turks and the people of the West, as an argument in favour of peace. In Montaigne's "Essays." (Book II., Chap. 36), we read:—

"Nothing is more widely known and believed than the story of Troy, of Helen and her wars, though peradventure they never existed. Our children are still called by the names invented by Homer more than three thousand years ago, and everybody has heard of Hector and Achilles. Not only a few races here and there, but nearly all nations seek their parentage in the stories he invented. Mahomet II., sultan of the Turks, writing to Pope Pius II. said, 'I am filled with surprise at seeing how the Italians band together against me, inasmuch as we

---

* A. Büchner, "Les Troyens en Angleterre," p. 88.   † Joly.

have sprung from the same Trojan origin, and that I have a like interest with them in avenging the blood of Hector on the Greeks, with whom, nevertheless, they side against me.'"

There is probably some confusion in these recollections of Montaigne's, and there is reason to believe that the letter he mentions and quotes of Mahomet II., was addressed to a king of France instead of to the Pope. And certainly Palma Cayet, a chronicler in the sixteenth century, writes that "the Turks considered the French as the only European nation worthy of their friendship, making use of these words in the Turkish tongue : the French and the Turks are brothers." And Sully relates in his "Économies Royales" how the Sultan sent his doctor to Henry IV. as an ambassador, "in order to confirm the ancient alliance between the house of Othman and that of France."

While the Franks claimed Francio, the Normans Antenor, and the Turks Troilus, Britain celebrated another Trojan hero as her ancestor, a great-grandson of Æneas, Brut, Brutus, or Brito, the hero of a poem by Robert Wace,* a Norman *trouvère* in the twelfth century. This Brut, according to the poet, changed the name of Albion to that of Britain after his own, much in the same way that Lutetia became Paris in remembrance of the son of Priam. The most illustrious descendants of Brito, were Locrinus, one of his sons ; Hudibras, a contemporary of Solomon's ; King Lear, made famous by Shakespeare's tragedy ; Gorboduc, who was brought upon the stage by Sackville, in the well-known piece mentioned in a former chapter ; Lucius, the first Christian Prince ; and lastly,

---

* "The stories told by Geoffrey of Monmouth were in the Latin tongue. They were put first into French verse by Geoffrey Gaimar. They got afterwards to France, and, added to from Breton legends, were made into a poem and decked out with the ornaments of French romance. In that form they came back to England as the work of Wace, a Norman trouveur, who called his poem 'The Brut,' and completed it in 1155."
—Rev. Stopford Brooke's "Primer of English Literature."

King Arthur, founder of the order of the Knights of the Round Table. Thus, the links in the genealogical chain that unites one of the most fruitful periods of mediæval poetry with the legends and myths of antiquity, become visible. In England, as on the continent, the story of the Trojan descent was not merely a poetic fiction, but was a popular belief and an article of patriotic faith, which even made its way into the most serious transactions in diplomacy, in politics, and in war. Edward III., for instance, in a letter addressed to Pope Boniface, brought forward the alleged Trojan origin of England as one of the most convincing demonstrations of her superiority over Scotland. These old legends had sunk so deeply into the minds of all men, that the fame of the Trojans, of their valour and of their superior prowess in all athletic exercises, became proverbial, and furnished the drama with a popular term of comparison ; as, for example, in Ben Jonson's " Every Man in his Humour," in which Cob the water-carrier, in order to recognize with vigorous praise the merits of the old judge, who is full of common-sense and good humour—a kind of personification of " Merry Old England," — calls him " the honestest old brave Trojan in London " (Act IV., Sc. 4).

In the time of the Renaissance men never dreamed of submitting this mediæval tradition to a critical examination, but on the contrary adopted it enthusiastically, and the Trojan legends were never held in higher honour than at the end of the fifteenth and beginning of the sixteenth centuries. They continued to live, and even to thrive, until the next century. In England they were introduced upon the stage, and it may have been in the theatre that Shakespeare learned the traditional origin of his country.

In France, perhaps the most remarkable and certainly the most extraordinary writer in the time of Louis XII., the vehement and emphatic Jean le Maire des Belges,

interesting on his own account as well as for having had
the honour of forming the taste of the delicate and fantastic poet Ronsard, teaches us, in his strange work
entitled "Illustrations de Gaule et Singularités de Troie,"
which he dedicated to the very noble and more than very
super-illustrious princess, Madame Marguerite Auguste
daughter of the Emperor Maximilian, that—

"in the days of ancientry the flower of the nobility of Asia came
over and settled themselves in Europe, whence they have not since
stirred," and that, "the glorious resplendence of nearly all the princes
at present reigning over western nations consists of the recollection of
the great Trojan deeds."

In writing this, Jean le Maire is perfectly serious; he
brings forward the support of as many authorities to
prove the genealogy of Œnone and the authenticity of
her marriage with Paris, as he does to prove the deeds
and exploits of Pepin le Bref. This mingled seriousness
of tone and absurdity of matter, the perpetual surprises
of a style alternately preposterous and delightful, at one
time full of the quaint pedantic rhetoric of the Limousin
scholar at whom Rabelais flung his gibes and mockeries,
and at another, full of the exquisite grace of the old
French tongue, and always bearing the mark of curious
and delicate workmanship, added to the inconceivable
confusion of a book in which history and poetry, sacred
matters and profane, the past and the present are all in-
extricably interwoven together,—all this makes of the
" Illustrations de Gaule " a volume of rare entertainment,
and positively amusing, not indeed to read, for that would
be impossible, but to dip into here and there, picking out
delicious little fragments. Take, for example, the description of the youthful Paris :—

" Now, to return to Paris and his companions, often they bathed,
says Scamander, in the river Xanthus and swam across it, or they
plunged into it, swimming between two waters; and all along the banks
of the river they fished for the many-clawed and sidelong-moving
crabs. Then, afterwards, Paris would wrestle naked on the green grass

with the strongest of his companions, or would take part in throwing the bar, in playing at quoits or at tennis. . . . Then the beauteous nymphs and fairies of the land of Cébrinois came down from their mountains, deserted their streams and waterfalls, left their forests and groves and their divers haunts, to come and see the great beauty of Paris. The one pointed him out to the other with great admiration. For he was white as the kernel of a nut, and had golden hair which was wavy and full of little curls. His limbs were well made, full and shapely as befitted his age, and so fair a thing was nowhere else to be seen in the world. Paris and his companions could well see the aforesaid gracious nymphs and fays among the willows and hiding behind the trees and peeping out from the thickets, but they dared not show they saw them, nor did they venture to address them, for they were overtaken by youthful timidity."

And this, it must be remembered, is no merely poetic fancy, but is a matter of history, of universal history moreover, related by a man gifted no doubt with imagination, but who gives his information in simple good faith and with perfect conviction. Jean le Maire desired that the princes of the West should form a crusade to reconquer, not the Holy Sepulchre, but the town of Priam, the country of their forefathers.

"It would be a fine pastime for the right noble and right illustrious French and British nations, proceeding from the true legitimate blood of Troy, to go and see, in passing through the countries of Hungary, Esclavonia and Albania, the homes of their first princes and progenitors; and from thence to penetrate into Greece to *contemplate the ruin of that audacious nation* which formerly had the honour of overthrowing and destroying the great city of Troy; and from thence to pass over to Constantinople by the Hellespontine Sea, that is to say, the arm of Saint George, and then to plant their victorious standard on the dry land of Asia Minor . . . and to recover by just arms the rightful inheritance and the twelve kingdoms possessed of old by King Priam, grandfather of Francus, Hector's son."

In the middle of the sixteenth century, Rabelais, in the "New Prologue" of his fourth Book, says—

"I will tell you what is written in the fables of the wise Æsop, the Frenchman, that is to say the Phrygian and Trojan, from which people, according to the most veracious chroniclers, the noble French are descended."

The satirical intention of this passage is obvious, but a little later on, in the latter half of the sixteenth century, Ronsard set to work quite seriously to write his "Franciade," a poem that has been ignorantly regarded as the pedantic fancy of a scholar more deeply versed in Greek and Latin matters than in French, but which was in reality quite as national as the "Æneid," for the minds of men in France in the sixteenth century were more preoccupied with the Trojan origin of their race, than were those of the Romans on the morrow of Pharsala and of Actium.*   It was the express wish of Ronsard to write a national poem, and he had in fact every reason to believe that the "Franciade" fulfilled the conditions to perfection.

"A good poet," he writes in his preface, "always builds his work upon the foundation of some old annals of the past, or on some deeds of renown known far and wide, which have gained a firm foothold in men's minds. . . . *Founded and based upon our ancient annals,* I have built up my 'Franciade;'" and elsewhere, "Seeing that the French people hold it as an assured fact that, as the old annals tell us, Francion the son of Hector, followed by a company of Trojans after the sacking of Troy, landed upon Palus Mæotides, and advanced into Hungary, I have lengthened the canvas, and have shown how he came into Franconia, and then on to Gaul where he founded Paris.   Desiring to immortalize my fame, based upon common report and the old belief in the chronicles of France, I knew not where to find a more excellent subject than this."

The Trojan tradition outlived Ronsard ; it reappeared at the beginning of the seventeenth century in Pierre de Laudun, Lord of Aygaliers, who again took the subject of the "Franciade" and treated it in nine books, in the year 1604.   The date is purposely mentioned here as it is coincident with the period of greatest activity and maturity of Shakespeare's poetic life.

But the existence of the tradition was drawing to its close.   Up to this date it had met with but few sceptics,

---

* Gandar on "Ronsard, considéré comme imitateur d'Homère."

such as Boccaccio,* Rabelais, and Etienne Pasquier,† but in the middle of the seventeenth century it finally died out, and in 1666, André du Chesne, a French historian, writing a "History of England, Scotland and Ireland," expresses his surprise that it should have lasted so long.

To sum up in two lines the result of all these quotations, we may say that every nation believed itself to be descended from the Trojans, and that in Hector Shakespeare was honouring an ancestor.

We must now turn to consider what were the *literary* sources of the tradition, either in classical antiquity or in the earlier Middle Ages. The first place must clearly be given to Homer. He is distinctly the father of it, for as far as we can see, without the "Iliad" the Trojan legends would never have existed. But the pedigree has not descended in a straight line, for Homer was left unread in the Middle Ages, and the bard that sang Achilles' praises would evidently not have inspired Europe with its feeling of resentment against Greece, or have suggested its pious glorification of fallen Troy.

This was the work of Virgil, in the first place. Virgil was the teacher and the sacred oracle of the Middle Ages —the "divine master," as Dante calls him. Not only were his works for fifteen or sixteen hundred years taken as "the basis of grammatical instruction, of literary culture, and of poetical education,"‡ but the Æneid was received and accepted as a sublime allegory, containing all the treasures of human wisdom and knowledge in the hidden depths of its meaning, and the

---

* " Although, he said, he did not much believe it, he would not absolutely deny it, seeing that all things are possible to God."

† Pasquier would have liked " the opinion to be more closely looked into."

‡ Article by M. Gaston Pâris in the " Révue Critique," Feb. 28, 1874, on M. Comparetti's " Virgilio nel medio evo."

poet himself figured in men's imagination as a supernatural being and a precursor of Christianity.

"His book," says Gaston Pâris, "was held in great veneration, and was believed to possess prophetic powers; persons consulted it as to the future, as they did the Bible, by opening it at a venture. All through the Middle Ages, Virgil remained encircled by this unparalleled aureole."

At the time of the Pagan Renaissance, the mystical element in the cultus of Virgil naturally dropped out of sight, but his paramount authority in classical matters remained untouched. It was Virgil, and Virgil only, that was held up as a model by every treatise on the Art of Poetry in the sixteenth century. Scaliger sacrificed Homer at the altar that he erected, in so many words, to the "divinity of Virgil.*

See, too, the enthusiasm with which Ronsard speaks of Virgil, " The first captain of the Muses," and with which he quotes certain of his lines, which no one, he says, can read " without every hair on his head standing up on end with admiration." It is quite natural that a nation or an individual mind when in the exuberance of youthful imagination and taste, should feel a stronger and more sympathetic attraction in the case of Latin antiquity, which is nearer, more modern in spirit, and more easily felt, than in that of Greek antiquity. Goethe, we know, in his youth preferred Virgil to Homer, and Shakespeare belonged to an epoch in which a just appreciation of the " Iliad " was almost impossible.

People did not know Greek in the Middle Ages,† and Homer was a mere name. They spoke vaguely " of the time of Homer and Solomon." When Charlemagne's

---

* Hallam: "Introduction to the Literature of Europe," Vol. II., p. 259. Sainte-Beuve, " Étude sur Virgile," p. 296.

† For the general truth of this assertion, and the few exceptions in detail, see Egger's " Hellénisme en France."

courtiers amused themselves by playing at antiquity, and every one had to choose a godfather, Homer's name appears amongst those that were borrowed.* He is mentioned by the author of the "Chanson de Roland," and also in the "Roman de la Rose;" in Dante we meet once with his name, but this isolated notice of the "Lord of Highest Song" only serves to bring out with greater force the high position given by Dante to Virgil, his guide through the eternal land, and the only father of poetry in his sight. The "Iliad" was only known through an abridged version, of eleven hundred Latin lines, apparently composed in the first century of the Christian era, and which, through a strange and at that time not unfrequent confusion of names and dates, was actually attributed to Pindar. Homer was looked upon more as an historian than as a poet—a fact which throws a curious and very instructive light upon the state of men's minds in the Middle Ages. To make no difference between poetry and reality, between history and an epic poem, belongs by right to a poetical age, when men are still simple and childlike, and the critical spirit is still dormant. And for the same reason there was, strictly speaking, no literary sense in mediæval times—no distinguishing of a fine work from a poor one. Like children, the early Middle Ages cared only for the matter, not for the form, and with them the best and finest book was the one that contained the greatest number of stories. The two poor impostures of the Latin decadence, by the so-called Dictys of Crete and Dares of Phrygia, were universally preferred to Homer, over whom they had the advantage of relating the whole account of the Trojan war; and their having given themselves out as eye-witnesses to the siege was quite sufficient to make them be accepted as greater authorities. Even on the

---

* Joly, p. 148.

threshold of the sixteenth century, Jean le Maire des Belges still writes :—

"The poet Homer lived a hundred years after the wars of Troy, but Dictys of Crete and Dares of Phrygia have written down all that they saw and heard done, one on either side, during the siege. The book by the aforesaid Dares, who was of Trojan race, was found, written in his own hand, in the University of Athens in the time of Julius Cæsar, by a famous orator named Cornelius Nepos, a native of Verona in Italy, who translated it himself from Greek into Latin, and then sent it to Rome to the very noble historian Crispus Sallust. The work of Dictys the Cretan came to light some time afterwards, to wit, in the time of the Emperor Nero. This Dictys was a stipendiary knight of King Idomeneus of Crete, and was present at all the battles."

Looking upon Homer in the light of a historian as they did, the Middle Ages actually reproached him for the poetical licence he allowed himself, in the many improbabilities of his account and especially in the intervention of the gods at various critical moments.

Benoit de Sainte-More, at the opening of his poem, says that Homer has related the history of the destruction of Troy, but that it would never do to trust him too implicitly, although he was a right good clerk ; for his work does not tell true, and we know very well that he was not present at the siege ; the proof of his want of veracity is, that he made the gods fight with men, which is absurd and impossible. But the truth, continues Benoit, the truth is this : some one ransacking a chest in Athens found in it an old Greek book, and he saw that it was a history of the siege of Troy, related punctually day by day.*

These two fictitious accounts have enjoyed a longer life than the Trojan traditions themselves, and their long usurpation of authority and renown would form a very curious chapter in the history of literary reputa-

---

* Introduction to the "Nouvelles françaises en prose du XIVe. Siècle," by L. Moland and C. d'Héricault, p. lxi.

tions. Not only did the Middle Ages swear but by them, while the Renaissance esteemed and cherished them more highly than ever, but they were adopted also by the seventeenth century: Madame Dacier honoured them with a long and careful commentary; they were installed, on the authority of Bossuet and the Duc de Montausier, amongst the ranks of classical authors *ad usum Delphini*; and in 1712, by order of Peter the Great, they were translated into Russian.

In the good old days, they were not both held in equal estimation, although they were both eye-witnesses of the siege, the Middle Ages liking Dictys less well than Dares (the worst in a literary point of view, as we are told by those who have read them), for the good reason that Dictys was a Cretan and Dares a Phrygian. Dictys saw things from the standpoint of a companion-in-arms to Idomeneus, while Dares showed himself favourable to his old King Priam. In Dares, the carrying off of Helen is represented as a just revenge on the part of the Trojans, from whom the Greeks had stolen Hesione; it is from the island of Cytherea, not from the house of Menelaus, that Paris elopes with Helen. Paris is one of the bravest of warriors, and Hector is even more valiant than he appears in Homer. Troilus, of whom Dictys says scarcely anything, becomes a hero; a truce is demanded seven times by the Greeks and only three times by the Trojans; and finally, Achilles is what we see him in Shakespeare, a traitor and a coward, in love with one of the daughters of Priam, and capable of slaying his enemy by treachery.*

The best of the matter is, that Homer met with correction and reproof if he allowed himself to contradict the evidence of Dares. Jean Sanson, a French translator during the Renaissance, who was the first to turn into

---

* Hermann Dunger: "Die Sage, etc.," p. 16.

French "The Iliads of Homer, a Greek poet and *great historiographer*, with the preliminary accounts given by Guido, *sovereign* historiographer" (note the shade of distinction), interrupts his translation to administer a sharp rebuke to Homer when Achilles, in the twenty-second book of the "Iliad," gains an advantage over Hector; he protests against "a partiality which is abundantly refuted by the contrary assertions of so many eye-witnesses," and quite in a rage exclaims :—

"Then tell me, Homer, why thou hast thus exalted Achilles. . . . Thou doest wrong in exalting a traitor and leaving alone the valiant nobles who were worth ten thousand of him !"

Homer is apostrophized in a like strain of indignation by the Italian Guido and the English poet Lydgate.

Throughout the Middle Ages, to make Hector play a glorious part and Achilles an ignoble one, was the order of the day. Dictys, although generally favourable to the Greeks, greatly diminished the honour of the victory gained by Achilles, who, according to him, lay in wait for Hector and surprised him as he was crossing a river, thus attacking him without any great risk. In the narrative given by Dares, Achilles kills Troilus—not Hector—by treachery; but this is of little importance, the villainy in either case being the same. As in Shakespeare, he calls upon his Myrmidons to fall upon his adversary; Troilus's horse is wounded and falls, throwing off his rider, who gets entangled in the reins, when Achilles hurries up and kills him.

In Benoit de Sainte-More, Achilles triumphs over Hector by surprise; his mode of proceeding does not quite amount to a positive act of treachery, but is eminently unfair.

"Hector had overthrown one of the kings, and wished to take him prisoner. He seized him by the aventayle, and dragged him out of the throng, no longer covering himself with his shield. When

Achilles, perfidious Achilles, noticed this, he charged him on his steed; the hauberk could not withstand such a blow, and the liver and the lungs were scattered all over the saddle bow. Alas! Alas! what misery!" exclaims the poet, quite touched by his own narrative.

In Raoul le Fèvre, Achilles orders his soldiers to surround Troilus. "And this did they, and Achilles himself cut off the head of the hero, and tied it to his horse's tail. In sooth, if Achilles had had any nobleness in him, he would not have done this villainy." Jean le Maire, rejoicing over the death of Achilles, which was secretly compassed by Hecuba, exclaims: "Thus was he deceived with false and wicked treachery who had before behaved in the same way to the very noble Hector, whose death was now avenged."

In opposition to the infamous conduct of Achilles the Middle Ages held up the honour and virtues of Hector, "the flower of chivalry in all the world." No one did more to render the Trojan hero illustrious than Benoit de Sainte-More, who left this portrait of him:—

"A better man could not be imagined. He surpassed all men in valour; he had yellow wavy hair, large shoulders and well-made body, with shapely limbs. . . . He carried arms day and night, and never loved rest nor idleness. Nothing was wanting to his liberality, for if the whole world had been his, he would gladly have bestowed it all upon good people. So great was his courtesy and so complete, that the Greeks were but churls compared to him. In good sense and perfect moderation he surpassed every creature." Benoit adds, "It is true that he stammered a little, and that his eyes looked not quite straight, but it was not unbecoming to him."

All the heroes were brave, but the distinguishing feature in Hector's character, as pourtrayed in mediæval tradition, was his possession of a wisdom and moderation equal to the prowess of his arm. In this he forms a contrast to Troilus, who represents the mere outburst of passion,—a difference which has been well preserved by Shakespeare in the fine scene in the second act, where Priam is holding a council of war. The first conception of this scene was given by Dares, and it is found with its characteristic details in all his followers. Shakespeare places it in the midst of the Trojan war—Dares, before the beginning of hostilities; but the personages, sentiments, characters, and passions are the same. Troilus vehemently takes the part of Paris, and opposes the timid counsels of Helenus the priest, by arguments *ad hominem*, as in Shakespeare.

In Raoul le Fèvre, he says: "Is it not the custom of priests to fear battles, out of cowardice; to enjoy the pleasures of life, and to fatten upon good wines and good meats?" Hector is invariably ready—and this is another characteristic of this modest and courteous hero —to sacrifice his own opinion to that of the majority. His opinion, in Shakespeare, is that the war should cease; in Dares, that it ought not to be begun: but in both cases, after having put forward the most sensible and solid arguments, he finally gives in to his two hot-brained young brothers Troilus and Paris.

The traditional prudence and judgment of the hero is set forth with a touch of satire in the "Histoire de la Destruction de Troie la Grande, translatée du latin en français et mise par personnaiges, par Maistre Jacques Milet, estudiant ès loix en la Ville d'Orleans, l'an mil quatre cens cinquante." Priam, having assembled his sons, informs them that their aunt, Hesione, has been carried off, and exhorts them to deliver her from captivity, in which she is kept by Telamon. But Hector takes a different view of the matter, and prudently advises the preservation of peace with the Greeks, by leaving his aunt in their keeping, and advances the following weighty arguments in support of his opinion:—

"I say that Hesione now is not worth so very much that we need run into such perils for her sake. She is full fifty years old, and her life is drawing to its close, therefore we should be much to blame if on her account we went through such torments. If she were a young girl that might marry again, we might all, of one accord, go and fight for her. But there is no one who, if he were paid ever so much, would wish to have her. Better therefore to forget her, than to die fighting on her behalf."

In mediæval traditions Hector is rough only with his wife. Whether this touch was intentionally preserved by Shakespeare we cannot say; but however it may be, the fact remains that to Andromache's tender supplications that he will not go forth to fight, he returns only rough and harsh answers.

A thousand proofs might be given of the ancient popularity of Hector and of Troy, but it will be sufficient here to single out one that shall carry conviction with it: in the pack of cards still used in France, in which each court-card bears a name, we see Hector figuring by the side of Launcelot; and surely this tells us, in more expressive language than that of history or of literature, that in the "good old times" the heroes of the Trojan war were no less widely known and liked than the Knights of the Round Table.

> "Let him who will, maintain,
> While such proofs still remain,"

that there is anything strange or obscure in Shakespeare's Trojan sympathies, and that the true explanation does not lie in the historical and literary traditions of the Middle Ages, which were still fresh and blooming in the sixteenth century.

CHAPTER XI.

TROILUS AND CRESSIDA.   SHAKESPEARE'S IMMEDIATE
SOURCES.   LITERARY JUDGMENT OF THE PLAY.

THE date of "Troilus and Cressida" is extremely uncertain, and has been the subject of a good deal of controversy.   The play appeared in 1609, under the title
of "The Famous Historie of Troylus and Cresseid.   Excellently expressing the beginning of their loves, with
the conceited wooing of Pandarus, Prince of Lycia.
Written by William Shakespeare."

The poet had as little to do with this lengthy and
inaccurate title—for Pandarus was not prince of Lycia—
as he had with its appearance in print, which was
apparently the work of some enterprising bookseller,
who stole the play from its proprietors before it had been
acted, and had it printed with a very singular preface,
in which the following curious passages occur :—

"A never writer to an ever reader.   Newes.   Eternall Reader, you
have here a new play never stal'd with the stage, never clapper-clawed
with the palms of the vulgar, and yet passing full of the palm comical.
. . . So much, and such savoured salt of wit is in his comedies, that
they seem, for their height of pleasure, to be born in that sea that
brought forth Venus.   Amongst all, there is none more witty than
this; and had I time I would comment upon it, though I know it
needs not (for so much as will make you think your testern well
bestowed) but for so much worth as even poor I know to be stuffed
in it.   It deserves such a labour, as well as the best comedy in Terence
or Plautus.   And believe this, that when he is gone, and his comedies

out of sale, you will scramble for them and set up a new English inquisition. Take this for a warning, and at the peril of your pleasure's loss and judgment's refuse not, nor like this the less, for not being sullied with the smoky breath of the multitude, but thank fortune for the scape it hath made amongst you: since, by the grand possessors' will, I believe you should have prayed for it rather than been prayed. And so I leave all such to be prayed for (for the states of their wits' healths) that will not praise it. Vale."

Two points of interest may be disentangled out of this strange rigmarole: first of all, it shows that in Shakespeare's lifetime, admirers were not wanting who appreciated his genius and foretold the glorious destiny that awaited him; and it further teaches us that the poet's works did not belong to him, but were the exclusive property of a company of players, who kept a jealous guard over their monopoly; for the "grand possessors" of whom the preface speaks were in all likelihood the "King's players," the company to which Shakespeare belonged and that acted at the Globe Theatre. And this is doubtless the reason of what, at first sight, seems so puzzling—that so small a number of his plays should have been printed by himself and in his lifetime,* and also that the first complete edition of his works only appeared seven years after his death, and was edited by two actors, Heminge and Condell.

Before Shakespeare's "Troilus and Cressida" Decker and Chettle had written a play under the same title, which was shortly changed for that of "Agamemnon." This play is lost, and consequently it would be difficult to say to what extent Shakespeare made use of his immediate predecessors: to discover in the work of a poet, traces of an earlier composition of which absolutely nothing remains to us, belongs to the "grand style" of criticism, and is a fine exercise of mental gymnastics, and

---

* With the exception of "Troilus and Cressida" and of "King Lear," none of his plays were separately published after the year 1603.

one in which German athletes excel, but which I confess
I feel quite powerless to imitate.

In searching for the immediate sources whence
Shakespeare received the materials for his "Troilus and
Cressida" we have to distinguish two distinct sets of
traditions, one of which relates to the two lovers and the
other to the Trojan war. In Shakespeare's time the
story of the two lovers had become a household word.
It formed the subject of more than one ballad in the
sixteenth century, and was one of the most popular
stories of the day, so that the names of the three
principal personages, Troilus, Cressida, and Pandarus, had
become proverbial. There can be little doubt that
Chaucer's poem principally furnished Shakespeare with
his love-plot; and there is not the slightest occasion to
suppose that he had a direct knowledge of the original
of Benoit de Sainte-More, which had been buried in
oblivion for centuries past; and here we must again
insist, how admirable is the sure and penetrating instinct
with which the poet re-discovered the frank original
conception that lay hidden under a heap of alterations,
all more or less for the worse.

As to the personages and events of the Trojan war,
they were chiefly known to Shakespeare through
William Caxton—the first English printer, and who died
in 1491,—who, towards the end of the fifteenth century,
translated into English the collection of the "Histories of
Troy" of "the venerable man Raoul le Febvre, priest
and chaplain to the Duke of Burgundy." To Caxton the
prose writer, may be fittingly added the name of the
poet John Lydgate, a monk, and a disciple in poetry of
Chaucer's; he flourished about the year 1430, and at the
beginning of the fifteenth century translated the then
celebrated work of Guido Colonna into verse, under the
title of "Troye Book." So Caxton, we see, translated
le Fèvre, and le Fèvre translated Guido, and Guido

translated Benoit who rifled Dares who rifled Dictys;[*] and it was thus that the mediæval traditions of the Trojan war filtered down to Shakespeare. It is to these chivalric romances that belong the stories of Achilles' love for Polyxena, the relationship between Hector and Ajax, the nationality and expatriation of Calchas, Priam's council of war, Hector's visit to the Greek camp, the dream of Andromache, the circumstances of Hector's death, and many other details of more or less importance. It will be sufficient to make one quotation from Caxton, and the scene chosen is that in which Andromache implores her husband not to go forth that day to battle.

"Andromache saw that night a marvellous vision, and her seemed if Hector went that day to the battle he should be slain. And she, that had great fear and dread of her husband, weeping, said to him, praying that he would not go to the battle that day: whereof Hector blamed his wife, saying that she should not believe nor give faith to dreams, and would not abide nor tarry therefore. When it was in the morning, Andromache went to the King Priamus, and to the queen, and told to them the verity of her vision; and prayed them with all her heart that they would do so much at her request as to dissuade Hector, that he should not in any wise that day go to the battle, etc. It happened that day was fair and clear, and the Trojans armed them, and Troylus issued first into the battle, after him Eneas. . . . And the King Priamus sent to Hector that he should keep him well that day from going to battle. Wherefore Hector was angry, and said to his wife many reproachful words, as that he knew well that this commandment came by her request; yet, notwithstanding the forbidding, he armed him. At this instant came the Queen Hecuba, and the Queen Helen, and the sisters of Hector, and they humbled themselves and kneeled down presently before his feet, and prayed and desired him with weeping tears that he would do off his harness, and unarm him, and come with them in to the hall: but never would he do it for their prayers, but descended from the palace thus armed as he was, and took his horse and would have gone to battle. But at the request of Andromache, the King Priamus came running anon, and took him by the bridle, and said to him so many things of one and other that he made him to return, but in no wise he would be made to unarm him."

---

[*] Dares proceeded from Dictys, Homer, and Philostratus.

This scene fills no fewer than 271 lines in the epic poem of Benoit de Sainte-More.

> "When Andromache found she could obtain no grace, neither by bawling nor by her cries, she smote great blows upon her breast with her two fists, and made great mourning and ado, and tore her hair and pulled and tugged."

Here we see the grip of the Middle Ages: Greek beauties never tore themselves to pieces, and were not in the habit of bawling. But a recollection of Homer is evoked further on in Benoit's poem, by the introduction of Hector's little son Astyanax,—a classical detail which one cannot help wishing Shakespeare had reproduced :—

> "Weeping very tenderly, she takes the child upon her arm and falls at his feet, and then says to him : 'Sire! by this little child begotten of thy flesh, have mercy on the child. Never will he see thee with his eyes if thou goest to join those yonder, of thee he will remain an orphan, cruel-hearted, wild wolf! . . . . Why wilt thou die so soon? Why wilt thou so soon leave me and him, your mother, your sisters and your father?' "

This is decidedly better, though it would not do to quote Homer immediately after it; or rather, he ought to be quoted, and that without any apology, for such literary comparisons are full of instruction, and a quotation from the "Roman de Troie" may be followed by one from the "Iliad" without any disparagement being intended towards the old Norman *trouvère* :—

> "Silent he smiled as on his boy he gazed :
> But at his side Andromache, in tears,
> Hung on his arm, and thus the chief addressed :
> . . . . . . 'To me nor sire is left,
> Nor honoured mother ; . . .
> But Hector, thou to me art all in one,
> Sire, mother, brethren! thou, my wedded love!
> Then, pitying us, within the tower remain,
> Nor make thy child an orphan, and thy wife
> A hapless widow.' . . .
> To whom great Hector of the glancing helm :

Think not, dear wife, that by such thoughts as these
My heart has ne'er been wrung ; but I should blush
To face the men and long-robed dames of Troy
If, like a coward, I could shun the fight. . . .
Yet in my inmost soul too well I know
The day must come when this our sacred Troy,
And Priam's race, and Priam's royal self,
Shall in one common ruin be o'erthrown.
But not the thoughts of Troy's impending fate,
Nor Hecuba's nor royal Priam's woes,
Nor loss of brethren, numerous and brave,
By hostile hands laid prostrate in the dust,
So deeply wring my heart as thoughts of thee,
Thy days of freedom lost, and led away
A weeping captive by some brass-clad Greek:' . . .
Thus, as he spoke, great Hector stretched his arms
To take his child; but back the infant shrank
Crying, and sought his nurse's sheltering breast,
Scared by the brazen helm and horse-hair plume
That nodded, fearful, on the warrior's crest.
Laughed the fond parents both, and from his brow
Hector the casque removed, and set it down,
All glittering, on the ground ; then kissed his child
And danced him in his arms: then thus to Jove,
And to the Immortals all, addressed his prayer :
'Grant, Jove, and all ye Gods, that this my son
May be, as I, the foremost man of Troy,
For valour famed, his country's guardian king;
That men may say " This youth surpasses far
His father," when they see him from the fight,
From slaughtered foes, with bloody spoils of war,
Returning, to rejoice his mother's heart.
Thus saying, in his mother's arms he placed
His child ; she to her fragrant bosom clasped
Smiling through tears."*

In Shakespeare, Hector's body is tied to the tail of
Achilles' horse, and dragged all along the field of battle.
A tradition which dates back to classical antiquity,
relates that the body of the Trojan hero was dragged

---

* "Iliad," Book VI., translation by the Earl of Derby.

three times round the walls of Troy, by Achilles; but this is not the case in Homer. The legend probably arose from a confused recollection of two distinct passages in the " Iliad," in one of which Hector, flying before Achilles, three times makes the round of the city walls, and according to the other, when Hector has fallen, Achilles drags his body behind his chariot towards the ships, and afterwards to the tomb of Patroclus, where he destines him " to be torn by dogs, piecemeal."

In accordance with chivalric traditions, Shakespeare mounts Hector, and all the other heroes of his mock-heroic play, on horseback, instead of making them fight in chariots; and he even preserves the traditional name of Hector's horse, Galathe (Act V., Sc. 5), which was thus named by Benoit de Sainte-More. " Hector was mounted on Galatée, a gift from the fairy Morgana, who loved him greatly and held him very dear."* It was one of the goodliest and strongest horses in the world, we are assured by Caxton.

In the midst of the battle, Shakespeare's Agamemnon exclaims :—

> " Renew, renew ! The fierce Polydamus
> Hath beat down Menon : bastard Margarelon
> Hath Doreus prisoner ;
> And stands colossus-wise, waving his beam
> Upon the pashed corses of the kings
> Epistrophus and Cedius : Polixenes is slain ;
> Amphimacus, and Thoas, deadly hurt ;
> Patroclus ta'en, or slain ; and Palamedes
> Sore hurt and bruised : the dreadful Sagittary
> Appals our numbers ; haste we, Diomed,
> To reinforcement, or we perish all."

There is too much clatter and clanking, too much of the clashing of cymbals, as it were, in this passage, but it is the delight and joy of learned persons, on account of

---

* The " Roman de Troie," line 7990.

the more or less ancient classical allusions with which it teems, moulded by the spirit of the Middle Ages.

We will confine ourselves here to the " dreadful Sagittary " which is a mixture of the classical centaur and of the monsters created by the Gothic imagination of our ancestors.

Caxton relates that from " beyond the royalme of Amasoune, came an auncient Kynge, wyse and discreete, named Epystrophus, abrought a thousand knyghtes, and a mervayllouse beste that was called Sagittayre, that behynde the myddes was an horse and to fore, a man: this beste was heery like a horse, and had his eyen rede as a cole, and shotte well with a bowe: this beste made the Grekes sore aferde, and slewe many of them with his bowe."

The monster is described in much the same terms by Lydgate, who, " reherses " his " auctour " Guido. But the Sagittary also is an invention of Benoit's, and no trace of it is to be found in Dares. Like the episode of Troilus and Cressida, it is one of his own fancies, one of the " bons dits " with which the *trouvère* thought himself at liberty to embellish and enrich the thread of his story.

" The King of Lyconia brought with him a Sagittary exceeding fierce, and horrible to see: for from his middle upward he was man, covered with no other clothing but hair, and all the rest of the body was shaped like a horse. The face was black, and the eyes shone in his head like two flames, so brightly that he could be seen four leagues off, and he was so passing hideous that no living thing in the world could have looked on him without quaking with horror. He carried in his hand a bow, not made of wood but of waxed leather, and at his side he carried a hundred arrows of fine steel. . . . Greatly afeared were those of the Greek army when they saw this gruesome devil, who wrought such havoc amongst them with his bow. For with one shot he killed four men, so that in a few hours very many were slain, and out of his mouth came a poisonous foam with which he touched his arrows. And if these torments had lasted much longer, not one of the Greeks would have escaped alive, for in this one day he had killed of them more than twelve thousand."

This is a thoroughly mediæval conception, such as the Middle Ages, with their love of the monstrous and the grotesque, delighted in ; the elements of the picture were borrowed from antiquity, but the centaur of class-ical poetry underwent an amazing and highly coloured treatment from the heavy brush of Benoit de Sainte-More.

Chaucer, Caxton, and Lydgate were not, however, the only immediate sources accessible to Shakespeare, nor was the Trojan war known to him solely through mediæval traditions; there was another fountain-head to which he had recourse, the purest and most classical of all, none other, in fact, than Homer's " Iliad " itself.

In 1598 appeared Chapman's translation of the first seven books of the " Iliad," and the description of the shield of Achilles. Chapman belonged, by virtue of his tastes and classical tendencies, to the school at the head of which stands Ben Jonson. His " Homer " is held in high esteem by competent judges, who rank it far above his dramatic works. That delicate and exquisite critic Charles Lamb speaks of it with enthusiasm, and says—

" Chapman would have made a great epic poet, if, indeed, he has not abundantly shown himself to be one; for his Homer is not so properly a translation as the stories of Achilles and Ulysses re-written. The earnestness and passion which he has put into every part of these poems would be incredible to a reader of mere modern translations. His almost Greek zeal for the honour of his heroes is only paralleled by that fierce spirit of Hebrew bigotry with which Milton, as if personating one of the zealots of the old law, clothed himself when he sate down to paint the acts of Sampson against the uncircumcised. The great obstacle to Chapman's translations being read is their un-conquerable quaintness. He pours out in the same breath the most just and natural and the most violent and forced expressions. He seems to grasp whatever words come first to hand during the impetus of inspiration, as if all other must be inadequate to the divine mean-ing. But passion (the all in all in poetry) is everywhere present, raising the low, dignifying the mean, and putting sense into the absurd."

From this it appears that Chapman's translation is not a more literal one than the generality of translations at that date, but that it is animated by a breath of the true spirit of poetry and by an enthusiastic admiration for Homer and his heroes. And this admiration is the more worthy of remark because it was far from being general at that time, when literary tendencies, unless they happened to be Gothic, were Latin, and sympathy was universally enlisted on the side of the Trojans; so that Chapman forms an exception to the period he lived in. When he completed his translation in 1611, he brought it out under the title of "The Iliads of Homer, Prince of Poets," which evinces a different spirit from that of Jean Sanson, the first French translator of the Iliad, who, as was noticed in the preceding chapter, only called Homer a "great historiographer." *

That Shakespeare had read at least the first seven books of Chapman's translation is beyond all doubt;† one great proof of which is the character of Thersites in "Troilus and Cressida." No such personage appears in any of the mediæval romances; and the Thersites of the Comic Interlude acted in 1537, has nothing beyond his name in common with the Thersites of the Iliad; a mere cowardly braggadocio, he is perfectly distinct from the reviler, of Homeric tradition. But it is the Homeric Thersites, in his characteristic garb of a reviler, only with all his peculiar features immeasurably deepened and multiplied, that Shakespeare has represented in his play. Nor is the character of Thersites the only thing that Shakespeare appears to have borrowed directly from Homer. In Benoit de Sainte-More, and in his followers, Achilles is roused from his long inaction and recalled to the combat by the sight of the exploits performed by Troilus; but in Shakespeare, as in Homer, it is the wish to avenge the death of Patroclus that incites his "drowsy

---

* See page 210.

† He may also very likely have known the remainder, before 1611, through his friendly and intimate relations with Chapman, who was one of the frequenters of the Mermaid Tavern.

blood." The splendid apparition of the Prophetess
Cassandra in the midst of the conference held by Priam
is also, with great show of probability, generally referred
to the Homeric poem. I may, however, remark that, in
glancing through the "Roman de Troie" as given by
M. Joly, I met with Cassandra represented with all her
accustomed characteristics and prophetic language. The
followers of Benoit are hardly likely to have left her out,
and, in this case, Shakespeare, though receiving the
character of Cassandra from mediæval traditions, might,
through his supreme poetic instinct, have found accents
for her, worthy of the antique Cassandra, without
necessarily having recourse to the "Iliad" for inspiration.
The part that Ajax, instigated by the Greek chiefs, plays
towards Achilles is another incident which there is every
reason to believe was directly borrowed from Homer.
And in the scene in which Achilles receives Hector in
his tent, and after feeding his eyes on him bursts out
with—

> " Tell me, you heavens, in which part of his body
>   Shall I destroy him ?   Whether there, or there, or there ?"

there would seem to be a reminiscence of the scene
in the "Iliad" in which Achilles, when on the point of
killing Hector, seeks out a vulnerable place, and expresses
himself in no less ferocious a manner :—

> " Gleamed the sharp-pointed lance, which in his right
>   Achilles poised, on godlike Hector's doom
>   Intent, and scanning eagerly to see
>   Where from attack his body least was fenced.
>   All else the glittering armour guarded well,
>   Which Hector from Patroclus' corpse had stripped ;
>   One chink appeared, just where the collar-bone,
>   The neck, and shoulder parts, beside the throat,
>   Where lies exposed the swiftest road of death."

Here Achilles smites him, and Hector falls prone into
the dust. His one entreaty to Achilles is not for what

is left to him of life, but that his corpse may be restored to his parents, that they

> "May deck with honours due my funeral pyre."

To which Achilles answers :—

> "Knee me no knees, vile hound ! nor prate to me
> Of parents ! Such my hatred that almost
> I could persuade myself to tear and eat
> Thy mangled flesh : such wrongs I have to avenge."

It may well be asked whether so great a height of barbaric cruelty as this was ever reached by Shakespeare or by the Middle Ages.

But although Shakespeare took some of his details straight from Homer, the whole spirit of his play is far more in keeping with the chivalric romances than with the heroic poems of the Greeks: his warriors speak and act like the knights of mediæval tradition, and these modes of thought and action—so strangely out of place at the siege of Troy—constitute a fundamental anachronism,* to which more than to anything else the play owes its anomalous and fantastic character. The ludicrous challenge delivered by Æneas may be contrasted with that given by Hector in the seventh book of the "Iliad." Æneas expresses himself like a gallant and somewhat swaggering knight, but Hector is brief and earnest, and chiefly solicitous for the restoration of the body of the vanquished combatant to his friends, reverence for the rites of burial being an ever-present care in the minds of the ancients, and a question of primary importance in the religious beliefs of antiquity.

But though Shakespeare clearly inherited more from the Middle Ages than from classical antiquity, it would be a great mistake to conclude that]he wrote his play in any spirit of partisanship, or from any wish to protest

---

* See Chapter V.

against the excessive and exaggerated imitation of the
ancients into which the Renaissance had already fallen,
and in which it was destined to continue; and if he
introduced knights into the scene, he did it much after
the fashion of Cervantes, in a not unkindly spirit of
humorous mockery. After all, who is there that escapes
being laughed at in this play? He was favourable to
the Trojans, it is true, but it was only a relative favour,
as when a passer-by separates two street-arabs who are
fighting, and administers correction, the one that receives
only ten cuts from his cane may be said to be favoured
compared to the other that gets twenty-five.

Amongst all the heroes of the Trojan war in either
camp, Hector is the only one for whom Shakespeare—
from force of tradition—shows some respect. And it is
just this universality of his irony that should acquit him
from the suspicion of harbouring any satirical intention
towards Homer individually. In saluting one person
you must perforce turn your back upon another, but if
you salute none, no one has any right to feel aggrieved,
and Shakespeare was on far too easy terms with every
one to admit of Homer, who had plenty of shrewd sense,
conceiving himself affronted by him.

The classical fervour of Chapman may have made
Shakespeare smile, but the fervour in an opposite direction, of the priests of the romantic movement, who would
one day sacrifice the posterity of Homer on the altar
of Shakespeare, would, if he could have foreseen it in
a dream, have caused him a *homeric* peal of laughter.
To search in "Troilus and Cressida" for the smallest trace
of a systematic profession of his principles, literary or
otherwise, is thoroughly to misunderstand him, and completely to fail in recognizing one most special feature of
his genius—the indifference with which he regarded all
prescribed rules and theories, an indifference co-extensive
with his powers of creation. What did our discussions

on the respective value of Dares and of Dictys, of Virgil and of Homer, matter to him? If he had known any Arabian legends concerning the Trojan war he would have used them, had they pleased him and suited his purpose. I imagine that Shakespeare, after the publication of Chapman's Homer, or even before with the manuscript, would devour the book with the eagerness with which he attacked everything that fell in his way to be read,—not with a view to collecting literary arguments but in order to enrich himself with poetic subjects. He created works of art; he was not an exponent of a literary system: and for him the "Iliad" was only one of the most important materials for the construction of a comedy that pleased his fancy.

This comedy stands by itself amongst Shakespeare's plays, forming a class of its own. It possesses almost none of the usual qualities that distinguish the Shakesperian comedy. There is far keener and fuller handling of individual character, and a deeper current of irony, than is usual in the delicate and playful frolics of poetic fancy, which are as innocent of satire as of any deep significance, of which a "Midsummer Night's Dream" is the type. We should look in vain in such plays as "Love's Labour's Lost," "As You Like It," or "Twelfth Night" for any figures so distinct and true and living as those of Pandarus, of Troilus, and above all of the fascinating, wicked little beauty, Cressida. The comic element in Shakespeare's plays generally consists entirely of sparkling repartees, of witty sayings—or sometimes of very poor ones,—but in "Troilus and Cressida" we find *comical personages,* and our laughter is evoked naturally by the different situations and by the whole turn of things. We may find less amusement than Achilles did in Patroclus's imitation of Agamemnon and Nestor, but when Ulysses tells Agamemnon and Nestor of the way in which they are caricatured, for the purpose of enraging

them, Ulysses being apparently full of indignation but
all the time really laughing in his sleeve, it makes up a
scene doubly and trebly comic. New words would have
to be coined fitly to describe the exquisite drollery of the
compliment paid by Ulysses to Ajax :—

> " I will not praise thy wisdom
> Which like a bourne, a pale, a shore, confines
> Thy spacious and dilated parts."

And when to all this riot and revel of merriment and
sarcasm, we add the beauty of such superbly tragic
episodes as the appearance of Cassandra, and the
lamentation of Troilus over the death of Hector, we
can only be struck afresh with amazement at the
many-sidedness and overflowing generosity of Shakespeare's genius.

Marvellous work as it is, "Troilus and Cressida" is
far from being faultless as a composition; the strange
mixture displayed in it of originality and of carelessness,
has given rise to much hesitation as to the date to be
assigned to it in the chronology of Shakespeare's plays.
Is it to be classed as a youthful product, or as the fruit
of the poet's maturity ? Mr. Furnivall, with great
plausibility, supposes that it was written at two different
times, separated by an interval of sixteen years. The
author would seem to have collected materials from
opposite sources without caring whether they contradicted
each other or not ; as, for example, though mention is made
in the beginning of the first act of Hector's continual
combats, this does not prevent Æneas from saying, in
the third scene, that the hero "in this dull and long-con-
tinued truce is rusty grown." The picture of Troilus
drawn by Ulysses (Act. IV., Sc. 5) is taken from the
heroic traditions of the mediæval epics, and is consequently out of harmony with the character of the
simple-hearted and doting young lover as revealed in the
comic scenes of the play. It is with the most solemn

good faith that Ulysses praises him for his firmness of word, his patience, and his judgment.

Another point in "Troilus and Cressida" that has been criticised is its double plot, and the utterly separate nature of the interests developed in it, having the episode of the lovers on the one hand, and the combats and deliberations of the Trojans on the other. This criticism may be equally applied to all Shakespeare's comedies; they invariably contain two, and sometimes contain three, more or less distinct and separable groups of personages. In the play under consideration, the two plots, though not more firmly welded together than in other instances, seem to me to be in very happy juxtaposition; and there is great ingenuity in the way in which the parallel is drawn (the idea of which was not, however, originated by Shakespeare),—in conceiving this counterpart in Troy of the story of Helen, in setting the pretty Trojan girl over against the beautiful Greek, Troilus against Menelaus, and Diomedes against Paris. The seduction of Cressida by Diomedes avenges Helen's flight with Paris. "Nothing but treachery! all incontinent varlets!" as the chorus exclaims through the voice of Thersites.

One of the secrets of art is to produce great effects through small means, and in this respect the fun and drollery of Shakespeare's play shine forth in brilliant contrast to a celebrated work, the thought of which has more than once crossed my mind in the course of this long study of "Troilus and Cressida,"—I mean Offenbach's opera of "La Belle Hélène." The comparison of different modes of treating the same subject is a fruitful field, always abounding in fresh surprises, and these chapters would be incomplete if, after having touched upon the ancient Greek "Iliad" and that of the Middle Ages and that of the Renaissance, we passed over in silence the "Iliad" of the present day, as acted in the Théâtre des Variétés. In the amusing burlesque Offenbach has set to music, the actors wear ridiculous costumes, and astonish both eye and ear; a blacksmith drags across the stage Jupiter's thunderbolts which he has had to mend, and Achilles has his heel encased in iron.

" *Ajax.* What a noise you make in walking!

Cal. I know what it is! his heel is clad in iron.

Achil. Well, what then? What would you have done in my place? . . . Since my mother was imprudent enough to leave out my heel when she plunged me into the Styx. It would have been so easy to have popped me in both ways, first like this, and then like that.

Orestes. That certainly is a thought that should have occurred to a mother.

Ajax. Great merit indeed, to be brave when one is invulnerable! He had only one weak point, and that was his heel. And now he has had that clad in iron. And he calls himself a hero!

Achil. Son of Telamon! you will have to answer for this.

Ajax. Never in all my life. Whoever thinks of fighting against a wall?

Achil. You beg off then?

Ajax. Certainly."

Shakespeare contrives to make his Greeks ridiculous with less material cost, and seeks no help from any farfetched means. While the authors of " La Belle Hélène " exaggerate and burlesque the vulnerable point of Achilles, Shakespeare proceeds in quite a different manner, and simply denudes his characters of their robes of state and heroic garb, and presents them in all the simplicity of their ordinary domestic life. No more than this is needed to deprive them of their heroic status, and to make them pass instantaneously from the higher epic spheres into the every-day world of comedy. The comical effect is the result of the surprise felt by the spectator at so unexpected a sight, accustomed as we are to associate the names of Agamemnon and of Achilles with ideas of grandeur and solemnity. In itself, there is nothing ludicrous in the fact of Agamemnon begging

Menelaus, when he hears a trumpet blown during his conference with the chiefs, to step out and see what it means; or of his reminding Diomedes, when he sends him as an ambassador to Troy, to dress himself in a befitting manner; nor is it ridiculous, in itself, that Ulysses should be deep in the perusal of a philosophic treatise as he takes his walk, or that the chiefs of the Greek army should take a turn after dinner round the camp to enjoy a little fresh air, and yet, nevertheless, all these details make us laugh because of the contrast they form to the traditional comportment of the heroes. Precise details and a picturesque familiarity are fatal to the grave and dignified aspect of a subject, as Buffon, the naturalist, who was of a solemn turn of mind, was well aware, and which led him to recommend his colleagues, the members of the French Academy, always to make use of the most general terms in their writings. It is very curious to observe how the admission of some little word of too definite a nature into the midst of a tirade which is otherwise grand and impressive, is sufficient entirely to destroy the intended effect. In "Les Martyrs," Chateaubriand describes how the wives of the Barbarians, into whose camp the Romans have forced their way, rush past the enemy and put themselves to death with their own hands. The picture is grand and imposing; but the writer, most unfortunately, shows us the same woman holding the fugitive Sicambre *by his beard*, and from this moment all is lost, the notion makes us laugh, and so, farewell to the sublime! So delicate is the boundary line between the sublime and the ridiculous, the tragic and the comic. The figures in Shakespeare are always very individual, because he never shrank, even in his tragedies, from freely introducing a comic vein. Perfect individuality of character is impossible when the blending of the two styles is carefully avoided. If, as Gervinus remarks, Homer's heroes are

more individual than those of Sophocles, the reason
undoubtedly is that the father of epic poetry allowed
himself more elbow-room, and was not afraid of laughing
a little; for in Homer also, there is a comic vein, or rather I
should say, a plenteous stream; and comedy and tragedy
alike flow in a full current from the "Iliad" and the
"Odyssey." Individualizing touches abound among the
personages of "Troilus and Cressida:" Pandarus suffers
from the rheumatism and has a cold in his eye; Ulysses
recognizes Diomedes at a distance by his manner of
rising on the toe in walking. It is possible, as Rümelin
suggests, that this may contain a personal allusion to the
then actor of the part; in the same way that Hamlet is
said to be "fat and scant of breath," a description that
applied to the famous actor Richard Burbadge.

"Troilus and Cressida" is, to sum up, the playful
recreation with which a great genius amused himself in
his lighter moods, when, finding in the traditions of the
two lovers and of the Trojan war a framework that
struck his fancy, he filled it up, somewhat hastily indeed,
but lavishing upon it all he has taught us to expect
from him, of dramatic life and wealth of ideas, of wit,
of pathos and of poetry. To seek for any deep hidden
meaning in this play implies an utter misconception of
its character. In order to appreciate it, it is necessary
to enter into Shakespeare's *humour* and frankly to throw
off all literary and moral preconceptions, without pretending to greater seriousness than he did himself. Then
our admiration can be freely given to a poet who is so
perfectly distinct from all his characters, and is so
completely independent and at his ease, moulding his
subject after his sovereign will and pleasure and we are
of one mind with Goethe when he said to Eckermann,
"If you wish to know Shakespeare's utter freedom of
thought, read 'Troilus and Cressida.'"

CHAPTER XII.

THE scene is in Athens, in the house of the rich and magnificent Timon, where visitors throng as to a king's palace. Never did citizen spend his fortune or practise hospitality with a more regal profusion and extravagance. No porter guards his gate—

> "But rather one that smiles and still invites
> All that pass by."

A poet, a painter, a jeweller, a merchant, senators and lords, and a cynical philosopher all meet in the hall of the palace, where the master of the house soon makes his appearance, and accosts all his various visitors with the greatest affability. His very first words and deeds proclaim him the friend and benefactor of men; giving five talents to the servant of Ventidius, to pay his master's debts and free him from his creditors; and promising to bestow upon Lucilius, one of his own servants, a sum of money sufficient to induce the old Athenian with whose daughter Lucilius is in love to accept him as a son-in-law. The jeweller offers Timon a jewel, the poet proffers a dedication, and the painter a newly finished picture, to one and all of which Timon accords a gracious reception. To the painter he remarks—

> "Painting is welcome.
> The painting is almost the natural man;
> For since dishonour traffics with man's nature,
> He is but outside: these pencilled figures are
> Even such as they give out."

But these wise-sounding words are mere commonplaces, unreal and lightly-spoken sentiments, coming
from a man in the height of prosperity, like Timon, and
with as superficial a knowledge as his, of the lives and
characters of men, and they contain no hidden depth or
bitterness of meaning. He has never been brought in
contact with the ruder lessons of life, and in fact he
knows nothing, and has suffered nothing. No trace of
real intellectual culture is apparent in any of his speeches,
while his whole conduct betrays an utter ignorance of
the ways of the world. With him, life is a beautiful
dream, and if the thoughts that he mechanically repeats
of the natural depravity and deceitfulness of men are
wise in themselves, it is but the unconscious wisdom of a
dreamer talking in his sleep.

Among the persons to whom Timon, in his universal
and indiscriminating hospitality, throws open his doors,
is the Cynic, Apemantus, who, with the brutality of
language affected by the sect of philosophers to which he
belonged, warns his host of the ruin to which his blind
generosity is hurrying him. But Timon turns a deaf ear
to all he says. In the retorts and gibes of Apemantus,
Shakespeare has carefully preserved the style of biting
and laconic sententiousness, ascribed by tradition to
philosophers of the Cynical school. "What time o' day
is 't, Apemantus?" asks one of the lords. "Time to be
honest," replies Apemantus. "Fare thee well, fare thee
well," says another lord to him. "Thou art a fool to bid
me farewell twice," says Apemantus. "Shouldst have
kept one for thyself, for I mean to give thee none." In
Lyly's play of "Alexander and Campaspe," Diogenes is
made to speak in just the same manner.

The banquet is served, and Ventidius, whom the
generosity of Timon has freed from imprisonment,
Alcibiades, and various senators and lords, seat themselves at the table of their genial and light-hearted host.

Timon, who is ever gracious and courteous, even to those
who abuse his kindness, invites Apemantus to join them,
but as the Cynic refuses, preferring to remain in a corner
apart, whence he can observe the company, and pour out
his flouts and warnings, Timon gives orders for him to
have a table by himself: "Thou art an Athenian; therefore welcome : I myself would have no power: prithee,
let my meat make thee silent."

> "*Apem.*　I scorn thy meat; 'twould choke me, for I should
> Ne'er flatter thee.—O you Gods l what a number
> Of men eat Timon, and he sees them not!
> It grieves me to see so many dip their meat
> In one man's blood; and all the madness is,
> He cheers them up too."

Meanwhile the guests make loud protestations of their
gratitude and devotion to Timon, who answers warmly :—

> "O, no doubt, my good friends, but the gods themselves have pro-
> vided that I shall have much help from you : how had you been my
> friends else. . . . Why, I have often wished myself poorer, that I might
> come nearer to you. We are born to do benefits : and what better or
> properer can we call our own than the riches of our friends? O, what
> a precious comfort 'tis to have so many like brothers, commanding one
> another's fortunes!"

Timon is so touched by this thought that it brings
the tears into his eyes: tears are contagious, especially
after dinner, and one of the lords declares that the words
of his noble friend have moved him much. "*Much!*"
ironically repeats Apemantus.

Timon is of a sensitive and affectionate nature. It
would be wronging him, and grossly to mistake the
delicate shades of his character, if we were to attribute
his munificence to selfishness and a love of ostentation,
or to vanity and a wish to be flattered, courted, and
adored. His heart is full to overflowing, and he is, in
truth, the least calculating and the most enthusiastic of
mortals. Entirely without either prudence or modera-

tion, he is as vehement and indiscriminating in friend-ship as in all else, lavishing his heart on all around him without thought or question. The spontaneity and extent of his affections have conjured up before him a phantom of *Humanity*, in the vaguest acceptation of the word, and his special virtue is *philanthropy*, also taken in its vaguest sense. But this virtue, when it shows itself in an exaggerated form, presupposes a meagre understanding of the realities of life. Every man is not lovable, any more than every man is hateful, and a person whose judgment is clear and sane will always distinguish between them, and not pour out his love or hatred blindly. Had Timon been capable of a little observation and reflection, had common sense not been with him so completely subservient to the emotional part of his nature, he would have seen at once, without the need of bitter experience to teach him, that a true friend is a very rare possession, and that to squander the best treasures of the heart upon every chance passer-by is not the way to obtain any friendship worthy of the name.

Timon exchanges gifts with his guests, for they make a point of offering him presents—in order to receive sevenfold in return ; generosity with them being only that common generosity which consists, as has been said of gratitude, in a lively sense of benefits to come. Of this they make no secret : " If I want gold," says a senator (Act II., Sc. 1)—

> " Steal but a beggar's dog
> And give it Timon, why, the dog coins gold :
> If I would sell my horse, and buy twenty more
> Better than he, why, give my horse to Timon,
> Ask nothing, give it him, it foals me straight
> And able horses."

Flavius, the faithful steward, alarmed at his master's reckless extravagance, tries in vain to warn him and to press upon him a knowledge of the true state of his affairs : Timon pays no more heed to the pleading voice of his steward than to the coarser tones of Apemantus.

> "*Flav.*   I beseech your honour,
> Vouchsafe me a word; it does concern you near.
>   *Tim.* Near! why, then, another time I'll hear thee."

The catastrophe is now drawing nigh. Timon's creditors foreseeing that "it cannot hold," decide on asking at once for their money back. Their messengers, who have received instructions to take no denial, arrive at Timon's house just as he is about to entertain Alcibiades and a brilliant company at a banquet, but Flavius not wishing to interrupt the feast begs them to "cease their importunacy till after dinner," in which entreaty Timon joins, characteristically adding to Flavius, "See them well entertained." When the feast is over, Flavius takes Timon aside, and much to his master's amazement enlightens him as to the poverty-stricken condition of his coffers.

> "*Flav.* The greatest of your having lacks a half
> To pay your present debts.
>   *Tim.*   Let all my land be sold.
>   *Flav.* 'Tis all engaged, some forfeited and gone;
> And what remains will hardly stop the mouth
> Of present dues : the future comes apace. . . .
>   *Tim.* To Lacedæmon did my land extend.
>   *Flav.* O my good lord, the world is but a word!
> Were it all yours, to give it in a breath,
> How quickly were it gone! . . .
>   *Tim.* Come, sermon me no further: . . .
> Unwisely, not ignobly, have I given. . . .
> . . . . . . You shall perceive how you
> Mistake my fortunes, I am wealthy in my friends."

The plan to which Timon in his childlike simplicity has recourse, is simply to send to his good friends Lucullus, Lucius, Sempronius, and to beg them to let him have fifty talents. He is now about to learn what such friends are worth. "One cloud of winter showers, these flies are couch'd."

The scenes in which Timon's servants are dismissed by these three lords, are extremely comic, at least in the opinion of French readers, though, it must be observed, they find little favour with English critics, who even doubt their having come from the hand of Shakespeare. Whether they are really written in a manner unworthy of the great poet is a matter for English commentators to decide, and as a rule they cry out against the language as bare, homely, prosaic, familiar and colourless. But putting aside the question of style, on which French critics are little qualified to judge, the ground-work of these scenes greatly pleases the countrymen of Molière, to whose comedies it bears a close resemblance: and here we may pause for a moment to notice the difference between the spirit of French and that of English or German comedy. In France, comedy is especially a gently modulated satire, a study of the customs and thoughts and ways of mankind; it is a product of the intellect rather than of the imagination, and of careful observation rather than of fancy, while in England and Germany it is essentially a work of the most brilliant imagination, a sort of strange fireworks, resplendent with poetry, with playful and fantastic incidents, and jokes of keenest wit.

An admirable stroke of humour may be noticed in the speech of Lucullus when, lamenting the extravagant habits of Timon, he says, "Many a time and often I ha' dined with him and told him on't; *and come again to supper to him of purpose to have him spend less.*" And again, where Lucius, in speaking of the refusal given by Lucullus to Timon's request, says—

"For my own part, I must needs confess I have received some small kindnesses from him, as money, plate, jewels, *and such-like trifles, nothing comparing to his*" (that is, to the presents Lucullus has received from Timon). He begs Timon's servant to *commend him bountifully* to his good lordship, and to express his great regret that he " cannot pleasure such an honourable gentleman."

But the most impudent and barefaced of all, in his excuses for refusing to give aid to Timon, is Sempronius, who angrily declines because forsooth Timon did not apply to him in the first instance. The note here struck may be exaggerated but it is not a false one, and more than one example can be found both in Molière and in Plautus of an equally hard and cruel bit of comedy.

Timon, meanwhile, is sore beset by his creditors, whose messengers, in obedience to the instructions received from their masters, become more and more urgent and importunate, but it is easy to see that they are ashamed of the task they have to perform, and to each other they openly acknowledge their distaste to it : in fact, throughout the whole course of the tragedy Shakespeare evidently intended to show that though all feelings of honour and gratitude may be banished from the heads of the rich and powerful, they are not so easily abolished from the memories of those in the humbler ranks of life.

Timon, in a transport of rage, is driven wild by all these demands, not one of which he is able to satisfy, and his absolute and indiscriminating temper hurries him into a course the direct opposite of all he had followed before. Deceived in his dreams of universal love and beneficence, he falls with all the weight of an ill-balanced judgment into the opposite error and exaggeration, and presents the most striking example to be met with on the stage, of a sudden transition from one extreme to the other. But the misanthrope will not shut himself up for ever in his cave in the woods, without having first confounded the ingratitude of men, and without giving a brilliant and terrible setting to his rupture with mankind. And to this end, he orders Flavius to invite all his friends once more.

The banquet is laid in a magnificent room in Timon's house, and then, when the guests, whom the sight of "all covered dishes" has set in happy expectation of "royal cheer," lift the covers and to their amazement and confusion find the dishes full of warm water, Timon bursts out into bitter, frantic invective :—

> " *Tim.* May you a better feast never behold,
> You knot of mouth-friends !   Smoke and lukewarm water
> Is your perfection.   This is Timon's last ;
> Who stuck and spangled you with flatteries,
> Washes it off, and sprinkles in your faces
> > [*Throwing water in their faces.*
> Your reeking villainy.   Live loathed, and long,
> Most smiling, smooth, detested parasites,
> Courteous destroyers, affable wolves, meek bears,
> You fools of fortune, trencher-friends, time's flies,
> Cap-and-knee slaves, vapours, and minute-jacks !
> Of man, and beast, the infinite malady
> Crust you quite o'er !—What, dost thou go ?
> Soft, take thy physic first—thou too,—and thou ;—
> > [*Throws the dishes at them, and drives them out.*
> Stay, I will lend thee money, borrow none.—
> What, all in motion ?   Henceforth be no feast
> Whereat a villain's not a welcome guest.
> Burn, house ; sink, Athens ! henceforth hated be
> Of Timon, man, and all humanity."

After this splendid and lurid farewell to the world, the misanthrope retires to a cave in the woods.   There he continues to pour out his curses on mankind ; and his hatred of the whole human race vents itself in the most violent, the most unbounded, the most passionate imprecations.   But to what purpose is all this foaming and raging ?   It does no harm to the world nor good to himself.   In contrast to Timon and his idealistic nature, Shakespeare shows us the practical man of action in Alcibiades, who in analogous circumstances behaves in a very different manner.   Like Timon he has suffered from the ingratitude of his fellow-citizens, the Senate having

banished him from Athens in spite of the services he had
rendered to the Republic, but while Timon is holding up
his hands to Heaven in a transport of impotent fury and
indignation, Alcibiades collects an army and marches
against Athens. With less nobility of nature than
Timon, Alcibiades has far more judgment, and is more
moderate and more just in his hatred; this " complete
soldier " as Gervinus calls him, " a man of coarse texture,
in no way enthusiastic about the extreme end of things,"
and caring only for himself, has not the raging thirst for
blood, and for unspeakable horrors of every kind, that
consumes the generous philanthropist who has been
completely maddened by the discovery that his dream of
friendship was a delusion. For Alcibiades is capable of
discernment, and can sort out of the crowd those who are
his friends or his enemies, and those who are simply indifferent to him; and never having given his love unreservedly to men, he now feels no temptation to pursue
them with indiscriminate hatred. While Timon calls
down maledictions even upon the babe at the breast
and upon innocent virgins, Alcibiades, the conqueror of
Athens, will not wreak his vengeance at random upon
his fellow-citizens, and is desirous only of punishing his
enemies.

As Professor Dowden has remarked, Alcibiades is to
Timon what Laertes and Fortinbras are to Hamlet, what,
in fact, all the practical men of action in Shakespeare's
plays are to the idealists and dreamers,—natures less
attractive and sympathetic, but still worthy and estimable, to whom the justice of the poet grants final
success, while the enthusiasts fall victims to their own
exalted imaginations.

Chance furnishes the misanthrope with a means of
doing evil to the race of human beings that have become
so odious to him. In digging the ground for roots—now
his only food—he alights upon gold, which he hails as a

R

weapon with which he can wage war upon mankind.
Some of it he gives to thieves, as payment in advance of
all their future crimes, to the commission of which he
encourages and incites them with a turgid frenzy. But,
by an admirable touch, the excess of Timon's rage
awakens better thoughts in the minds of the thieves.
"He has almost charmed me from my profession, by
persuading me to it," says one, "I'll believe him as
an enemy and give over my trade," says another. So
futile is Timon's rage; but, at the same time, so potent
is the influence that emanates from the noble nature
of the man in spite of himself! The weapon that he
intended to do the work of destruction changes in his
powerless and consecrated hands into an instrument of
blessing.

Some of those who formerly fawned upon him, hearing that he is again possessed of gold, try to approach
him, but Timon drives them away with taunts and
blows.

A long scene takes place between Apemantus the
cynic, and Timon the misanthrope, which is more renowned than really remarkable; but the fiat of criticism
has gone forth concerning it, and decreed its perpetual
admiration. The two man-haters discuss with much
plain-speaking which is the truer philosopher of the
two, and finally Timon beats Apemantus off with a
shower of stones. In the last century, Burke, who was
a refined critic as well as a great orator, commended, as
we are told by Dr. Johnson, "the subtlety of discrimination with which Shakespeare distinguishes the present
character of Timon from that of Apemantus whom, to
vulgar eyes, he would now resemble." Critics were thus
fairly warned that if they failed to see the divergencies
of character between Timon and Apemantus, they would
be classed among the vulgar. The two parts have
accordingly been examined with the utmost care, and

various shades of difference, that really are to be found between them, have been discovered, and may be summed up as follows : the misanthropy of Apemantus, who is a species of human porcupine, a philosopher of the sect that called itself by the name of "The Dog," is merely an affectation of originality ; he indulges in stinging remarks and insolent truths only in order to satisfy his vanity and to attract attention, even at the risk of getting kicked for it ; while Timon's hatred is real, arising from the destruction of his faith in human nature, and his hatred is fatal to him because to love was a necessity of his nature. His misanthropy is directed against humanity in general, while that of the Cynic expends itself in petty personal insults : the one is the venomous outcome of wounded vanity, the other flows from a higher source —an intense feeling of disappointed love.

These distinguishing marks may, with the help of a little imagination, be made out, taking each character as a whole ; but they are by no means apparent in the particular scene in question, which confuses them instead of bringing them into clear relief, and which is moreover tediously long, monotonous, and diffuse.

A far finer scene is that which takes place between Timon and his former steward. When the servants separate after their master's downfall, and take leave of each other, the sense of their own misfortune seems overpowered by pity at the thought of his misery, thus showing, in contrast to the selfishness and baseness of the crowd of parasites, that menial souls are not invariably to be met with in those who wear the outward livery. Flavius, after sharing with them the little money he has of his own, determines to follow his master ; but when he approaches the cave in which he has hidden himself, Timon comes out, raging like a wild beast at the sight of a man approaching him. When Flavius protests he is an honest poor servant of his, Timon rejoins—

> "Then I know thee not.
> I ne'er had honest man about me: ay, all
> I kept were knaves to serve in meat to villains . . .
>   *Fla.* I beg of you to know me, good my lord,
> To accept my grief, and, whilst this poor wealth lasts,
> To entertain me as your steward still.
>   *Tim.* Had I a steward
> So true, so just, and now so comfortable?
> It almost turns my dangerous nature wild. . . .
> Forgive my general and exceptless rashness,
> You perpetual-sober gods! I do proclaim
> One honest man,—mistake me not,—but one;—
> No more, I pray,—and he's a steward."

Surely here we see a glimmering hope of Timon's
recovery, for he begins to *distinguish.* Formerly, in
his mania of universal benevolence and love, he deemed
such men as Lucullus and Sempronius equally worthy of
his affection as this true and trusty soul; and afterwards,
in his misanthropic frenzy, this same faithful fellow
appeared equally worthy of his hatred as Sempronius,
Lucullus, and all humanity. But now a sudden ray of
light shoots through the darkness of his mind, and he
makes the immense discovery that all men are not the
same, and that there is one, at all events, who deserves
to be singled out from the rest. If the wellsprings of
life were not attacked, so important a change would
justify the hopes of his complete return to sanity and
reason. But, unhappily, Flavius has arrived too late to
save his master, whom misery and madness have marked
for death. When the Athenian senators offer to make the
most brilliant reparation for their former ingratitude, and
to load him with honours and power, he only answers
with bitter mockeries, giving as his final charge :—

> "Come not to me again: but say to Athens,
> Timon hath made his everlasting mansion
> Upon the beached verge of the salt flood,
> Whom once a day with his embossed froth
> The turbulent surge shall cover; thither come
> And let my gravestone be your oracle."

Whether behind these words of his, and also when he says :—

> " Why, I was writing of my epitaph ;
> It will be seen to-morrow,"

there lurks an intention of suicide, or whether they are merely the expression of a presentiment of his fast-approaching end, is of little import, for in either case his death is equally his own doing. His noble but weak nature was utterly wanting in the practical common sense which enables men to discern and follow the right path, and also in the energy so indispensably necessary if we hope to bear up against the reverses of fortune, and to guide, rather than to be drifted along by, the current of events.

In the mean time, Alcibiades marches against Athens, which he enters as a conqueror. One of his soldiers has discovered Timon's grave on the sea-beach, and gives the general the epitaph, of which he took the impression in wax :—

> " Here lies a wretched corse, of wretched soul bereft :
> Seek not my name : a plague consume you wicked caitiffs left !
> Here lie I Timon ; who, alive, all living men did hate :
> Pass by, and curse thy fill ; but pass, and stay not here thy gait."

Having read this epitaph, Alcibiades pronounces a funeral oration on the misanthrope :—

> " These well express in thee thy latter spirits,
> Though thou abhorr'dst in us our human griefs,
> Scorn'dst our brain's flow, and those our droplets which
> From niggard nature fall, yet rich conceit
> Taught thee to make vast Neptune weep for aye
> On thy low grave, on faults forgiven. Dead
> Is noble Timon ; of whose memory
> Hereafter more. Bring me into your city,
> And I will use the olive with my sword ;
> Make war breed peace ; make peace stint war ; make each
> Prescribe to other, as each other's leech.
> Let our drums strike."

CHAPTER XIII.

TIMON OF ATHENS.　SOURCES FROM WHICH THE PLAY WAS DERIVED.

PLUTARCH, in his life of Antonius, says :—

"Antonius, he forsook the city and company of his friends, and built him a house in the sea, by the Isle of Pharos, upon certain forced mounts which he caused to be cast into the sea, and dwelt there as a man that banished himself from all men's company : saying that he would lead Timon's life, because he had the like wrong offered him that was before offered unto Timon, and that, for the unthankfulness of those he had done good unto, and whom he took to be his friends, he was angry with all men and would trust no man. This Timon was a citizen of Athens, that lived about the war of Peloponnesus, as appeareth by Plato and Aristophanes' comedies : in the which they mocked him, calling him a viper and malicious man unto mankind, to shun all other men's companies but the company of young Alcibiades, a bold and insolent youth, whom he would greatly feast and make much of, and kissed him very gladly. Apemantus, wondering at it, asked him the cause. Timon answered him, 'I do it because I know that one day he shall do great mischief unto the Athenians.' This Timon sometimes would have Apemantus in his company, because he was much like of his nature and conditions, and also followed him in manner of life. On a time when they solemnly celebrated the feasts of the dead, and that they two then feasted together by themselves, Apemantus said unto the other : 'O here is a trim banquet, Timon !' Timon answered again : 'Yea, so thou wert not here.' It is reported of him, also, that this Timon on a time (the people being assembled in the market-place about despatch of some affairs) got up into the pulpit for orations; and silence being made, every man listening to hear what he would say, because it was a wonder to see him in that place. At length, he began to speak in this manner: 'My lords of Athens, I have a little yard at my house, where there groweth a fig-tree, on the which many citizens have hanged themselves; and because I mean to make some building on the place, I thought good to let you all understand it, that before the fig-tree be cut down, if any of you be desperate, you may there in time go hang yourselves.'

"He died in the city of Halæ, and was buried upon the sea-side. Now, it chanced so, that the sea getting in, it compassed his tomb round about, that no man could come to it; and upon the same was written this epitaph :—

'Here lies a wretched corse, of wretched soul bereft :
Seek not my name; a plague consume you wicked wretches left.'

It is reported that Timon himself, when he lived, made this epitaph; for that which is commonly rehearsed was not his, but made by the poet Callimachus :—

'Here lie I Timon, who alive all living men did hate:
Pass by and curse thy fill, but pass and stay not here thy gait.' "

This account is not the only one given of Timon by classical writers; Lucian has a dialogue entitled "Timon, or the Misanthrope." At the opening of the dialogue, the misanthrope calls upon Jupiter from his cave, and reproaches him, in language of more than Aristophanic irreverence, for letting his thunders sleep.

"Any scoundrel going to perjure himself, would now as soon dread the snuff of a last-night's candle as thy all-consuming flashes. In short, you seem to fling at them, instead of the tremendous thunder-bolt, a burnt-out torch, of which no one fears either the fire or the smoke; the worst that can befall them, if it hits, is to get a smutty face. . . . What else can we think of it but that you are grown purblind and hard of hearing with age?"

As a consequence of this inaction on the part of the master of gods and men, crime flourishes upon the earth. "But," pursues Timon, "to dwell no longer 'at present on the common cause, and come directly to my own— how have I been served?" He had been rich in former days, and had made a generous use of his wealth in trying to make men happy; but after having squandered immense treasures upon his friends, he became poor, and was no longer recognized by the ungrateful recipients of his bounty.

"If by chance I meet them in the street, they pass by me as we pass by the dilapidated monument of a man long since dead and forgot; without so much as stopping to read the inscription. Nay, several, if they spy me at a distance, take a different way."

Thus he has been driven by necessity into the desert, where he at least gains the one advantage of not being forced to see—

"those scoundrels who are battening in the prosperity they so ill deserve. Come, then, O son of Chronos and Rhea! and at length shake off this long and heavy slumber; blow your extinguished thunderbolt again into flame, or light it afresh at Etna; and, by a tremendous flash of indignation, show yourself once more that lusty and vigorous Jupiter you were when young,—unless you are minded to have the fictions of the Cretans believed, who even show strangers your tomb." "Mercury!" cries out Jupiter, "who is that dirty fellow below, at the foot of Hymettus, with a goatskin about his loins, bawling up to us? Some talkative, saucy clown! Probably a philosopher, or he would never have dared to blurt out such blasphemies against us."

Mercury wonders that Jupiter does not recognize Timon, who so often formerly regaled him with festive offerings, and sacrificed whole hecatombs to him. Jupiter exclaims :—

"Things are strangely altered with him! What has happened to reduce him to such a miserable condition?" "I might say," answers Mercury, wisely, "his good nature and general philanthropy, his commiseration for all who were in want, have brought the poor man to ruin; the plain truth, however, is, that it is his folly, his excessive complaisance, and his imprudent choice of friends, that has done it. The simple man never perceived that he was lavishing his favours on crows and wolves, and mistook all the vultures that were preying upon his liver for friends who kept him company merely from kindness and goodwill, while in reality they only came to gormandize. When they had completely gnawed all the flesh from his bones, and carefully sucked out all the marrow, they flew away and left him a dry skeleton, unknown and disregarded."

Jupiter declares he will not behave towards Timon as those execrable sycophants have done. He has not forgotten the " many hind-quarters of beef and mutton, the delicious smell whereof I have still in my nostrils." He bids Mercury take Plutus, the god of riches, with him, and instal him with all speed in Timon's dwelling. As to the flatterers and ungrateful companions of his days of prosperity,—

"they shall smart for it as soon as I can get my thunderbolt repaired; * for the two great rays of it were broken, and the whole of its edge got blunted, when I launched it a little too furiously at the head of Anaxagoras, who wanted to persuade his scholars that we gods did not exist. I missed him, because Pericles held his hand over him, and the lightning was almost broken to shatters against a huge block of marble."

Plutus is very surly about obeying Jupiter's order, and says that Timon has insulted him, so he will not go to him.

" Do you suppose he will ever cease from pouring me into a basket full of holes? I am persuaded that he will act just as if I poured water into the tubs of the Danaïds." Jupiter, however, insists. " Go, I say, once more. Do as I bid you. And, Mercury, do you, on your way back, bring the Cyclops from Ætna, that they may repair and point my lightning for me as sharp as possible, as I shall soon have occasion for it."

On the way, the two travellers engage in a conver-

---

* There is nothing new under the sun. Did the ingenious authors of the parody before alluded to, know that Lucian had preceded them in the idea of sending Jupiter's thunderbolts to the blacksmith? In Act I., Sc. 2, of "La Belle Hélène," Calchas enters, saying, "And the thunderbolt? Have they brought back the thunderbolt?" "Not yet." "What! not yet? We can't do without it to-day. It is going to be very hot. I must have my thunderbolt. The blacksmith Euthycles promised it me faithfully—but here he comes." Euthycles enters with a roll of sheet-iron which represents the thunderbolt, and begins shaking it about. "Will you leave off," cries Calchas. "People will think it is Jupiter. This kind of effect must be used sparingly."

sation full of meaning : Mercury pities Plutus for being
both blind and lame, to which Plutus answers :—

"I am not always lame, Mercury, but only when I am sent by
Jupiter on an errand to somebody. Then, I know not why, but all at
once it feels as if I had no bones in my legs : I halt on both feet, and
walk so slowly that he who is waiting for me is grown an old man
before I arrive. Whereas, on taking my departure, you would suppose
I had wings, and I fly quicker than a bird."

As to his blindness, that, he acknowledges, is complete,
so that he often makes a mistake when Jupiter sends
him to enrich some one, and arrives at a wrong destination.

"I stroll up and down, groping to and fro, till by chance I meet
somebody, who, without more ado, takes me home with him, and
offers up a thankoffering to you, Mercury, for the unexpected good
fortune."

This time, in order that no mistake may arise, Mercury
says to him, "Lay hold of the skirts of my coat, and
stick fast till I have discovered Timon's solitary retreat."

The celestial messengers alight in Attica. The allegory, of which Plutus is the principal figure, is completed
by a circle of abstract personages, such as Poverty,
Labour, Patience, Wisdom, Courage, etc., who surround
the misanthrope. When Poverty sees Plutus coming,
she says, "I have nothing further to do here. Do you,
Wisdom and Labour, follow me." Timon, on his side,
begins by picking up stones with which to pelt the new
arrivals; but Mercury stops him :—

"No nonsense of that kind, Timon! . . . Hate mankind, who
have so injured you, if you like ; but why hate the gods, who are
ready to relieve you ? Hold out your hand, good Timon, and accept
your good fortune. The gifts sent by Jupiter are not thus to be
rejected."

But Timon is not easily convinced; he has learnt to
mistrust Plutus, who "was the cause of all his ills," while
Poverty on the contrary acted generously and wisely

towards him. Mercury, however, persuades him to comply and to become rich again, suggesting, as a final
inducement, that "at least he will have the pleasure of
seeing his fawning dissemblers burst with envy." This
said, he flies back to heaven. Plutus, now left alone
with Timon, bids him "Dig away! strike deeper in!" in
order to find Thesaurus, the god of gold, hidden in the
earth. . . . Behold him! Thesaurus shines resplendent
in the sunlight.

The discovery of the treasure fills Timon with joy,
but in no way alters his misanthropy. Far from being
softened, the hatred he has sworn to all mankind expresses itself more fiercely than ever :—

"Should I see a man ready to perish by fire, and implore me to
extinguish the flames, I will with all my might extinguish them—
with oil and pitch: and if a furious wintry flood should be overwhelming a man before my eyes, and he should call to me with
outstretched arms for help, I will just shove his head down so that he
shall never raise it again from the water. Only in this way can I
retaliate their behaviour to me. This law has Timon, the son of
Echecratides, of the Colyttean district, decreed and published; and
the said Timon, having united the president and the community in
his sole person, has ratified the same."

Meantime, the news flies far and wide that Timon
has again become rich; flatterers, parasites, false friends,
getting scent of his wealth, betake themselves to his
cave. The same thing happens in Shakespeare's tragedy;
and Timon, both in Lucian and in Shakespeare, receives
his visitors with blows and showers of stones. The
most amusing flatterer of the misanthrope newly crowned
with riches is Demeas, the orator, whose profession has
taught him to delight in fine phrases, and to take the
inventions of his own eloquence for realities. The conversation between him and Timon is a capital piece of
comedy.

"*Dem.* Health to you, Timon! the great ornament of your race,
the pillar of Athens, and bulwark of all Greece! Both of the councils

and the whole corporate assembly have been long anxiously waiting for your return. But, first of all, listen to the decree which I have proposed in your favour: 'Forasmuch as Timou, the son of Echecratides, of the commonalty of Colyttos,—a man who, whether for probity, politeness, or sagacity, has no equal in all Greece,—has constantly and in various ways rendered conspicuous services to the commonwealth; and has, moreover, signalized himself by gaining the prize in one day at Olympia, in boxing, in wrestling, in running, and in driving both with a pair of horses and with four-in-hand——'

Tim. I! who have never seen the Olympian games in all my life!

Dem. What matters that? You will see them some day or other. The more you insert of this sort in a decree the better. 'Moreover, he fought with great gallantry last year for the republic against the Acharneusians, and cut to pieces two whole battalions of the Peloponnesian troops——'

Tim. What! I, who never carried arms, and was never inscribed upon the muster-roll!

Dem. . . . 'For all which considerations it has been thought fit and decreed by the council and the people, in the first place, to cause to be erected a golden statue of the said Timon, and, further, to crown him with seven golden crowns.' . . . Thus ruus my decree. I intend to present my son to you, whom I have called Timon after you.

Tim. How is that, Demcas? Since to my knowledge you have never been married.

Dem. No, but I hope to marry next year, so good luck betide me, and to have a family of children; and my eldest born, who is sure to be a son, I shall call Timon.

Tim. [*Aiming a blow with his spade at him.*] Whether this may help on your marriage, my fine fellow, I cannot say.

Dem. Mercy on me! What is that for? Do you think to play the tyrant of Athens, by beating free people? You, whose free birth and citizenship are questionable, to say the least. But depend upou it, I will be even with you. You shall smart for this, and for setting the Acropolis ou fire, too!

Tim. The Acropolis never has been set ou fire, you sycophant!"

Towards the end of the dialogue, Apemantus, under the name of Thrasycles, appears. The cynic's enmity to men, and to the goods and pleasures of life, is a shallow pretence. He is simply a humbug, as may be guessed from his advice to Timon:—

"If you will hearken to good counsel, throw incontinently all your gold into the sea, as unnecessary and useless to a good man, to whom all the treasures of wisdom are open. You need not go out far into the sea,—only just step knee-deep into the water, close to the shore, when there is nobody by but me." .

The satire, it must be confessed, is a little thickly laid on. It is not in his dialogue of 'Timon' that Lucian has given us his most vivid picture of the cynic; for this we must turn to "The Sale of the Philosophers," in which the philosophical sects of every kind and species are sold by auction. The sale takes place by Jupiter's order, and Mercury plays the part of auctioneer, crying up the value of his wares and knocking each down to the highest bidder.

When it comes to Diogenes' turn, Mercury calls out: "There, gentlemen, I present to you a brave man, an excellent man, a well-bred free man. Who buys?"

A purchaser comes forward and inquires of Diogenes what he can teach, and what he is good for.

"Well," says Diogenes, "your chief acquirements will be these: you must be audacious and insolent, blurt out the most saucy speeches in the face of every one, from the prince to the beggar, for that will attract attention and procure you a reputation for intrepidity. Your speech must be quaint, the tone of your voice snarling and doggish; your expression must be scowling and surly, and your manner suited to your face; in one word, in everything be brutal and churlish. You must bid farewell to all shame, modesty, and decency, and blush at nothing. Frequent the most populous places, but when there, walk as if alone in the midst of the crowd, and acknowledge nobody as your friend. . . . Perform boldly before all the world what everybody else would blush to do even in secret."

"Fie! Fie!" exclaims the buyer in disgust, "I call all this infamous and beastly."

Dio. It is at any rate very easy, and within the power of every one. You need no learning, nor reasoning, nor any such nonsense; and you take the shortest way to glory. Be you ever such a blockhead, a tanner, a costermonger, a blacksmith, or a money-broker, nothing will prevent you from becoming a wonder in the eyes of the gazing multitude, if only you have impudence enough and are quick and ready with insolent repartees.

Buyer. You would be of no service to me in any of these qualifications; . . . but with your broad shoulders you might be useful as a gardener. I cannot afford to give more than twopence for you, but if the auctioneer will take that . . .

Mercury. A bargain! You may have him for twopence! We are glad to be rid of him—a noisy chap who is for ever railing at people and loading them with abuse."

These are the principal pages left to us by antiquity referring to the Misanthrope and the Cynic. Many others might be cited, but these are amply sufficient as specimens of the *classical* sources of a tragedy, the genealogy of which offers no particular interest, and raises no question of critical nicety. Alcibiades, Apemantus, the anecdote of the fig-tree, Timon's tomb and his epitaph are all in Plutarch; the conception of the misanthrope as a deceived and disappointed philanthropist, his withdrawal to a wild and desolate place, his finding a treasure, and the blows he gives to his ungrateful and self-seeking friends are in Lucian. But whether Shakespeare had direct recourse to Plutarch and Lucian is very doubtful. As we do not conceive the honour of the poet to be greatly concerned in the point as to whether he knew Greek, it may frankly be admitted, without attaching more importance to the answer than belongs to the question, that, in all likelihood, here as elsewhere, there were intervening links between him and antiquity. In the first place, Shakespeare only knew Plutarch through the translation of a translation, as has been conclusively demonstrated by Dr. Farmer, who is prouder of his discovery than if he had written "Timon of Athens." This play, according to Shakespearian chronologists, must have been written about the year 1608, that is, at a time subsequent to the finishing of his three Roman tragedies, and when he had had his English Plutarch for the last eight years or more. But before this, in 1575, the history of Timon, as related in Plutarch's "Life of Antonius," had appeared in Painter's

"Palace of Pleasure," a collection of "pleasant histories and excellent novels," the twenty-eighth of which is entitled, "of the strange and beastlie nature of Timon of Athens, enemie to mankinde, with his death, buriall, and epitaphe." It would be difficult to tell a story worse than poor old Painter, whose account is only an attenuated version of Amyot's dilution of Plutarch. The amiable retort, already quoted, of the Misanthrope to the Cynic is thus spun out by him :—

> "On a day, they two being alone together at dinner, Apemantus said unto him : 'O Timon, what a pleasant feast is this, and what a merry company are we, being no more but thou and I.' 'Nay,' quoth Timon, 'it would be a merry banquet indeed if there were none here but myself.'"

Not content with amplifying his text, he proceeds to comment upon it :—

> "Wherein Timon showed how like a beast indeed he was : for he could not abide any other man, being not able to suffer the company of him which was of like nature."

When he comes to the anecdote of the fig-tree, the brilliant idea occurs to him of telling his readers beforehand the purpose to which the tree was put—"He had a garden adjoining to his house in the fields, wherein was a fig-tree, whereupon many desperate men ordinarily did hang themselves,"—so that all the point of the story is lost; but Painter, thinking it still too pointed, effectually tones it down by his manner of telling it :—

> "He said that he purposed to cut down his fig-tree, to build a house upon the place where it stood. 'Wherefore,' quoth he, 'if there be any man among you all in this company that is disposed to hang himself, let him come betimes, before it be cut down."

Procumbit humi bos.

In Shakespeare's time, the history of Timon the Misanthrope was one of the popular stories of the day. Allusion is made to him in an epigram, dated 1598, and in the play of "Jack Drum's Entertainment" (1601) we meet with the line —

> "Come, I'll be as sociable as Timon of Athens."

No English translation of Lucian's dialogues had as yet been made, but dramatists who were better Greek scholars than Shakespeare, though not such good poets, had read them and given the first rough draft of Timon's history to the stage, moulded upon the satirist of Samosata. In 1842, a manuscript and anonymous play called "Timon," which is to all appearances anterior to that of Shakespeare, and is believed to have been written about the year 1600, was edited by Dyce, in the works of the "Shakspere Society." It contains all the general features of Timon's history as given by Lucian—his wealth and liberality at the beginning, his retreat to the woods, his discovery of gold, and the driving away of his sycophantic friends with blows and stones, etc.; and there is one scene in particular which bears a certain coarse and ridiculous resemblance to Timon's farewell banquet in Shakespeare. The *dramatis personæ* are, Laches, his faithful servant, whose part is the same as that of Flavius, and a crowd of parasites, among whom may be noticed the name of Demeas, the orator, who plays so amusing a part in Lucian's dialogue. Timon, when ruined, prepares a feast for his friends for the last time, and says to them :—

> "*Tim.* What man is he can wail the loss of wealth,
> Guarded with such a friendly company?
> I'll thrive my gold, it shall not wring one tear
> From these mine eyes, nor one sigh from mine heart:
> My friends stick close to me, they will not start.
>   *Dem.* Is he mad? We knew him not this morning:
> Hath he so soon forgot an injury?"

While waiting for the banquet to be served, the following conversation goes on :—

> " *Phil.* I love a piece of beef.
>   *Gelas.* I honey-sops.
>   *Pseud.* Give me a phœnix stewed in ambergris.
>   *Dem.* I love an artichoke pie soaked in marrow.
>   *Herm.* I pray thee, put a pheasant on the table.
>   *Stil.* I pray thee, let not mustard be wanting,
>   *Speus.* Be mindful of fat bacon : I do love
> To line my chops well with the grease thereof."

They then seat themselves, and Timon bids Laches bring
in the artichokes ; then, taking the dish, he says :—

> " These artichokes do no man's palate please.
>   *Dem.* I love them well, by Jove !
>   *Tim.* There, take them then,"

and he throws at their heads stones painted like artichokes :—

> " Nay, thou shalt have them, thou and all of ye !
>   Ye wicked, base, perfidious rascals,
>   Think ye my hate's so soon extinguished ?"

The guests rush off, crying, "O my head !" "O my
cheeks !" "Woe and alas ! my brains are dashed out."

> " *Tim.* Ye are a stony generation,
>   Or harder, if aught harder may be found ;
>   Monsters of Scythia, in hospital,
>   Nay, very devils, hateful to the gods.
>   *Laches.* Master, they are gone.
>   *Tim.* The pox go with them :
>   And whatsoe'er the horrid-sounding sea
>   Or earth produces, whatsoe'er accursed
>   Lurks in the house of silent Erebus,
>   Let it, O let it all sprawl forth here ! here
>   Cocytus flow, and ye black fords of Styx !
>   Here bark thou, Cerberus ! and here ye troops
>   Of cursèd furies, shake your fiery brands !
>   Earth's worse than Hell ; let hell change place with earth,
>   And Pluto's regiment * be next the sun."

Timon vows to hate mankind for ever, and to flee

---

* *i.e.* sway, rule.

S

from the society of men. Laches declares he will follow
him through sword, through fire and death :—

> "If thou go to the ghosts I'll be thy page,
> And lackey thee to the pale house of hell.
> Thy misery shall make my faith excel."

Besides the general resemblance in composition and idea,
there is one particular line in Shakespeare's scene which
looks like a confused recollection of this anonymous play.
According to Shakespeare, it is warm water that Timon
serves up to his guests and throws in their faces, but one
of them exclaims as he makes his escape, "One day he
gives us diamonds, next day *stones*"—a singularly inappropriate metaphor for water, unless we suppose the
water to have frozen on the way; but it would apply
with perfect propriety to the painted artichokes that the
Timon of the manuscript drama, showered down with
might and main on the heads of his guests.

Shakespeare, like Molière, is a robber on a grand
scale, not a poor literary pilferer but a jolly free-booter,
taking what he likes wherever he finds it. There is little
sense in the efforts made by critics, from time to time, to
prove that so far from his being indebted to his predecessors, they on the contrary stole from him, and that
the plays which are usually looked upon as poor attempts
preliminary to his, are in reality crude imitations of him.
Shakespeare was less of an inventor and more of an
artist than is generally supposed, and as Emerson
remarks, fully used the mass of old plays then in
existence, which gave him the needful ground in popular
tradition on which to work, and supplied a foundation
for his edifice, and which—

"in furnishing so much work done to his hand, left him at leisure
and in full strength for the audacities of his imagination." "A great
poet, who appears in illiterate times, absorbs into his sphere all the
light which is anywhere radiating."

The clever French writer M. Philarète Chasles, giving a slightly paradoxical expression to the same idea, declares that Shakespeare *invented nothing*, that what he did was to bestow a sublime and delicate setting upon the jewels he obtained from others, and that the very vocation of genius is to arrange and imitate, to study and to examine, but not to invent.

The rough imperfect works by which the master-pieces of art are almost invariably preceded may be compared to the abortive attempts, in which Nature seems to try her hand as a prelude to the formation of more perfect beings.

" It really looks," says Sainte-Beuve, in speaking of a precursor of Lamartine, " as if literary history, when on the eve of a grand creation, and about to produce and bring forth some fresh great personality, made experiments, as Nature seems to do, in crude preliminary attempts on a smaller scale, and in approximate but uncertain and undetermined models, which dimly foreshadow the coming genius, at whose advent they all crumble to pieces as useless before ever arriving at final completion."

All trace of a Greek spirit and of the local colouring of Greece are as absent in " Timon of Athens " as in " Troilus and Cressida ; " the names of the characters are Latin, and Alcibiades, the practical man intended as an antithesis to the idealism of Timon, has none of his well-known characteristics. It is strange that, as far as Greek antiquity is concerned, all that Shakespeare borrowed from Plutarch should consist in an incidental passage in the " Life of Antonius." Neither the heroes of the Median wars, nor the century of Pericles, nor Cimon, nor Pelopidas, nor Alexander stirred his poetic imagination ; he felt more at home with Rome and the ruder character of the Roman people.

CHAPTER XIV.

TIMON OF ATHENS.   LITERARY CRITICISM.   SHAKESPEARE'S
PERSONALITY IN HIS PLAYS.

"TIMON of Athens" would make a grand libretto for
an opera, but it fails as a play. It presents the single
instance amongst Shakespeare's tragedies of a play
characterized by qualities of a more brilliant than solid
description; the mind at first is dazed by its grandeur,
but like all works of factitious brightness it loses greatly
on a second reading. The impression it makes is the very
reverse of that produced by "Troilus and Cressida," which,
when we first read it, strikes us as so extraordinary and
so impertinent that we are shocked and repelled by it,
and it is only after a time that we become aware of the
charming treasures that lie hidden in its fantastic depths.
"Timon of Athens" is not unlike a drama of the
French romantic school; and is the only one of Shakespeare's plays of which this could be said: picturesque
and sonorous, it appeals to the eye and to the ear, with the
rich and gorgeous setting of its scenes, and with the
lyrical ring of its poetry, its eloquence and declamation.
Forsaking his accustomed mode of proceeding,—the close
and careful following of moral reality and truth, of
human nature and individual character,—Shakespeare
here gives way to exaggeration, after the manner of the
Romantic idealists; the knowledge shown of the hearts

aud minds of men is shallow, and the hero walks upon stilts. Excessively simple in structure, it is the triumph of antitheses; the action confining itself to the development of the most violent contrasts to be met with on the stage—a frenzied misanthropy succeeding a fanatical philanthropy, the palace of a lively and courteous host suddenly changing to the cave of a wild beast, love and hatred, laughter and weeping, joy and rage, and, as Victor Hugo would say, *light* and *darkness*. What magnificent scenes, and what a poem for the music of a Meyerbeer or a Beethoven ! Considered as an opera, the very points that constitute its poverty as a play, change into so many advantages,—no complication of plot, situations most clearly and distinctly drawn in symmetrical contrast, more feeling than thought, more of a lyrical cry in its voice than a strict rendering of human nature, a mood too exalted or too intense for the articulate language of prose or verse, and which can only find its true utterance in that art of which Victor Hugo has so well said, "Music expresses that which cannot be said and yet cannot be kept silent." What a subject for the musical interpretation of a Wagner is presented by the Banquet Scene, when Timon's anger, which for a time he has dissembled under a courteous and smiling exterior, all at once bursts forth like a thunder-clap. It is easy to imagine the suggestions of vague disquietude that the orchestra would shed over this false gaiety, through which the rumbling of the approaching storm would be dimly heard.

And after the dazzling splendour of his last banquet, and the terrible crash and din of his farewell to the world, we are transported to the silence of night, to the woods, and the gloomy cave of the misanthrope—all of which would furnish motives for a majestic overture to the first act. And, for the grand and solemn finale, we have Timon's tomb, chosen by himself, on the sea-beach

where once a day the rising tide shall sweep over it, and
where this great soul has at last attained eternal rest!
"Timon of Athens" possesses every qualification necessary to tempt a great composer, even down to the
suggestion of a ballet when Cupid and a group of
Amazons dance before Timon and his guests.

It is natural to draw a parallel between this tragedy
and "King Lear," just as two pictures by the same master
might be compared, in which the emotions and situations
are the same, although the figures are different; and
every Shakespearian critic has been struck by the
resemblance.

"There is the same vivid contrast of light and darkness," writes
M. Francois V. Hugo, who develops the antithesis with great talent
and ability, "Lear and Timon are both precipitated by a like catastrophe from the radiant summit of prosperity into the unfathomable
night of misery. As in Lear's case, Timon suddenly exchanges princely
wealth for the miserable condition of a vagabond; he is scourged by
the same tempest, blinded by the same hurricane. The morbid
melancholy that has its issue with King Lear in raging madness,
bursts out with Timon into a furious misanthropy. In this frightful
delirium, the one receives the like powerless devotion from his steward
Flavius, that the other finds in his vassal, Kent. And they both die of
grief, equally betrayed by those whom they have loved."

The effect produced by these two tragedies as of a
destructive hurricane sweeping by, is finely given in
this passage; but there is a still further analogy between
Lear and Timon in that they are both equally unreasonable, equally senseless, not only after the blow
has been struck, but before—very madmen from the
outset. Nothing can be more childish than the conduct
of King Lear in the first scene, when he divides his
kingdom as he might a cake, between his daughters,
promising the largest share to the one that loves him
most. "In this scene," says Goethe, "Lear's folly is so
great that later on, we cannot but feel that his two

eldest daughters and their husbands have some right on their side." Timon acts in precisely the same manner.

" He resembles a man," says Rümelin, " who throws all his goods and his money out of window to the passers-by in the street, and who, when his treasures are exhausted, innocently looks to the passers-by to give him back what he threw to them. He is deceived in his expectation, and thereupon loses what little reason he ever had." " In fact," he adds, in the same key as Goethe when speaking of Lear's daughters, " it is impossible to help feeling that the persons act very reasonably who refuse to give money to one who threw it about so wildly until he had squandered it all away."

This is the chief defect of the play. " King Lear " at all events presents an interesting and very carefully-studied picture of the progressive stages of mental malady; while Timon, on the contrary, falls from one extreme to the other with a passionate impetuosity that does away with any sort of gradation and degree. The absence of culture, of common sense, of knowledge of the ways of mankind, places Shakespeare's Misanthrope far beneath the Alceste of Molière: he has less distinction of mind, and his moral nature is narrower and poorer; he is at once less attractive and less worthy of esteem. The misanthropy of Alceste has its roots in a keen, strong sense of what is true and upright; that of Timon is but the rage of a spoilt child, who sees his dream crumble into pieces. The general good feeling and right-mindedness of Alceste so completely overbalance the peculiar twist in his mind which Molière pretends to be ridiculing, that we admire and respect him in spite of it. He reasons with Philinte, and discusses the merits of Oronte's sonnet; Eliante especially honours him with her regard, and Célimène distinguishes him from among the crowd of her lovers, and acknowledges that she treats him very badly. Timon inspires no feeling but that of pity. No one dares approach him, and even if any did, the most skilful physician of either

body or soul could avail him nothing. The Angel of
Charity alone could have sufficient courage to speak to
him, or sufficient self-sacrifice to minister to his needs.
Flavius—the finest character in the play—comes too
late to fulfil this sacred mission.

Goethe, who was a great admirer of Molière's "Misanthrope," called it "a true tragedy, both in its depth of
ideas and by the course of the plot;" but he thought
far less highly of "Timon of Athens," which he treated
somewhat lightly as a comedy, meaning, doubtless, that
with its unnatural and impossible exaggerations, it was
wanting in true force and earnestness, and that the hero
was less real.

And here this chapter might terminate, were it not
for a conjecture that has been started by ingenious commentators with regard to "Timon of Athens," which
opens up an interesting discussion, though one that can
scarcely lead to any certain conclusion. Their hypothesis is, that in the character of Timon Shakespeare
was expressing his own personal feelings, and that at
the time the play was written (about the year 1608), he
was himself passing through a misanthropic phase.
Hallam, who we know was little given to fanciful or
adventurous flights, was, I think, the first to hazard this
conjecture touching Timon of Athens, but it has been
constantly repeated in connection with other characters
of Shakespeare's plays, such as Hamlet, Jaques, Vincentio, etc.; and is, altogether, one of the prettiest
questions round which a skilful critic, well acquainted
with the poet's works, can let his imagination play.

There are many ideas in literature which have, and
can have, no intrinsic value, and the good or evil fortune
of which depends entirely upon the greater or smaller
amount of skill and talent with which they are worked
out. Among the number may be reckoned all the
theories that have been made, and will yet be made, as

to the character of Shakespeare. So irritating a problem naturally stimulates the curiosity of critics, and this exercise of their ingenuity can hardly be taken amiss; still, in the absence of conclusive documents, it would be hopeless to expect to arrive at any definite solution.

The attempts made to build up the personal character of Shakespeare, out of the different little hints and disclosures with which his plays are supposed to furnish us, are generally met by the objection that dramatic art is essentially impersonal, and that the very reason of Shakespeare's greatness as a dramatic poet is the impossibility of identifying him with any one of his characters, above all of whom he soars in complete independence.

" Never," writes Scherer, for instance, in his " Études Critiques sur la Littérature," " did any genius give himself up to art with more supreme indifference to everything but art itself. To Shakespeare, as he himself tells us, the drama is simply a mirror held up to Nature, who is reflected in it in all her varied aspects. So complete, indeed, is the impersonality of his plays, that it is impossible to gather from them any information as to his ideas, his passions, and his character."

" Of all the modern, and perhaps ancient, poets, Shakespeare," says Dryden, " was the man who had the largest and most comprehensive soul." Coleridge called Shakespeare myriad-minded, and spoke of his oceanic mind not less on account of the ceaseless movement than for the vast extent of his genius. Emerson says—

" Shakespeare has no peculiarity, no importunate topic; . . . no veins, no curiosities : . . . no mannerist is he," adding, with rare felicity of expression, " a good reader can, in a sort, nestle into Plato's brain, and think from thence ; but not into Shakespeare's. We are still out of doors." (" Representative Men.")

Schiller protests against the notion of searching after Shakespeare in his works :—

" As the Deity," he writes, " hides himself behind the edifice of the universe, so does the objective poet hide himself behind his works

. . . and we must be unworthy of his works, or unable to understand
them, or else sated by them, if we are tempted to ask after the author.
Such, for instance, is Homer among the ancients, and Shakespeare
among the moderns; two natures widely different and separated by a
deep abyss in time, but in perfect agreement in this one particular.
When, at a very early age, I first made Shakespeare's acquaintance, I
was repelled by his coldness and insensibility." *

To this—the simplest and most certain mode of
regarding the subject—other commentators answer :
dramatic objectivity is a big word only too easily hurled
at those who undertake to reconstruct a poet's personality from his plays.   Shakespeare was human, and
doubtless nothing common to humanity was foreign to
him. The sort of god that you imagine—a creator impassible and indifferent—is a being above—or beneath
—humanity; in every case, a myth, a conventional
personage, a figure of speech, a flower of rhetoric; and
in actual fact and reality, men are not Olympian to such
an unlimited extent. They have their tastes and foibles,
their secret or avowed predilections and antipathies. It
is all very fine to descant upon the impersonality of the
drama, but it is impossible for the individuality of the
author not to betray itself, if only in the choice of
subjects. There must be some reason why, at one period
of his life, Shakespeare wrote an almost uninterrupted
course of lively and brilliant comedies, and at another
composed only tragedies; and it is natural to suppose
that the choice in either case corresponded to different
peculiar mental conditions. Not even Homer, nor
Shakespeare, can rid himself of his own nature by any
mysterious transcendent virtue of genius.† The man
is always present beneath the work of the artist, and
all that requires to be done is to discover him. We

---

* See Chapter III., " Shakespeare and the Unities."
† " Even Shakespeare cannot transcend himself."—Dowden, " Shakespeare : His Mind and Art," p. 164.

acknowledge that with Shakespeare this is singularly difficult, and demands an exceptional degree of penetration; but if, by dint of care and trouble, it is possible to be done, there is nothing vainly presumptuous in the attempt to do it.

This answer is plausible, and to a certain extent true. Theoretically, it is reasonable to admit that Shakespeare's dramas ought to contain revelations of his personality, but, in point of fact, the alleged results are so poor and insignificant, and, it must be confessed, so doubtful, that they cannot be accepted as in any way adequately solving the problem, and the wiser part is to give up attempting its solution. All the inferences drawn touching his character, tastes and thoughts, and with regard to the different phases and incidents of his life are so entirely hypothetical that we shall do well to take them only as ingenious theories, elegant lucubrations of the mind, worthy to be listened to with pleasure, if logically put together and ably carried out, but which no one can seriously be required to accept as the positive truth.

The best known and the most common of these conjectures is that which identifies Shakespeare with Hamlet, of which his identification with Timon of Athens is merely a variation or different reading, Timon belonging, like Hamlet, to the race of dreamers, of idealists. And this is the reason why Gervinus, a deep thinker, but of a practical and positive temperament, prizing concrete reality, politics and history above all things, felt obliged to protest against this suggestion. As a German, he saw the danger of proposing the Prince of Denmark to his fellow-countrymen as the ideal of their favourite poet, and boldly taking the converse of the commonly received opinion, declared that Shakespeare's personal preference was not for the man of contemplative character, but for the man of action,—not for Hamlet, but for Henry V.

We have now a new commentator in Professor

Dowden, who, in his "Shakespeare: His Mind and Art," steers clear of either extreme and takes a middle course, offering a very ingenious and well-thought-out theory of the poet's character, which cannot· fail to be read with pleasure by all, and which those who will may adopt.

Professor Dowden begins by setting aside as equally false two extreme and contrary views of Shakespeare's character: one is that of M. Taine, who, true to his pre-dilection for tracing out the beast in man, delights in representing Shakespeare as free from all restraints of reason and morality, as a man of inordinate passions and extravagant imagination. According to the other paradox, Shakespeare would seem to have been a sort of manufacturer of poetry, a wise and prudent man of business, taking to the stage as the way to fortune, just as others with a slightly different order of genius take to dealing in sugar or wool, and troubling himself but little about anything except the money his plays brought him. Professor Dowden reconciles these two views by taking the portion of truth contained in each. He remarks that, in 1604, when Shakespeare had already become a wealthy man, he brought an action against Philip Rogers for the sum of £1 15s. 0d.

"Shakspere evidently could estimate the precise value for this temporal life of £1 15s. 0d.; and in addition to this he bore down with unfaltering insistance on the positive fact that the right place out of all the universe for the said £1 15s. 0d. to occupy lay in the pocket of William Shakspere."

But Professor Dowden adds that in this same year the poet was engaged upon his "Othello" and his "Lear." The attention he paid to the little sum of money due to him in no way interfered with his vision of Lear upon the heath and of Othello slowly enveloped in the traitor's coils.

"Our conclusion therefore is," says Professor Dowden, "that Shake-speare lived and moved in two worlds—one limited, practical, positive, the other a world opening into two infinites, an infinite of thought and an infinite of passion. He did not suppress either life to the advantage of the other; but he adjusted them, and by stern and persistent resolution held them in the necessary adjustment."

For Shakespeare's natural tendency, Professor Dowden goes on to say, was to lose himself in the infinite of thought and the infinite of passion. The prose of practical life had no attraction for him, and it was only by a prolonged effort of reason and of will that he came to assign it its due place. "His series of dramatic writings is one long study of self-control,"—a lesson, as it were, in which he schools himself, contrasting idealists, dreamers, sublime and passionate natures, whose destiny is to perish, with practical characters and men of action, to whom success in this world is assured. We must not say with Gervinus, that Shakespeare *likes* Henry V. *better* than Hamlet; on the contrary, in his heart he prefers Hamlet, but he *respects* Henry V. the most. Shakespeare's secret favourites are Hamlet and Romeo, Brutus, Timon of Athens, and all who are of the race of victims to the ideal, though his acknowledged admiration is for Henry V., Theseus, Hector, Fortinbras, Alcibiades, and all the heroes of solid fact and reality. Shakespeare is stern to the idealists whom he loves, just because he was conscious of the strongest temptation to be an idealist himself; and his admiration of the great men of action is immense—albeit a little cold and resembling esteem rather than love—because he himself was not primarily a man of action. He loves Hamlet and Timon of Athens passionately and with all his heart because of their close affinity with his own nature—they are as he is; his admiration for Alcibiades and Fortinbras proceeds from deliberate consideration and reasons to some extent outside himself, because they are what he struggles to be.

Such is the latest theory of Shakespeare's character as deduced from his plays. Attractive as it is, it will infallibly be followed by others, for it is of the very nature of imaginative works to be incessantly renewed for the delight of mankind.

Most readers are wishful to raise the veil that hides Shakespeare's personality, but, far from adding to the poet's greatness, the process would only detract from it, for the mystery that surrounds his character and life tends to enhance the power of his spell over men's minds: *omne ignotum pro magnifico habetur.* The learned men of the present day who make such efforts to know more of his history and character, and to whom the thought of studying him in any other light never occurs, ought hardly to lay the flattering unction to their soul that they are subserving his glory: the more devout critic, in whose soul the sources of poetic feeling have not been dried up by the dry and positive spirit of the age, approaches Shakespeare as he would a sanctuary, and a little obscurity seems to him not unbefitting to the vastness of the place; a flood of light let in to every nook and cranny would but make him regret the vanished shade. But the cultus of great men in the present day is characterized by a prosaic demand for clear conclusions and precise information; passionate admirers of Molière endeavour with untiring energy to clear up the obscure points in his life, and passionate admirers of Shakespeare strive to reduce his immense work to an intellectual and moral whole—to trace the development of a doctrine from the succession of his plays, and to present his series of writings in the light of a personal apprenticeship, or school of discipline for life. For my own part, I can only say that the less commentators succeed in their task so much the greater does the poet appear.

A recent critic (H. von Friesen) has made a great discovery: he has laid his hand upon a line which he considers settles the question as to which Church the poet belonged to by birth. Was Shakespeare a Protestant or a Roman Catholic ? Juliet (Act IV., Sc. 1) says to Friar Laurence, "Shall I come to you at evening mass ? " *Evening mass !* No Roman Catholic would ever have made use of such an expression; consequently Shakespeare was a Protestant. But in the "Merchant of Venice," Lorenzo says to Jessica (Act V., Sc. 1) :—

> " Look how the floor of heaven
> Is thick inlaid with patines of bright gold."

On this M. Montégut remarks :—

> " A patine is the small gold disk kissed by the faithful in the sacrament of the eucharist. This is one of the many details in Shakespeare which refer to ancient Catholic civilization and betray the poet's Catholic origin."

So Shakespeare was a Roman Catholic. But in the same play Portia says to Shylock (Act IV., Sc. 1)—

> " Therefore, Jew,
> Though justice be thy plea, consider this—
> That in the course of justice, none of us
> Should see salvation."

These words savour not only of Protestantism but even of Calvinism, and contain the whole doctrine of justification by faith.

In the last scene of " Henry VIII." it is predicted that under the reign of Elizabeth " God shall be truly known." Therefore Shakespeare was a Protestant. M. Riaux has nevertheless written a book to prove he was a Roman Catholic. In this I am inclined to think he is mistaken, and further on we shall be led by considerations of an entirely different nature to conclude, with infinite probability, that Shakespeare *started from Protestantism*, soon to raise himself far above either of the rival factions of the Christian Church ; but the general and glorious fact brought prominently forward by a discussion of this kind is, the immense impersonality of the poet whose works do not enable us to pronounce with any certainty even as to the communion in which he was born.

As Shakespeare was much occupied in his earlier plays with the question of marriage, and because he wrote the "Taming of the Shrew," and in the "Comedy of Errors" set forth the baneful effects of jealousy, and in "Henry VI." exclaimed—

> "For what is wedlock forcèd but a hell,
> An age of discord and continual strife?
> Whereas the contrary bringeth bliss
> And is a pattern of celestial peace"
>
> (Pt. I., Act V., Sc. 5),

it has been concluded that he was unhappy in his marriage, and had reason to complain of his wife. It may be so, but it renders the profession of a dramatic author terribly compromising if he can represent no passion without immediately being accused of having painted it from his own heart or domestic fireside. In this case, as Narcisse in "Britannicus" bestows great praise upon the excellent poison of Locuste, there is nothing to prevent us from maintaining that Racine secretly gave himself up to the same practices as the Marquise de Brinvilliers.

The greatly debated point concerning the politics of Shakespeare will be noticed further on, when we are studying the last of his three great Roman tragedies, "Coriolanus."

CHAPTER XV.

PERICLES, PRINCE OF TYRE.

It would be quite legitimate, if need were, to let our examination of Greek and Latin antiquity, as found in Shakespeare's works, include two plays, which cannot indeed be said to be derived from classical sources, but which yet belong to that vague transitional period in which the latest times of antiquity melt into the earliest Middle Age: these two plays are "Titus Andronicus" and "Pericles, Prince of Tyre." It being perfectly optional whether we take them or leave them alone, the middle course will here be adopted of examining only the last-named drama, as being the more interesting of the two; "Titus Andronicus," having, however, been named, a few words may first be said concerning it.

It is unnecessary to give any analysis of the play, which is simply a tissue of horrors. In no reader, however little educated, could it possibly excite the slightest emotion; all pity and all terror absolutely cease when the horrible is carried to such lengths, and its outrageous atrocity is even capable of provoking a fit of laughter.

Once when Mérimée wished to ridicule the extravagances of the romantic drama, he wrote "La Famille de Carvajal," and lest some simple-minded reader should take his jest for earnest, he took the precaution

T

of prefacing it by a letter in which he thus writes to himself:—

"Sir,—I am fifteen years and a half old, and mamma does not like me to read novels or romantic dramas; everything, in fact, that is horrible and amusing I am forbidden to read. They pretend it sullies the imagination of a young girl, but I do not believe a word of what they say, and as I always have access to papa's library, I read as many books of the kind as I possibly can. You cannot imagine how delightful it is to read a forbidden book in bed at midnight. But unfortunately I have quite exhausted papa's library, and I do not know what I shall do now. Could not you, who write such delicious books, compose a little play for me or a little novel, that shall be very black and terrible and full of crimes and love, something in the style of Lord Byron? I should be immensely obliged to you, and I promise to recommend you heartily to all my friends.

"P.S. I should like it to end badly, and especially that the heroine should die 'unhappily.'"

But "Titus Andronicus," unfortunately for itself, is anything but an ironical work intended to play the part of the drunken Helot, and under the guise of caricature to render the barbarities then permitted in the drama ridiculous and repulsive : it is written in earnest and aims at being terrible ; it rivals the most atrocious inventions of the playwrights of the day, but scarcely exaggerates them. Examples of cruel ferocity are easily to be found, as, for instance, in one of Chettle's tragedies, in which the hero has an iron crown heated red hot, and then pressed down upon the head of a rebellious lord. In one of Ford's plays, a husband stabs his guilty wife and tears out her heart, which he sticks on to the point of his lance. Barabbas in Marlowe's "Jew of Malta" poisons a whole convent of nuns to make sure of poisoning his recently converted daughter Abigail; he also goes about and poisons wells, and invents a sort of movable floor which at a given signal is to give way and precipitate "into a deep pit past recovery" all the guests he has invited to a grand banquet. He himself ends by falling head-

long into a caldron, in which he is boiled alive. In
" Tamburlaine," which, in the words of the King of
Jerusalem, is full of " merciless infernal cruelty," the hero
enters in his chariot drawn by captive kings with bits
in their mouths, with the reins in his left hand, and in
his right hand a whip with which he scourges them.

It appears from a passage in Ben Jonson, written in
1614, that a tragedy named " Titus Andronicus " had
appeared " five and twenty or thirty years " before, which
carries back the date to 1589 at least, at which time
Shakespeare was twenty-five years old; but whether
this monstrous drama was really written by him and is
to be taken as his first essay in tragedy may well be
doubted. It offers no *internal* evidence of Shakespearian
authorship, but two *external* authorities have led to its
being ascribed to him. First, Meres, in his " Wits'
Treasury," in 1598, mentions " Titus Andronicus " among
the number of Shakespeare's plays; and secondly, it was
admitted into the first folio published by Heminge and
Condell in 1623. In spite of these proofs however, I
decline to believe that " Titus Andronicus " was written
by Shakespeare. All internal evidence negatives any
such notion, and it is therefore necessary to explain
through what confusion it became possible for Meres and
the compilers of the first folio to attribute it to him.
Shakespeare when he came up to London was poor, and
was glad of any work that would bring him in money,
and at this time the more lucrative his employment was
and the quicker it was accomplished, the better it suited
him. Plays more or less defective were given him to
remodel for the stage, and amongst others he is generally
supposed to have touched up some of Greene's tragedies,
who reproached him bitterly for beautifying himself with
the feathers of others. This slight share in works, of
which the original authors for the most part remain
unknown, was quite enough, in an age not possessed of

our present delicate scruples with regard to literary
property, to cause their authorship to be ascribed to
Shakespeare. Poetry during the Middle Ages was so
thoroughly impersonal and anonymous, that in order
to appropriate a poem it was only necessary to
modernize the style; and in this respect the sixteenth
century had as easy a conscience as the Middle Ages,
which explains how, for instance, thirty ballads by
Charles of Orleans got mixed up with the works
of Octavien de Sainte-Gelais. Even in Athens, the very
centre of art and civilization, any one who had introduced
a few corrections of his own into a play of Sophocles or
of Euripides, was actually at liberty to bring it forward
on the stage under his own name. A remarkable fact
that may continually be observed in our own times, and
which will aid us in understanding this peculiar state of
things, is that the literary names which are the least
inquired after are those of new dramatic authors; it
frequently happens that a play may have a successful
run at the theatre for some time before even professional
literary critics know exactly whom it is by. It is
known by its title, not by its author. This is never the
case in other branches of literature. An unknown
writer may in the space of twenty-four hours make his
name famous by a successful novel, but a single dramatic
success will never suffice to gain him personal celebrity.
In the same year that the first complete edition of
Shakespeare's works appeared, Bacon, in one of his
philosophical works, deals incidentally with the theatre in
general, and with modern poets in particular, but he
makes no allusion whatever to his great contemporary.
It is quite possible that he may have known his masterpieces, and yet have been unaware of his personal
existence, or, at least, ignorant of the unparalleled position
he occupied in dramatic literature. For aught we know
Bacon may have attributed "The Jew of Malta" to

Shakespeare, "The Merchant of Venice" to Marlowe, and "Othello" to Greene. This indifference, which is so invariably manifested in a greater or lesser degree towards the authors of new dramatic works, and which was much more intense in the sixteenth century than at the present time, adequately explains how the work of another writer, which had been merely given to Shakespeare to touch up, came to be ranked among his own earlier productions.

It is not because "Titus Andronicus" is a bad play that I am unwilling to attribute it to Shakespeare—its badness would at least possess the interest of showing from what a lowly beginning the great poet started,— but because it is opposed to all that we know of the mood and temper of the young Shakespeare at the time that it is considered possible he should have conceived it. He began with bright and graceful trifles, with laughter and love: his first works were comedies and joyous hymns in honour of the senses. Frolicsome and poetic fancies like "Venus and Adonis," "A Midsummer Night's Dream," "Love's Labour 's Lost," "A Comedy of Errors," betray nothing analogous to the dark and stormy period traversed by Goethe and by German literature in general, and which found expression in "Werther." * It was only later on that Shakespeare was inspired by the tragic muse, and his taste never at any time led him to the introduction of scenes of horror.† A critic of the adventurous school might feel tempted to exercise himself in hunting out in "Titus Andronicus" every

---

* "The supposed *Sturm und Drang* period of Shakspere's artistic career exists only in the imagination of his German critics. The early years of Shakspere's authorship were years of bright and tender play of fancy and of feeling."—Dowden, "Shakspere: His Mind and Art."

† Of atrocity, strictly speaking, there is absolutely none in Shake-speare's plays, except in the scene in "King Lear," in which the Duke of Cornwall tears out Glo'ster's eyes and treads them under foot.

finger-touch of the young poet, but that the scheme of
the play is not Shakespeare's, and that no one scene
stands out from the rest, unmistakably revealing the
master's hand, is a full and sufficient reason for our here
passing it by, without stopping to inquire into the
sources whence it was derived.

"Pericles, Prince of Tyre," is also a doubtful play,
which, taken as a whole, strikes us as little worthy of
Shakespeare. It contains, however, at least one scene
of which the probability that it bears his stamp is
sufficiently great. How the hero came by his name of
Pericles remains a mystery. It has been suggested that
it was a printer's mistake for Pyrocles, the name of the
hero in Sir Philip Sidney's "Arcadia." However this
may be, the real name of the Prince of Tyre, as handed
down by tradition, is neither Pericles nor Pyrocles, nor
anything resembling it, but Apollonius. The most
ancient record known of the story of Apollonius of Tyre
is to be found in a Greek romance of the fifth or sixth
century, A.D. Later on, in the twelfth century, Godfrey
of Viterbo, secretary to the Emperors Conrad III., Frede-
rick I., and Henry VI., the author of the "Pantheon"—
a universal chronicle in Latin verse, beginning with
Adam and finishing about the year 1186 of the Christian
era—found room in it for the tale of Apollonius. Almost
at the same time it also appeared in Latin prose in
the "Gesta Romanorum," of which it formed the 154th
chapter. It was extremely popular in the Middle Ages,
and was repeated in every form and in every language.
We need here only mention the poet John Gower (died
1408), who gives it in verse in his "Confessio Amantis,"
and upon whose narrative the author of "Pericles"
founded his play. The old romance of Apollonius of
Tyre is so closely followed in the play that a sketch
of the outlines of the story, as told by any one of its
innumerable narrators, will serve at the same time as
an analysis of the play.

Apollonius of Tyre, fearing evil at the hand of Antiochus, King of Syria, whose wrath he has incurred through the discovery of his secret crimes, leaves his own dominions, of which he hands over the government to his true and faithful friend, Helicanus, and sets sail for Tharsus. Here were reigning a king and queen, who, with the author of the play, we will call Cleon and Dionyza. A famine was raging in Tharsus, but the vessels of Apollonius were laden with corn, which he generously distributed amongst the starving inhabitants. After spending some time at Tharsus, in the midst of the feasting and rejoicing that took place in the now joyful town, which had been restored instantaneously to all its ancient prosperity by this one cargo of corn, Apollonius proceeds to Cyrene. But on his way he encounters a fearful storm, and his vessel, after losing all its masts, runs upon a rock and breaks to pieces, drowning all on board except Apollonius, who catches hold of a plank and manages to reach the shore of Cyrene in safety.

A grand tournament was just about to be held, to celebrate the birthday of Thaisa, daughter to the good King Simonides ; * and, as the sea conveniently casts up on the shore the prince's own suit of armour, Apollonius joyfully dons it and repairs to the lists. He is, of course, of all the princes and knights the handsomest and the bravest; and, equally of course, the Princess Thaisa immediately falls in love with him."

" The young girl, who had never known what love was, and had gone to bed expecting to fall asleep as usual, found that sleep was chased from her eyes by the vivid thoughts succeeding each other in rapid succession in her mind, of the face and form, the manners, gentleness and grace of Apollonius. The next day, rising much earlier than was her wont, she went to her father, whom she greeted

---

* I follow the play in the names of all the secondary personages.

humbly with pretty coaxing ways; and when he inquired why she had come, contrary to custom, so early to his room, she had her answer all ready and said, ' Sire, if to love one's equal be a sin to be punished, I am worthy of punishment. . . . And, not to detain you, sire, you know the merits, virtues, knowledge, and nobleness of Apollonius, Prince of Tyre; he it is that I love, and—forgive me—to such a degree, that if I do not marry him, this day will be the last one of your daughter's life.'"

The King willingly gives his consent, and as Apollonius on his side is perfectly ready, the marriage takes place, "to the great happiness and content of the bridal pair, and to the joy of all the Cyrenians."

About six months after this happy event, messengers arrive from Tyre, bringing the good news that Antiochus is dead, he and his daughter having both been struck by lightning, and that the inhabitants of Antioch have elected Apollonius as their king; also that his own subjects beg of him to return to Tyre and resume the sceptre.

Full of gratitude to his good fortune, which thus bestowed two thrones upon him and called him away from the whims of his father-in-law, Apollonius says farewell to the "good King Simonides," and departs with Thaisa his wife. But they have scarcely left the harbour of Cyrene when a terrific storm arises, the effect of which upon poor Thaisa is to bring on a premature confinement. A beautiful little girl is born amid the uproar of wind and wave, but "the mother could neither caress nor kiss her child, for she lay senseless, stiff and cold as one dead, and so in truth they thought she was." Apollonius faints with grief over her inanimate body; but when he regains his senses, as the storm is still raging, the sailors declare that the body must be thrown overboard at once to appease the wrath of heaven. Against superstition all reasoning is futile, and the unhappy prince is obliged to acquiesce; so he lays in a coffin the body of his beloved wife,—

" royally dressed and apparelled as beseemed so noble a lady ; and he laid therein many coins to pay for her burial wherever the coffin should come to land, and wrote inside that she was the wife of the unhappy Apollonius, who besought him who found her to give her burial."

The coffin is washed up on the coast of Ephesus, where it is found by the physician Cerimon, who opens it, and reading what is written therein, begins to make preparations for burying the Queen in a manner befitting her rank, when—

" accidentally passing his hand over her heart, he fancied that it beat ; and upon further examination found there was indeed a slight breath-ing, albeit very faint and feeble, as though life were struggling against death. He ordered the servants to place torches all around, and to burn aromatic spices, so that the warmth and the sweet odour should awaken the slumbering senses of the lady, and liquefy the coagulated blood which had caused this long trance. So well did it answer, that little by little the princess began to move and breathe slightly."

In a few hours she regains life and consciousness, and in a few days is perfectly recovered. Thus restored to life by the care of the good physician Cerimon, she becomes a priestess in the service of Diana, in whose temple she spends her life.

Meanwhile, Apollonius, inconsolable at the loss of his young wife, arrives off Tharsus with the little Marina, which is the pretty name given to her in the play be-cause "she was born at sea." He confides his infant-daughter to the care of Cleon and Dionyza, as he has now no intention of returning to Tyre or of living in any fixed place, but will travel from place to place till he find the spot where the body of his wife came to land ; and until then, he takes an oath to leave his hair and beard uncut.

The King and Queen of Tharsus have a daughter of much the same age as Marina, so that the two children are brought up together ; but Marina, as she grows up, quite eclipses her companion, both in beauty and in wit, which so excites Dionyza's jealousy that she resolves to make away with the charming young girl who throws her own daughter into the shade. She accordingly hires a slave to kill Marina. The wretch lures his prey down to a desert place on the sea-shore, but just as he is about to accomplish his purpose he is interrupted by a band of pirates, who carry off the young girl with them to Mitylene, where they sell her into infamous hands, and where she undergoes great and terrible trials; through all of which, however, her invincible purity and innocence bear her triumphantly.

Apollonius, who all this time has been vainly searching for the place where his wife was buried, now returns to Tharsus to see Marina. The wicked Dionyza makes him believe that the child died in her infancy, and even shows him her tomb, bearing an epitaph written by the Queen herself. Thus bereft of every tie of affection and love, Apollonius gives himself up to despair, and returns on board his ship. The waves carry him to the coast of Mitylene, where Lysimachus, the governor of the town, perceives the royal vessel at anchor in the roadstead, and is prompted by curiosity to visit it. He finds on board a man prostrate on his couch, crushed down by the weight of an immense sorrow, unwashed, dishevelled, and speechless. On learning that the cause of this intense grief is the loss of his wife and daughter, Lysimachus by a happy inspiration bethinks him of sending for Marina, in the hope that the sorrow of this unhappy father may have a moment's alleviation at the sight of one, who may perchance remind him of the child he has lost. Marina is sent for and arrives, when a very beautiful scene takes place, and the father recognizes his daughter.[*]

---

[*] This final recognition gives a classical air to "Pericles." "We learn from Aristotle," writes M. Gaston Boissier, "and from the practice of Latin authors, that comedies almost invariably wound up with recognitions; it was generally a young girl that was lost in a crowd, or carried off by pirates, who, after having been sold as a slave, is recognized in the last act and restored to her parents."

The physical and mental restoration of Apollonius begins upon this first gleam of happiness. But there is yet more in store for him : in obedience to an order given to him by Diana in a dream, he repairs to Ephesus to offer a sacrifice to the goddess in her temple ; and here he finds his wife. Never did romance have a happier ending. The wicked King and Queen of Tharsus expiate their crime by a violent death ; Marina marries the governor of Mitylene ; Apollonius trims his beard, and places his daughter and son-in-law upon the throne of Tyre, his subjects, with model patience and constancy, having awaited his return for more than fifteen years.

So runs the romantic tale which charmed the imagination of the Middle Ages, and which was turned into a drama in the beginning of the sixteenth century.

The first edition of "Pericles" was published in 1609, under the title of "The late and much admired play called Pericles, Prince of Tyre. With the true relation of the whole history, adventures, and fortunes of the said Prince ; as also the no less strange and worthy accidents in the birth and life of his daughter Marina. As it hath been divers times acted by his Majesty's servants at the Globe, on the Bank-side. By William Shakespeare." There was a second edition of "Pericles" in the same year, and four new editions appeared in 1611, 1619, 1630, and 1635, all bearing the name of Shakespeare. It was not, however, included among the plays of either the first or the second complete edition of his works, the folios of 1623, and of 1632, and only makes its appearance in the third folio in 1664.

From these facts and dates nothing can be concluded either for or against the authenticity of the play : the quarto editions containing Shakespeare's name are no proof that it is his, as similar adoptions of the name of a poet of renown were by no means rare at that time ; while, on the other hand, the omission of " Pericles " from the first two folios is no proof that it is apocryphal, as some material difficulty of which we know nothing may have stood in the way of its admission, as, for instance, the rights of some other bookseller. And these rights would be all the more keenly looked after, as " Pericles " was a great success, as is attested by various contemporary documents. An anonymous poem called " Pymlico," published in 1609, speaks " of the crowd of gentles mixed with grooms," who swarmed to see " Pericles;" and the prologue to an old comedy, " The Hog has lost his Pearl" (1614), expresses the hope that the play may be " as fortunate " as " Pericles."

The chief element for the solution of this little problem in the history of literature—the authorship of " Pericles "—is an examination of the play itself. The invention and composition of the tragedy and its notions of morality are all equally childish. As to invention there is none ; the author has simply followed the old romance, neither adding nor altering a single incident. Nor is there any greater notion of composition; the events of the drama succeed each other chronologically, one by one, in precisely the same order as in the narrative, which is the greatest sign of inexperience that a dramatic poet can possibly give. The author of " Pericles " proceeds in exactly the same manner as those dramatists so ridiculed by Sir Philip Sydney, and relates the whole string of incidents without sparing us a single detail. There is no sort of unity in it, not even the unity of action,*—it is like the showing off of a magic lantern with an indefinite number of pictures, and the more slides there are in the box the better the

---

* " A fable is not *one*, as some conceive it to be, merely because the hero of it is one. For numberless events happen to one man, many of which are such as cannot be connected into one event, and so likewise there are many actions of one man which cannot be connected into one action."— Aristotle's " Poetics," § 5.

children are pleased. So great is the dramatic feebleness of the poet in his childish reproduction of the romance of Apollonius, that not being able to represent on the stage more than a fraction of the events, while at the same time he can only render his play intelligible by letting them all be known, he is obliged to have recourse to dumb show, and to prologues to carry on a considerable part of the plot. Dumb show belongs to the very infancy of dramatic art.

"It was the chief element in the shows that took place in the fourteenth and fifteenth centuries. It held a large place in those mixed productions which during the time of the Renaissance, preceded and led on to the formation of the modern theatre; it even thrust itself, strange to say, into translations of ancient classical authors, aud notably invaded Seneca's ten tragedies, translated by Jasper Heywood between the years 1559 and 1566; and actually insinuated itself into the "Phœnissæ" of Euripides, in its reproduction by Gascoigne in 1566, under the title of "Jocasta." It parades itself at the beginning of each of the five acts of "Gorboduc" (1561). . . . In "Hamlet," the play acted before the King and Queen is preceded by a dumb show rehearsing all the principal scenes." *

The explanatory prologues in "Pericles" are spoken by the old poet John Gower, from whom the play was borrowed. In the list of persons represented at the beginning of the play, Gower is called the Chorus but, as has already been remarked, this is a very inexact and inappropriate title, and it would be better to say that he plays the part of prologue, his office being simply to relate what has not been seen, or to announce what is going to be seen, and having nothing in common either with the Greek chorus, which took part to a certain extent in the plot, nor with the chorus in Seneca's tragedies and those of the Renaissance, which were a form of rhetorical digression. The chorus, or what is so called by Shakespeare, in Henry V., in the "Winter's

---

* François Victor Hugo.

Tale," and in " Romeo and Juliet," could be omitted
without hurting the sense of the play, but it is indispensably necessary for the understanding of Pericles.   For
instance, in the middle of the fourth act, Gower appears
and informs us that " Pericles is now again thwarting the
wayward seas," to reach Tharsus and see his daughter,
" all his life's delight ; " then follows a dumb show.

" Pericles enters at one door with his train : Cleon and Dionyza at
the other.   Cleon shows Pericles the tomb of Marina, whereat Pericles
makes lamentation, puts on sackcloth, and in a mighty passion (of
sorrow) departs."

Then Gower again takes up his parable, and says—

" See how belief may suffer by foul show !
This borrowed passion stands for true old woe ;
And Pericles, in sorrow all devoured, . . .
Leaves Tharsus, and again embarks.   He swears
Never to wash his face nor cut his hairs. . . .   •
                            Now please you wit
The epitaph is for Marina writ,
By wicked Dionyza."

And the poor old twaddler bends down and reads out the
inscription on Marina's monument for the information of
the audience.   So important an incident had necessarily
to be introduced, but with how little art the introduction
is effected !   A scene that to a great dramatic poet would
have afforded such splendid opportunities—Pericles,
deceived by false friends and plunged into the depths of
despair beside the tomb he believes to be his daughter's,
is here represented in pantomime !   Instead of unfolding
it before our eyes and ears in all the fulness of its
tragedy, the author simply gives us a meagre account, by
the clumsy means of a prologue accompanied by a dumb
show ; the veriest tyro in dramatic art could hardly hit
upon a more unskilful arrangement than this.   The
epilogue at the end of the play, with its narrow notions

of morality, contains a last parting instance of the same simple-minded character :—

> " In Antiochus and his daughter, you have heard
> Of monstrous lust the due and just reward ;
> In Pericles, his queen and daughter, seen
> (Although assail'd with fortune fierce and keen)
> Virtue preserved from fell destruction's blast,
> Led on by Heaven, and crown'd with joy at last. . . .
> For wicked Cleon and his wife, when fame
> Had spread their cursed deed, and honour'd name
> Of Pericles, to rage the city turn ;
> That him and his they in his palace burn.
> The gods for murther seemed so content
> To punish them ; although not done, but meant.
> So on your patience ever more attending,
> New joy wait on you ! Here our play hath ending."

In every way,—in thought and in expression,—this is thoroughly puerile. This winding-up in the style of Mrs. Trimmer, and this strictly equitable Providence treating every one according to his deserts, rewarding virtue and punishing crime, belong to a childish conception which we are most assuredly not accustomed to find in Shakespeare.

When the fourth act, with its coarseness and grossness, is also added to the charge of the author of " Pericles," it is easy to understand why many critics, in the absence of imperious external evidence, should have excluded this play, as unworthy, from the works of Shakespeare. Pope omitted it in his edition of the poet's works, and calls it in his preface " a wretched play."

" Pericles," however, is far from being uniformly bad. The third act is interesting ; the fifth act is touching, and contains one great scene full of the most admirable poetry—the scene in which Pericles recognizes his daughter—which can bear comparison with the passages of purest and most acknowledged beauty in any of Shakespeare's plays.

Three hypotheses have been advanced in order to explain this great inequality in " Pericles ;" the first and oldest of which I reserve until we have examined the other two, as it is the one that after all I am most inclined to accept, and I accordingly begin with the second, which is that started by Steevens. He suggests that "Pericles" was the production of some earlier playwright, which Shakespeare improved, especially in the last scenes, and gave to the theatre in 1609. Hallam and Collier agree in this opinion, against which there is not much to be said, and which can very well be maintained, but it hardly seems the most probable. It is scarcely likely that Shakespeare should in 1609, towards the end of his career—after "Hamlet," "Othello," and "King Lear," have laid hands upon the imperfect work of another writer ; this sort of partnership or literary pillaging is more conceivable at the beginning of his dramatic career.

The third hypothesis is quite recent. At a meeting of the New Shakspere Society (May 8, 1874), Mr. Fleay read a paper * in which he rejected without criticism the explanation given by Steevens, and proposed as *certain* the theory that—

"Shakspere wrote the story of Marina, in the last three acts, minus the prose scenes and the Gower. This gives a perfect, artistic, and organic whole. . . . But this story was not enough for filling the necessary five acts from which Shakespeare never deviated : he therefore left it unfinished. . . . The unfinished play was put into the hands of another of the 'poets' attached to the same theatre, and the greater part of the present play was the result; this poet having used the whole story as given in Gower and elsewhere."

This is Steevens's theory reversed ; the great master, instead of touching up the sketch of an inferior writer, was the first to conceive the original dramatic idea which some clumsy workman afterwards filled up. The hypo-

---

thesis is clearly attractive, for it is infinitely more agreeable to see Shakespeare originating works which were spoilt by those who came after him than improving those of others. Inversions of this kind would appear to be greatly in vogue in the New Shakspere Society. The still more daring and original theory maintained by Mr. Fleay with regard to "Timon of Athens," of which he has made bold to reconstruct the text as Shakespeare first wrote it, has already been mentioned, and he has in like manner published among the "Transactions of the New Shakspere Society" the primitive and original portion of "Pericles," under the title of "The Strange and Worthy Accidents in the Birth and Life of Marina, by William Shakespeare."

Mr. Fleay's mode of procedure in the discussion is scarcely modest, but it is based upon a true knowledge of the human mind. He is aware that our natural impatience and indolence of mind make definite conclusions the most acceptable, that no one is grateful to a critic for having doubts and expressing them, and that the surest way of communicating ideas to the world is to promulgate them in a tone of authority; and accordingly he never hesitates nor minces matters, while the habitual forms of his expression are "no doubt," "decidedly," "unquestionably." He not only decides that such and such a scene is not Shakespeare's, but actually goes so far as to be quite clear as to who the real author is. So well does he know the style of every fourth-rate author contemporary with Shakespeare, that he can pronounce with the utmost confidence that this is undoubtedly by George Wilkins, but that is unquestionably by William Rowley. This is unquestionably, to use Mr. Fleay's expression, an efficacious method, and carries conviction home to the minds of the majority of readers. But let us consider the matter a little.

Mr. Fleay maintains, for instance, that the prose

U

scenes in the fourth act of "Pericles" are "decidedly" not by Shakespeare, apparently for the reason that they are of too coarse a nature, and that such a subject would be repugnant to the natural delicacy of the poet; but the fact that a picture is coarse can hardly be taken as a sufficient proof that Shakespeare had no hand in it. Nowhere in his plays do we see any signs of an easily startled modesty, blushing and veiling itself from every subject of a questionable character. In "Measure for Measure" we find quite as revolting a situation as that in the fourth act of "Pericles." Shakespeare, like Molière and Rabelais and Aristophanes, and most of the great poets, is in fact a cynic,—not, indeed, that he is immoral, he never invests "passion or weakness with attractions which might captivate us and lead us morally astray." (Gervinus, p. 892.) With him vice remains vice, and in his plays we meet with no virtuous crimes or poetic sins: in the words of Coleridge—

"keeping at all times in the high-road of life, in Shakespeare vice never walks as in twilight; nothing is purposely out of its place, he inverts not the order of nature and propriety, does not make every magistrate a drunkard or a glutton, nor every poor man meek, humane, and temperate; he has no benevolent butchers, nor sentimental rat-catchers."

Shakespeare is distinctly not immoral, but this does not prevent him from being cynical. He calls things by their true names, and paints a picture frankly and truthfully; he is as bare and open as Nature, and, like her, uses neither veil nor varnish. "True genius is never decent," Schiller boldly remarks, "for corruption only is decent." To this general remark it should also be added that the situation in the fourth act of "Pericles" is the crowning point of Marina's sad history, without which her sufferings would be comparatively slight. Shakespeare, having begun to depict the trials she went through, was obliged to show us the greatest of them all. And upon examination of the act in question, the opinion that it is by Shakespeare may even be confirmed rather than shaken; the situation once admitted, it must be acknowledged to be drawn with rare energy, and to contain one especially fine passage, worthy of either moralist or poet: "Are you a woman?" Marina asks of the mistress of the house, who answers, "What would you have me be an I be not a woman?" "An honest woman, or not a woman."

Mr. Fleay further remarks that Shakespeare would never have married Marina to Lysimachus; but that this incident formed part of the old story of Apollonius, which the author of "Pericles" closely followed in every particular, is surely sufficient to make such an outcry unreasonable.

But although Mr. Fleay has not proved his theory, his labours have not been all in vain, for he has done good service to the poet, or rather to his admirers, in pointing out the purest and most authentic beauties of "Pericles." In the scene of the storm, in which Marina is born in the midst of the waves (Act III., Sc. 2), and still more in the scene in which she is recognized by her father, the hand of Shakespeare is manifest. And this opinion is confirmed by Mr. Tennyson, whose authority as a poet carries no inconsiderable weight with it.

At the same meeting of the New Shakspere Society, in the discussion on "Pericles," Mr. Furnivall communicated the following interesting details :—

"When I first saw Mr. Tennyson last winter, he asked me during our talk whether I had ever examined 'Pericles' with any care. I had to confess that I had never read it, as some friends whom I considered good judges had told me it was very doubtful whether Shakspere wrote any of it. Mr. Tennyson answered, 'Oh! that won't do. He wrote all the part relating to the birth and recovery of Marina and the recovery of Thais. I settled that long ago. Come upstairs and I will read it to you.' Upstairs to the smoking-room we went, and there I had the rare treat of hearing the poet read in his deep voice, with an occasional triumphant, 'Isn't that Shakespeare?' 'What do you

think of that?' and a few comments—the genuine part of 'Pericles.'
I need not tell you how I enjoyed the reading, or how quick and sincere
my conviction of the genuineness of the part really was. But I stupidly
forgot to write down the numbers of the scenes. However, when the
proof of Mr. Fleay's print of the 'Birth and Life of Marina' came,
its first words, 'Thou God of this great vast,' brought the whole thing
back to me, and I recognized in its pages the same scenes that
Mr. Tennyson had read to me."

And now, going back, we come to the first hypothesis,
the earliest one of all, and which I myself consider the
best of the three—without, however, being ready to shed
my blood in its defence, or being desirous of hewing to
pieces those critics who share another opinion.

According to this conjecture, Shakespeare is the sole
author of "Pericles," but between the first idea of the
work and its final execution lies an interval of twenty
years or so; it is an attempt of his inexperienced youth,
taken up again and finished by the master in 1609.
Malone was the first to offer this suggestion, but he afterwards withdrew it in favour of that of Steevens. Knight
re-vindicated Malone's theory, but left one point unex-
plained : by his incomprehensible desire that "Pericles"
should have been acted once for the first time at the
beginning of Shakespeare's dramatic career, and that its
representation in 1609 should have been only a revival,.
he undermines the whole argument. It is impossible to
reconcile this notion with the testimony of contemporary
witnesses, who agree in calling it a new play ; and if it
had appeared on the stage before the close of the sixteenth century, Meres, in enumerating Shakespeare's
works in 1598, would hardly have forgotten to mention
so popular a piece. For the simplest and most rational
explanation of the matter we must turn to M. François
Victor Hugo, who sheds light upon every point in his
excellent remarks preceding his translation of "Pericles:"

"Mr. Knight's bold conjecture," he writes, "is entirely superfluous.
It does not necessarily follow that because 'Pericles' was written by

Shakespeare when he was young, that it must therefore have been acted in Shakespeare's youth. Without going far to seek I could furnish evidence to show that a long interval may elapse between the conception of a work and its publication. Ever since 1839 I have known of the first four acts of a drama which is, I think, entitled 'The Twins,' which is still awaiting completion at the bottom of a certain portfolio. For one reason or another its termination up to this time has been postponed, and the play which was begun in the second period of the author's style will necessarily be finished in the third. I may be allowed to lay stress upon this fact, although perhaps a somewhat personal one, because it contains the very explanation that Mr. Knight sought for in vain. For some reason, for some caprice perhaps, or some trifling hindrance, this play of 'Pericles' which was conceived by Shakespeare when quite a young man, remained in an unfinished state for many years; so that it was only in the seventeenth century that he was able to work up the piece which he had in all probability sketched out before the year 1590. And this is why it could only see the light in 1609, although its creation belonged to the days of Shakespeare's youth, and also explains why it should exhibit such striking disparity of style."

Dryden, who was in a position to be well-informed, being a contemporary of three old actors who had formerly been comrades of Shakespeare, and whose testimony ought therefore not to be lightly rejected, positively says in his prologue to Sir Charles Davenant's " Circe," that " Shakespeare's own muse his 'Pericles' first bore." One of the finest parts, it appears, of the celebrated actor Burbadge was that of the Prince of Tyre, and it is indeed easy to conceive how the representation of a hero ageing act by act, more from the effect of sorrow than of time, and being finally restored to youth and life by the successive transports of two immense, unlooked-for joys, might be a triumph of acting. Gervinus suggests that Shakespeare may have chosen this play simply for the sake of giving this part to Burbadge (p. 111), but in 1590 Burbadge had not yet appeared, and Gervinus himself admits that " it is difficult to believe " that in the beginning of the seventeenth century, in the full maturity of his power, Shakespeare should have written a play so full of defects both of style and of plot, simply for the purpose of furnishing an actor with an advantageous part. But once admit that " Pericles " had been sketched out twenty years before, and there is no absurdity in the conjecture that the poet's wish to give a friend and comrade a splendid opportunity for displaying his talents may have been the determining cause which made him put the finishing touch to his work.

CHAPTER XVI.

SHAKESPEARE AND PLUTARCH.

FOR the material of the three Roman tragedies, "Julius
Cæsar," "Antony and Cleopatra," and "Coriolanus,"
Shakespeare drew exclusively upon Plutarch. An interval of at least half a dozen years separates the first
tragedy from the other two, the latest in point of date
being "Coriolanus," which would appear not to have
been written before 1608. For reasons stated further
on, I shall take these three plays in the order in which
they were written, and not in that of historical facts.
An English translation, by Sir Thomas North, of the
"Lives" of Plutarch appeared in 1579. This, as I have
already said, was not taken from the Greek text, but
was simply a version of the French translation by
Amyot, whose genius had at once invested it with all
the importance of an original work. North made no
attempt to revert to the Greek, and frankly called his
book, "The lives of the noble Grecians and Romans compared together by that grave, learned philosopher and
historiographer, Plutarch of Chæronea. Translated out
of Greek into French by James Amyot . . . and out of
French into English by Sir Thomas North, Knight."

No sign of Shakespeare having read Plutarch appears in his plays until we come to "Julius Cæsar," in
the beginning of the seventeenth century. The ingenious conjecture by which M. Philarète Chasles endeavours to explain in what manner this translation of

Sir Thomas North's came to attract Shakespeare's attention, has already been alluded to. From him we learn of the copy of Montaigne's "Essays" in the British Museum, which contains Shakespeare's signature, and the date 1603 written by his own hand, besides his marks with the pen, and various marginal notes. It is a folio copy, published in English by Florio, an Italian who was acquainted with several languages. But even without this palpable proof—this copy of Montaigne annotated by the hand of Shakespeare—no doubt could be entertained as to his knowing the "Essays," as several evident recollections of them, and even quotations, are to be found in his plays—notably in the "Tempest," in which a fragment of the chapter "On Cannibals" is introduced. M. Chasles imagines that Shakespeare's curiosity was aroused by Montaigne's praises of Plutarch, and his attention was thereby called to North's translation, which had been published twenty-four years before. He looks upon the year 1603, in which Shakespeare read Montaigne's "Essays"—pen in hand,—as a turning-point in his literary and moral development, from which the direction of his genius into a new channel may be dated. Up to that time, the poet had mistaken his path, frittering away his time and talent in the by-ways of fancy, of comedy, and of the historical drama; but his meeting with Montaigne was a revelation to him—a journey, as it were, on the road to Damascus, and the deep sources of tragedy were laid open to his gaze by the great French moralist. M. Philarète Chasles would willingly insinuate that we are indebted to Montaigne, not only for "Julius Cæsar," but also for "Hamlet," and for all Shakespeare's great works up to the "Tempest." But this conjecture is based on too slight a foundation. An earlier date by a year or two than 1603 is assigned, with every appearance of probability, by the most recent efforts of criticism, to the first representation of "Julius Cæsar." M. Chasles might, it is true, reply that the edition of 1603 to which Shakespeare's copy belonged, was a reprint, and that the first English edition having appeared in 1601, he might still have known the "Essays" when he wrote "Julius Cæsar;" besides, putting translations aside, he doubtlessly knew French well enough to run through them in the original before studying them more closely in his English copy. But all this is nothing but conjecture, and the influence it attributes to Montaigne over the development of Shakespeare's genius is a gratuitous supposition quite unjustified by the few traces in his writings of his having read the "Essays." However, be it as it may with the part played by Montaigne between Shakespeare and Plutarch one thing is abundantly clear, and that is that Shakespeare only knew Plutarch at third-hand,—through the English version of Amyot's translation. Ample proof of this has been given in a former chapter, in considering the question that animated criticism of the pedantic sort to such a ridiculous degree, as to whether Shakespeare knew Greek. There is no necessity to repeat the evidence here, or to show how closely the poet followed the translation even down to its mistakes, or to point out the numerous passages which are simply transcribed from it. The interest attaching to this comparison of texts was merely superficial, and the subject of the present chapter is of deeper and graver import, in which Shakespeare is no longer to be compared with North or Amyot, but with Plutarch—the poet with the historian. The matter is no longer one of words, but concerns the inmost heart of things.

In his Roman tragedies, with the exception of a few instances to be mentioned further on, Shakespeare has generally followed Plutarch so faithfully and minutely that they are almost, so to speak, only the lives of Cæsar.

of Brutus, of Antony, and of Coriolanus *dramatized*. If a poet of the rigid French school were to borrow the materials for a tragedy from Plutarch, we can picture to ourselves what his mode of procedure would be. From the varied and ample information supplied by the Greek historian, he would choose out a few salient points and some clearly defined set of circumstances; then, rigorously excluding all the rest, with this single situation and his selected features he would make up a fine work maybe of its kind, but of which the essential beauty would consist in its unity, simplicity, and clearness; it would be a dramatic extract from Plutarch, but it would not be Plutarch himself dramatized. But Shakespeare's method is far less austere, and of greater width; a masterly breadth of touch everywhere characterizes his handiwork. It would be a manifest absurdity to say that he made no choice and excluded nothing, since selection, and therefore also exclusion, is an elementary, an essential condition of every work of art; but the multiplicity of detail in his plays is so amazing that the thought never occurs to us that all this abundance is only a choice out of yet vaster treasures, and that the knowledge and memory and imagination of the poet were incomparably greater than any tangible result he has left of them. We forget that his ideal was always infinitely beyond the work he actually accomplished, and that he had in his own mind stores of materials a thousand times richer and more varied than his dramas; and it is because we overlook all this, that the impression given us by his dramatic translation of Plutarch is that of a most prodigal use of materials, which appears—but it is in appearance only—to exclude nothing, and to aim at reproducing everything.*

---

* "Art cannot get on without abstraction. A choice must inevitably be made among all the many elements of human life, but the truth of art consists in preserving the greatest possible number of them."—Vinet.

Having said this, the critical remark may now fearlessly be ventured on, that however true Shakespeare
may generally be to the profoundest rules of art in his
mode of laying the historian under contribution, it would
be difficult to deny that he sometimes a little overdoes
the borrower's part, and rather encumbers his plays with
his gleanings. The mind cannot stand it; it is incapable of following indefinitely a succession of dazzling
pictures as in a magic lantern, and it is impossible to
read "Antony and Cleopatra," in which Shakespeare
has followed Plutarch more closely and completely than
in any other of his Roman tragedies, without a sense
of fatigue. To enumerate all the passages in which
Shakespeare has followed or imitated Plutarch, in
"Julius Cæsar," in "Antony and Cleopatra," or in
"Coriolanus," would be a long and tedious business, and
in fact, to say what he has added or altered would be
the shorter plan; but the all-important point is, that
Shakespeare, who usually treated the sources of his
materials with but scant courtesy, showed the utmost
deference and submission towards Plutarch. He never
wittingly allowed himself any essential modification of
the given facts, and his wish would seem to be to trans-
form—if such a thing were possible—the whole account
into a drama. It may be safely said, that in his Roman
tragedies, he followed Plutarch far more closely than he
did even the old English chroniclers in his plays drawn
from English history.

The reason of this is not far to seek;—it lies in
Plutarch's genius, in his poetical imagination, which was
his dominant quality and the source alike of his defects
and of his merits; and also in his tastes and instincts
as a moralist, to which his capacities as an historian were
subordinate.

Shakespeare found history already half turned into
poetry in Plutarch, whose greater love for moral truth

than for historical accuracy was what specially recommended him to Shakespeare as well as to Montaigne,
who, in his charming essay " On Books," says :—

" But they who write lives by reason they take more notice of
counsels than events, more of what proceeds from within doors than
what happens without, are the fittest for my perusal ; and therefore, of
all others, Plutarch is the man for me."

" In the same way that a painter chiefly seeks after
resemblance in the features of the face and in the eyes, in
which the nature of the man most sensibly manifests
itself," Plutarch more particularly studies " the distinctive
marks of the soul in the smallest facts, in witty answers
and lively off-hand remarks, which often show a man's
character more clearly than murderous combats, or great
battles, or the taking of towns." These are Plutarch's
own words ; and M. Gréard, from whom I have borrowed
the quotation, adds :—

" He was the first among ancient historians who ventured to introduce familiar details into history ; and he passes, without the
slightest embarrassment, from the humblest particulars to the most
lofty considerations." *

These words exactly apply to the method pursued
by Shakespeare himself, and might be used to describe
one of the characteristics of his art and style in tragedy.

" Plutarch," says also Jean Jacques Rousseau, " excels in such
details as no one would now dare to enter into. There is an inimit-
able charm in portraying great men by little things, and he is so
happy in his choice that often a word, a smile, a gesture is enough to
give the character of his hero. Hannibal reassures his frightened
army with a jest, and leads it laughing to the battle which lays Italy
at its feet ; Agesilaus riding with his children on a stick, makes me
love the conqueror of the great king ; Cæsar, passing through a little
town in the Alps, betrays the ambitious impostor who gave out that
his desire was only to be equal with Pompey ; Alexander swallows
the suspected dose of physic without a word,—and this is the grandest

---

* " La Morale de Plutarch."

moment of his life. Aristides, in writing his own name on the shell, completely justifies his surname of The Just ; Philopœmen, throwing off his cloak, chops up wood in his host's kitchen. This is the true art of painting character ; the expression of a man's face is not revealed in its principal features, and it is in trifling matters that the nature of the man discloses itself rather than in the great actions of life. Public affairs are too common and too much a matter of course, and yet it is considered beneath the dignity of our present writers to mention any others."

Having begun to quote the opinions of celebrated writers on the subject of Plutarch's talents, I must not omit the eloquent and well-known passage in which M. Villemain praises his picturesque qualities and the mine of artistic wealth he offers both to painter and poet :

" What finer and more animated pictures could there be than the farewells between Brutus and Portia, the triumphs of Paulus Æmilius, Cleopatra in her galley sailing along the river Cydnus, or the scene so graphically told of Cleopatra leaning out of the window of her inaccessible tower and exerting all her strength to draw up the cord to which the wounded and dying Antony was fastened ? And besides these, there are many other admirably vigorous descriptions and brilliant pictures, added to which are the familiar little details, which he gives in the most simple and natural manner, taking men in the very act, and painting the depths of their characters by showing all their littlenesses. This peculiar faculty of his, which has been universally recognized, has perhaps tended to hide his wonderfully graphic power and the brilliancy of his style, but it is to just this twofold character of eloquence and of truth that the influence he exercises over all lively imaginations is due. No other example need be cited than that of Shakespeare, who was never more truly inspired than he was by Plutarch, to whom he owes his most sublime and lifelike scenes in ' Coriolanus ' and in ' Julius Cæsar.' . . . The secret of the immense interest excited by Plutarch's ' Lives ' is to be found in the vivacity of his style combined with his felicitous choice of the greatest subjects that can occupy the thought and the imagination. He has drawn the portrait of mankind, and has well recorded the grandest characters and the noblest actions of the human race."

Of the Roman tragedies, as of all the great works of Shakespeare, the pre-eminent beauty consists in the delineation of character ; but before entering upon a psychological analysis, and studying each character in turn carefully and thoroughly, it will be well to give a few instances of the skill with which Shakespeare has turned Plutarch's narrative into a dramatic work, taking them from the very surface of the play, so as not in any way to encroach upon the study of the characters which will constitute our whole examination of the Roman tragedies.

The portentous events that preceded and announced the death of Cæsar are thus related in North's Plutarch :

" Certainly destiny may easier be foreseen than avoided, considering the strange and wonderful signs that were said to be seen before Cæsar's death. For, touching the fires in the element, and spirits running up and down in the night, and also the solitary birds to be seen at noon-days sitting in the great market-place : are not all these signs perhaps worth the noting in such a wonderful chance as happened ? But Strabo the philosopher writeth, that divers men were seen going up and down in fire : and furthermore that there was a slave of the soldiers that did cast a marvellous burning flame out of his hand, insomuch that they who saw it thought he had been burnt ; but when the fire was out, it was found he had no hurt. Cæsar himself also, doing sacrifice unto the gods, found that one of the beasts which was sacrificed had no heart : and that was a strange thing in nature, how a beast could live without a heart."

Here we have the account in its bare simplicity and somewhat cold enumeration of details, faults which not all the imagination of Plutarch could entirely prevent, resulting as they do from the inevitable inferiority of the historical style to that of dramatic poetry. Let us now see the movement and colour, the life and passion, given to things by Shakespeare (Act I., Sc. 3).

" *Cicero.* Why are you breathless ? and why stare you so ?
    Casca. Are not you moved, when all the sway of earth
Shakes like a thing infirm ? O Cicero,
I have seen tempests, when the scolding winds
Have rived the knotty oaks ; and I have seen
The ambitious ocean swell, and rage, and foam
To be exalted with the threat'ning clouds :

But never till to-night, never till now,
Did I go through a tempest dropping fire.
Either there is a civil strife in heaven ;
Or else the world, too saucy with the gods,
Incenses them to send destruction.

    Cic. Why, saw you anything more wonderful ?

    Casca. A common slave (you know him well by sight),
Held up his left hand, which did flame and burn
Like twenty torches join'd ; and yet his hand,
Not sensible of fire, remain'd unscorch'd.
Besides (I have not since put up my sword),
Against the Capitol I met a lion,
Who glared upon me, and went surly by
Without annoying me : and there were drawn
Upon a heap a hundred ghastly women,
Transformed with their fear ; who swore they saw
Men all in fire walk up and down the streets.
And yesterday the bird of night did sit,
Even at noon-day, upon the market-place,
Hooting and shrieking.   When these prodigies
Do so conjointly meet, let not men say
' These are their reasons,—They are natural,'
For I believe they are portentous things
Unto the climate that they point upon.

    Cic. Indeed, it is a strange-disposèd time :
But men may construe things, after their fashion,
Clean from the purpose of the things themselves.
Comes Cæsar to the Capitol to-morrow ?

    Casca. He doth ; for he did bid Antonius
Send word to you he would be there to-morrow.

    Cic. Good night, then, Casca ; this disturbed sky   •
Is not to walk in.

    Casca.   Farewell, Cicero."

Mark the profound harmony between Nature and the agitated souls of men, and the tragic events about to happen.   Men cannot rid themselves of a confused and undefined feeling, which at times is sweet and soothing, but more usually terrible, as of a mysterious union exist- ing between all parts of the universe, and of the interest taken by the heavens above in the affairs on the earth beneath.   It is this strange sympathy between the

physical and moral worlds that gives its deep meaning
to the speech of a philosopher to an artist :—" You are
greatly behind your time if you think that it is of
no interest to know what sort of weather it was in
Rome on the day that Cæsar was assassinated." Shakespeare, with the instinct of a great poet, has carefully
and solemnly noted each hour that passes, from the eve
of Cæsar's death up to the moment when the first blow
is struck—night, dawn, eight o'clock, nine o'clock.*

But no passage expressive of these subtle feelings and
impressions is more remarkable than one that occurs in
the same tragedy, which, though very short and apparently insignificant, becomes full of meaning when rightly
apprehended.

The conspirators enter Brutus' garden at night, where
he is awaiting them, and while Cassius and he converse
aside in a low voice, the others stand about and talk.
And what do they say ? We might expect them to utter
imprecations against tyranny and the tyrant, to bind
themselves with oaths, and to flourish their swords
about, so as to perform well their part of conspirators,—
conspirators, moreover, of subordinate importance,—before
the public, as an ordinary poet would not fail to make
them. But Shakespeare is not an ordinary poet, and his
genius has inspirations that completely disconcert all the
common notions of rhetoric ; not that he aims at originality, but he closely watches Nature, and Nature reserves
many surprises for those who have only studied theatrical
effects.

Pointing to the horizon, Decius says :—

" Here lies the east : doth not the day break here ?
    Casca. No.
    Cin. O, pardon, sir, it doth ; and yon grey lines
That fret the clouds are messengers of day.

---

* See Dowden's " Shakspere : His Mind and Art," p. 295.

Casca. You shall confess that you are both deceived.
Here, as I point my sword, the sun arises,
Which is a great way growing on the south,
Weighing the youthful season of the year.
Some two months hence, up higher toward the north
He first presents his fire ; and the high east
Stands, as the Capitol, directly here." (Act II., Sc. 1.)

Nothing could be more natural : when men have their minds burdened with the load of some great enterprise, they are glad to avoid speaking of it amongst themselves, and it is when they are most absorbed in thought that conversation has the greatest tendency to turn upon trivial and indifferent matters. Every one experiences this over and over again in his life : when suffering or witnessing some great sorrow, when attending the service of the dead, the very intensity of our feelings prevents us from speaking of them, and we only talk at such times of mere nothings, of the heat, the cold, the weather.

In the "Tartufe," Cléante, when he comes to see Orgon for the express purpose of speaking to him about some serious family business, opens the conversation with the remark : " The flowers are very backward still in the country."

Arnolphe, in " L'École des Femmes," wishes to speak to Agnes of a subject that he has terribly at heart, and takes a walk with her, when the following conversation ensues :

" *Arn*. What a pretty walk this is !
Ag. Very pretty.
Arn. What a beautiful day !
Ag. Very fine.
Arn. Any news ?
Ag. The little kitten is dead.
Arn. That is very sad ; but, after all, we are all mortal, and each one takes care of himself. Didn't it rain when I was in the fields ? "

But in the scene from " Julius Cæsar " there is something more than an accurate observation of nature,—

X

it is full of an intense poetry. This discussion of the
conspirators before the dawn, on the Ides of March, as
to the precise point of the horizon in which the sun
would rise, eloquently proclaims the importance of the
day in the annals of mankind. Nor, surely, are we
pushing criticism too far in attributing a symbolical
meaning to the last words spoken by Casca, " The high
east stands, as the Capitol, directly here," and in seeing
in these significant words, the meaning of which might
be more fully brought out by the tone and gesture of
the actor, an allusion to the new era by which he hoped
and believed the death of Cæsar would be followed—the
glorious dawn of Liberty.*

Casca's dramatic account of the prodigies given by
Plutarch, is not the only one in the tragedy: Calphurnia
too, Cæsar's wife, relates what she has heard, when
frightened by a dream, she tries to deter her husband
from going to the senate :—

> " There is one within,
> Besides the things that we have heard and seen,
> Recounts most horrid sights seen by the watch.
> A lioness hath whelped in the streets ;
> And graves have yawn'd and yielded up their dead :
> Fierce fiery warriors fight upon the clouds,
> In ranks, and squadrons, and right form of war,
> Which drizzled blood upon the Capitol :
> The noise of battle hurtled in the air,
> Horses did neigh, and dying men did groan ;
> And ghosts did shriek and squeal about the streets.
> O Cæsar ! these things are beyond all use,
> And I do fear them."

Yielding to his wife's entreaty, Cæsar consents to
stay at home. We will turn first to the account given
by Plutarch :—

" But in the mean time came Decius Brutus, in whom Cæsar put
such confidence, that in his last will and testament he had appointed

---

* See the remarks made on this passage by Mr. Knight and Mr. Craik.

him to be his next heir, and yet was of the conspiracy with Cassius and Brutus: he, fearing that if Cæsar did adjourn the session that day, the conspiracy would be betrayed, laughed at the soothsayers, and reproved Cæsar, saying, ' that he gave the Senate occasion to mislike with him, and that they might think he mocked them, considering that by his commandment they were assembled, and that they were ready willingly to grant him all things, and to proclaim him king of all his provinces of the Empire of Rome out of Italy, and that he should wear his diadem in all other places both by sea and land. And, furthermore, that if any man should tell them from him, they should depart for that present time, and return again when Calphurnia should have better dreams, what would his enemies and ill-willers say, and how could they like of his friends' words ? And who could persuade them otherwise, but that they would think his dominion a slavery unto them, and tyrannical in himself? 'And yet if it be so,' said he, 'that you utterly mislike of this day, it is better that you go yourself in person, and, saluting the Senate, to dismiss them till another time.' Therewithal he took Cæsar by the hand and brought him out of his house."

Whosesoever the fault may be, whether it be with the historian or with the translator, this account is wanting in light and shade, and even in clearness and precision, especially when contrasted with the force and life with which Shakespeare has endowed it in its dramatic form :—

" *Decius.* Cæsar, all hail ! Good morrow, worthy Cæsar :
I come to fetch you to the senate-house.
　　Cæsar. And you are come in very happy time,
To bear my greeting to the senators,
And tell them I will not come to-day :
Cannot is false ; and that I dare not, falser ;
I will not come to-day : tell them so, Decius.
　　Cal. Say he is sick.
　　Cæs. 　　　　　　Shall Cæsar send a lie ?
Have I in conquest stretch'd mine arm so far,
To be afeard to tell greybeards the truth ?
Decius, go tell them Cæsar will not come.
　　Dec. Most mighty Cæsar, let me know some cause,
Lest I be laugh'd at when I tell them so.
　　Cæs. The cause is in my will, I will not come ;
That is enough to satisfy the senate.

> But, for your private satisfaction,
> Because I love you, I will let you know;
> Calphurnia here, my wife, stays me at home:
> She dreamt to-night she saw my statue,
> Which like a fountain, with an hundred spouts,
> Did run pure blood; and many lusty Romans
> Came smiling, and did bathe their hands in it.
> And these does she apply for warnings and portents,
> And evils imminent; and on her knee
> Hath begg'd that I will stay at home to-day.
>   *Dec.* This dream is all amiss interpreted;
> It was a vision fair and fortunate:
> Your statue spouting blood in many pipes,
> In which so·many smiling Romans bathed,
> Signifies that from you great Rome shall suck
> Reviving blood; and that great men shall press
> For tinctures, stains, relics, and cognizance.
> This by Calphurnia's dream is signified.
>   *Cæs.* And this way have you well expounded it.
>   *Dec.* I have, when you have heard what I can say:
> And know it now; the senate have concluded
> To give, this day, a crown to mighty Cæsar.
> If you shall send them word you will not come,
> Their minds may change. Besides, it were a mock
> Apt to be render'd, for some one to say,
> 'Break up the senate till another time,
> When Cæsar's wife shall meet with better dreams.'
> If Cæsar hide himself, shall they not whisper,
> 'Lo, Cæsar is afraid?'
> Pardon me, Cæsar: for my dear, dear love
> To your proceeding bids me tell you this;
> And reason to my love is liable.
>   *Cæs.* How foolish do your fears seem now, Calphurnia!
> I am ashamèd I did yield·to them.—
> Give me my robe, for I will go."

The anxiety of Portia, Brutus' wife, whilst her husband, whose terrible secret she has extracted from him, is at the Capitol, is well told by North, in a charming and vivid manner:—

"Portia being very careful (anxious) and pensive for that which was to come, and being too weak to away with so great and inward grief of mind, she could hardly keep within, but was frighted with every little noise and cry she heard, as those that are taken and possessed with the fury of the Bacchantes; asking every man that came from the market-place what Brutus did, and still sent messenger after messenger to know what news."

We are thankful for anything so full of life and stir as this, but in the drama it is fuller still. (Act II., Sc. 4.)

" *Por.* I prithee, boy, run to the senate-house;
Stay not to answer me, but get thee gone ;
Why dost thou stay ?
    Luc.   To know my errand, madam.
    Por. I would have had thee there, and here again,
Ere I can tell thee what thou should'st do there.—
O constancy, be strong upon my side !
Set a huge mountain 'tween my heart and tongue !
I have a man's mind, but a woman's might.
How hard it is for women to keep counsel !—
Art thou here yet ?
    Luc.   Madam, what should I do?
Run to the Capitol, and nothing else ?
And so return to you, and nothing else ?
    Por. Yes, bring me word, boy, if thy lord look well,
For he went sickly forth : and take good note
What Cæsar doth, what suitors press to him.
Hark, boy ! what noise is that ?
    Luc. I hear none, madam.
    Por.   Prithee, listen well.
I hear a bustling rumour, like a fray,
And the wind brings it from the Capitol.
    Luc. Sooth, madam, I hear nothing.
              Enter Soothsayer.
    Por.   Come hither, fellow. . . .
What is't o'clock ?
    Sooth.   About the ninth hour, lady.
    Por. Is Cæsar yet gone to the Capitol?
    Sooth. Madam, not yet; I go to take my stand
To see him pass on to the Capitol.
    Por. Thou hast some suit to Cæsar, has thou not ?
    Sooth. That I have, lady : if it will please Cæsar
To be so good to Cæsar as to hear me,
I shall beseech him to befriend himself.

Por. Why, know'st thou any harm's intended towards
    him ?
Sooth. None that I know will be, but much that I fear
    may chance.
Good morrow to you. . . .
    Por. I must go in.—Ah me, how weak a thing
The heart of woman is ! O Brutus !
The heavens speed thee in thy enterprise !
Sure the boy heard me :—Brutus hath a suit
That Cæsar will not grant.—O, I grow faint :—
Run, Lucius, and commend me to my lord ;
Say I am merry : come to me again,
And bring me word what he doth say to thee."

The tragi-comic incident of the death of the poet
Cinna is also made more of in Shakespeare than in
Plutarch. The difference will be noticed further on,
when we come to study the part played by the people
in the Roman tragedies, and it will serve to show how
Shakespeare occasionally modified the matter given by
the historian, for his fidelity to his model is, after all,
by no means absolute ; important reservations have to
be made on this point, and several noticeable exceptions
must be observed. For instance, Plutarch says positively
that Coriolanus, when desirous of obtaining the consul-
ate, conformed without resistance to all the usages of the
law : Shakespeare's Coriolanus, on the contrary, revolts
against the idea of soliciting the votes of the people, and
is infinitely more haughty and imperious all through
the play, from beginning to end, than he is represented
in Plutarch.

The plebeians of the early days of the Republic, with
their strong sense of their rights, but also of their duties,
passionately attached to their country and its laws,—
firm, grave, resolute men, who offered a perfectly quiet
and pacific resistance to the pretensions of the nobles by
their orderly retreat to Mons Sacer,—the old Romans who
could hardly have been the dregs of humanity, since

from them sprang Rome in all her greatness, become in Shakespeare's plays the mob of a modern London or Paris ; a blind mass incapable of any political thought, led by low and obscure instincts, swayed by demagogues this way and that, stupid, base, and above all dastardly, in spite of Plutarch's express statement to the contrary.*

In Plutarch, Antony is frankly despicable and even positively odious, while Shakespeare adds many happy and delicate touches which render him, if not an alto-gether lovable, at least an interesting and well-nigh a beautiful character. Again, Plutarch insists upon the paternal tie by which, according to a scandalous story of the time, Brutus was united to Cæsar; to this, Shake-speare has thought it unnecessary to make the slightest allusion.

In every case of deviation from Plutarch, Shakespeare finding himself placed, as it were, between poetry and history, which are sometimes at variance, invariably followed the higher laws of poetry; in some instances unconsciously, and in others with a clear knowledge of what he was doing. He was, doubtless, perfectly aware that he was heightening the character of Coriolanus, that he was idealizing that of Antony, and increasing the grandeur of that of Brutus; but it was probably without knowing it or intending it, that he was unjust towards the plebeians of the early Republic, and changed them into a common street rabble. But here, also, his instinct as a poet guided him aright,—taking Shakespeare's con-ception of the subject, some such alteration was impera-tively called for, in order to justify the torrents of scorn poured out by Coriolanus upon the people, and to

---

* Shakespeare's injustice towards the plebeians of early Rome has been particularly well shown by Kreyssig, in his commentary on Corio-lanus. See his " Vorlesungen über Shakespeare," Vol. I., pp. 468 and following.

prevent his character from appearing in too offensive a light, and in order also to secure the concentration of our whole admiration on this colossus of haughtiness and passion, without a moment's disturbance from the world of mediocrities by which he was surrounded and isolated.* That a poet is not an historian, and that he is not called upon to write an historical work, is a truth that can never be too often repeated. And it is on account of this, and because nothing could aim less at being a course of Roman history than Shakespeare's Roman tragedies, that there is no occasion to invert their order, and substituting the succession of historical facts for that of their composition, to study " Coriolanus " before " Julius Cæsar." To take these tragedies as a text or pretext for historical commentary would be a very formidable undertaking, which would involve more rectifying of mistakes than marks of approval, but besides this and more than this, it would be one of those deadly sins against poetry which are too often committed at a time when literary criticism, strictly so-called, is universally neglected and its place usurped by every kind of learned research which belongs to quite another region. Shakespeare has been lauded by many critics for his vast knowledge of Roman affairs, but there is quite as much error in these praises as there is truth ; all that appeals to the poetic sense, such as the grandeur of soul of a Brutus, the patriotism of a Volumnia, the aristocratic pride of a Coriolanus, has been seized by Shakespeare, and as admirably rendered as it could have been by Corneille. The remarkable affinity, moreover, that exists between the genius and character of the English people and that of the Romans, stood him in peculiarly good stead.

" A certain hardness without any poetry," writes Heinrich Heine, "an avidity in sanguinary pursuits, an indefatigable energy and

---

* See Hallam's " Literature of Europe," Vol. III., p. 329.

firmness of character, are qualities that distinguish Englishmen of to-day as much as they did the ancient Romans; only these last were land rats rather than water rats, but as to the utter absence of amiability it is as strongly marked in the one case as in the other.'

Shakespeare has portrayed his Romans truthfully, in so far as they are Englishmen,—so far goes his historical exactitude, and no further. As to the incongruous details with which these plays abound, I attach no importance to them whatever, but the case is very different when it comes to confusing, as he has done, the early days of the Republic with those of the Empire, and no greater mistake could be made than to confound the proud brave plebeians of Rome, at the beginning of her greatness, with the degraded populace of the Rome of later times.

With the exception of this one blunder, which is the only one of any consequence, Shakespeare's tragedies are *poetically true.* Poetic truth is not quite the same thing as historical truth, and it is poetic truth alone that should be demanded of a poet who chances to borrow the subject of his plays from history. History offers an immense proportion of insignificant details which contain no interest and no ideas, and are consequently of not the slightest value in the sight of art, and the true function of the poet is to penetrate to the centre of this vain and useless heap, and to seize the very soul of things : he idealizes by leaving aside all that is superfluous, by disengaging the essential elements, by being clearer than history and truer,—that is to say, by giving to the thought a greater prominence and a firmer solidity than it is practically possessed of—an operation that has been compared by Vinet to that of the extraction from carbon of the diamond. The tragedy of "Antony and Cleopatra," for instance, produces a more vivid impression upon the imagination than any accounts given by history do, of an era drawing to its close, of an order of things about to

crumble away, which is the special aspect of the period
that the artist wished to present.   Ronsard, in his "Pré-
face sur la Franciade," after showing how the historian
follows the actual fact at every step, while the poet
devotes himself to what is possible and likely to be true,
adds this excellent remark :

> " Many people think that the historian and the poet pursue the
> same calling, but this is a great mistake, for they are two workmen
> who have nothing in common, except that neither the one nor the
> other *may ever go contrary to the truth of things.*"

So that upon both poetry and history, though aiming at
different sides of truth, it is equally incumbent to be
true.   And indeed, in more than one sense poetic truth
may be said to have the superiority over historical
truth :—

> " The difference between the historian and the poet," says Aristotle,
> " is not that one speaks in verse and the other in prose.   The real
> distinction is, that the one relates what has been, the other what
> might have been.   On this account poetry is more philosophical and a
> more excellent thing than history, for poetry is conversant with the
> universal, history with the particular."

Aristotle is right, poetry is more general than history,
and in this sense is more philosophical.   But not in this
sense only, for poetry has the same superiority over
history that ideas have over facts, that mind has over
matter, and that the human reason and conscience have
over the blind course of events.

   This thought has been most eloquently developed by
Bacon, who, not content with saying with Aristotle that
poetry relates what *might* have happened, boldly declares
that it relates what *ought* to have happened.   Our introduction to the study of Shakespeare's Roman tragedies
may fitly close with this magnificent passage from the
"Advancement of Learning" (The Second Book, iv. § 2):

> " The use of this feigned history (as he calls poetry) hath been to
> give some shadow of satisfaction to the mind of man in those points

wherein the nature of things doth deny it, the world being in proportion inferior to the soul; by reason whereof there is, agreeable to the
spirit of man, a more ample greatness, a more exact goodness, and a
more absolute variety, than can be found in the nature of things.
Therefore, because the acts or events of true history have not that
magnitude which satisfieth the mind of man, poesy feigneth acts and
events greater and more heroical. Because true history propoundeth
the successes and issues of actions, not so agreeable to the merits
of virtue and vice, therefore poesy feigns them more just in retribution
and more according to revealed providence. . . . And therefore poesy
was ever thought to have some participation of divineness, because it
doth raise and erect the mind, by submitting the shows of things to
the desires of the mind; whereas reason doth buckle and bow the mind
into the nature of things."

CHAPTER XVII.

JULIUS CÆSAR.

NONE of Shakespeare's three Roman tragedies would appear to have been printed before the famous folio of 1623, the first complete edition of his plays. There are sufficiently cogent reasons for thinking that "Julius Cæsar" was written at latest in 1601, which is the date of Weever's "Mirror of Martyrs," a forgotten poem recently discovered by Mr. Halliwell, which in all probability alludes to the most famous scene of "Julius Cæsar" in the lines :—

> "The many-headed multitude were drawne
> By Brutus' speech, that Cæsar was ambitious;
> When eloquent Mark Antonie had showne
> His vertues, who but Brutus then was vicious?"

And this discovery confirms an inference that had already been drawn by Payne Collier from Drayton's poem of the "Barons' Wars" (published in 1603), in which a passage occurs apparently inspired by the lines in which Mark Antony describes the character of Brutus (Act V., Sc. 5). The date assigned to the two other tragedies is that of about seven or eight years later.

But even if external evidence were wanting in support of their relative order in point of time, it would be abundantly apparent from a comparison of the plays themselves, that "Julius Cæsar" must have been written a considerable time before the others. Shakespeare's language grew more and more concise, rich, and full. The style of "Julius Cæsar" is characterized by simplicity and breadth of touch, and each sentence is clear, easy, and flowing, with the thought clothed in perfect and adequate expression: the lines are as limpid as those of "Romeo and Juliet," but without their remains of rhyme and Italian conceits. Of all Shakespeare's works, none has greater purity of verse or transparent fluency. It belongs to what may be called Shakespeare's second and most perfect style. "Antony and Cleopatra" and "Coriolanus," on the contrary, belong to his later period, in which his works abound in metaphors, and in abrupt and elliptical expressions, to such an extent that their meaning is in places difficult to make out.

These questions of date are not without their interest: it is not a matter of indifference to know that "Julius Cæsar" is closely connected with "Hamlet" in point of time. In the latter play, which was published in its final form in 1604, the poet's imagination is still full of the thought of Cæsar; as, for instance, in the first scene, in which, after the ghost has vanished, Horatio says :—

> " A mote it is to trouble the mind's eye.
> In the most high and paling state of Rome,
> A little ere the mightiest Julius fell
> The graves stood tenantless, and the sheeted dead
> Did squeak and gibber in the Roman streets," etc.

Again, in Act III., Sc. 2, Polonius boasts of how well he acted in the university :—

> " *Pol.* I did enact Julius Cæsar; I was killed in the Capitol: Brntus killed me ; "

not to mention Hamlet's moralizing in the churchyard

on the dust of Alexander and of "Imperial Cæsar."
But "Hamlet" and "Julius Cæsar" stand to each other
in a far closer relationship than that implied by stray
reminiscences and details; they belong to the same
current of reflections and ideas, and the poet's thought
in each lies in the same direction. In the earlier one,
Shakespeare has drawn a noble nature grappling with
a duty enforced in no actual and binding category, and
which, from its doubtful and uncertain character, deeply
troubles the conscience of the hero, who questions and
considers and weighs it over and over again: Brutus
has a passionate love for justice, but is led astray by the
exacting demands of a too delicate and lofty soul. In
the other tragedy, the same note is again struck, but
with this considerable variation, that with Hamlet,
although the duty is more imperious, yet his uncertainty
is greater: he, too, thirsts after the Ideal, but with him
the generous instincts of the heart are mingled with
all the graceful refinements and superb disgusts, all the
baffling turns, of an over-subtle brain, and the end of
his hesitations is a rapid moral decadence. Brutus, after
his deliberation, acts resolutely; he greatly errs, but he
preserves our esteem and sympathy to the end: Hamlet
—always deliberating—errs in a far graver manner by
never acting at all, and our respect for him finally goes.
Both of them are men of meditative and studious nature,
called by circumstances to a line of action repugnant to
their whole character. But of this deep inner affinity
that unites "Hamlet" with "Julius Cæsar," there is
none between "Julius Cæsar" and the two later Roman
tragedies. "Antony and Cleopatra" and "Coriolanus,"
both written about the same time, proceed from an
entirely new order of thoughts and reflections, their
motive being the portrayal of selfishness, which in the
one case presents itself in an amiable, open, and attractive character, and in the other, in a proud and reserved

one. All these plays are pre-eminently ethical studies, not historical sketches.

The mode in which I purpose studying the Roman tragedies is simply that of taking each personage in turn, and following him throughout his part. All æsthetic criticism of Shakespeare must be founded on the study of his characters, for it is his subtle and varied delineation of them that forms his special and supreme merit. On this point, his pre-eminence has never been disputed,— not even when every other quality of his dramatic talent was most severely called in question. The eighteenth century and the nineteenth century are here in full accord, and no one has written of Shakespeare as a creator of souls better than Pope in his preface to Shakespeare's works :—

"His characters are so much nature herself, that it is a sort of injury to call them by so distant a name as copies of her. Those of other poets have a constant resemblance, which shows that they received them from one another, and were but multipliers of the same image; each picture, like a mock rainbow, is but the reflection of a reflection. But every single character in Shakespeare is as much an individual as those in life itself; it is as impossible to find any two alike; and such as, from their relation or affinity in any respect, appear most to be twins, will, upon comparison, be found remarkably distinct. To this life and variety of character, we must add the wonderful preservation of it, which is such throughout his plays that, had all the speeches been printed without the very names of the persons, I believe one might have applied them with certainty to every speaker."

Macaulay gives a still more lively and striking expression to the same thought when he, in his turn, observes that although in defining the characters of Hotspur and of Faulconbridge almost the very same terms would have to be employed, yet the two men resemble each other so little, that there is perhaps not a single word spoken by Hotspur which would not be out of place if given to Faulconbridge. The most hostile critic that

Shakespeare has met with in our own times, Gustave Rümelin, reproaches him with the inadequate and improbable motives by which his characters are occasionally led; he blames him for not having always sufficiently matured the conception or compressed the plot of his plays, but he never refuses him the creative gift.

This gift, this power, is the very summit of dramatic art, and it is to the poet who possesses it in the highest degree that the crown of victory belongs. To create *one* character is no small achievement, but Shakespeare scatters them up and down his ideal world with the lavish hand of Nature herself. In the whole realm of literature there are not so very many characters we can count, and amongst the number how enormous a proportion we owe to Shakespeare! In reading the works of even the greatest novelists and most famous dramatists we meet with not many personages, drawn with such truth, such originality and life, as to take and for ever retain in our imaginations bodily form and expression as of living persons, whose features and bearing, whose tones and gestures are more familiar to us than those of our actual friends, and whom we are quite sure have really existed, and whom we fancy we have somewhere seen.

To weave the rich and intricate tissue of a clever plot requires no mean skill, or so to combine varied and complicated situations, as, without tiring the reader or offending his good sense, to hold his attention in suspense throughout a series of surprises, leading up to an unexpected but not unnatural climax. But greater still, incomparably greater, is the creation of characters, the peopling of the ideal world with beings who shall live for ever, and the gift of such reality to these phantoms that the persons that we call real, for the specious reason that they possess a body, look like shadows by their side. And to give them so distinct an individuality, that beneath all general outward resemblances, each one of them should be stamped with his own special and distinguishing mark, and that this small but definite number of deathless types should represent the very limited circle of human passions, and yet, at the same time, the inexhaustible variety of nature, is the true miracle of art and the divine element in genius,—poetry then becomes creation, and poets win a place among the gods.

CÆSAR.

The character of Cæsar offers a comparatively ungrateful subject with which to begin a psychological study of the Roman tragedies; not, indeed, that it is wanting in interest when Shakespeare's meaning comes to be fathomed, but because it is strange and unexpected, and perplexingly unlike the ordinary idea we fashion to ourselves of the Roman hero; the first impression it leaves upon the mind is that of a vague surprise and disappointment.

Cæsar enters without any imposing grandeur, and his first words betray a weak and superstitious spirit. He says nothing of any importance, and passes by. Then Cassius tells Brutus the story of Cæsar's fool-hardiness, which led him, "on a raw and gusty day," to challenge Cassius to swim across "the troubled Tiber chafing with her shores," and of his physical weakness which obliged him to implore help from Cassius. He goes on to tell how—

> " He had a fever when he was in Spain,
> And, when the fit was on him, I did mark
> How he did shake : 'tis true this god did shake :'
> His coward lips did from their colour fly ;
> And that same eye whose bend doth awe the world
> Did lose his lustre : I did hear him groan."

Y

The immortal ghost of his victim appears one night to him in his tent, and Brutus, terror-struck, exclaims:

> "Ha! who comes here? . . .
> It comes upon me!   Art thou anything? . . .
> Speak to me what thou art."

And the spectre answers :—

> "Thy evil spirit, Brutus; . . .
> To tell thee, thou shalt see me at Philippi."

At the supreme moment in the senate, Cæsar is not without a certain dignity, but it is the dignity of an Oriental despot, intoxicated with absolute power, and there is no real greatness in the majestic airs he affects, or in his inflexible refusal to repeal the sentence of banishment passed on Publius Cimber. And so, at the beginning of the third act, after having appeared only in three scenes, the hero of the tragedy, or at least the personage who has given his name to the play, dies, assassinated. This is surely very strange, and we may be very sure that it has not been passed by in silence on the part of critics. Shakespeare has been reproached with wronging Cæsar, by showing only the lowest and meanest sides of his character, and in making him speak in a ridiculous and inflated manner that is quite at variance with that simplicity of style in which his commentaries are written, of which Montaigne remarks that it is peculiar to great captains when relating their own deeds, "for what they have done is more glorious than what they say." Boswell says :—

"There cannot be a stronger proof of Shakespeare's deficiency in classical knowledge than the boastful language he has put in the mouth of the most accomplished man of all antiquity, who was not more admirable for his achievements than for the dignified simplicity with which he has recorded them."

"Fénélon's censure of our plays," says M. Villemain, "on account of the pompous and emphatic manner in which they make their Romans talk, applies with far greater force to Shakespeare's 'Julius Cæsar.'"

Rümelin ridicules this custom of common tragedians, of making the chief characters use big words, into which, he says, Shakespeare was unable to avoid falling.

M. Mézières writes :—

"Shakespeare presents us with a conventional Cæsar very different from that of Plutarch—a proud and arrogant Cæsar whose strained and exaggerated language forms a marked contrast to the simplicity of the 'Commentaries,' which was so well preserved by the Greek historian. He never tells us of the lofty thoughts with which, to the very last, the mind of the master of the world was occupied, nor mentions the new conquests that his genius was preparing when he was struck down by the swords of the assassins. And more than this, he completely ignores his generosity and clemency, and the openness of a great nature which trusts its enemies too entirely to take any precautions against them. It is but a poor defence of this rendering of Cæsar's character, to say, with certain critics, that the subject of the play being the life of Brutus, and not that of Cæsar, Shakespeare was right in showing the feeble side of Cæsar's character, his vanity and arrogance, and his ambition after regal honours, in order to justify the conspirator's conduct. To decide that only part of the truth shall be told is no excuse for the decision. The poet was under no obligation to follow the plan he adopted, and it is simply futile to attempt to place his work beyond reach of censure by the plea of a choice which he need not have made unless he had wished. In any case, it must be acknowledged that he, in this instance, contrary to his custom, fails to be impartial. I admit that he recovers his impartiality in Antony's admirable speech to the people; but, after all, it is poor justice to praise Cæsar dead, and to call the tragedy by his name by way of attesting that greatness which should have been made more apparent in the part played by Cæsar alive."

Here we have the adverse criticism in all its strength; but it is not, I think, wholly unanswerable.

In the first place, it must be observed that Shakespeare's plays give proof—and that repeatedly—of his knowledge of "Cæsar's Commentaries," and of his being fully aware of the hero's historical importance. In "Henry VI." (Pt. 2, Act. IV., Sc. 2), he mentions the Commentaries by name, when quoting a sentence from them; and in "Richard III.," Julius Cæsar is referred to in the significant dialogue between Edward Prince of Wales and his terrible uncle (Act III. Sc. 1)—

> " *Prince.* Say, uncle Gloster, if our brother come,
> Where shall we sojourn till our coronation?
>   *Glo.* Where it seems best unto your royal self.
> If I may counsel you, some day or two
> Your highness shall repose you at the Tower. . . .

Prince. I do not like the Tower, of any place :—
Did Julius Cæsar build that place, my lord ?

Glo. He did, my gracious lord, begin that place;
Which, since, succeeding ages have re-edified.

Prince. Is it upon record ? or else reported
Successively from age to age, he built it ?

Glo. Upon record, my gracious lord.

Prince. But say, my lord, it were not registered ;
Methinks, the truth should live from age to age,
As 'twere retail'd to all posterity,
Even to the general all-ending day.

Glo. [*Aside.*] So wise so young, they say, do never live
    long. . . .

Prince. That Julius Cæsar was a famous man :
With what his valour did enrich his wit,
His wit set down to make his valour live :
Death makes no conquest of this conqueror ;
For now he lives in fame, though not in life."

The passage has been already cited from " Hamlet "
in which Horatio speaks of " the mightiest Julius ; " and
he is referred to in " Antony and Cleopatra " as " broad-
fronted Cæsar." Coming, finally, to the very tragedy
under discussion, even if the mighty Julius does not
appear to advantage in his own person, still the events
by which his death is preceded and followed, the dis-
turbances in nature and the civil war let loose, show
clearly enough that in the poet's mind, it was no insignificant man that fell.*

Why, then, did Shakespeare deliberately set to work
to disparage his hero ? For, whether right or wrong, it
is evidently the result of choice on his part; and it is
impossible to ascribe to mere negligence a contrast so
disproportionate as that existing between the Cæsar who
makes his appearance in a few short and rapid scenes,
and the grand ideal Shakespeare himself had of him,

---

* Hudson's " Shakespeare : His Life, Art, and Characters," Vol. II.,
p. 225; also Dowden's " Shakespeare : His Mind and Art," p. 285.

which ideal he well knew was shared in by all his audience, and would continue to be held by them in spite of everything.

The first explanation of this singular anomaly may be found in history, for Shakespeare's Cæsar contradicts the testimony of historians less than is commonly alleged. Plutarch gives us to understand that a few days before his death—that is, just about the time at which the play begins, a great alteration took place in Cæsar's character : he had "a covetous desire to be called king,"—king, indeed, was not enough ; every one knows that Cæsar aspired to nothing lower than the honours paid to divinity itself. The solemn oration which he gave, while still quite a young man, over the grave of Julia, shows that these aspirations date back to the first years of his public life.

> "My aunt Julia by the mother's side came of royal blood, and by the father's was related to the gods themselves ; for her mother was of the house of the Marcii, descended from Ancus Martius, King of Rome, and her father was of that of the Julii, who sprang from Venus, and of which we are a branch. So that kings whose persons are sacred, and they the greatest of men, and the gods whom we worship and in whose hands are kings themselves, both concur to render our family great and illustrious." (Suetonius.)

Suetonius further relates how, one evening, Cæsar "mounted the Capitol by torchlight, forty elephants carrying flambeaus on each side." It was towards the end of his life that he said such things as that "the commonwealth was become an empty name, without either reality or appearance," and that "men ought to take care what they said to him at that time of day, and look upon his dictates as laws."

> "He not only," Suetonius continues, "arrogated too great honours upon himself as the continual exercise of the consulship, the perpetual dictatorship, the power of censor under a more specious name, the title of Emperor and Father of his Country, his statue amongst the

kings, a partionlar box for himself at the theatre; but accepted of others too big for the circumstances of bare mortality to support : as a chair of gold in the senate and assemblies of the people, the carrying of his effigies in solemn procession at the Circenscan games, templos, altars, images of himself placed near the gods, a consecrated couch for his godhead's statue to repose upon, his priest common to other deities, and the credit of having one month in the year called after his own name. . . . But the most flagrant odium he drew upon himself was from his haughty deportment to the senators."

Here, however, we will rather turn to Plutarch, who relates the same thing :—

"When they had decreed divers honours for him in the senate, consuls and prætors, accompanied with the whole assembly of the senate, went unto him in the market-place, where he was set by the pulpit for orations, to tell him what honours they had decreed for him in his absence. But he sat still in his majesty, disdaining to rise up unto them when they came in, as if they had been private men."

This is the Jupiter that Shakespeare found in history and represented in his tragedy. It pleased him to lay stress upon the physical weakness and human infirmities of this divinity, which he also found indicated in Plutarch. Suetonius likewise, relates that towards the end of his life Cæsar was subject to sudden swoons, and to a sleep so troubled that he often awoke in terror, and that twice he had epileptic fits, in a public assembly of the people.

It is easily seen that in carefully preserving these details and in adding even further maladies, such as fever and deafness, Shakespeare's intention was to bring into prominent notice this clay, this dust, this mud, on which Hamlet was one day to philosophize: "Thou art but a mortal god, O Cæsar, and already thou crumblest into dust ! "

But I think it is possible to penetrate deeper into the poet's thought than this. Not only in body but also in mind was Cæsar becoming enfeebled in those last days of his life ; he was superstitious and frightened, he had lost all foresight and firmness of purpose, and took refuge in a grandiloquent and empty declamation; his mental collapse was everywhere evident. And yet, when the conspirators put a violent end to this poor exhausted spirit, which was dying of itself, the Republic gained absolutely nothing: the Emperor is no more, but the Empire is begun—Cæsar is dead, long live Cæsar!

By this, Shakespeare, with a depth of insight and observation, before which thought stands astounded and abashed, meant to show that the days of liberty in Rome were irrevocably ended, and that for the future the cause of her bondage would no longer be the commanding genius of a ruler, but the inward alteration in the public mind and disposition. What must have been the bitterness of spirit experienced by Brutus when, in answer to his proclamation of liberty from the Forum, he heard the stupid people cry in their enthusiasm, "Let him be Cæsar!" Had the empire depended only upon the genius of one man, Brutus, in killing Cæsar, might have saved the Republic, but in point of fact the Empire was rooted in the general state of things. It was in not perceiving this that the error of Brutus lay, and from this also resulted the utter failure of his enterprise. It is not the spirit of any one man, but the spirit of a new era about to begin—the spirit of *Cæsarism*—that fills Shakespeare's play and gives it its unity and moral significance, and therefore it is that this tragedy, in which Cæsar appears in only three scenes, and neither says nor does anything of importance, is called "Julius Cæsar" and not "Marcus Brutus."

From the very first scene we feel the shadow of Cæsarism hanging over Rome, ready for a state of servitude. The people are in the streets, keeping holiday as on some great feast day, dressed in their best clothes, and decorating Cæsar's statues. The tribunes, Flavius and Marullus, are indignant at the sight, and roughly rebuke

their fellow-citizens, but far from being the mouthpiece of
the Republican spirit, they are only former followers of
Pompey, whose great name they use as a weapon against
Cæsar's partisans.

> " O, you hard hearts, you cruel men of Rome,
> Knew you not Pompey ? Many a time and oft
> Have you climbed up to walls and battlements,
> To towers and windows, yea, to chimney-tops,
> Your infants in your arms, and there have sat
> The livelong day, with patient expectation,
> To see great Pompey pass the streets of Rome, . . .
> And do you now put on your best attire ? . . .
> And do you now strew flowers in his way,
> That comes in triumph over Pompey's blood ?
> Be gone !
> Run to your houses, fall upon your knees,
> Pray to the gods to intermit the plague
> That needs must light on this ingratitude."

There is a scene in Plutarch by which any other poet
than Shakespeare might have been led astray, for it
would almost appear from it as if the Roman people were
still capable of choosing between freedom and slavery, in
favour of freedom :—

> " So Antonius came to Cæsar, and presented him a diadem, wreathed
> about with laurel. Whereupon there rose a certain cry of rejoicing,
> not very great, done only by a few appointed for the purpose. But
> when Cæsar refused the diadem, then all the people together made an
> outcry of joy. Then Antonius offering it him again, there was a second
> shout of joy, but yet of a few. But when Cæsar refused it again the
> second time, then all the whole people shouted."

This is what may be called a regular trap laid by
history to catch poetry in, and Voltaire, with all his wit,
fell right into it, and even out-did Plutarch in these lines
from " La Mort de Cæsar : "—

> " Du peuple que l'entoure Antoine fend la presse ;
> Il entre, ô honte ! ô crime indigne d'un Romain !
> Il entre, la couronne et le sceptre à la main.

On se tait, on frémit. Lui, sans que rien l'étonne,
Sur le front de César attache la couronne,
Et soudain, devant lui se mettant à genoux :
' César, régne,' dit il, ' sur la terre et sur nous.'
Des Romains, à ces mots, les visages pâlissent,
De leurs cris douleureux les voûtes retentissent ;
J'ai vu des citoyens s'enfuir avec horreur,
D'autres rougir de honte et pleurer de douleur.
César, qui cependant lisait sur leur visage
De l'indignation l'éclataut témoignage,
Feignant des sentiments longtemps étudiés,
Jette et sceptre et couronne, et les foule à les pieds.
Alors tout se croit libre, alors tout est en proie
Au fol enivrement d'une indiscrète joie."

But Shakespeare was not to be imposed upon by this apparent love of the Roman people for liberty, the shallowness of which at this time he truly divined : his account of the scene in the Forum is an admirable instance of the sovereign authority with which poetry, as Bacon has so splendidly pointed out, corrects history, not by falsifying its spirit, but by rendering it more at one with ideal truth.   The wonderfully vivid account full of grim humour, given by Casca, of Cæsar's refusal of the crown (Act I., Sc. 2), lets us plainly see that the cheering of the populace had nothing solid, nor even intelligent, about it, and that if Cæsar had been only bold enough to set the crown upon his head, the same rabble that applauded his respect for the law would have been equally ready to applaud his violation of it.

Cæsar dead, the people's one fear is that " a worse may come in his place; " that another must necessarily succeed him seems to be taken for granted.*   This is the spirit of Cæsarism, the spirit that Brutus could not slay. It would even seem as if, after the violent death of the

---

* Gervinus.

feeble body, the spirit of Cæsar grew immeasurably, covering the whole tragedy with its shadow.*

In the last three acts, in which Cæsar is no longer numbered amongst the living, his power and influence are far greater than in the first two. "Woe," cries Antony (Act III., Sc. 1)—

> "Woe to the hand that shed this costly blood!
> Over thy wounds now do I prophesy,—
> Which, like dumb mouths, do ope their ruby lips,
> To beg the voice and utterance of my tongue,—
> A curse shall light upon the limbs of men;
> Domestic fury, and fierce civil strife,
> Shall cumber all the parts of Italy, ...
> And Cæsar's spirit, ranging for revenge,
> With Até by his side, come hot from hell,
> Shall in these confines, with a monarch's voice,
> Cry 'Havoc,' and let slip the dogs of war."

"O, Julius Cæsar!" says Brutus himself, when standing over the dead body of Cassius—

> "Thou art mighty yet!
> Thy spirit walks abroad, and turns our sword
> In our own proper entrails."

---

* The posthumous greatness of the demi-god has been very finely expressed by a poet not often cited for praise. Scudéry, in his tragedy, "La Mort de César" (1636), which contains many beautiful lines and striking scenes, makes a citizen give the senators this account, with which the play closes:—

> "Sénateurs, apprenez la plus grande merveille
> Que peut-être jamais ait frappé votre oreille;
> Hier au soir, ennuyé de voir tant de méchants,
> J'allay passer la nuit dans la douceur des champs:
> Mais revenant au point que la clarté s'allume,
> Mon œil a vu César, plus grand que de coutume,
> D'un port majestueux, d'un regard éclatant,
> Qui s'élevait sur Rome, et qui, dans un instant,
> Par cette agilité dont une âme est pourvue
> A traversé les airs, ayant lassé ma vue:
> Mais au même moment s'est fait voir à mes yeux
> Un astre tout nouveau qui brillait dans les cieux."

The immortal ghost of his victim appears one night to him in his tent, and Brutus, terror-struck, exclaims :

> "Ha! who comes here? . . .
> It comes upon me!   Art thou anything? . . .
> Speak to me what thou art."

And the spectre answers :—

> "Thy evil spirit, Brutus; . . .
> To tell thee, thou shalt see me at Philippi."

CHAPTER XVIII.

• JULIUS CÆSAR (*continued*). BRUTUS. CASSIUS.

BRUTUS.

THE personage of Cæsar, as seen in the last chapter, presents no coherent whole, of mingled qualities, good and bad, such as constitute a character properly so-called; and indeed the Roman hero would seem to be effaced and reduced almost to a nonentity. The strange whim that led Shakespeare to show Cæsar in his weakness rather than in his strength has, as already observed, considerably shocked certain of his critics, who have unhesitatingly condemned his conception of the character as superficial and false.

That it is quite possible for Shakespeare sometimes to make mistakes, either through inattention or through ignorance, I am quite willing to admit; his infallibility is no article of my creed, and there is perhaps not a single play of his which seems to me entirely perfect in every point: if there is one weakness more than another against which I would specially be on my guard, it is that enthusiasm of a common kind which consists in admiring everything and in justifying everything in the author chosen for study. Nothing is more calculated to render criticism insipid and to deprive it of all authority than this indiscriminate mode of praise. Shakespeare's plays, like Molière's—and to a much greater extent than those of Molière—are full of scenes which must have been composed and written at too rapid a rate not to be defective in some part or other.   It was impossible for these men, mixed up as they were with the active and all-devouring life of the theatre, always to have time to elaborate their works patiently in the silence of the study.   It was not so much that they *wrote* them, that they shaped them with their pen, as that they threw them, so to speak, all boiling and in a state of fusion on the stage, as into the mould in which they were to receive their form.   And consequently their literary labours bear, here and there, signs, easily discerned, of haste and of pressure of the moment, signs which it would be vain to deny and which systematically-admiring critics do wrong to forget.

To find fault with the conceptions of such poets as Molière and Shakespeare is not, however, a matter to be lightly entered upon, and a man may well look twice or thrice before doing so.   It is a noticeable fact, and one from which criticism might learn an important lesson in modesty and prudence, that of two judgments concerning a great writer, one of which blames him for the very same thing for which the other praises him, and justifies his praise, it is invariably the approving criticism that strikes us as most significant and most thorough ; not, perhaps, necessarily as the most true, but it presents itself under a more exquisite, a more distinguished, and a more original aspect, which prepossesses us in its favour.   The reason of our preference is very simple : all adverse judgment of poetry is, from its very nature, negative, and in the main superficial, evil being a pure negation, and the faults being only too obvious, lying, as they generally do, on the surface.   But the case is otherwise with its beauties, which are positive and real, and often lie hidden, so that he who enables us to see them is bestowing upon us a solid possession, and we feel that he must at least have penetrated to a certain depth to have discovered these pearls of great price.

As concerns the personage of Cæsar, no very extraordinary penetration was required to make the discovery. A little attention only was needed to justify Shakespeare's rendering of the character, and to reveal all the hidden beauty and the moral and poetic significance in that presentation of the Roman hero, shorn of his usual grandeur and importance, at which over-hasty critics have taken exception. It is evident that Shakespeare intended by the very weakness of Cæsar to show the strength of Cæsarism, and in the fall of the individual to mark the irresistible advance of the principle.

But here let me be clearly understood, for it must not be imagined that this evident intention on Shakespeare's part implies that it existed in his mind with the same clearness that it does in the explanations and commentaries of critics. It is true that the exaggerated and erroneous notion which has often been held of Shakespeare's unbridled and unconscious imagination necessitates a special insistance upon his insight and lucidity of mind, but it would be only falling into the contrary error—and one no less grave—to attribute to Shakespeare a clear and complete consciousness of his own beauties. Genius does not know itself entirely throughout, and in this blissful ignorance a portion of its strength resides. To see too clearly into itself would have a disastrous effect, for reflection, to a certain extent, is fatal to inspiration.

" The poet," says Goethe, " should look upon all his lofty perceptions and imaginations and great thoughts as so many unhoped-for gifts from above, and purely as children of God, who must be received with respectful joy and veneration. There is in them a sort of demoniac power, which leads men where it will, while they believe themselves to be acting of their own accord. . . . When Shakespeare had his first thought of ' Hamlet,' when the idea of the whole scheme came into his mind as an unexpected impression, and when in a moment of sublime emotion he perceived the various combinations, the different cha-

racters and the final catastrophe, it was a pure gift from above, over
which he had had no direct influence, although, of course, for such a
sight to be possible presupposes the existence of a mind like his."—
(Conversations with Eckermann.)

To think out into clear relief all that genius has more
or less dimly conceived, and, Mercury-like, to be the
interpreter of the gods to men, is the highest aim of
æsthetic criticism. The true critic will never let himself
be stayed or troubled by the common objection, "You are
giving to poets a meaning which they never intended."
What matter whether they intended it or not, as long as
it is in their works? To develop fully and freely, to
analyse with boundless liberality, all that study can disclose, is the inalienable right of criticism; and it will
never be led astray if only it has due sympathy and
respect for the writer it is dealing with, and in no case
need it ever fear that it can exhaust its subject. The
function of a critic may very fitly be compared to that of a
great actor: if Shakespeare and Racine had seen their
plays interpreted by Garrick, Talma, Rachel or Sarah
Bernhardt, we cannot help thinking that they might
themselves have been a little astonished at all the wonderful things they had written; but they would have
made no objection or complaint, I fancy, on this account.
And this same good service is precisely what criticism
should endeavour to perform; to show poets themselves
how admirable their own works are, is at once its highest
and most legitimate ambition.

If, for various reasons, Cæsar's personality is not a
strongly accentuated one, the case is very different with
Brutus: his is a complete and finished character, and one
of the finest in all Shakespeare's plays.

In order to understand Brutus, it is well not to lose
sight of his relationship in point of date and of moral
sentiment with Hamlet. Brutus, like Hamlet, has been
said to be "a man of study, who, in spite of his natural

repugnance, has become a man of action, and has been carried by the stream of events into circumstances foreign to his nature." These words are not taken, as might be supposed, from a Shakespearian commentator, but were written by a narrator of the history of Brutus. And it is noteworthy that this description, in which M. Gaston Boissier* sums up his whole judgment concerning the Brutus of history, is at the same time the very best that can be given of the Brutus of poetry. There is no essential difference between the two; Shakespeare has simply omitted one or two traits which might have confused or altered the moral unity of the character, but he had nothing to add, and all that we are about to say of the Brutus of the drama will be found true at heart of the Brutus of actual history : the two portraits make but one.

Brutus had a passion for reading, and for books, but there are many different ways of liking books and reading ; some, for instance, delighting in them as materials for dreamy speculation, as did Hamlet and all his posterity down to Werther, René, and Obermann ; others prizing them for the sake of the mental culture they afford, like Cicero and other men of letters ; others again for the satisfaction of a craving after knowledge, like Terentius Varro, and scientific men of all periods. But Brutus was influenced by none of these motives ; what he asked for from books was food for moral meditation, and their aid in perfecting himself in virtue. Philosophical writers were those he valued above all others, and among these his especial favourite was Plato.

He was greatly given to self-examination and self-study, contemplating and observing himself so intently that the one great pre-occupation of his life might be said to be how to make himself a more noble character. To be noble, that is, to be just, upright, brave, generous, and all

---

* " Ciceron et ses Amis, étude sur la Société Romaine du temps de César."

the rest, implies indeed in one word the fulfilling of the
whole duty of man; still, in this very habit of making one's
own personality the centre of the world, and of regarding
things in general only in connection with oneself, there
lurks a kind of moral egoism, and the germ of a very
serious failing. By dint of so entirely directing his
attention inwards, Brutus became blind to outward
things, and lost the sense of reality. His idealism led
him, when confronted by the needs and requirements of
practical life, to commit very grave oversights; he
observed facts badly, and had no good sound judgment,
and was of all men the one who could least understand
and read the characters of others: witness, for example,
his enthusiastic praises of Cicero's son on account of a
few brilliant hopes to which he had at first given rise,
and he was quite unable to penetrate beneath the
deceitful surface and to discover the young man's
essential mediocrity.

His self-engrossed and meditative habits so isolated
him from the outer world, as to make him oblivious of
the duties of friendship, for which Cassius gently reproached him (Act I., Sc. 2). The reason, however, was
no lessening of affection on his part, only that—

> " Poor Brutus, with himself at war,
> Forgets the shows of love to other men."

In striking contrast with Henry V., who on the eve of
the battle of Agincourt visited his soldiers to cheer and
inspire them with the same courage and spirit that
glowed within himself, Brutus was always reading and
pondering. We see him in Shakespeare, on the eve
of the battle of Philippi, seated in his tent, taking up
a book and begging his servant to draw sweet strains
from his instrument to soothe away his cares. In
Plutarch, he is the same; on the day before the battle
of Pharsala, when every one else thought only of the

great struggle which was to decide the fate of the Republic and of the world, he was able to abstract his mind from all surrounding circumstances, and "wrote all day long till night, writing a compendium of Polybius."

Men of this temperament are not the predestined leaders of a party, and Brutus would never of himself, or from the unassisted promptings of his own nature, have become the head of the conspiracy against Cæsar. He would have let things follow their course, silently grieving in his heart at the direction they were taking, but doing nothing to prevent it. When he hears the shouts of the people, he says calmly—

> " I do fear the people
> Choose Cæsar for their king."

Cassius, eager and impetuous, catches at the expression, exclaiming—

> " Ay, do you fear it?
> Then must I think you would not have it so."

But Brutus answers gently—

> "I would not, Cassius ; yet I love him well."

And in this melancholy regret and dreamy sadness, Brutus, if left to himself, would have passed his days.

But the conspiracy needed him for its leader. Plutarch relates that—

> " When Cassius felt his friends, and did stir them up against Cæsar, they all agreed and promised to take part with him, so Brutus were the chief of their conspiracy. For they told him that so high an enterprise and attempt as that required a man of such estimation as Brutus, to make every man boldly think that by his only presence, the fact were holy and just. If he took not this course, then that they should go to it with fainter hearts ; and when they had done it, they should be more fearful : because every man would think that Brutus would not have refused to have made one with them, if the cause had been good and honest."

This gives an idea of the moral authority Brutus possessed, and of the respect he universally inspired. As Casca says (Act I., Sc. 3) :—

> " O, he sits high in all the people's hearts :
> And that which would appear offence in us,
> His countenance, like richest alchemy,
> Will change to virtue and to worthiness."

A passage from M. Boissier's historical study here comes in most appropriately :—

" Every eye was fixed on this earnest young man, with the pale, grave face, who was so unlike all the others. In accosting him, it was impossible to resist feeling an emotion, which seemed strangely out of keeping with his age,—that of respect. Even his elders and superiors, even Cicero and Cæsar, in spite of their glory, even Antony who so little resembled him, and his very opponents and enemies, were unable to shake off this feeling in his presence."

What Antony, in spite of all his levity, could not choose but admire and respect in Brutus was his disinterestedness, and his admiration is the more significant as coming from a foe, and a man of wild and corrupt life.

" Antonius spake it openly divers times," says Plutarch, " that he thought, that of all them that had slain Cæsar, there was none but Brutus only that was moved to do it, as thinking the act commendable of itself; but that all the other conspirators did conspire his death for some private malice or envy that they otherwise did bear him."

Shakespeare has made magnificent use of this passage at the end of his tragedy, when, standing by the dead body of Brutus, Antony says—

> " This was the noblest Roman of them all ;
> All the conspirators, save only he,
> Did that they did in envy of great Cæsar ;
> He only, in a general honest thought,
> And common good to all, made one of them.
> His life was gentle ; and the elements
> So mix'd in him that Nature might stand up,
> And say to all the world, ' This was a man ! ' "

In the war between Cæsar and Pompey, Brutus gave what may rightly be called an heroic proof of disinterestedness. He loved Cæsar and he detested Pompey, whom he could never forgive for having put his father to death; but he had the moral' strength to sacrifice his private affections to the good of his country, and considering Pompey's cause as the juster of the two, he took part with him. Acts like these could not fail to gain for him the respect and admiration of the great Roman people; and when the conspirators wished to speak to the people after Cæsar's death, it was Brutus that the crowd would alone consent to listen to; when another tried to speak, his voice was immediately drowned in cries and hooting.

But to insist too exclusively upon this nobility of nature in Brutus, and on the universal respect which he excited, might leave a false impression of his character if its qualifying and counterbalancing elements were not at the same time carefully noted.

Brutus was an eminently lovable person, which is rarely the case with those who inspire very great respect, for men's hearts, it must frankly be confessed, are not as a rule, attracted by moral perfection; it is indeed admired and venerated,—but coldly, and at a distance. The comparison is too humiliating for poor humanity to feel very great interest in the sight of irreproachable virtue; and so true is this, that Aristotle forbade the tragic poets to present blameless and altogether perfect heroes, lest they should weary their audience. But in order to bring the Brutus of history within this excellent rule, Shakespeare has no occasion to make any alterations; all he had to do was to clothe in the language of poetry the features of his character given by Plutarch.

Brutus was in reality a sensitive nature, gentle and tender-hearted as a woman; he had great apparent self-control, but it was due to his reason as a philosopher, which triumphed over his nature by an heroic effort of will, and this man of iron was in truth only a reed, and a reed that never grew so rigid as not at times to be felt to tremble. Nothing less resembles the real Brutus than the stiff inexorable stoic of the school of Seneca, that Voltaire has drawn with superficial eloquence in cold and rigid lines. He was beloved of the people and of his friends, "because he was a marvellous lowly and gentle person," as North has it. He had a horror of violence and bloodshed, and sickened at the sight of suffering and destruction. When the necessities of war obliged him to lay siege to a town in Asia Minor, and the inhabitants themselves set fire to it, the scene of unspeakable horror that ensued—men, women, and children throwing themselves into the flames, or casting themselves headlong from the walls—so roused Brutus' pity and sorrow that he rode round the walls, "and held up his hands to the inhabitants, praying them to pardon their city and to save themselves."

Nothing perhaps in the whole roll of dramatic poetry equals the tenderness given by Shakespeare to Brutus, that tenderness of a strong nature which the force of contrast renders so touching and so beautiful.* Note the kindliness of tone with which he speaks to his attendants, carrying his gentleness so far as to ask their pardon for his absence of mind (Act IV., Sc. 3)—

> " *Bru.* Look, Lucius, here's the book I sought for so;
> I put it in the pocket of my gown.
>   *Luc.* I was sure your lordship did not give it me.
>   *Bru.* Bear with me, good boy, I am much forgetful."

Fully to appreciate this short passage it is only necessary to remember that it was on the eve of the battle of Philippi, and the day after Portia's death, that Brutus thus begged his servant to bear with him for his

---

* "O that goodness of great natures! Their emotion, with which if they chose they might make the earth shake, is at times so soft and so sweet that it is like the rocking of a cradle."—Victor Hugo.

forgetfulness. He asks Lucius for a little music, which he loved, and even this detail has its significance when contrasted with the brief remark made by Julius Cæsar respecting Cassius, " he hears no music."

> " *Bru.* Canst thou hold up thy heavy eyes awhile,
> And touch thy instrument a strain or two?
> *Luc.* Ay, my lord, an it please you.
> *Bru.*   It does, my boy :
> I trouble thee too much, but thou art willing.
> *Luc.* It is my duty, sir.
> *Bru.* I should not urge thy duty past thy might;
> I know young bloods look for a time of rest."

So Lucius sings, and falls gradually asleep over his music; Brutus, with the tenderness of a mother, rises carefully not to awake the boy, and gently draws the instrument from his hands, for fear he should break it in his sleep, then sits down again, and taking up one of his beloved books, goes on with it where he had last left off.

This " marvellous lowly and gentle " nature inclined him to acquiesce too readily in the wishes of others :—

" He could offer no resistance," says M. Boissier, " to those he loved. His mothers and his sisters had great influence over him, and more than once led him into error; he also had numerous friends to whose advice Cicero reproached him with paying too great attention; they were well-meaning people, but without any knowledge of affairs, only Brutus was too tenderly attached to them to be able to free himself of their counsels."

Cassius was quite alive to this trait in his character, and in his soliloquy, in which he considers how he can win the high-minded Brutus over to the conspiracy, exclaims—

> " Well, Brutus, thou art noble; yet I see
> Thy honourable metal may be wrought
> From that it is disposed."

The plan adopted by Cassius, who was a skilful reader of men's characters, was to lure Brutus by in-

voking his sense of honour and duty. If he appealed
to any lower motives Brutus would turn a deaf ear,
but by speaking to his conscience, Cassius at any rate
ensured a hearing. In Shakespeare, Cassius is the sole
inventor of a plot, which in Plutarch is represented as
being the work of many, cleverly contrived to stir up
Brutus to action.

Cassius begins by telling Brutus, who is standing
by him grave and thoughtful as usual, that all the
citizens of "best respect" in Rome look to him, and
count upon him to free his country from its yoke, but
that he is prevented by his modesty of mind and by his
habit of living within himself from being aware of the
general attention of which he is the object. By degrees
Cassius comes nearer to his point and speaks more
urgently—

> "O! you and I have heard our fathers say,
> There was a Brutus once that would have brook'd
> The eternal devil to keep his state in Rome,
> As easily as a king."

And here begins the tragedy in the soul of Brutus. He
hated tyranny, but he loved Julius Cæsar. Shakespeare
has passed Plutarch's hint over in silence, as to Brutus
being Cæsar's own son, not considering any complication
of emotion of this kind necessary to the dramatic
interest, and wishing to preserve the tragedy in purer
and more ideal regions, by not allowing the conscience of
his hero to be disturbed by the too obtrusive pleadings
of a love enforced by the ties of nature.

The soliloquy in Act II., in which Brutus debates
the point raised by Cassius and finally makes his resolve,
is an extremely puzzling one. This avenger of the
Republic gives utterance to not a single republican
sentiment, and is exclusively occupied with the question
of the alteration that Cæsar's nature might undergo, if
he were given the crown. As in the eyes of Brutus the

attainment of the crown would only serve as a ladder to
Cæsar's ambition, he decides that he must be prevented
from reaching "the top-most round." To this metaphor
of the ladder, he adds another metaphor, drawn from the
sun that hatches the serpent's egg, and the conclusion of
the whole discourse is—

> "Therefore think him as a serpent's egg,
> Which, hatched, would as his kind grow mischievous;
> And kill him in the shell."

Brutus might surely have faced the position of affairs
far more simply by frankly looking at it from a republican point of view. One is inclined to speculate,
whether in this strange meditation on the dangerous
effect the crown might have on Cæsar's nature, Shakespeare intended to show the subjective tendency of
Brutus' mind, and his habit of scrutinizing things below
the surface; or whether it may not be an illustration of
the hold that his affectionate and gentle disposition had
over him. It would almost seem that, in his love for
Cæsar, he could suffer his acceptance of the crown, if
only he were sure that Cæsar would not abuse his power.
He weighs calmly and impartially the considerations on
either side, admitting that—

> "To speak truth of Cæsar,
> I have not known when his affections sway'd
> More than his reason."

But the stern republican fibre of his nature checks this
confidence and makes him dread the possible consequences to the liberty of the people, and in the end
triumphs over all hesitation. According to this view
we see him, indulging indeed to a certain extent the
psychological bent of his mind, but it is directed towards
practical ends. The acquisition of kingly power may
change Cæsar's nature, and if so, what would be the effect

on the nation? The chances are that it would be of the most disastrous kind, therefore "kill him in the shell."

However, be it as it may with his soliloquy, Brutus, when he has once made up his mind, is henceforth inflexible. Here we see the wide difference between him and Hamlet; his heart is bleeding, the thought of what he is about to do, at times makes him shudder with horror, but the thing is decided and he will never draw back. "Grave and deliberate," writes M. Boissier, "he always advanced gradually, but once resolved he gave himself up to his idea fully and unrestrainedly; he would isolate himself from everything else and concentrate his whole force upon it. The more he reflected, the deeper grew his devotion to it, until he heard nothing but the inexorable logic which prompted him to put it into action. His was one of those minds of which Saint-Simon says that they are carried along by a *fanatical sequence of thought*, and Cæsar said of him "what he he wishes, he willeth it vehemently."

That Brutus, when chief of the conspiracy, should allow the conspirators to bind themselves by no oath, declaring that the conscience of each man and the rightfulness of their cause affords ample security for the accomplishment of the deed, and sanction of the bonds that unite them, is a fine and characteristic touch. The serious question now arises, what is to be done with Antony? Cassius, a man of acute judgment and foresight, though with but little magnanimity in his composition, goes straight to the point, and gives it as his opinion that he too should die: "Let Antony and Cæsar fall together," and the event proved how right Cassius was. But here, notwithstanding all the grandeur of his character, Brutus gives the first signs of mental blindness, the blindness of a mind entirely shut up within the walls of its own generous chimæras.

> " Let us be sacrificers, but not butchers, Caius.
> We all stand up against the spirit of Cœsar ;
> And in the spirit of men there is no blood :
> O, that we then could come by Cœsar's spirit,
> And not dismember Cœsar."

The beautiful dream of this idealist is to fight against ideas without fighting against men. He despises Antony, because of his dissolute habits and consequent worthlessness in the austere eye of Brutus, but in this he makes the fatal mistake of judging as a moralist instead of as a statesman, and of failing to perceive that Antony's wild life was no guarantee whatever of intellectual mediocrity.

" There is nothing so rare in the world," says the old Duc de Broglie, " nothing so difficult as for a man to wish for what he wishes ; by which I mean wishing for it with all its consequences, good or bad, pleasant or unpleasant, and to accept without a murmur all its attendant evils."

In spite of what Cœsar said of him, Brutus did not really possess this rare virtue of wishing for what he wished, in the Duc de Broglie's sense of the words, and the only true one,—that of never quailing before the measures which lead to the desired end. He had, undoubtedly, an admirable firmness of resolution, and nothing could be finer than his attitude in the senate on the morning of the Ides of March, when the conspirators, alarmed by a passing word from one of the senators, think they have been betrayed; even Cassius loses his head and talks of killing himself, but Brutus remains calm, he takes in the situation with perfect coolness, and perceiving that the alarm is false, keeps up the spirit of his companions, who were ready to slink away, overcome with fear. But in order thoroughly to wish for what one wishes, it is not enough to be firm; a little foresight and knowledge of likely results is also requisite. And here Cassius was better off than Brutus, for he had the power of forecasting the inevitable consequences of actions: as Professor Dowden remarks, he is the political Jacobin, anxious to carry out to its fullest extent the enterprise which the gentler nature of Brutus would willingly have kept within the limits of the Girondins. Brutus' plan—if he had one—was of such an abstract and utopian nature, that it was equivalent to having none at all, and was based upon a complete misconception of the circumstances and needs of the time. It was the plan of an idealist who fancied himself living in the Republic of Plato, instead of being in the midst of all the tumult of a town in revolution.

This plainly shows itself after Cæsar's death, when Brutus commits the enormous imprudence of allowing Antony to speak at Cæsar's funeral. Cassius at once measured the consequences of this error, and says to Brutus, "You know not what you do."

But, whatever it may be in the future, up to the present time at all events, "politics," as M. Guizot says, "is not the work for saints," and, in the words of Socrates, "it is impossible to conduct public affairs with the same honesty as those of private life." Human nature being what it is, those nobler souls whose abstract love of liberty would lead them to bestow it fully and completely upon their enemies, and who cannot understand that there are occasions in which things must be carried with a high hand, and in which the application of their great principle is impossible, had far better keep clear of public matters, at least in such cases of peculiar emergency.

With angelic candour, Brutus trusts Antony, because he knows only his own heart, and he knows well that *that* is to be trusted. "He cannot credit or conceive the base facts of life. He has no instrument by which to gauge the littleness of little souls." (Dowden, p. 291.)

Antony is accordingly allowed to speak to the people, Brutus imposing on him but the one condition of speak-

ing no evil of the conspirators, while saying all the good
he can of Cæsar. For his own part, Brutus flatters himself that he will obviate the danger dreaded by Cassius,
by first mounting the pulpit himself, and explaining to
the people—and this one sentence paints the whole man
—"the reason of our Cæsar's death." The *reason,*—to
speak of reasons to a crowd! It is even to such a point
as this that Brutus is carried by his illusions; his ignorance of men's hearts and his blindness to actual facts, we
have already seen, but until now he had given no proof
of his absolute want of common sense. So little does he
know of men, that when addressing the multitude he
speaks to them as to so many philosophers like himself,
he sternly forbids himself any persuasive eloquence of
animated gesture or pathetic tones, because he himself
despises any appeal made to the imagination or to the
passions, and cares only for what recommends itself to
his reason. His speech is a model of the most finished
conciseness and studied coldness; but the irony of facts
brings about as unexpected a turn of affairs as ever
humiliated the eloquence of a public orator. His speech
was received with loud applause, it is true, but silence
would have been better. Brutus spoke of one thing, and
all the people understood another: when he spoke of
liberty, of the love of country and of justice, the people
understood him as asking for power and honours; when
he spoke of the glory of having cast down tyranny, the
people thought to please him by offering to make him
Cæsar!

It may be worth while to note in passing that the
laconic and sententious style in which Brutus addresses
the people was suggested to Shakespeare by a passage in
Plutarch, as Mr. Hudson has observed:—

"In some of his speeches he counterfeited that brief compendious
manner of the Lacedæmonians. As when the war was begun, he wrote
to the Pergamenians in this sort: ' I understand you have given Dola-

bella money: if you have done it willingly, you confess you have offended me; if against your wills, show it by giving me willingly.' Another time, again, unto the Samians: ' Your councils be long, your doings be slow, consider the end.'"

Professor Dowden adds, " This peculiarity of style is not confined to Brutus' address to the people. It appears, for example, in his final and deliberate reply to Cassius (Act I., Sc. 2):—

> " That you do love me, I am nothing jealous !
> What you would work me to, I have some aim. . . .
>   What you have said,
> I will consider; what you have to say,
> I will with patience hear."

Brutus, when too late, recognized the error he had been guilty of, in allowing Antony to give a funeral oration over Cæsar's body. Little by little he learned, through bitter experience, to know the actual facts of life, and all his illusions one by one dropped off from him. Invariably led on by his noble nature, he persisted in following its generous impulses; not till it was too late did he discover that the view taken by the more earthly-minded Cassius had unfortunately been true. Such is his history up to the last day of his life, on which, in a final fit of blindness, he decided, contrary to the advice of Cassius, that the army should advance to Philippi.

The death of Brutus was not merely the penalty he paid for a series of imprudent and mistaken actions, but was also the expiation of a great crime. Dante and Virgil, after having travelled through the eight circles of hell, and having arrived at the lowest abyss of all, perceive the three-faced monster, " the Emperor of the realm of sorrow," who " at every mouth a sinner champed,"—

> " Bruised as with ponderous engine; so that three
> Were in this guise tormented. But far more
> Than from that gnawing, was the foremost pang'd
> By the fierce rending, whence oft-times the back

Was stript of all its skin. 'That upper spirit
Who hath worst punishment,' so spake my guide,
'Is Judas, he that hath his head within
And plies the foot without. Of th' other two,
Whose heads are under, from the murky jaw
Who hangs, is Brutus: lo ! how he doth writhe
And speaks not. The other Cassius, that appears
So large of limb. But night now re-ascends ;
And it is time for parting. All is seen.'" (Canto XXXIV.)

Dante, it may be thought, is very severe upon our poor noble Brutus. Many extenuating circumstances could indeed easily be pleaded in his favour, and there is no human tribunal at whose bar he would not stand absolved, to say nothing of those that would decree him laurel wreaths and statues. But from an absolute, ideal point of view like Dante's, abstracting all adventitious circumstances of place, time and persons, the regicide would deserve a place of honour in the nethermost hell, for no crime could be greater than his—that of high treason against the Divine King, for he who had committed it would be guilty of trying to make himself wiser than God, and of taking the place of the Most High in the government of the world. He would have tried by suppressing present evil to assure the well-being of the future. But what did he know, and what certitude could he have that he was making no mistake ? He was not in the secret of the universe, for who has known the thought of the Lord, or been the counsellor of the Most High ?

CASSIUS.

Cassius had none of the noble qualities that distinguished his friend ; he was not a high-minded nor a magnanimous man, and was far less finely touched in all matters of feeling. "A choleric man," writes Plutarch,

" and hating Cæsar privately, more than he did the tyrant
openly. It is also reported that Brutus could evil away
with the tyranny and that Cassius hated the tyrant."
This plainly shows itself in the scenes in which Cassius,
the real instigator of the conspiracy against Julius Cæsar,
endeavours to win first Brutus and then Casca over to his
designs, when the accent of envy sharpens his every
word.

When he relates the story of his having saved Cæsar's
life, he harps continually upon the jealous string of
I, I, I, and later on, when speaking to Casca, he talks of
Cæsar as—

> "A man no mightier than thyself, or me,
> In personal action. . . .
> And why should Cæsar be a tyrant then ? "

This is not the language of an outraged sense of
right, nor even that of a man whose reason is unsatisfied,
but simply that of a disappointed vanity and selfishness
which can brook no superior power in others. It is not
an enthusiast who speaks like this, but merely a dis-
contented man.

In addition to this personal hatred and desire for
vengeance, Cassius is devoid of any merciful scruples :—
to the question, " Shall no man else be touched, but only
Cæsar ? " he unhesitatingly answers that Mark Antony
should also fall, not on account of any aversion that he has
for the man, but because the thought of Antony's assassination naturally presents itself to his hard cold reason
as an indispensable corollary to that of Cæsar. Brutus,
with more of merciful generosity than of political insight,
objects to this proposal and saves Antony's life. If
Brutus by his moral authority had not carried his point
in this instance as in every other, it would be impossible
to say where Cassius might have stopped. He was
standing on the ridge of a slope whence the descent
seemed likely to stretch out to an indefinite distance.

Had this first dangerous person been sacrificed to the safety of the Republic, other victims would doubtless have followed: after Antony would have come Octavius; after the Dictator's friends would have come the members of his family, who were at least equally to be dreaded. It is the idealism of Brutus joined to Cassius' indifference to human life that brings about the reign of terror in times of revolution. Brutus had that narrow fanaticism that would upset the world in order triumphantly to establish a principle, but his sentiment of humanity held him back, on the brink of the system of wholesale destruction, and he recoiled from it in horror; never would he become the Saint-Just of a revolutionary tribunal. He belonged in reality to the race, not of those who kill, but of those who die, for an idea. Cassius, a mere political malcontent, and on that account far less to be feared theoretically than his enthusiastic companion, became practically far the more terrible of the two, being restrained by none of those scruples which, while they did honour to Brutus' character, at the same time paralysed his activity.

Looked at from the political point of view, which differs widely from the moral point of view, Cassius, the skilful man of action, with his penetration and promptitude, undoubtedly had the advantage over Brutus, who was only a noble-hearted dreamer. Cæsar rightly said of him—

> " He is a great observer, and he looks
> Quite through the deeds of men ; he loves no plays,
> As thou dost, Antony ; he hears no music :
> Seldom he smiles. . . .
> Such men as he be never at heart's ease
> Whiles they behold a greater than themselves ;
> And therefore are they very dangerous."

His knowledge and skill as a great observer and reader of men's characters are plainly visible, as already noticed, in

2 A

the mode in which he lays siege to Brutus; letting drop
no word suggestive of personal interest, and appealing
exclusively and entirely to his love of liberty and honour.
He proceeds in a very different manner with Antony,
whom, now that the question of his life or death had been
settled in favour of clemency, the conspirators desire to
attach to their side. Brutus, who is always ready to
believe in the upright feelings of others, as they are those
of his own heart, which is the only heart he knows,
ingenuously urges upon Mark Antony the existence of
good reasons for Cæsar's assassination (Act III., Sc. 1):—

> "Though now we must appear bloody and cruel, . . .
> . . . . . . yet see you but our hands, . . .
> Our hearts you see not, they are pitiful. . . .
> Only be patient, till we have appeased
> The multitude, beside themselves with fear;
> And then we will deliver you the cause
> Why I, that did love Cæsar, when I struck him,
> Have thus proceeded. . . .
> Our reasons are so full of good regard,
> That were you, Antony, the son of Cæsar,
> You should be satisfied."

Brutus invariably forgets that men in general feel and
think after a much less elevated fashion than does a
reasoning and speculative nature like his, and are infinitely more accessible to interested motives than to
what is strictly right and just; it never occurs to him
that they are more swayed by passion than by reason.
Cassius says only one word to Antony, but it is the very
word appropriate to the circumstances and to the particular man; he flatters him, and dangles before his eyes
the most adroitly chosen motive for tempting his vanity:—

> "Your voice shall be as strong as any man's
> In the disposing of new dignities."

It is this possession of a thorough knowledge of men
and things that so eminently distinguishes Cassius from
Brutus, and though, morally, he was worth much less

than his friend, he was beyond all dispute more astute and skilful.

But this is not the whole of his character : something still remains to be said, which gives rise to a general remark of the highest importance in studying Shakespeare's dramatic genius.

Had Cassius been only an envious and jealous man, one who threw himself into violent political opposition out of feelings of mere personal discontent,—if his heart had been absolutely shrivelled up with selfishness, and left frozen by the absence of all human sentiment,—his undoubted diplomatic talents would never have succeeded in attracting our sympathy, and in spite of his cleverness we should have felt no moral interest in him whatever. But—and this must be carefully noted—he does manage to inspire a moral interest, and is not so remote from the circle of our sympathies as might at first be imagined. Doubtless we grant him none of the deep and loving respect that we pay to Brutus, but he nevertheless deserves, and obtains from us, a certain amount of esteem. If now we turn to seek the means by which Shakespeare gives him this new and unexpected aspect, we shall find that it is effected by dint of several very delicate touches, which, without destroying the fundamental unity of his character, *seem slightly to contradict it.*

For instance, Cassius cherishes a personal animosity against Cæsar, presenting in this respect a marked contrast to Brutus, who, without any dislike to the man, and on the contrary with the tenderest affection for him, has the purest and most disinterested hatred of tyranny; yet neither is Cassius altogether devoid of a share in this nobler range of feelings, and objects to tyranny as well as to the tyrant. Shakespeare here follows Plutarch, who, in North's charming roundabout version, relates that—

"Cassius, even from his cradle, could not abide any manner of tyrants; as it appeared when he was but a boy, and went into the same school that Faustus, the son of Sylla, did. And Faustus, bragging among other boys, highly boasted of his father's kingdom : Cassius rose up on his feet, and gave him two good wirts on the ear. Faustus' governors would have put this matter in suit against Cassius : but Pompey would not suffer them, but caused the two boys to be brought before him, and asked them how the matter came to pass.   Then Cassius said unto the other : ' Go to, Faustus. Speak again, an thou darest, before this nobleman here, the same words that made me angry with thee, that my fists may walk once again about thine ears.' Such was Cassius' hot, stirring nature."

Energy of this kind is more attractive than the cold calculations and sorry resentments of self-interest, and Shakespeare has carefully preserved all its advantages to the subordinate hero of his tragedy, who is as fiery and passionate as a second Achilles ; nor is it only a heated impulse of the moment,—a fervent and noble spirit, worthy of Brutus himself, is distinctly discernible in some of his sayings, as for instance in his answer to Casca, who remarks (Act I., Sc. 3) :—

> " *Casca.* Indeed they say the senators to-morrow
> Mean to establish Cæsar as a king :
> And he shall wear his crown by sea and land,
> In every place, save here in Italy.
>   *Cas.* I know where I will wear this dagger then ;
> Cassius from bondage will deliver Cassius :
> Therein, ye gods, you make the weak most strong ;
> Therein, ye gods, you tyrants do defeat :
> Nor stony tower, nor walls of beaten brass,
> Nor airless dungeon, nor strong links of iron,
> Can be retentive to the strength of spirit :
> But life, being weary of these worldly bars,
> Never lacks power to dismiss itself.
> If I know this, know all the world besides,
> That part of tyranny that I do bear
> I can shake off at pleasure."

There is a resemblance in several minor respects be-tween Cassius and Brutus : when Cæsar says, " he thinks too much . . . he reads much . . . . such men are dangerous," he says it of Cassius not of Brutus ;

and in fact, in the portrait that he draws of him in
contrast to Antony, he describes a man who deserves
nearly as much respect for his austere private life as
Brutus himself. And although he has none of the rich
humanity which distinguishes Brutus, and may appear
like a sort of formidable living logical machine, when,
in the name of the public welfare, he inaugurates the
series of revolutionary crimes by coldly voting for Antony's death, his intellect, nevertheless, has not entirely
frozen his heart; he loves Brutus greatly, with the love
of a brother, and submits to his moral ascendency
although himself the elder of the two, with a humility
that does him honour. He yields to him in everything
without any protracted resistance, even when right is
on his own side; and we almost lose sight, in his intense
interest in all that concerns his friend and in the warmth
and sincerity of his sympathy, of the unpardonable sin
he committed in involving Brutus in a plot so wholly
repugnant to his nature.

But what is perhaps still more surprising is that,
while Cassius thus approaches Brutus, to a certain extent Brutus too, on his side, shows at times some
resemblance to Cassius. He too can be violent, and can
lose his temper and be unjust; even he, the upright
and lofty-minded Brutus, flies into a passion quite unworthy of him, and is guilty of injustice towards his
best friend. Cassius, pained beyond all words, bends
before the storm, and it is he that plays the finer part,
until Brutus, repenting him of his anger and returning
to his true nature, speaks the word of peace.

In all Shakespeare's plays there is no finer and more
memorable scene than this quarrel between the two
leaders and their reconciliation; in none does the sovereign art, the truly divine power of this greatest among
all painters of character more fully disclose itself, and
no other exemplifies to a greater degree a secret that

belongs to him alone among dramatic poets. This scene, of which no critic will ever fathom all the depths, inspired Coleridge with unbounded admiration :—

"I know no part of Shakespeare," he writes, " that more impresses on me the belief of his genius being superhuman than this scene between Brutus and Cassius. In the gnostic heresy, it might have been credited with less absurdity than most of their dogmas, that the Supreme had employed him to create, previously to his function of representing, characters."

The groundwork of the scene Shakespeare found in Plutarch :—

"About that time Brutus went to pray Cassius to come to the city of Sardis, and so he did. . . . Now, as it commonly happened in great affairs between two persons, both of them having many friends and so many captains under them, there ran tales and complaints betwixt them. Therefore, before they fell in hand with any other matter, they went into a little chamber together, and bade every man avoid, and did shut the doors to them. Then they began to pour out their complaints one to the other, and grew hot and loud, earnestly accusing one another, and at length fell both a-weeping. . . . One, Marcus Phaonius, that took upon him to counterfeit a philosopher, in despite of the doorkeepers came into the chamber, and with a certain scoffing and mocking gesture which he counterfeited for purpose, he rehearsed the verses which old Nestor said in Homer :—

My lords, I pray you hearken both to me,
For I have seen mo years than suchie three.

Cassius fell a-laughing at him; but Brutus thrust him out of the chamber. . . . The next day after, Brutus did condemn and vote Lucius Pella for a defamed person, for that he was accused and convicted of robbery and pilfery in his office. This judgment much misliked Cassius, . . . and therefore he greatly reproved Brutus for that he would show himself so straight and severe in such a time as was meeter to bear a little than to take things at the worst. Brutus answered, that he should remember the Ides of March, at which time they slew Julius Cæsar, who neither taxed nor robbed the country, but only was a favourer and suborner of all them that did rob and spoil by his countenance and authority. And if there were any occasion whereby they might honestly set aside justice and equity, they should have had more reason to have suffered Cæsar's friends to have robbed and done what wrong and injury they had wished, than to bear with their own men."

By the time we come to this scene—Act IV., Sc. 3,—
we are well acquainted with the characters of Brutus
and Cassius in their original integrity, and with their
essential differences. Brutus we know to be an idealist,
of a calm and gentle disposition, loving justice blindly,
and firm and rigid in the fulfilment of what he conceives
to be his duty; Cassius is a practical politician, of a
fiery nature, self-interested and clever, and not over-
scrupulous in the choice of means, if only he can attain
his end. Plutarch offers a fine opportunity for bringing
these differences forward still more emphatically, and
any other poet but Shakespeare would have been sure
to have seized it, pruning away every detail that might
conflict ever so slightly with the given basis of each
character, and adding at need new touches to bring them
into still sharper relief. For with most dramatic poets
the first and great consideration is unity and clearness;
when they have conceived a type their first care is to
idealize it, and accordingly they set to work to simplify
and generalize it, stripping it of every individual peculiarity, and rigorously rejecting all those little contradictions and slight inconsistencies which give the delicate
and fugitive expressions of life and reality. All their
portraits are taken in profile, because the profile gives
the real character, the fixed and abiding element of the
human countenance.

Shakespeare's method is utterly different: he is too
sure of his brush not to paint his portraits fearlessly
in full face, with all their varying and fleeting expressions.
What he seeks above everything is not unity and clearness, but truth and life. A truth is only true, it has
been said, when it also contains its contrary; in other
words, all that is absolute and cut-and-dried is false, and
truth can only consist of half-tones and delicate distinctions. Shakespeare carries the truth of his characters
so far that the point of perfection, of richness and of

fulness is reached, at which they contain *their own contradiction.*

He knew that in real life men are not always logical and consistent, and was quite aware of the frailty and weakness of even the best and strongest amongst them, so he shows us Brutus unfaithful for the moment to his nature and to his principles, and as far less reasonable than the man who is distinctly inferior to him morally; in point of fact, in the quarrel with Cassius, he boldly makes the usually just and generous-hearted man completely in the wrong.

Brutus is wrong both in the matter and in the manner of his complaint. He who was the first to give the example of lawlessness and licence, in violently departing from the law by a crime, has no right, in the midst of the horrible confusion of the civil war which he himself has caused, to exact from his lieutenant a rectitude of conduct which he has not shown himself; and it belongs not to the murderer of Cæsar to say to violence and disorder, "Thus far and no further." He reproaches Cassius with procuring the necessary money for the campaign by dishonourable means; but without any wish to extenuate Cassius' culpability, it must be observed, that the true culprit is the war. He who wishes to keep his hands clean should never go to war, and he who once ventures upon it must frankly face the necessity of committing many a censurable action. The war once begun, money became absolutely indispensable; obtained it must be, no matter by what means. Brutus himself was so alive to this necessity, that his complaints against Cassius fall with sudden descent from the pure and sublime regions of absolute principles to that of prosaic and personal considerations, and he bitterly reproaches his colleague with having refused the money for which he had sent to ask him.

Amazed at such flagrant injustice, Cassius exercises

all his self-control and restrains his anger; his replies, at first sharp and hasty, soften by degrees, and he gradually calms down and endeavours to calm his friend. He would almost appear to have some intuition of the state of grief poor Brutus is in, and to understand that it is a passing and abnormal excitement which will wear itself out, and the cause of which will sooner or later be explained to him.

The explanation is soon given. Brutus comes to himself and gives his hand to his friend, and then only, when peace is established between them, he utters in a broken voice, three words, to which his great and silent sorrow adds nothing, but which are all-sufficient to account for the profound perturbation of his mind,—"Portia is dead." Then, at this heart-rending news, Cassius understands everything, he forgets everything, and with sublime self-abnegation exclaims: "How 'scaped I killing, when I cross'd you so?" It is he, the one who has been wronged, that begs pardon of Brutus. His friend's sorrow becomes his own, and the reconciliation of these two great men is sealed by the grief they have in common.

When we seek the reason of Shakespeare's incontestable and uncontested pre-eminence among all other poets as a delineator of character, we discover in the last hiding-places of analysis, that it consists in the largeness and breadth of his treatment. He alone dares to introduce into his portraits the little seeming contradictions, which terrify ordinary reasoning because of their apparent inconsistency with the general outlines of the character, although in reality they enhance the resemblance by keeping closer to nature.

The consistency of Shakespeare's characters is universally admired, as there is every reason it should be; it is obvious and strikes the mind at once, while the contradictions here spoken of are almost imperceptible;

but it is their very imperceptibility that makes it incumbent upon critics to dwell upon them with especial care; for without destroying the inner unity of the characters, these light and delicate touches break through all superficial harmony and reveal a still greater art than what is usually the object of admiration.

Who would ever have guessed beforehand—to refer to only the slightest incident of this incomparable scene —that at the entrance of the officious mediator, who comes and preaches peace to the two generals when they have already made peace, that it would be Brutus—the patient and gentle Brutus—that would be the most exasperated; or that it would be Cassius,—the violent and choleric man, that would endeavour to protect the meddlesome intruder, saying, " Bear with him, Brutus: 'tis his fashion"?   But when the particular circumstances are taken into consideration, all surprise at the anomaly vanishes.   The fact is given by Plutarch, the reason of it by Shakespeare.

This, then, is the whole truth, the living truth. There is no settling on a general and accepted type, with a determination to follow it blindly, in an inflexible and mechanical manner: but every modification that the type might undergo in any given circumstances, is carefully observed and noted.   What Shakespeare, with his inexhaustible wealth of poetry, can effect for so apparently ungrateful a subject as Cassius, is amazing, for he actually succeeds in making us feel even a kindly interest in the hard and unsensitive egoist.   For, after all, in spite of his hardness and selfishness, Cassius is a man too, and nothing human can be wholly foreign to the creations of the greatest of dramatic poets, the only one whose work any one has ever ventured to compare to that of the Divine Creator.

It belongs to the nature of poetry to be more concise

than history, to be less varied, and to go deeper below the surface; and we see Shakespeare, in his treatment of Plutarch, following the great canon of art which teaches that in historical tragedy the facts must be epitomized and brought into close relation with each other. He obtained the necessary materials for his drama principally by a process of elimination, and on the whole, he added less than he left out of the historian's account. But notwithstanding this, his poetry, more than that of any other poet, was enabled by virtue of that largeness of touch in the presentment of character which has already been signalled as the dominant feature of his genius, to offer history a warm and hospitable reception.

In philosophy Cassius belonged to the sect of the Epicureans, and believed neither in another life nor in a Divine Providence; but this, as Plutarch relates, did not prevent him, on entering the senate on the morning of the Ides of March, from "casting his eyes upon Pompey's image, and making his prayer unto it, as if it had been alive;" or from being a good deal disturbed in mind by the sinister omens which occurred before the battle of Philippi. Shakespeare was careful not to suppress so natural an inconsistency. "O ye immortal Gods!" Cassius exclaims, instinctively glancing upward, when horror-struck at the news of Portia's death: and on the plains of Philippi, before the action, he says to Messala (Act V., Sc. 1)—

> " You know that I held Epicurus strong,
>   And his opinion : now I change my mind,
>   And partly credit things that do presage.
>   Coming from Sardis, on our former ensign
>   Two mighty eagles fell ; and there they perch'd,
>   Gorging and feeding from our soldiers' hands,
>   Who to Philippi here consorted us ;
>   This morning are they fled away, and gone ;
>   And in their stead do ravens, crows, and kites,
>   Fly o'er our heads, and downward look on us,

As we were sickly prey ; their shadows seem
A canopy most fatal, under which
Our army lies, ready to give up the ghost."

A similar inconsistency appears to exist between the
philosophical doctrines of Brutus and his practical
sentiments when he blames Cato for committing suicide,
and in almost the same breath announces his resolution
to put an end to his own life should he lose the battle of
Philippi, but the discrepancy here arises from Shakespeare having been misled by the passage in North's
Plutarch, which is obscured by being badly printed.
What Brutus there really says, is that when he was a
young man and inexperienced in the world he blamed
Cato for killing himself, but that now, being in the midst
of danger, he was of a contrary mind; but owing to the
clumsiness of the printing, Shakespeare understood him
to be expressing a present disapproval of Cato instead of
one of past years.*

---

* See " Julius Cæsar," Clarendon Press Series, p. 195.

CHAPTER XIX.

JULIUS CÆSAR (*continued*).   CASCA.   CICERO.   PORTIA.

CASCA.

IF it were not a somewhat hazardous conjecture when applied to the most impartial of dramatic poets, one would be inclined to suspect that the type of character to which Casca belongs was a peculiar favourite of Shakespeare's. In the. first place, he is a humourist, he has a strong sense of the comedy of human life, and of the nothingness of the things of this world. It is he that relates in a tone of transcendent mockery, to Brutus and Cassius who are not at all in a mood to laugh with him, the great event of the feast of Lupercal, and describes how Antony offered the crown to Cæsar. Brutus is shocked at his levity of tone, and when Casca leaves them, he expresses his disapprobation with all the weighty injustice of a stern moralist, who takes everything seriously and who as a matter of course is invariably wrong in his judgments of men. Cassius, who has no obtuseness of this sort, answers that what shocks Brutus in him is only put on, and that he may be safely counted on for any bold or noble enterprise. Casca, when enrolled amongst the conspirators, soon justifies this opinion of him, and is the one to strike the first blow. This mingled good-humour and practical energy, this strength and solidity of character underlying all his merry jests and laughter, cannot but represent not only one of Shakespeare's favourite types, but the special type of his predilection, if we admit, with his most learned commentators, that Henry V., in whom these characteristics are most strongly marked, was his ideal.

Casca is moreover an aristocrat in true disdainful English fashion. He expresses the most elegant contempt, which is all the more cutting because he speaks without any bitterness, and with a smile on his lips, for the folly of the crowd, and for their dirty hands and sweaty night-caps and stinking breath : " It had almost choked Cæsar; for he swooned, and fell down at it : and for mine own part, I durst not laugh, for fear of opening my lips and receiving the bad air."

One of the rare expressions to be met with in Shakespeare, which would seem to indicate a personal sentiment, occurs in this narrative of Casca's : " If the tag-rag people did not clap him, and hiss him, according as he pleased and displeased them, as they used to do the players in the theatre, I am no true man."

M. Guizot, after describing the populace which composed the pit in English theatres in the sixteenth century, and which contemporary writers designated by the name of *stinkards*, adds :—

"In the lot of actors, working for the amusement of such a public, there must have been much that was unpleasant, and to what he suffered in this way we may be allowed to attribute the aversion for popular assemblies which Shakespeare shows so strongly in his plays."

To what extent Shakespeare shared in Casca's aristocratic disdain, and how far personal antipathy caused him to depart in his portrayal of the people, from the poetic impartiality which is one of his highest titles to glory, is a curious question, but one which it would be premature to attempt to answer before we come to examine the play of " Coriolanus," in which the people play an important part.

One last thing to be noticed concerning Casca is the wonderful effect that the prodigies foretelling the death of Cæsar have upon him; they work a complete revolution in his nature, and give a suddenly meditative turn to his usual airiness of tone : his irony is in reality only a thin and superficial covering, which falls at the first serious occasion and lets the true nature of the man be seen.

CICERO.

Cicero only makes his appearance in the tragedy as listening to Casca's account of the marvellous sights of the night he had been witnessing; he answers his religious terror with a philosophical commonplace :—

> " Indeed, it is a strange-disposèd time :
> But men may construe things, after their fashion,
> Clean from the purpose of the things themselves."

There is nothing highly original or daring in this remark, but its very insignificance seems to belong to Shakespeare's conception of the character; besides which, though the Roman orator may say nothing very important himself, he is twice mentioned in the play in terms sufficiently explicit to make his faults and failings known. When Casca describes the scene at the offering of the crown to Cæsar, Cassius inquires—

> " Did Cicero say anything ?
> *Casca.* Ay, he spoke Greek.
> *Cas.* To what effect ?
> *Casca.* Nay, an I tell you that I'll ne'er look you i' the face again; but those that understood him smiled at one another, and shook their heads : but, for mine own part, it was Greek to me."

It has been thought ridiculous in Shakespeare to make Cicero speak Greek, but this is to overlook the possibility of a characteristic touch being intended by it. To speak at a time like that in Greek, in a language not to be understood by the common people, and in a manner that made those who did understand smile meaningly at each other, implies a skilfulness and a regard for prudence quite at one with the traditional, and more or less historically true, representation of the friend of Atticus.*

The conspirators did not dare, Plutarch tells us, to acquaint Cicero with their conspiracy,—

"for they were afraid that he, being a coward by nature, and age also having increased his fear, he would turn and alter all their purpose, and quench the heat of their enterprise, seeking by persuasion to bring all things to such safety, as there should be no peril."

But such an endeavour is absolutely fatal to a spirit of enterprise, and to action of every kind: Hamlet did nothing, because he sought "by persuasion to bring all things to such safety, as there should be no peril."

Cassius, for once making a mistake and failing in his usual penetration—though the mistake, after all, might be on the part of the poet,—is inclined at first starting to enroll Cicero among the conspirators, but Brutus objects :—

> " For he will never follow anything
> That other men begin." '

In this instance, Brutus was enabled by the natural antipathy which he felt towards Cicero, in spite of his friendly relations with him, to estimate him more accurately than even Cassius did, the close observer of men. Pure men of letters like Cicero, who are chiefly con-

---

* Voltaire had no higher idea of Cicero than Shakespeare had: see the lines in his tragedy of " Brutus " :—

> " Cicéron qui d'un traître a puni l'insolence,
> Ne sert le liberté que par son eloquence :
> Hardi dans le sénat, faible dans le danger,
> Fait pour haranguer Rome et non pour la venger,
> Laissons à l'orateur qui charme sa patrie
> Le soin de nous louer quand nous l'aurons servie."

cerned with the improvement of their mental faculties, are looked upon askance by stoics like Brutus, whose whole aim is moral perfection.

" Cicero's friendship with Brutus," says M. Boissier, " was a very disturbed and stormy one; and violent discussions broke out more than once between them, although they held many opinions in common. These dissensions naturally arose from the diversity of their characters : never did two friends less resemble each other; Cicero was pre-eminently fitted for society, possessing all the necessary qualities for social success, great flexibility of opinion, a wide tolerance for others, and sufficiently easy terms for himself, besides a talent of steering safely between all parties, and a naturally indulgent, easy-going disposition which made him understand everything and accept almost everything. Though he wrote very indifferent verses, he was of a poetic temperament, strangely versatile in his impressions, and irritably sensitive; his mind was swift and supple and far-reaching, quick to conceive, but equally quick to abandon his ideas, and passing with a bound from one extreme to the other. He never formed a serious resolution without repenting of it the next day. Whenever he took a side in any matter, he was warm and decided at the beginning, and then gradually grew colder and colder."

Cicero is accordingly left out of the conspiracy for the reason given by Brutus :—

" For he will never follow anything
That other men begin."

But neither would he begin anything himself; he would rather remain inactive, which in the time of civil troubles, when calm wisdom is only a form of selfishness, and when men should be able to range themselves unreservedly on the side that is least wrong, is always a culpable mode of conduct. His fate, however, was to die by the sword, like those who live by the sword, but with this difference—that theirs is an honourable death, while his was inglorious. Such is the moral lesson taught by Cicero's death, in Shakespeare's tragedy.

PORTIA.

Portia as she appears in Plutarch is, I think, an even finer and more interesting character to study than she is in Shakespeare. The poet has undoubtedly endued the historian's account with the more vivid life of the drama, and has given more force to her words, more distinctness to her actions, but he could add no further feature of any importance to her character. History furnishes a complete and finished portrait of Portia, to which poetry may give a warmer glow and richer colouring, but which in its essential lines it can never improve. It is only fair that this should be openly and clearly stated, that Plutarch may have the full credit of his victories in a most unequal combat, in which it would seem that his highest success could only consist in not being entirely beaten. But not only does the poet's rendering not surpass his model, but it seems to me to fall a little short of it, and to leave out some of its beauties, which apparently belong peculiarly to the form of narrative and refuse to be transplanted into dramatic regions. It requires all the wooden inflexibility of a systematic admiration not to regret the absence, in Shakespeare's tragedy, of the beautiful scene in which Brutus and Portia take leave of each other at Elea :—

"There Porcia, being ready to depart from her husband, Brutus, and to return to Rome, did what she could to dissemble the grief and sorrow she felt at her heart: but a certain painted table * bewrayed her in the end, although until that time she showed always a constant and patient mind. The device of the table was taken out of the Greek stories, how Andromache accompanied her husband Hector when he went out of the city of Troy to go to the wars, and how Hector delivered her his little son, and how her eyes were never off him. Porcia, seeing this picture, and likening herself to be in the same case, she fell a-weeping: and coming thither oftentimes in a day to see it, she

---

* Picture.

wept still. Acilius, one of Brutus' friends, perceiving that, rehearsed the verses Andromache speaketh to this purpose in Homer :—
> 'Thou, Hector, art my father, and my mother, and my brother,
> And husband-eke, and all in all : I mind not any other.'

Then Brutus, smiling, answered again : 'But yet,' said he, 'I cannot for my part, say unto Porcia, as Hector answered Andromache—
> Tush, meddle thou with duly weighing out
> Thy maids their task, and pricking on a clout.

For, indeed, the weak constitution of her body doth not suffer her to perform in show the valiant acts that we are able to do : but for courage and constant mind, she showed herself as stout in the defence of her country as any of us.' "

The Portia of Plutarch, in the way in which she understood and exhibited married love, certainly represents the most beautiful type of a wife easily conceivable, and yet she belongs to the ancient world. Before the publication of various important works, among which that of M. Havet,* on the origin of Christianity, and that of M. Boissier, on the religion of Rome,† must be specially mentioned, had begun to spread abroad more exact notions on the subject, there existed in commonly received opinion an abyss between the condition of women in ancient and their condition in modern times ; and it was ordinarily believed that women were looked down upon by classical antiquity, and that respect for them was due to Christian and Germanic influences.

Apparent proofs were not wanting in support of this prejudice. If we consult the laws of Greece and Rome, we shall see women everywhere kept in what one is inclined to call a barbarous state of legal inferiority, and never considered free to act alone and to dispose of themselves.

"In marriage, as understood by the ancients," writes M. Lallier, the author of an interesting essay on " La Condition de la Femme dans

---

* "Le Christianisme et ses Origines," Paris, Michel Lévy, 1871.

† "La Religion Romaine d'Auguste aux Antonins," Hachette, Paris, 1874.

la Famille Athénienne au Vᵉ. et au VIᵉ. Siècle," "the wife counted
as nothing. Her feelings were never consulted, nor was she chosen
for her own sake, but simply accepted as a necessary instrument for
the continuation of the family and of the city; nothing further seems
to have been expected of her, nor was she supposed to have any other
virtue : her duty was fulfilled when she had given birth to her sons.
. . . There was no question of mutual inclination or motives of affection;
the married couple did not come together to share each other's thoughts
and feelings, or to be mutual helps in the trials of life, but were simply
acquitting themselves of a patriotic and religious obligation, in provid-
ing future citizens for the state, who would take their fathers' places,
and in their turn offer domestic sacrifices. . . . But from the moment
that marriage is degraded into a civic duty, and becomes nothing but
an obligation which it is impossible to evade without sinning against
religion and against the State, the charm of domestic life is done away
with, and at the same time the influence of the wife is greatly lessened.
The Athenian lent himself to marriage in much the same spirit as that
in which one pays a debt,—slowly and reluctantly.   The interest of
the Republic required the introduction of a wife into his household,
and so far he obeyed its behests, but he strictly measured the share she
would have in his life, and when these limits were once settled he
troubled himself no further with the cares of his family."

At Rome, the Censor Metellus, in the time of the
Gracchi, preached matrimony to his fellow-citizens in
these terms, as quoted by Montesquieu, and often
repeated since :—

"Citizens, if we could live without having wives, we should all
avail ourselves of the possibility, *ea molestia careremus*, but since
Nature has chosen to make it as impossible to do without them as it is
disagreeable to live with them, let us sacrifice the pleasures of our
short life to the interests of the Republic, which endures for ever."

If we turn from legislators to philosophers, we shall
find many contemptuous passages in their writings, in
which wives are slightingly spoken of and the idea of
marriage reduced to a very low level indeed.   Socrates
says to one of his friends, as though it were quite a
matter of course, "Is there anybody that you talk less to
than to your wife ? "   When Plato wishes to describe a
democratic society, over which the magistrates, like

awkward cupbearers, have spilt the wine of liberty so that it has become intoxicated with it, and utterly lost its reason, he represents the slave refusing to obey his master, and the wife alleging her equality with her husband, as the climax of disorder. And Aristotle is still more impertinent: " There certainly may be some honest women and slaves," he says, " but it may be said in general that women are an inferior species, and that the slave is altogether bad." The Roman philosophers express themselves in their speculative writings in the same strain as the Greeks.*

And when after having read these impertinent remarks, we enter with Tacitus into the new world of Germany, with all its veneration for women and its deep sense of the majesty of marriage, the contrast certainly appears complete. Later on, the Germanic idea received the fullest consecration from Christianity, so much so that the supreme expression of respect for women may be found in the incident related in the biography of a mystic German in mediæval times :—

"One day he met a woman in the dirtiest street of the town, and immediately stepped into the mud to let her pass in the only part that was dry. She, seeing this act of humility, said to him, 'My father, what are you doing? You are a priest and a monk. Why do you give up the path to me, who am only a weak woman?' Brother Henry answered, 'My sister, it is my custom to honour and venerate all women, because they remind my heart of the powerful Queen of Heaven, the Mother of my God.'"†

But to mix up all the different periods of classical antiquity together, and then to say of it, as a whole, that it despised women, and showed itself incapable of conceiving an elevated ideal of marriage, would be to make a great mistake; many distinctions and reservations have to be made before arriving at a conclusion on this matter, —the distinction between law and custom, between the

---

* Gaston Boissier.   † Heinrich, "History of German Literature."

paradoxes of philosophers and the general feeling of the community, between the heroic age of Greece and the succeeding periods of its history, and finally the distinction between Athens and Rome.

In studying closely the life of ancient societies, we find that the laws were often considerably at variance with the prevailing custom, the consideration claimed for women by manners and habits going far beyond their legal rights; in which conflict it was custom that invariably carried the day. In our own times, as M. Lallier ingenuously remarks—

" A very erroneous notion would be entertained of the important part played by women in French society, if we were to judge simply by the articles of the civil code which define the respective rights and duties of husband and wife."

And France is probably not the only country to which the remark applies. In point of fact, the paradoxes of philosophers signify nothing. Witticisms of a commonplace kind on the good and bad qualities of women are as frequent now as they were in former days, all resolving themselves in their final analysis into the sentence pronounced by Hesiod, which is weighty and full of wisdom as any maxim of the seven sages of Greece : " There is nothing in the world better than a good woman, or worse than a bad one." And even Aristotle, in spite of his depreciatory remarks already cited, speaks of the tenderness between man and wife, and of the harmony of soul necessary for happiness; while Pythagoras dwells with great eloquence upon the love with which a man should regard the woman who has left her father's house for his sake, and who loves him even more dearly than her parents, the authors of her existence.

No women were more surrounded with respect than those of Homer's heroic world; but later on, a grave alteration took place in this respect in the manners of the Greeks, so that the most important distinction to be made in speaking of the condition of women in antiquity comes to be that between Athens and Rome.

In Rome, women were treated with far greater consideration than in Athens. The Athenians shut their women up in the apartments specially reserved for them, and esteemed it their highest honour to have nothing said of them, good or bad. Rome knew nothing of the institution of the gynecium, and frankly associated women with the life of men, and in the atrium, the centre of a Roman house, used as a general sitting-room for the family, and as a reception-room for either friends or strangers, the married woman—the Matron, as the Romans reverently called her—took her place beside her husband. The Romans always had a very high ideal of marriage, which they regarded as the blending of two lives into one, and it is to their legal writers that we owe the well-known definition : " Marriage is a union for the pursuit of things human and divine—*juris humani et divini communicatio . . . uxor socia humanæ rei atque divinæ.*"

The personal importance of women continually increased in Roman society : the time at which they played the greatest part in history was towards the close of the Republic and the beginning of the Empire :—

" We see them," wrote M. Saint-Marc Girardin,[*] " taking part in conspiracies and civil wars, as for instance Servilia in Sallust's ' War of Catalina,' and Fulvia in the proscriptions. They also took part in the court-intrigues under Augustus and the other Cæsars, as is seen in Livia and Agrippina. Their new-found independence was used by some to subserve their love of pleasure ; by others, their ambition ; and by others again, to contribute to the dignity of married life : take, for example, Pauline ready to die with Seneca, or Arria who, to encourage her husband to kill himself, stabbed herself with a sword and then, drawing it covered with blood from her breast, gave it to her husband, saying, ' Take it, Pœtus ; there is nothing painful in it.' "

---

[*] " Cours de littérature dramatique," Vol. IV., p. 262.

To this heroic race belonged Portia ; but what adds a peculiar attraction to the grandeur of her character is that in her case, as in that of Brutus, heroism extinguished none of the gentler feelings of humanity : nothing could be less theatrical than her stoicism, and her whole nature was intensely sensitive—it was this, indeed, that killed her.   How acute her feelings were may be seen in her deadly anguish on the morning of the Ides of March, and in the tearful farewell she took of Brutus when leaving Elea ; we know, too, that she died, as Brutus himself says, of grief, causing her own death in the madness of despair.

Plutarch tells us of her heroism in giving herself a wound in the thigh to make sure that no pain or grief could overcome her ; and in Shakespeare the scene is given with all the perfection of dramatic language (Act II., Sc. 1) :—

> " *Por.*   Upon my knees
> I charm you, by my once commended beauty,
> By all your vows of love, and that great vow
> Which did incorporate and make us one,
> That you unfold to me, yourself, your half,
> Why you are heavy. . . .
>   *Bru.* You are my true and honourable wife ;
> As dear to me as are the ruddy drops
> That visit my sad heart.
>   *Por.* If this were true, then should I know this secret.
> I grant I am a woman ; but, withal,
> A woman that lord Brutus took to wife :
> I grant I am a woman ; but, withal,
> A woman well reputed,—Cato's daughter.
> Think you I am no stronger than my sex,
> Being so father'd and so husbanded ?
> Tell me your counsels, I will not disclose them :
> I have made strong proof of my constancy,
> Giving myself a voluntary wound
> Here, in the thigh : can I bear that with patience,
> And not my husband's secrets ?
>   *Bru.*   O ye Gods,
> Render me worthy of this noble wife ! "

In this splendid metamorphosis of a simple narrative into a dramatic scene, the poet naturally accentuates every point of Portia's character, and especially her sense of the dignity of marriage and of what is owing to her as a wife.

"Shakespeare's Portia," says M. Saint-Marc Girardin, "ventures further than the Portia of Plutarch in claiming her share in her husband's perils; and, in fact, in her notions of her rights and of her duties, there is much of the Christian and even of the English wife."

That Shakespeare's Portia is a Christian and an Englishwoman may be true—I have no wish to dispute it,—but between her and her prototype I see no essential difference, but one in degree only. And, as I have said before, what strikes me as even more marvellous than Shakespeare's poetry is the existence and portrayal of such a character in the heart of pagan antiquity. Ever since ancient times there have been those who did honour to marriage, even as there have been some—and, in point of fact, many—in modern days who have not entirely reached Plutarch's ideal in his treatise on love, in which he protests against any lower and meaner doctrine of marriage than that of its being the union of two hearts.

If we wish to see a case presenting the most complete and amusing contrast to the relations between Brutus and Portia, we can also find it in that collection of all possible characters, Shakespeare's plays. We have only to turn to "Henry IV." (Act II., Sc. 3), where Hotspur abruptly tells his wife he is about to start in two hours' time, without telling her why he leaves or where he is going. A man of rash and hasty disposition, with none of the refinements of thought and culture, without any need or wish for an ideal love, he is not likely to have such a wife as Brutus had, or to be capable of such veneration as Brutus was; and accordingly he treats his wife more as a child than as a woman :—

" Come, wilt thou see me ride ?
   And when I am a horseback, I will swear
   I love thee infinitely.   But hark you, Kate;
   I must not have you henceforth question me
   Whither I go, nor reason whereabout :
   Whither I must, I must; and, to conclude,
   This evening must I leave you, gentle Kate.
   I know you wise ; but yet no further wise
   Than Harry Percy's wife : constant you are,
   But yet a woman : and for secrecy,
   No lady closer ; for I will believe
   Thou wilt not utter what thou dost not know ;
   And so far will I trust thee, gentle Kate !
      Lady.   How ! so far ?
      Hot.   Not an inch further."

Hotspur thought with Racine that a woman is " a
body which is all tongues," and would have said with La
Fontaine, " Nothing weighs more heavily than a secret,.
to carry it far is difficult for ladies."   But here I stop,
for if I were to quote French authors, beginning with the
greatest, I should find more satirical hits at women in
one single period, than in the whole of antiquity, Greek
or Roman ; and what is worse, I should also find a constant tendency, which neither England, nor Rome, nor
even light and gay Athens ever exhibited, to turn the
sacred institution of marriage into ridicule.

CHAPTER XX.

SHAKESPEARE, as we have seen in speaking of Cassius, in order to make his characters more lifelike, and truer to nature, had no hesitation in representing them in so many different moods and aspects as *almost* to verge upon inconsistency. I am always careful, in expressing this idea, to modify it by some little qualifying word, as it is obvious that the inconsistency must never be allowed to be too obtrusive. The apparent contradictions must be delicate enough to admit of reconciliation with the leading features of the character, as otherwise, under the plausible pretext of gaining variety, there would be nothing but anarchy and confusion. Shakespeare's characters never fail to fulfil the two essential laws of unity and clearness; only, unity, as understood by him, is larger and richer than that of other dramatic poets, and his clearness allows the mingling of many different colours in a strikingly bold manner.

So many different elements go to make up the character of Antony, that it would be difficult to form a distinct notion of it, without first disengaging from its adjuncts its fundamental and characteristic feature.

The essential definition of this strange and many-sided personage may be given summarily as a noble nature destitute of any moral sense.* Is nobility of

---

* "A man of genius, without moral fibre."—Dowden, p. 289.

nature, it may be asked, compatible with an absence of moral principle? It may appear strange to place the two terms in such close juxtaposition, but the state of things thus implied is of only too real occurrence.

There are men who are passionately affected by every thing that is beautiful—fine forms, fine sentiments, fine actions, fine characters, excite their enthusiastic admiration,—but in whom the pure and simple love of what is right, is not manifest to the same extent, or indeed to any extent at all, and with whom the moral element, which according to the more elevated doctrine of ideal beauty, enters into the composition of all true beauty worthy of the name, has neither part nor lot in their affections. These men are capable of enthusiasm for a fine trait of virtue, not because it is virtuous but because it is fine; they themselves would be capable of acts having all the appearance of virtue—they could be magnificent, generous, chivalrous, even heroic,—but all the time it would be nothing but a brilliant falsehood, for their conduct has no moral principle for its basis, and is determined by an attraction which charms their imagination, and not by the idea of duty ruling in their conscience. Besides the morality enforced by duty, nothing is commoner or better known than that dictated by self-interest or by pleasure; but there yet remains another system of ethics, which is less studied and has, too, fewer disciples than these, and it is of this æsthetic morality, as it may be called, that Antony is the type.

But now that we have penetrated to this secret spring of his nature, we must guard ourselves against seeing that only, and be careful not to shut our eyes to all the other lights and shades of his character, under the specious pretext of their being too coarse or too obvious, and so make too refined a personage of this man, who was moreover an Epicurean in the common acceptation of the term.

Antony had a robust body and temperament;—

"he had a goodly thick beard," says Plutarch, "a broad forehead,
crooked-nosed, and there appeared such a manly look in his countenance,
as is commonly seen in Hercules' pictures, stamped or graven in metal.
Now it had been a speech of old time, that the family of the Antonii
were descended from one Anton, the son of Hercules, whereof the
family took name. This opinion did Antony seek to confirm in all his
doings : not only resembling him in the likeness of his body, but also
in the wearing of his garments."

It may be added that besides all these points of resemblance to his great ancestor, he principally imitated him
in his relations with Omphale.

The licence of his manners is, however, far less offensive in Shakespeare than in Plutarch. The poet has toned
down or omitted all that could make him contemptible
or odious—his wild orgies, and several instances given
in history of his ferocious cruelty, violence, and plunder,—
and has only left him vices of a more agreeable and pleasing kind.

Of an open nature, happy and expansive, he is one of
those amiable egoists who desire the happiness of others
as an element of their own well-being.

The entrance of this roman Don Juan in "Julius
Cæsar" almost recalls that of Alfred de Musset :—

> "Tendant sa coupe d'or à ceux qu'il voit sourire,
> Voulant voir leur bonheur pour y chercher le sien."

His first words are to reassure Cæsar with regard to
Cassius :—

> "Fear him not, Cæsar, he's not dangerous;
> He is a noble Roman, and well given."

Antony asks nothing better than to live on good
terms with all parties alike, republicans as well as Cæsar.
It is such folly, he thinks, for a man to go about creating
a hard and embittered existence for himself, by indulging
in feelings of rancour or animosity or ambition, or
through an over-scrupulous attention to justice, when

everything around him is inviting him to enjoyment. Ambition is utterly foreign to Antony's nature, and he would have been the last man to have preferred being first in his village to being second in Rome; his one aim was pleasure, and he had no desire for power or honours beyond such as might give free scope to his tastes; besides which, for voluptuous natures like his, the second place, which offers nearly all the privileges of regal power without its cares, is distinctly more desirable than the first. And so we see him gladly remaining second to Cæsar, and after Cæsar's death, hastening to call Octavius to succeed in the dictatorship: the division of the Empire suited him exactly, but the thought of securing the whole for himself would never have occurred to him.

This tendency always to take the second place was not so much due to conscious intention on Antony's part, as it was the result of his natural inclination. He was a born disciple, ever ready, that is, to yield unresistingly to the sway of any genius that he recognized as greater than his own, and delighting in hero-worship. Besides his gift for subordination, he has, as Professor Dowden remarks, an enthusiasm for great personalities, such as a Julius Cæsar, or a Cleopatra. Fear probably played a greater part than love in the ascendency that his wife Fulvia had over him,—a virago who carried matters with a high hand, and fought in the field like a man, while he was away in Alexandria behaving like a weak woman; but at the news of her death he breaks out into regrets, exclaiming, "There's a great spirit gone!" ("Antony and Cleopatra," Act I., Sc. 2). The thought of her stirs his æsthetic imagination, and he appears, on the whole, to be far less rejoiced at being rid of her, than to be sincerely affected by the loss of so rare a character. There was something more than mere beauty and charm, there must have been an intellectual power in the fascination Cleopatra exercised over him, and by which he was so completely subjugated. Weak, in spite of his bodily strength, "weak, and needing like ivy, the support of others,"* the presence of some one person that he could serve or adore was a necessity of his nature. It was to this deeply rooted instinct that, as Gervinus remarks, his worship of the great Alcides as a tutelar deity, and the invocations he addressed to him, were probably due.

His sentiments with regard to Octavius, his colleague, and later on his rival and foe, were of a very mixed kind; in his heart he hated and despised him; the pale, beardless youth, cold, reserved, and hypocritical, with neither talent nor martial courage, was absolutely alien to Antony's nature. There was no one but "barren-spirited" Lepidus, who was but an ass to be "led or driven, as we point the way," "a slight, unmeritable man," for whom he had a greater contempt. But, at the same time, he was fully alive to the fact that it was Octavius whose fortune was in the ascendant, and he yielded to him on every occasion: on the plains of Philippi it is sufficient for Octavius to say, "I will do so," to make Antony give up to him the right wing of the army, which he had intended to take himself. He, the experienced and valiant general, consents to take a post of secondary importance and to fight against Cassius, while his young and presumptuous colleague, who was as wanting in courage as he was in skill, awaits the attack of Brutus. Later on, when he has at last resolved to leave Egypt and Cleopatra for a while, and to return to Rome, he asks pardon from Octavius, "so far as befits mine honour to stoop in such a case," and entering of his own accord into the plans of the new Cæsar, allows himself to be married to his sister Octavia.

---

* Alfred de Musset.

" My amazed spirit trembles before hers," says Racine's
Nero in "Britannicus," speaking of Agrippina, which
reminds one of Antony's interviews with the soothsayer
(" Antony and Cleopatra," Act II., Sc. 3)—

> " *Ant.*   Say to me
> Whose fortune shall rise higher, Cæsar's or mine ?
>   *Sooth.* Cæsar's.
> Therefore, O Antony, stay not by his side :
> Thy dæmon (that thy spirit which keeps thee) is
> Noble, courageous, high, unmatchable,
> Where Cæsar's is not ; but near him thy angel
> Becomes a Fear, as being o'erpower'd ; therefore
> Make space enough between you."

The personage of Antony fills both " Julius Cæsar "
and " Antony and Cleopatra ; " in the first, he is dominated by an enthusiastic devotion to the still living spirit
of a great man who has himself passed away ; and in
the second, he is dominated by an impassioned devotion
to the Egyptian Queen.

No doubt can be felt concerning the reality of
Antony's affection for Cæsar, or the sincerity of his
grief at his violent death. Whether alone, or in the
presence of the messenger from Octavius, or among the
assassins, his lamentations are the same :—

> " O mighty Cæsar ! Dost thou lie so low ?   .
>   Are all thy conquests, glories, triumphs, spoils,
>   Shrunk to this little measure ? "

" Fare thee well," he exclaims with deep emotion, and
then, turning to the conspirators, asks if his death is to
be the next ; if so—

> " There is no hour so fit
> As Cæsar's death's hour ; nor no instrument
> Of half that worth as those your swords, made rich
> With the most noble blood of all this world. . . .
>   . . . Live a thousand years
> I shall not find myself so apt to die :
> No place will please me so, no mean of death,
> As here by Cæsar and by you cut off,
> The choice and master spirits of this age."

Sublime self-devotion!   But notice well how the imagination of this artistic nature was captivated by the splendid surroundings of the scene—to be struck here, close to Cæsar, by the swords enriched by the noblest blood of all this world, and by men who were the choice and master spirits of their age.   These last words were spoken by him in no spirit of flattery or of cringing; they are simply the expression of his sincere admiration for the conspirators, and especially for the chief and greatest of them all.   Let us turn to the field of battle at Philippi, where Antony, victorious and avenged, looks on the dead body, not this time of Cæsar, but of Brutus, and pronounces a solemn dirge over him:—

> "This was the noblest Roman of them all. . . .
> His life was gentle; and the elements
> So mix'd in him that Nature might stand up,
> And say to all the world, 'This was a man!'"

He not only gave magnificent words of praise to Brutus, but also, as Agrippa tells us, shed tears over him:—

> "When Antony found Julius Cæsar dead,
> He cried, almost to roaring; and he wept,
> When at Philippi he found Brutus slain."
>
> ("Antony and Cleopatra," Act III., Sc. 2.)

This paints Antony exactly: with his artistic temperament he could give admiration and tears alike to the victim and to the murderer; it was easy for him, devoid as he was of any moral standard, but with a splendid capacity of receiving vivid impressions from everything that was beautiful or grand, to combine these contrasts in feeling.   He looked upon the world as a stage, in which each person had a part to play, and in his sight the loss of such an actor as Cæsar was heightened rather than atoned for by the death of such an actor as Brutus.*   He can hold out his hand to Cæsar's

---

* See Dowden, p. 290.

murderers without our taxing him with hypocrisy,—the
æsthetic versatility of his nature shields him, do what he
may, from our distrust.

When he begged permission of Brutus to speak at
Cæsar's funeral he probably had no intention of turning
the opportunity to account; he never guessed the immense effect his eloquence would have upon the crowd,
but simply wished to fulfil the duties of a friend, while
Brutus granted his request the more willingly because
his own affection for Cæsar made him feel a little comfort
in the thought that the funeral rites of the great hero
would be worthily celebrated.   Cassius alone foresaw
what the result would be.   It was not till afterwards,
upon reflection, that Antony became aware of the advantage that their permission to him to address the people
gave him, and it was only in the course of his speech
that he perceived the lengths to which this advantage
might be pushed.

In order thoroughly to appreciate his famous speech,
with its strange admixture of good faith and astuteness,
of premeditated art and the sudden and irresistible inspiration of the moment, we must picture to ourselves
the unpropitious circumstances under which he laboured
at the beginning.   Brutus had stipulated with Antony
that he was to cast no blame upon the conspirators, and
had himself, the very moment before, publicly justified
the murder of. Cæsar, so that the people, upon seeing
Antony ascend the tribune, all cried with one voice,
" 'Twere best he speak no harm of Brutus here."   " This
Cæsar was a tyrant."   " We are blessed that Rome is
rid of him."   Then Antony begins his magnificent
address, his eloquence soon carrying his hearers with
him, and finally working them up to such a pitch of
excitement that they burst out into groans for Cæsar's
death and cries for revenge.   The people depart tumult-
uously to set fire to the traitors' houses, and Antony, as

he stands there left alone, says, with cynical indifference
—not the indifference of an ambitious man pursuing re-
lentlessly a definite aim, but of an elegant conjurer who
has succeeded in performing a brilliant piece of juggling
by means of the terrible and powerful weapon of a public
appeal to the passions of the people—

> " Now let it work !   Mischief, thou art afoot,
> Take thou what course thou wilt ! "

In the tragedy of " Antony and Cleopatra," we see
the Triumvir forgetful of all his duties as a Roman
citizen, as a politician and a soldier, and as one of the
heads of the government, and wholly given up to the
fascinations of a woman ; but even in this state of
bondage, the comparatively noble quality which has
been already pointed out as the peculiar and distinguishing element of his nature—his æsthetic sense of
morality, which enabled him to comprehend and to love,
and even wish to imitate, what is beautiful or honourable—never forsakes him, and it is the struggle between
his higher and lower instincts that makes him a true
tragic hero.

He flatters himself with no illusions, he is clear-
sighted and brave when evil days come upon him ; and
contrary to the general custom of those who have done
wrong, he desires to have the truth frankly told him, and
never gets angry upon hearing it.

> " These strong Egyptian fetters I must break,
> Or lose myself in dotage " (Act I., Sc. 2),

he exclaims in a supreme effort ; and if he does not
entirely break them, at least he has the strength to
escape for a time. Again, after Actium, he is overwhelmed by a sense of shame (Act III., Sc. 9) :—

> " I have offended reputation ;
> A most unnoble swerving. . . .
> Hark, the land bids me tread no more upon't,
> It is asham'd to bear me."

Trouble and distress generally make a man unjust, especially when he is the author of his own ruin, but from this weakness Antony is wholly exempt. He dies without one bitter word to Cleopatra, and he freely forgives Enobarbus, who has deserted him, heaping benefits instead of reproaches upon him, and accusing himself for the defection of so true a follower :—

> " Go, Eros, send his treasure after ; do it ;
> Detain no jot, I charge thee : write to him
> (I will subscribe) gentle adieus, and greetings ;
> Say, that I wish he never find more cause
> To change a master.—O, my fortunes have
> Corrupted honest men."

For those of his servants who remain faithful to him to the end, Antony is so full of gratitude, and expresses himself with such warmth, that they all burst into tears. Eros, whom Antony in despair begs to put an end to his life, falls upon his own sword and kills himself, rather than strike his master. Kind, generous, and magnificent, Antony was adored by all his soldiers :—

" Things that seem intolerable in other men, as to jest with one or other, to drink like a good fellow with everybody, to sit with the soldiers when they dine, and to eat and drink with them soldier-like, it is incredible what wonderful love it won him amongst them." *

When Shakespeare makes Antony give his young wife, Octavia, unlimited permission to spend as much as she will, it is thoroughly in keeping with several incidents mentioned in Plutarch : a liberality of disposition, amounting almost to prodigality, would seem to have been an hereditary tendency in Antony's family :—

" His father," writes North, " was not very wealthy, and therefore his wife would not let him use his liberality and frank nature. One day, a friend of his coming to him to pray him to help him to some money, having great need, Antonius by chance had no money to give him, but he commanded one of his men to bring him some water in.

---

* North's " Plutarch."

a silver basin ; and after he had brought it him, he washed his beard
as though he meant to have shaven it, and then found an errand for
his man to send him out, and gave his friend the silver basin, and
bade him get money with that. Shortly after, there was a great stir
in the house among the servants, seeking out this silver basin. Insomuch as Antonius, seeing his wife marvellously offended for it, and
that she would examine all her servants one after another about it, to
know what was become of it, at length he confessed he had given it
away, and prayed her to be contented."

Like father, like son ; the anecdote is well known which
relates how Antony ordered his treasurer to give one of
his friends " five and twenty myriads, which the Romans
call *decies* ; " and how, when the indignant treasurer
showed him the money in a heap together that he might
see what an extravagance he was committing, Antony
"perceiving the spite of the man, 'I thought,' said he,
'that *decies* had been a greater sum of money than it is,
for this is but a trifle : ' and therefore he gave his friend
as much more another time."

Shakespeare's Antony, faithful to Cleopatra with
romantic devotion, has no intention of letting his marriage with Octavia be other than a purely political
matter. That he should love her we see could not be,
but he entertained for her every kind feeling possible,
outside of love ; and her sad fate—condemned through
his very respect for her to a forlorn and neglected life
—inspired his poetic imagination with many graceful
similes. He compares her eyes to a gleam in April, her
tears to a spring, and the gentleness of her grief to the
swan's-down feather—

> " That stands upon the swell at the full of tide,
> And neither way inclines." (Act III., Sc. 2.)

We see but little of Octavia in the play, Shakespeare
not wishing to excite too strong an interest in her, lest
it should distract attention from the two principal characters.

The moral lesson taught by " Antony and Cleopatra "
is, according to Goethe, the incompatibility of a life of
action and a life of pleasure. This no one would be likely
to deny; it is obvious that in dallying with Cleopatra,
Antony wasted his time and fortune and lost his life
and honour, and the judicious remarks that Heinrich
Heine heard when he was at school are clearly not to
be gainsaid :—

"My old Professor did not at all like Cleopatra, and made us
expressly notice how, by giving himself up to her, Antony ruined his
whole public career, and how it entailed private misfortunes upon him,
and a miserable ending."

But without disputing the value of this moral lesson,
it may be remarked that his robust temperament enabled
Antony to reconcile voluptuous pleasures and hard work,
sensual enjoyments and the privations of a military life,
to a degree unknown to feebler constitutions.   In times
of war, Antony was seen drinking stagnant water, and
eating wild roots or even the bark of trees, and feeding
upon "such beasts as never man tasted of their flesh
before," and yet with all this he was so strong and
courageous that his cheek never even grew thin.   " His
soldiership is worth twice that of Octavius and Lepidus,"
says Pompey.

From an æsthetic point of view, nothing could be
finer or more proudly and bravely conceived, than Antony's resolution, upon Octavius arriving in Egypt after
the battle of Actium, to meet him next day in a final
and decisive combat, and by way of preparation to have
one more night of revelry :—

> " Cæsar sits down in Alexandria ; where
> I will oppose his fate. . . .
> I will be treble-sinewed, hearted, breathed,
> And fight maliciously. . . .
>   Come,
> Let's have one other gaudy night: call to me
> All my sad captains ; fill our bowls once more ;
> Let's mock the midnight bell."

This strain of knightly valour as of the days of chivalry, runs through Plutarch as much as Shakespeare, and the historian even mentions one detail which has been omitted by the poet, which is in full accordance with Antony's poetic and romantic nature. He and his friends, Plutarch tells us, abolished a society which they called "The Society of the Incomparable Life," and set up another, which they called "The Order of Those that will Die Together," "the which in exceeding sumptuousness and cost was not inferior to the first." In the end, Antony, who had no moral strength of his own to uphold him, and was consequently driven to seek support from those around him, lost all those that he had leant upon, one after the other, and was left standing alone. During this last night of revelry, even his tutelar deity, Hercules, forsook him :—

"The selfsame night, when all the city was quiet, it is said that suddenly they heard a marvellous sweet harmony of sundry sorts of instruments of music, with the cry of a multitude of people as if they had been dancing, and had sung as they use in Bacchus' feasts : and it seemed that this dance went through the city unto the gate that opened to the enemies. Now such as in reason sought the depth of the interpretation of this wonder, thought that it was the god unto whom Antonius bare singular devotion, that did forsake them."

All through the ending of Antony's life, Plutarch's account is as poetical as Shakespeare's, and we can pass indifferently from the drama to the history, and from the history to the drama, without encountering any change of style or tone; for in truth the hero himself is full of poetry : his language, his feelings, his conduct become more and more poetical as he approaches his last hour. He arms himself early in the morning, and Cleopatra helps him to put on his armour :—

> " *Cleo.* Is not this buckled well ?
> *Ant.* Rarely, rarely ;
> He that unbuckles this, till we do please
> To doff't for our repose, shall hear a storm. . . .

> This morning, like the spirit of a youth
> That means to be of note, begins betimes."

Antony gains a useless victory on land, while he is hopelessly and completely beaten at sea. Upon hearing the false news of Cleopatra's death, he resolves to die :—

> " I will o'ertake thee, Cleopatra. . . .
>   I come, my Queen. . . . Stay for me :
> Where souls do couch on flowers, we'll hand in hand,
> And with our sprightly port make the ghosts gaze :
> Dido and her Æneas shall want troops,
> And all the haunt be ours."

When Eros falls upon his sword to escape from the sorrow of killing his master, who implores him to perform that last service for him, Antony exclaims :—

>   " My Queen and Eros
> Have, by their brave instruction, got upon me
> A nobleness in record : but I will be
> A bridegroom in my death, and run into't
> As to a lover's bed."

He falls upon his sword, but does not die immediately from the wound.

Cleopatra, however, was not dead, but shut up with her women in her monument; upon hearing which, Antony orders his men to carry him there, that he may die at her feet. In the tragedy, Cleopatra sings a sort of funeral hymn in honour of Antony, overflowing with passion and poetry :—

> " His face was as the heavens : . . .
> His legs bestrid the ocean : his rear'd arm
> Crested the world : his voice was propertied
> As all the tunèd spheres, and that to friends ;
> But when he meant to quail and shake the orb,
> He was as rattling thunder. For his bounty,
> There was no winter in't : an autumn 'twas
> That grew the more by reaping : his delights
> Were dolphin-like ; they show'd his back above
> The element they lived in : in his livery
> Walk'd crowns and crownets ; realms and islands were
> As plates dropp'd from his pocket."

These are the impassioned tones of love; but Antony in
an exquisitely appropriate simile has drawn an equally
poetical and, at the same time, a more exact portrait of
himself (Act IV., Sc. 12):—

> "*Ant.* Eros, thou yet behold'st me?
> *Eros.*   Ay, noble lord.
> *Ant.* Sometime we see a cloud that's dragonish:
> A vapour, sometime, like a bear, or lion,
> A tower'd citadel, a pendant rock,
> A forked mountain, or blue promontory
> With trees upon't, that nod unto the world,
> And mock our eyes with air: thou hast seen these signs;
> They are black vesper's pageants.
> *Eros.*   Ay, my lord.
> *Ant.* That which is now a horse, even with a thought
> The rack dislimns; and makes it indistinct,
> As water is in water.
> *Eros.*   It does, my lord.
> *Ant.* My good knave, Eros, now thy captain is
> Even such a body."

No truer or more striking symbol could be chosen to
represent the *splendid nothingness** of his nature,
adorned as it was with every kind of brilliant qualities,
but utterly unstable and unsubstantial, with no solid
foundation; delighting in the transient and deceitful
forms of mere æsthetic beauty, which were but a vain
and empty show, in which greatness, generosity, and
high-mindedness were absolutely unconnected with any
moral element.

CLEOPATRA.

"HAD Cleopatra's nose been shorter," says Pascal, "the
whole face of the world would have been changed."
We have no precise information as to the shape and
size of Cleopatra's nose; medals and statues here are
wanting, and history, which tells us that Antony had an

---

* Gervinus' expression.

aquiline nose, forgets to say anything with regard to the
Queen of Egypt about this interesting feature, which is
doubly remarkable, from its function as the organ of
smell, and also, as Hegel justly remarks, from its
intermediary position between the forehead and the
chin. But we know that Cleopatra's beauty was not of
a regular character : hers was not the absolute perfection
of line, as was that of Venus, or of Helen, or even of
Octavia, who, Plutarch distinctly states, yielded neither
in youth nor in good looks to Cleopatra. Neither the
noble severity of ancient Greece, nor the majesty of
Rome, belonged to Cleopatra : after reading Plutarch's
account of her successful method of introducing herself
unseen into Cæsar's presence, wrapped up in a mattrass,
and so carried by Apollodorus on his shoulder, she
remains for ever associated in our imagination with an
idea of graceful littleness, of a sort of feline suppleness
and sinuosity. Other women may be of the antique
type of beauty and grandeur, but this little creature is
fascinatingly pretty. That wonderful chivalric romance,
written by a Greek historian in the first century and
called "The Life of Antony," is irradiated by the presence
of Cleopatra as by a premature apparition of modern
beauty,—animated and subtle, more mental than physical,
dazzling, less by purity of form than by ever-varying
expression. To speak of her as charming, as enchanting,
is to say little or nothing—she was an *enchantress*, a
charmer not of snakes but of men, and what was felt in
her presence was something more than attraction; she
was simply bewitching, and her spell was all the stronger
and the more irresistible because it wound itself round
its victim closer and closer by slow degrees.

"Her beauty," says Plutarch, "was not so passing as to be un-
matchable of other women, nor yet such as upon present view did
enamour men with her : but so sweet was her company and conversation that a man could not possibly but be taken. And besides her

beauty, the good grace she had to talk and discourse, her courteous nature that tempered her words and deeds, was a spear that pricked to the quick. Further more, besides all these, her voice and words were marvellous pleasant: for her tongue was an instrument of music to divers sports and pastimes, the which she easily turned into any language that pleased her."

"Enchanting Queen," "great fairy," "witch," "basilisk," "serpent of old Nile,"—such are the epithets continually applied to her in Shakespeare's play; to whom, Antony declares—

> "Everything becomes, to chide, to laugh,
> To weep; whose every passion fully strives
> To make itself in thee, fair and admired !"

That Antony should be all fervour and enthusiasm when speaking of Cleopatra is only natural, but the extraordinary thing, and that which more than everything else conveys an idea of the supernatural power of her spell, is that even those most opposed by nature to poetry and love, become equally enthusiastic when she is mentioned, and speak of her in the language of poets and of lovers. Enobarbus, a species of rough and honest humourist, if we ask him to tell us about Cleopatra, relates in glowing lines how she first met Antony upon the river Cydnus :—

> "The barge she sat in, like a burnish'd throne,
> Burnt on the water: the poop was beaten gold;
> Purple the sails, and so perfumed that
> The winds were love-sick with them: the oars were silver;
> Which to the tune of flutes kept stroke, and made
> The water, which they beat, to follow faster,
> As amorous of their strokes. For her own person,
> It beggar'd all description : she did lie
> In her pavilion (cloth of gold, of tissue),
> O'er-picturing that Venus, where we see
> The fancy outwork nature: on each side her,
> Stood pretty dimpled boys, like smiling Cupids,
> With divers-colour'd fans, whose wind did seem
> To glow the delicate cheeks which they did cool,
> And what they undid, did." (Act II., Sc. 2.)

This sailing down the Cydnus shows us Cleopatra in full dress, as it were, and is her official and ceremonious entrance on the scene; but her seductive wiles took every form, the most familiar as well as the most majestic: "I saw her once," says Enobarbus—

> "Hop forty paces through the public streets:
> And having lost her breath, she spoke, and panted,
> That she did make defect perfection. . . .
> Age cannot wither her, nor custom stale
> Her *infinite variety :*"

an admirable expression, this *infinite variety,* that all commentary would only weaken.

She was continually devising new delights, Plutarch tells us, to retain her hold over Antony. She would play at dice with him, drink with him, hunt with him. And sometimes, when he would go up and down the city in disguise, playing all sorts of pranks, Cleopatra would also array herself like a chamber-maid—

"and amble up and down the streets with him. . . . On a time he went to angle for fish, and when he could take none he was as angry as could be, because Cleopatra stood by. Wherefore he secretly commanded the fishermen that, when he cast in his line, they should straight dive under the water, and put a fish on his hook; and so snatched up his angling rod, and brought up a fish twice or thrice. Cleopatra discovered it straight, yet she seemed not to see it, but wondered at his excellent fishing: but she told her own people how it was, and bade them the next morning to be on the water to see the fishing. Antonius then threw in his line, and Cleopatra straight commanded one of her men to dive under water before Antonius' men, and to put some old salt-fish upon his bait. Antonius thinking he had taken a fish indeed, snatched up his line. Then they all fell a-laughing. Cleopatra laughing also, said unto him: 'Leave us, my lord, Egyptians, your angling-rod: this is not thy profession, thou must hunt after conquering of realms and countries.'"

Shakespeare has introduced all the little details given by Plutarch, even down to this anecdote of the salt fish. In all his plays no more striking example can be found of his bold and comprehensive treatment of character than his Cleopatra; and the more the Roman tragedies are studied, the stronger will the conviction grow that it is in this perfect ease and wide liberality of touch that Shakespeare's peculiar excellence consists. Cleopatra has furnished the subject of two Latin, of sixteen French, of six English, and of at least four Italian tragedies; the lesser works may be left aside, and we will go straight to the product of a great master. Ptolemy's sister is one of the principal figures in Corneille's " Pompée," but that a really lifelike portrait of her should be painted by Corneille was simply impossible : the habit into which the French drama had fallen of generalizing its figures into mere abstractions, and the constant tendency towards what was great and noble, which was one of Corneille's marked characteristics, effectually prevented such a thought from ever even occurring to him. With him she is always a Queen, an utterer of fine sentiments, as Molière would say, but she is scarcely a woman The constant dignity with which he invests her can only have belonged by fits and starts to the real Cleopatra, who was absolutely incapable of sustaining this lofty tone for ten minutes together.* Cleopatra, in the French tragedy, aspires to Cæsar's hand, but magnanimously undertakes to protect Pompey, who has sought refuge in Egypt after his defeat :—

> " *Cleo.* 'Tis true I love him, but my ardent flame,
> Though burning bright, can never blind my soul.
> To help the vanquished is a noble law
> Which I obey, consumèd still with love
> For him who vanquished him. And she who dares
> To place her love so high, must ne'er allow
> Suspicion even of one single fault
> To cling to her. Unworthy were it, both
> Of him and me alike, should I attempt
> To ensure his love by means of aught that's vile.

---

* Mrs. Jameson, " Characteristics of Women."

> *Char.* 'Tis strange if you love Cæsar to speak thus.
> Would you have Egypt armed in Pompey's cause,
> And shelter him from his avenging foe?
> The yoke of love you bear but lightly, madam.
> *Cleo.* A prince must needs be noble, like his birth,
> Controlling passion with a sovereign hand,
> And following only glory's golden path.
> Illustrious always when he trusts himself,
> Unheedful of the whispers from below;
> For when the people see him swerve from right,
> Corrupt advice from others is the cause.
> *Char.* With Cæsar then in love, and yet his foe——
> *Cleo.* A flawless love, a heart unstained and pure
> I give to him."

This is a good instance of the manner in which Corneille, who was a great epic poet rather than a dramatic one, ennobled all he touched.

The subject of Shakespeare's tragedy is the guilty love of Antony and Cleopatra, a subject that would have presented an almost insuperable difficulty to a poor little poet of a narrow and mediocre type; quite at a loss, and biting his pen the while, he would have said to himself, "What is to be done? Cleopatra is a very wicked woman, a *monster*, as Horace calls her,—a mixture of all we most hate and despise, she is a coquette, timid, cowardly, cringing, perfidious, tyrannical, cruel and wanton. To interest decent people in such a creature is clearly impossible, except by making a selection from among the contradictory features of her character, and since Plutarch speaks of her as being occasionally generous, tender and devoted, heroic and sublime, I must convert the exception into the rule, and put an expurgated Cleopatra on the stage." But Shakespeare reasoned in a very different manner. He started with the notion of Cleopatra as an enchantress, and he trusted with quiet confidence to the power of his poetry, and to his sure knowledge of the human heart, to make the same fascination that she exercised over her lovers be

felt by us: her faults, her vices, her crimes—what do
they matter? Everything with her becomes graceful
and alluring :—

> "Vilest things
> Become themselves in her; that the holy priests
> Bless her when she is riggish."

Besides which, it betrays a good deal of simplicity to
suppose that certain sins which are repulsive in a man
are equally odious when met with in a woman. A man
is ugly, and has hard work to atone for his natural
ugliness, but, as a poet has said—and it is no empty
compliment, but an astute psychological truth,—women,
do what they will, are always charming :—

> "On en peut par hasard, trouver qui sont méchantes ;
> Mais qu'y voulez vous faire? Elles ont la beauté."*

Shakespeare has not deemed it necessary to leave out
any of the stains, big or little, in Cleopatra's character, as
he was obliged to do in Antony's case; and this, instead
of depriving the lovely little monster of a single charm,
only makes her the more irresistible.

Her coquetry is a finished work of art: see how she
plays upon poor Antony, how she laughs at him, even
imitating and mocking him, and how she teazes him at
every turn with the name and recollection of Fulvia :—

> "What says the married woman?—you may go; . . .
> Let her not say 'tis I that keep you here,
> I have no power upon you; hers you are."

To inflame the passion they have excited, by running
counter to it, is the great secret of coquettes when sure of
their power. If Antony wishes for amusement and asks,
"What sport to-night?" Cleopatra advises him to hear
what the ambassadors from Rome have to say, but as
soon as ever he shows some faint disposition to go where

---

* Alfred de Musset.

duty and honour call him, she intoxicates his mind with
the thought of pleasure. She is far more learned in all
coquettish arts and wiles than her attendants, Iras and
Charmian, though they too are anything but inexperienced and unsophisticated maidens :—

> " *Cleo.* See where he is, who's with him, what he does.—
> I did not send you.—If you find him sad,
> Say I am dancing; if in mirth, report
> That I am sudden sick : quick, and return.
> 　　*Char.* Madam, methinks, if you did love him dearly,
> You do not hold the method to enforce
> The like from him. . . .
> In each thing give him way, cross him in nothing.
> 　　*Cleo.* Thou teachest like a fool : the way to lose him."
> 　　　　　　　　　　　　　　　　　　(Act I., Sc. 3.)

With this calm cruelty, this cat-like skill in playing
with her prey, is mingled a passionate unreasonableness,
enough to drive the most resolute patience mad. She
allows Antony neither to mourn over his wife's death,
nor to treat it with indifference : if he weeps for his wife
it is treachery towards Cleopatra, and if he weeps not,
she exclaims :—

> "O most false love !
> Where be the sacred vials thou shouldst fill
> With sorrowful water ? Now I see, I see,
> In Fulvia's death how mine received shall be.

This spoiled child is undoubtedly in love ; Antony, of
the race of Hercules, was just the man to please a feminine nature like hers, and the reality of her love, which
may be open to dispute as a matter of history, is beyond
all question in Shakespeare. Corneille wished to see
in Cleopatra a woman actuated entirely by political
motives :—

"In closely examining history," he writes, "I find that Cleopatra
was full of ambition but not of love, and that she made a diplomatic
use of her advantages in the way of beauty, in order to secure her fortunes. This becomes apparent, although not expressly stated by his-

torians, when we consider that she only gave herself to the two
foremost men of the world, Cæsar and Antony, and that after Antony's
overthrow she spared no artifice to entangle Octavius in the same fatal
passion, thus showing that it was Antony's power and position which
attracted her, and not his person."

But though statecraft may furnish subjects for very
fine lines, as Corneille has proved, it offers a very meagre
dramatic interest, and accordingly, with Shakespeare, the
passion of the two lovers forms the life and soul of the
play.   That Cleopatra's love for Antony may have been
due to a certain extent to political ambition, is quite
possible and even probable, but the poet had no wish to
show her under this aspect.   He presents her as a woman
rather than as a Queen, and makes no reference to what,
Plutarch says of there not being a single prince among
all Antony's kingly allies to whom she yielded in prudence and judgment.   The poet, for whose mighty touch
no contrasts, however intricate, were too difficult, may
perhaps justly be reproached for omitting to make this
further addition to the " infinite variety " of her qualities ;
but still it must be acknowledged that the suppression of
the ambitious and political side of her nature makes her
stand out in greater relief as a woman of an amorous and
impassioned disposition.

And so Cleopatra is in love with Antony.   When he
has left for Rome she scarcely knows how to endure his
absence, and wishes to drink mandragora to sleep away
the time.

> " *Cleo.*   O Charmian,
> Where think'st thou he is now ? Stands he, or sits he ?
> Or does he walk ? or is he on his horse ?
> O happy horse, to bear the weight of Antony. . . .
>   He's speaking now,
> Or murmuring, ' Where's my serpent of Old Nile ? '
> For so he calls me."

She wishes to know whether when he left he was sad
or merry, and upon Alexas answering "He was nor sad,

nor merry," she comments on this insignificant answer
with all the ingenious subtlety of love.*

> " O well-divided disposition!—Note him,
> Note him, good Charmian, 'tis the man; but note him:
> He was not sad; for he would shine on those
> That make their looks by his: he was not merry;
> Which seem'd to tell them his remembrance lay
> In Egypt with his joy: but between both;
> O heavenly mingle!—Bee'st thou sad, or merry,
> The violence of either thee becomes,
> As does it no man else. . . .
> Did I, Charmian, ever love Cæsar so?"

" O, that brave Cæsar!" repeats Charmian, mechanically echoing her mistress, and meaning no evil.

> " *Cleo.* By Isis, I will give thee bloody teeth,
> If thou with Cæsar paragon again
> My man of men!"

To send greetings to him every day, she will despatch
messenger after messenger, " or I'll unpeople Egypt."

In the scene between Cleopatra and the messenger
who brings the tidings of Antony's marriage with
Octavia, her fury and unreasonableness know no bounds.
Harpagon, thumping Maître Jacques, who, in obedience
to his master's orders, tells him candidly what is said of
him in the town; the Viceroy of Peru, in the " Périchole "
of Mérimée, banishing his secretary for a like service,
are models of wisdom and coolness compared to Cleopatra.
There is some shadow of excuse for their anger, as the
account given them is not the mere simple announcement
of a fact, but consists of a long preachment which the
secretary and Maître Jacques may have flavoured with

---

* " One alarming sign that a man is beginning to lose his head is
when, in thinking of some little fact, he sees it as white, and interprets
it all in favour of his love, but an instant afterwards perceives it as black,
and yet finds it equally conclusive in favour of his love."—Stendhal.

a spice of malice of their own; but the unhappy messenger to Cleopatra is as guiltless of the message as if he had given it to her under cover, closed and sealed. To insult him, beat him, and threaten him with a dagger shows a capability of exercising the same frenzy upon inanimate objects, such as pieces of furniture, mirrors, and china. No man, however furious, vents his rage in so senseless a form as this, which would seem to belong peculiarly to the anger of women and children. But at the same time, we must notice how passion dignifies every movement and action; the impetuous torrent of her wrath even makes what is immeasurably petty, mean, and ridiculous appear grand. No one would ever feel inclined to laugh at this scene, in which what might have been the subject for a comedy is transformed by the violence and force of Cleopatra's love into tragic cries and outbursts.

The thought of Octavia henceforth continually torments her. What is her rival like? She must have details and details without end; and accordingly sends Alexas after the messenger :—

> " Go to the fellow, good Alexas; bid him
> Report the feature of Octavia, her years,
> Her inclination; let him not leave out
> The colour of her hair. . . .
> Bring me word how tall she is." (Act II., Sc. 5.)

The only means of appeasing her insatiable curiosity is to bring back the messenger, whose fear has a good deal abated now that he has had time to reflect upon the secret, which is as simple as it is infallible, of how to please this terribly spoiled child. Taught by experience, he speaks welcome falsehoods of Octavia, and departs laden with Cleopatra's gifts.

In the year 1564, Sir James Melville, the ambassador of Mary, Queen of Scots, was admitted to an audience

of Queen Elizabeth, of which he has left an account in
his Memoirs :—

> " Then she entrit to dicern what kynd of colour of hair was re-
> puted best, and enquyred whether the Queen's or hers was best, and
> quhilk of them twa was fairest. I said the fairness of them baith was
> not their worst faltes. But she was ernest with me to declare quhilk
> of them I thocht fairest. I said she was the fairest Queen in England,
> and ours the fairest Queen in Scotland. Yet she was ernest. I said
> they were baith the fairest ladies of their courtes, and that the Queen
> of England was whiter, but our Queen was very lusome. She enquyred
> quhilk of them was of highest stature. I said, our Queen. Then she
> said the Queen was over-high, and that herself was neither over-
> high now over-laich. Then she asked what kind of exercises she used.
> I said that I was despatched out of Scotland, that the Queen was but
> new come back from the Highland, hunting, and when she had leasure
> fra the affaires of her country she red upon good bukis, the hystories
> of dyvers countries, and sometimes would play upon lute and virginelis.
> She spered gen she played well, I said raisonably for a Queen. . . .
> She asked whether the Queen or she plaid best. In that I gave her
> the praise. . . . She enquired at me whether she or the Queen danced
> best. I said the Queen danced not so hich and disposedly as she did."

Question may follow question, but of answers there are
never enough to satisfy the curiosity of a rival. No
sooner has the messenger to Cleopatra left her presence,
than she says to her attendant :—

> " I have one thing more to ask him yet, good Charmian ;
> But 'tis no matter : thou shalt bring him to me."

Poetically speaking, Antony's desertion of Octavia,
the consequent resentment of Octavius, Cleopatra's
jealousy and her determination to prevent at all hazards
a fresh reconciliation from taking place, were the causes
that brought about the battle of Actium ; and though
history may introduce wider and more general reasons
to account for the dissensions and the war, it never denies
the existence of these personal and special causes. Never
has there been a more striking instance of the fatal
power of a woman than in this immortal disaster. When

she regains her empire over Antony, Cleopatra never lets him leave her again, but keeps him always in sight, knowing that he is only to be retained by the continual witchery of her presence. She follows the army, heedless of all the embarrassment that her presence entails in the execution of strategic plans; in spite of Enobarbus, who can speak plainly enough when he chooses, and strongly inveighs against her appearance in the camp. Antony, however, justifies her presence and approves of it, and covers her with his protection. But he does more than this, and if it were not for the account given by the historian, his conduct in the matter would be taken as an invention of the poet's, so incredible are the lengths to which the blindness of his love leads him—for he actually gives up the ordering of the battle to Cleopatra. On land all the chances were in his favour—he held victory in his hand,—but it was the whim of the Egyptian Queen to insist upon a naval combat, and, contrary to the advice of all his captains, Antony decides to fight at sea.

In the midst of the engagement and while the advantage seems equally divided on either side, suddenly, to the amazement of the enemy, Cleopatra's sixty vessels are seen to turn, "hoist sail and fly."

"Antony," says Plutarch, "was so carried away with the vain love of this woman, as if he had been glued unto her, and that she could not have removed without moving of him also. For when he saw Cleopatra's ship under sail, he forgot, forsook, and betrayed them that fought for him, and embarked upon a galley with five banks of oars, to follow her that had already begun to overthrow him, and would in the end be his utter destruction."

What had happened was very simple; it was only that Cleopatra had felt frightened: she was not a woman of heroic type, and her nerves were not strong enough to bear the excitement of a battle for any length of time, —that was the whole secret. Those who seek for any

other explanation of the defeat at Actium, do so because
they start with the notion that on great occasions
Cleopatra could be truly brave, the splendid manner of
her death having acquired for her a false reputation for
courage; but her supposed heroism is only a brilliant
theatrical cloak wrapped round the most feminine little
person, presenting the most complete contrast to all man-
liness of character that ever wore a crown. We have
only to study closely her ending, as it is given by Shakespeare, and the mask falls—the woman remains and the
heroine vanishes.

After his victory at Actium, Octavius endeavours to
lure her away from Antony, and sends a messenger who
is most graciously received by the consummate actress,
and whom she charges with a submissive message to
Octavius. She gives him her hand to kiss, and as he is
pressing it to his lips, Antony enters.

A most violent scene ensues between the exasperated
lover and the frightened Queen. Twice in the play such
scenes occur; a guilty love like theirs could be no continual idyl, and sin must inevitably bear its bitter fruits.
Antony is superb in his rage, which is like the rage of
Jupiter the Thunderer. Cleopatra bows her head and
recognizes her master. He forgives her, speaks again of
fighting and of conquering, and the two hearts are
completely reconciled, until a fresh act of treachery or of
cowardice on her part causes so terrible an explosion of
anger from Antony that she rushes away, and shuts herself up with her women in her monument, and sends
word to Antony that she is dead.

When Antony is brought to her tower, dying from
his self-inflicted wound, she does not venture to open the
door, but she and her women draw him up by ropes
through the window.

But in spite of her precautions she is taken. First,
the envoys of Octavius, and then Octavius himself make

their way into the monument, and Cleopatra humbly bends the knee and speaks soft words to him.

An amazing little incident, not invented by Shakespeare but to be found in Plutarch, exhibits the inherent falseness of her nature with such frank impudence that it makes the reader smile, as it must have made Octavius himself smile. She gives up her gold and plate and jewels to Cæsar, protesting she has kept back nothing for herself, and calls upon Seleucus, her treasurer, to testify to the truth of what she says: but Seleucus is an honest-spoken man and cannot conscientiously confirm her statements. This exasperates her to such a degree that even in Cæsar's sight, and appealing to Cæsar, she exclaims against the ingratitude and perfidy of her slave, beating him and ordering him off, because he would not serve her with a convenient little lie.

Cleopatra wishes for death indeed, but her wish is due neither to the loss of Antony, nor to the loss of her kingdom, nor to the loss of her liberty; all these sorrows and humiliations she could have borne, but when she hears that Octavius intends taking her to Rome, all that would befall her if led in triumph through the streets of Rome, flashes through her imagination, and the bare thought of it is insufferable.* She had long been occupied with the study of poisons, seeking to discover one that would ensure a speedy and a painless death: the bites of serpents had particularly attracted her attention, and after various experiments on prisoners condemned to death, she had come to the conclusion that that of the asp was the most desirable. It produced no convulsions —nothing violent or horrible; it only caused a feeling of sleepiness, and a slight moisture on the face, and so pleasant was this drowsiness that the victim had no wish to be awaked out of it; to die like this was but another voluptuous pleasure.

---

* "Mrs. Jameson, "Characteristics of Women."

For the last time she puts on her royal robe and crown, and then, taking up an asp from the basket of figs just brought to her, she applies it to her breast, saying to Charmian who utters an exclamation of horror :—

> " Peace, peace !
> Dost thou not see my baby at my breast,
> That sucks the nurse asleep? "

Never was self-inflicted death more soft and gentle or more suggestive of the metaphor of sleep.

> " She looks like sleep,
> As she would catch another Antony
> In her strong toil of grace."

The final impression left upon the mind by this woman, in whom there was no real goodness or grandeur of character, is that of a grace and a fascination that never leave her from the beginning to the end, and in her last moments, that of majesty.   As an example of the magic power of beauty and of poetry Shakespeare's Cleopatra stands alone.

CHAPTER XXI.

ANTONY AND CLEOPATRA (*continued*). OCTAVIUS. LEPIDUS. ENOBARBUS.

OCTAVIUS.

IN the whole range of historical figures it would be difficult to find one more disagreeable, more ugly, and more repulsive than Cæsar's nephew, Octavius, who afterwards became the renowned Augustus, so chanted and glorified by the poets. Not that he was a monster of wickedness; comparatively speaking at least and placed by the side of the more thorough-going ruffians who were members of his august family, he could hardly be called so. But from a poetical point of view this is just where his fault lies; had he been more frankly and boldly wicked he would have been less detestable. Schiller has very truly remarked that a robber gains, poetically speaking, by being also a murderer, and that a man who lowers himself in our æsthetic esteem by some paltry rascality, may raise himself by the commission of a great crime. But in a mean shivering creature, who used to regale himself upon an ounce of bread and a few dried raisins, and in winter wore four tunics under his toga, it is impossible to feel any vivid interest. Military courage, we know, was not one of his virtues. His favourite maxims, " Precaution is better than boldness," " Make haste

slowly," etc. were of much the same unheroic character
as the saying that Louis XI. was so fond of repeating:
"In war the honour is his who gains the most by it."
Political sagacity can hardly atone for the absence of
physical courage, in the opinion of mankind in general,
which in this instance coincides with the judgment of
poetry; and, moreover, it may be gravely doubted whether
Octavius was as wise a statesman as he was said to be.
If ever in history there was a man predestined to win, it
was Octavius, and all his skill, which was of a negative
rather than of a positive order, simply consisted in
offering no obstacle to his good fortune, but in letting
things work for him, and in floating on the stream of
events which carried him on of itself. He has often, like
many other persons whose whole wit consists in preserving a judicious silence, been taken for a deep thinker,
but his solemn and mysterious manner only hides the
emptiness beneath. Nothing is more irritating for purposes of analysis than this kind of colourless character,
which has nothing original or worth studying about it,
and which defies all definition, because its indefinite
and varying features cannot possibly be brought into
any sort of unity.

For instance, Octavius was cruel from inclination
as well as from policy, and several instances of his cruelty
are related by Suetonius which Caligula himself might
have envied him; but he had his moments of moderation
and clemency notwithstanding, and it is to one of these
slight attacks of generosity that he owes the reputation
of magnanimity which he has obtained through the too
great benevolence of Corneille, who was ever on the
watch for what was grand and noble.

The death of his enemy Antony inspired him,
according to Suetonius, with feelings of delight, but
according to Plutarch, he withdrew into his tent and
wept and lamented. Shakespeare here, as always,

follows Plutarch; but his conduct is not of the slightest importance, nor is it even necessary to suppose that his tears were hypocritical: with his thin coating of sensitiveness he might easily be affected for an instant by the "breaking of so great a thing." A passive instrument in the hands of fortune, tame and colourless, without one ray of poetry in his nature, Octavius both in history and in Shakespeare is an absolutely vapid and insipid personage. To take him as the representative of an iron will, cold, patient, and certain of his aim, as some commentators have done, and to contrast him with the lavish splendour of a brilliantly gifted nature, whirled away by a fatal passion, like that of Antony, is assuredly to do him too much honour. We meet with many practical men of action in Shakespeare's plays who are tolerably worthy of forming a contrast to the more poetical but less sensible hero, such as Fortinbras in "Hamlet," Alcibiades in "Timon of Athens," and Cassius in "Julius Cæsar;" but we may be allowed to doubt whether Octavius had any very real practical merit, and whether the appearance he had of it was not entirely due to the egregious folly and infatuation of his opponent, by force of contrast with which, the faintest signs of ability or wisdom would become magnified. When Antony, after his defeat, challenged Octavius to single combat, it was not necessary for him to be a wise man, to shrug his shoulders at a challenge so obviously absurd,—not to be a hero was quite sufficient.

It was not Octavius, but the star of his destiny that won the battle of Actium: Cleopatra took flight, her lover followed her, and Octavius, as usual, had only to let the gods act for him. At most, he only fills in the tragedy the place of the principal agent in Antony's predestined downfall.

LEPIDUS.

Lepidus is at all events amusing; he is such an un-equivocal nonentity that he becomes positively comic. As soon as he makes his entrance on the scene in " Julius Cæsar " (Act IV., Sc. 1), his two colleagues in the Trium-virate send him about on errands. They begin by all three sitting round a table, making out a list of those condemned to death, but Antony soon sends Lepidus to Cæsar's house to fetch his will. It is amusing to see how Corneille, without the slightest satirical intention, makes Lepidus play the same menial part in his tragedy of "Pompée," in which Cæsar recommends Cornelia, Pom-pey's widow, to his care, saying, "Choose thou for her some fitting suite of rooms."

In "Julius Cæsar," as soon as he has left the room, the conversation between the two remaining triumvirs turns upon him :—

> " This is a slight unmeritable man,
> Meet to be sent on errands. . . .
> And though we lay these honours on this man,
> To cure ourselves of divers slanderous loads,
> He shall but bear them as the ass bears gold,
> To groan and sweat under the business,
> Either led or driven, as we point the way. . . .
> 　　　　　　　　Do not talk of him
> But as a property."

The poor man is regarded in the same light by the lackeys as by their masters, and laughed at for his abject servility :—

" 2 *Serv.* Why this it is to have a name in great men's fellowship: I had as lief have a reed that will do me no service, as a partizan I could not heave.

1 *Serv.* To be called into a huge sphere, and not to be seen to move in't, are the holes where eyes should be, which pitifully disaster the cheeks."

Antony never opens his lips without Lepidus exclaiming, "'Tis nobly spoken," and to all that Octavius proposes he cheerfully cries *Amen.* This open-mouthed and indiscriminate admiration on his part is ridiculed wittily enough in the running fire of laughter and jests kept up by Agrippa and Enobarbus :—

> "*Agr.*   'Tis a noble Lepidus,
> *Eno.* A very fine one : O, how he loves Cæsar !
> *Agr.* Nay, but how dearly he adores Mark Antony !
> *Eno.* Cæsar ? Why, he's the Jupiter of men.
> *Agr.* What's Antony ? The god of Jupiter. . . .
> *Eno.* Would you praise Cæsar, say, ' Cæsar ; '—go no further.
> *Agr.* Indeed, he plied them both with excellent praises.
> *Eno.* But he loves Cæsar best :—yet he loves Antony. . . .
> *Agr.*   Both he loves.
> They are his shards, and he their beetle."
>
>   ("Antony and Cleopatra," Act III., Sc. 2.)

The three triumvirs and Pompey figure in a wonderful scene, which is perhaps the most humorous in all Shakespeare's plays, attaching to the word humorous a meaning which may perhaps be thought narrow and inadequate, but which at any rate has the advantage of being precise and definite. Like Jean Paul and Heinrich Heine, I mean by humour a sense of the nothingness of all things, but a sense not sad or bitter, but light, and joyous, and poetic. The Preacher crying at the beginning of his book, "Vanity of vanities, all is vanity," is only half a humourist ; the peals of laughter and the fantastic fancy of the author of "Gargantua" must be added to this profound conviction of the nothingness of the universe, in order to form the real and complete humourist. There is something very individual and personal about the humorous spirit, and it can only belong to those natures whose originality is of a very strenuous and peculiar type. We cannot expect to find it in Shakespeare to the same extent as in Rabelais or in Sterne ; he is more in earnest than either of these sublime mockers ever was ; besides which, his plays are

too impersonal for so intensely subjective a spirit as
that of humour and one so destructive of all great art
and true beauty, to be admitted otherwise than occasionally.   But, on the other hand, Shakespeare was too
philosophical not to be impressed with the truth that in
reality "all is vanity," and his disposition was too
serene and unfettered for him not to laugh sometimes at
the folly of mankind and the nothingness of things.   In
his tragedies and comedies alike, we come across many
humorous personages who serve as his mouth-piece, and
give expression to this mode of viewing the ways of the
world,—Enobarbus, for instance, is one of these laughing
interpreters of his deep yet gentle irony,—but Shakespeare's humour is sometimes too general and wide-spread
to be limited to an individual character, and is inextric-
ably intertwined with the very soul of the play.   And
this is peculiarly the case with "Antony and Cleopatra."
The dominant impression made by it on the spectator
from the very beginning, and which never leaves him
till the final catastrophe is reached, is that of a world
crumbling to pieces in the midst of riot and revelry.*
It is not only one man, but an historical era, it is the
grandeur of ancient Rome, which is gaily accomplishing
its ruin amid laughter and songs, while soothsayers,
eunuchs and wantons all join hands and dance the
giddying round of the Egyptian Bacchanals.   And
this general impression of the play is condensed and
summed up in the symbolic and humorous scene of the
banquet given by Pompey to the triumvirs.

The incident of the banquet is mentioned in Plutarch,
but he merely suggests the subject, and the whole picture
itself, the conversation and behaviour of the chiefs,—with
the single exception of the proposal made to Pompey by
Menas the Corsair, and Pompey's answer,—is all Shake-

---

* Hazlitt.   See also Kreyssig, Vol. I., p. 438.

speare's own, and I know of no other poet who could have conjured up so daring, so characteristic, and so burlesque a scene.

The revellers begin by making Lepidus drunk, by getting him repeatedly to drink what Shakespeare calls "alms-drink," the extra amount of wine that one devoted boon companion drinks out of kindness to another whose share it is; just as in the Triumvirate (for everything in this scene has a satirical meaning) Lepidus was admitted in order to take off the load of envy and responsibility from his two colleagues.

While Lepidus is visibly approaching the condition of plenitude and ease in which a man soon lets himself roll gently under the table, Antony, whose head is stronger, enters like a well-bred man of the world upon an eminently instructive conversation with Octavius on the local customs and physical geography of Egypt. In the midst of this gay and careless scene comes the thrilling whisper in which Menas offers to make Pompey lord of all the world, by cutting the cable of the vessel and then falling on the throats of the three sharers of the world. Pompey gives an indignant refusal, and again health after health is drunk, until finally Lepidus is carried off in a completely helpless condition. Antony, whose robust temperament can stand an immense amount of wine, continues to drink to Octavius, who would willingly dispense with the compliment and groans under the "monstrous labour" imposed upon his delicate health by the demands of courtesy. Then the merriment grows wilder and wilder, and they fall to dancing "the Egyptian Bacchanals to celebrate their drink."

The music plays, and the revellers dance round and round, hand in hand, singing louder and louder the song to Bacchus :—

> " In thy vats our cares be drown'd ;
>   With thy grapes our hairs be crown'd :
>   Cup us, till the world go round ; ˙
>   Cup us, till the world go round ! "

Octavius with his accustomed prudence does his best
not to be dragged into this frantic jollity, but in the
company of madmen there is little chance of remaining
thoroughly sane : he too has drunk too much, for his
pale cheeks are on fire, but his mind is perfectly clear,
and he is quite aware of the state of things and sternly
disapproves of it :—

> " Pompey, good night.   Good brother,
> Let us request you off : our graver business
> Frowns at this levity.—Gentle lords, let's part ;
> You see we have burnt our cheeks : strong Enobarbe
> Is weaker than the wine ; and mine own tongue
> Splits what it speaks : the wild disguise hath almost
> Antick'd us all.   What needs more words?   Good night.
> Good Antony, your hand."

The two triumvirs leave the vessel, arm in arm,
staggering as they go, with just enough strength to keep
on their legs, and Enobarbus who perceives their un-
steady gait calls out to them to take care not to fall.

Grimm, in his literary correspondence, writes, " It may
be very ridiculous to make valets speak in the language
of heroes, but it is infinitely more ridiculous to make
heroes speak like the common people."   What would he
have said of a scene in which the heroes so far forget their
dignity as to drown it in a drunken carouse ?   Voltaire's
indignation is well known at Shakespeare's so-called
tragedies which are only " farces in which the burlesque
and the horrible are united," and in which we see " the
lowest rabble appearing on the stage by the side of
princes, and princes often using the same language as the
mob."   Judgments of this kind belong to a period in
which the characters of a tragedy were merely regarded

as so many lay figures, who were expected to act in a solemn and ceremonious manner, especial care being taken that they should speak in the most courtly style and be able to make court-curtseys; and they belong moreover to a country in which the spirit of society and of high-bred manners has always been peculiarly cultivated and prized, and this differs as widely from the humorous spirit as one of our garden plants does from a foreign wild flower. These adverse opinions, however, do not prevent the banquet on board Pompey's vessel from being a most excellent scene, and one even more thoroughly Shakespearian perhaps than the passages most celebrated for beauty in his plays, since in this particular kind of humorous presentation he is not only unrivalled, but has neither follower nor forerunner. "Vanity of vanities, all is vanity;" what more amazing or more grotesque commentary on this philosophical truth, which lies at the basis of the spirit of humour, could be found than this scene, in which the lives of the triumvirs depend upon a rope that Pompey had only to say the word to have cut, and in which Lepidus, "the triple pillar of the world," rolls dead drunk under the table, and is carried off on the back of a slave.

ENOBARBUS.

An interest of a double kind is presented by Enobarbus, with whom our psychological study of the tragedy of "Antony and Cleopatra" will be brought to a close, for he is the mouth-piece of Shakespeare's humorous views regarding men and events, and he is also a character in himself. The part played by him has been ingeniously compared to that of the chorus in Greek tragedy, one of the offices of which was to serve as a vent for the poet's thoughts and opinions; but this comparison would require many restrictions and reserves before it could be accepted. Shakespeare has never made any one of his characters pronounce the whole truth concerning any matter, as was required theoretically of the Greek chorus; *theoretically,* because as a matter of fact the Chorus in Æschylus is as much a person as any other in the drama, active, interested, and full of emotion; and in Sophocles it is often only a group of old men or young girls, with all the characteristic qualities of their age or sex. But from what we possess of Greek tragedy it has been found possible to extract an ideal standard, of which it may boldly be asserted that the habitual practice of Æschylus and Sophocles fell short. This conception of the Greek chorus which only genius could have formed, belongs to Hegel, the greatest of writers on the philosophy of art, and the pages in which he expresses it are among the finest ever produced by the highest literary criticism. Briefly to sum up their contents, it may be said with a conciseness which is necessarily somewhat obscure, that the various conflicting passions of the human soul which are separately personified on the stage, are reduced to their true perspective and are represented as a united whole by the classical chorus; and the justice and wisdom, of which the different characters of the drama only represent fragments, is set forth in all its entirety.

But to return to Shakespeare, the heart and core of his dramatic action never consists in the external conflict of moral feelings, and to not one of his characters is it given to expound and lay bare the whole of the truth; each sees only some portion of it which is hidden from the others, and none, consequently, conforms to the theoretical standard of the Greek chorus. Friar Laurence, who is supposed by Gervinus to represent in some sort a chorus, in "Romeo and Juliet," is a solitary old man, living in seclusion, ignorant of all concerns of active life, and leading a somewhat useless existence, gathering herbs in the fields; Shakespeare can never have intended to present this meditative old monk as the final oracle of wisdom; he is simply a character *sui generis*, and nothing more.* It has been pointed out in a former chapter how much is wanting to make Thersites, the arch reviler in "Troilus and Cressida," a faithful representative of the antique chorus, with which he happens to have a few superficial points of agreement. And in the same way, Enobarbus is first and foremost an individual character, one made up, that is, of mingled qualities, good and bad, and this of itself is enough to incapacitate him from performing the function of the ideal chorus, which by its very definition required absolute wisdom and absolute truth.

Still, to a certain extent, the poet's thought speaks out through Enobarbus; and it is just this mixture of a wisdom which scarcely seems to be his own but rather the promptings of some superior spirit, with a very definite and strongly marked individuality, that constitutes the originality of his character.

The day after Antony's marriage with Octavia, he predicts all that will happen. He shakes his head when Menas remarks that Cæsar and Antony are now for ever knit together, and says :—

"If I were bound to divine of this unity, I would not prophesy so. . . . you shall find the band that seems to tie their friendship together will be the very strangler of their amity." (Act II., Sc. 6.)

---

* "Shakespeare has never made the moderate, self-possessed, sedate person a final or absolute judge of the impulsive and the passionate ; the one sees a side of truth which is unseen by the other; but to neither is the whole truth visible. The Friar had supposed that by virtue of his prudence, his moderation, his sage counsels, his amiable sophistries, he could guide these two young passionate lives, and do away the old tradition of enmity between the houses. There in the tomb of the Capulets is the return brought in by his investment of kindly scheming."—Dowden's "Shakespeare: His Mind and Art," p. 121.

When Antony and Octavius agree to unite their
forces against Pompey, Enobarbus at once perceives the
weakness of the alliance, cemented as it was only by the
interest of the moment and a common dread, and warns
them of it :—

> " If you borrow one another's love for the instant, you may, when
> you hear no more words of Pompey, return it again : you shall have
> time to wrangle in when you have nothing else to do.
>
> *Ant.* Thou art a soldier only ; speak no more.
>
> *Eno.* That truth should be silent, I had almost forgot." (Act II.,
> Sc. 2.)

Lepidus is the especial butt of his humour. It is Enobarbus who compares him to the beetle of which Antony
and Octavius are the two wings, and remarks of the
servant who carries off Lepidus after the banquet that he
must be a strong fellow thus to bear " the third part of
the world." The termination of Lepidus's political career
was very appropriate to a man whom a Latin historian
calls the greatest of all nonentities, *vir omnium vanissi-
mus ;* Octavius deprived him of his power, gave him his
life which he begged upon his knees, and banished him
for ever to the island of Circe. At the news of this event
Enobarbus exclaims :—

> " Then, world, thou hast a pair of chaps, no more ;
> And throw between them all the food thou hast,
> They'll grind the one the other."

Enobarbus generally cloaks his real and serious meaning under the outward garb of satire, but occasionally he
speaks out openly enough, in no very measured terms.
He roundly tells Cleopatra the truth as to the inconveni-
ence and embarrassment her presence would occasion in
the camp ; and puts before Antony very distinctly the
madness of running the risks of a naval combat when his
greatest strength consists in his land forces. The disaster
at Actium occasions a violent outburst of grief and de-

spair from the brave warrior, whose lamentations and woe, and those of the other officers of Antony's army, recall the last pages of Æschylus' sublime tragedy of the "Persæ":—

> "*Eno.* Naught, naught, all naught! I can behold no longer:
> The 'Antoniad,' the Egyptian admiral,
> With all their sixty, fly, and turn the rudder:
> To see't, mine eyes are blasted.
>   *Scar.*   Gods, and goddesses,
> All the whole synod of them!
>   *Eno.*   What's thy passion?
>   *Scar.* The greater cantle of the world is lost
> With very ignorance; we have kiss'd away
> Kingdoms and provinces. . . .
>   Yon ribald-rid nag of Egypt,
> Whom leprosy o'ertake! in the midst o' the fight,—
> When vantage like a pair of twins appear'd,
> Both as the same, or rather ours the elder,
> The brize upon her, like a cow in June,
> Hoists sails, and flies.
>   *Eno.*   That I beheld:
> Mine eyes did sicken at the sight, and could not
> Endure a further view.
>   *Scar.*   She once being loof'd,
> The noble ruin of her magic, Antony,
> Claps on his sea-wing, and like a doting mallard,
> Leaving the fight in height, flies after her:
> I never saw an action of such shame;
> Experience, manhood, honour, ne'er before
> Did violate so itself.
>   *Eno.*   Alack, alack!"

Here we seem to catch the sound of the words broken by sobs, exchanged between Xerxes and the Chorus in the Greek tragedy: "Alas! alas! our fleet; alas, alas! our vessels have perished!"

Enobarbus portions out the share of responsibility attaching to each of the chief actors in the defeat at Actium, with a stern and rigid justice which the sentence pronounced by poetry and by history has since con-

firmed; the woman who took flight he considers as less
guilty than the man who followed her :—

> " The itch of his affection should not then
> Have nick'd his captainship. . . .
> 'Twas a shame, no less
> Than was his loss, to course your flying flags,
> And leave his navy gazing."

The story of this noble captain is a sad one. His
intentions were good, and he had a sincere affection for
his master, but he was too clear-witted not to perceive
all the hopeless folly of Antony's conduct; and he lived
too, at a time when a long succession of civil wars had
weakened the sense of devoted faithfulness to a flag, and
had demoralized the Roman armies, which were no longer
those of the Republic; and as the rival chiefs each
claimed to be fighting for Rome, a soldier might pass
indifferently from one camp to the other under the
belief that he was following his country's standard all
the time. Discipline, in fact, had entirely vanished;
Menas, when angered at Pompey's refusal to follow his
treacherous counsels, resolved to leave his service. Enobarbus is a man of infinitely greater honour and conscience, but although he represents all that a noble heart
could preserve in the way of chivalrous fidelity to a
madman like Antony, in that age of decadence in which
the notion of duty had become perverted among the
Roman soldiers by means of unrighteous wars, and in
which Egypt had enervated them both in body and
soul, and surrounded them with so many corrupting influences, yet he, even he, ends by deserting his master.
His first impulse after the defeat at Actium is to resist
the general movement towards desertion which passes
like a wave over Antony's army, and in which many of
the leaders pass over to the enemy. But when his
general is guilty of the signal folly of challenging the
conqueror to single combat, his reason revolts, and the

thought of deserting a master whom misfortune is power-less to teach, begins to present itself to his mind :—

> " That he should dream,
> Knowing all measures, the full Cæsar will
> Answer his emptiness !—Cæsar, thou hast subdued
> His judgment too. . . .
> The loyalty, well held to fools, does make
> Our faith mere folly :—yet he that can endure
> To follow with allegiance a fallen lord,
> Does conquer him that did his master conquer,
> And earns a place i' the story." (Act III., Sc. 11.)

In the end, Enobarbus succumbing to temptation, leaves Antony's camp, who in his generosity writes him an affectionate letter of farewell, and sends him all his chests and treasures. But the deserter had no need to wait for Antony's message to feel the pangs of repentance : his resolution was hardly formed and acted upon before he exclaims :—

> " I have done ill ;
> Of which I do accuse myself so sorely,
> That I will joy no more."

The tragedy does not say that he kills himself ; he literally dies of remorse in Cæsar's camp during the night, calling upon the moon as a witness of his repen-tance ; his last words form one of the most poetical and most touching little bits in Shakespeare :—

> " Be witness to me, O thou blessed moon,
> When men revolted shall upon record
> Bear hateful memory, poor Enobarbus did
> Before thy face repent. . . .
> O sovereign mistress of true melancholy,
> The poisonous damp of night disponge upon me ;
> That life, a very rebel to my will,
> May hang no longer on me : throw my heart
> Against the flint and hardness of my fault ;
> Which, being dried with grief, will break to powder,
> And finish all foul thoughts. O Antony,
> Nobler than my revolt is infamous,

Forgive me in thine own particular ;
But let the world rank me in register
A master-leaver, and a fugitive :
O Antony, O Antony ! "

And so, with his master's name upon his lips, he dies.
His figure is by far the noblest in the tragedy among
those that have more than a shadowy existence, for
Eros and Octavia, two other beautiful apparitions, only
pass and disappear.

Notwithstanding all its poetry and all its magnificent
glow and colour, " Antony and Cleopatra " is the weakest
of the three Roman tragedies. Its principal fault is that
of diffuseness. The innumerable facts and anecdotes
which Shakespeare found in Plutarch and inserted in his
tragedy, greatly interfere with its dramatic unity and
clearness ; as for instance the scene in the third act,
in which Ventidius returns from an expedition against
the Parthians, which is not only entirely superfluous but
also wholly devoid of any interest whatever. Michael
Angelo used to say, " a statue should be so made that
it could roll from the top of a mountain down to the
bottom, without breaking any of its limbs." And this
is a true image of the strict severity of composition by
which all the parts of a work of art, of a drama as well
as of a statue, should be bound and linked together.
By no work of art is this law more boldly transgressed
than by this tragedy of " Antony and Cleopatra." The
action comprises a period of more than ten years ; the
scene changes every moment, and the spectator is carried
incessantly from one end of the empire to the other
without a moment's rest, from Alexandria to Rome, to
Athens, to Cape Misenus, to the plains of Syria and to
various battle-fields. Its excessive irregularity is enough
to convert even the warmest partisans of dramatic
liberty to the doctrine of the unities of time and place.

Aristotle, in his distrust of our intelligence and of our knowing what is meant by a thing being entire, has taken the trouble to define the word in his " Poetics ":—

"By entire I mean that which has a beginning, a middle, and an end. A beginning is that which comes first, an end is that which comes last " (the definition is slightly abridged, but nothing essential is left out), " a middle is that which comes between the beginning and the end ; " and he judiciously adds, " whatever is beautiful, whether it be an animal or any other thing, composed of different parts, must have those parts arranged in a certain manner, and must also be of a certain magnitude. No very minute animal can be beautiful : the eye comprehending the whole too instantaneously to distinguish and compare the parts ; neither can one of prodigious size be beautiful, as, for instance, an animal of *many miles in length,* as all its parts cannot be seen at once, and the whole, the unity of the object is lost to the spectator."

An animal of many miles in length is an admirable description of " Antony and Cleopatra."

Nor does it present any tragic interest of the highest order ; the internal struggle which forms the essence of modern tragedy is not here an eminently ethical one ; the battle waged is not between duty and passion, or between two conflicting duties ; but is of a far commoner description, the clashing together of the temptations of pleasure and the dictates of self-interest, the voice of mere ordinary prudence.* In giving himself up to Cleopatra, Antony only forfeits the empire of the world, which is of less consequence than losing his soul ; from this point of view he is a less tragic hero than Enobarbus.

But the paramount claim of the tragedy to our admiration is the profusion of poetic wealth lavished upon the love of Cleopatra and Antony. Shakespeare is no pedantic and narrow moralist, and delights as much in the creation of Cleopatra, "the ideal of sensual attractiveness," as of Portia, "the ideal of moral loveliness,"

---

* Kreyssig, " Vorlesungen über Shakespeare," Vol. I., p. 438.

and he has no need, like Milton, of a chorus of Israelite captives to utter invective against the Egyptian Dalila.* This serene and placid impartiality, akin to that of the Creator, who makes His sun to shine upon the just and upon the unjust, is Shakespeare's highest glory. And it would be absurd after this, for criticism to assume the airs of a prude in speaking of these two great offenders. Their example can hardly be said to be dangerous, but if any one feels tempted to imitate them, I would only beg of him not to content himself with half measures, but to do the thing thoroughly. Pearls that have cost a few millions, and are absorbed in a single night of revelry, kingdoms and provinces to be "kissed away,"—this is all that is needed. Antony and Cleopatra are, in truth, so completely removed from all ordinary conditions of humanity, "sitting on thrones, outside the circle of the round globe," that we no more think of following them than we do of claiming the liberty of a comet to move in its eccentric orbit.†

Shakespeare, as Professor Dowden has remarked, enforces no moral lesson by means of cold, dry precepts or trite reflections, but he leaves the catastrophe to show us the inevitable end: the splendour of the feast is dimmed by no word of warning, the dancers whirl gaily by, the air is filled with strains of music and the perfume of roses—but we see a hand writing on the wall mysterious words in letters of flame, whereof the meaning is:—

" God hath numbered thy kingdom, and finished it ;

"Thou art weighed in the balances and art found wanting;

" Thy kingdom is divided, and given unto thine enemies."

---

* Dowden, pp. 313 and following.   † Hudson.

CHAPTER XXII

WE have now come to "Coriolanus," the third of Shakespeare's Roman tragedies, and the latest in point of date. The intention of the present chapter is simply to analyse the hero's character, and to seek in it the reason and explanation of his fate; for with Shakespeare men are invariably the forgers of their own chains, and are the victims of no other Nemesis than that of their own evil deeds. "Men, at some time, are masters of their fates," says Cassius,—

> " The fault, dear Brutus, is not in our stars,
> But in ourselves that we are underlings."

Although Antony might seek a salve for his vanity by ascribing all his misfortunes to the ascendency of Octavius' star, in sober truth he had none but himself to charge with his ruin.

In the case of Coriolanus, external circumstances, such as the inconstancy of the people and the treacherous conduct of the tribunes, may have palliated his misdeeds in his own eyes, and even to a certain extent may extenuate them in those of posterity; but leaving to another chapter the study of that complex personality, the restless and fickle mob, as also that of the tribunes who excited and led it at their pleasure, our present concern is solely with the moral responsibility of the violent and haughty patrician, as evidenced by an analysis of his character, and by the tragic story of his life.

Marcius, as he is called before his gallant behaviour at the taking of the town of Corioli gained for him the surname of Coriolanus, makes his entrance upon the scene in the midst of the excited populace, with contemptuous and insulting words upon his lips:—

> " What would you have, you curs,
> That like nor peace, nor war ? the one affrights you
> The other makes you proud. . . .
>   Who deserves greatness
> Deserves your hate : and your affections are
> A sick man's appetite, who desires most that
> Which would increase his evil. . . .
>   Trust ye ?
> With every minute you do change a mind ;
> And call him noble that was now your hate,
> Him vile that was your garland."

So far, there is no difficulty in admitting his contempt for the mob, proceeding as it does from a lofty sense of honour and of right. It is no petty pride of caste that vents itself in his burning words, but the pride of a noble nature : the man who thus expresses himself is an aristocrat in the best sense of the word, and we feel that with him the first title to nobility is courage—not the mere bearing of a noble name or coat-of-arms,—and that he would willingly agree with the father of Don Juan, that " birth goes for nothing if valour is absent." But at the same time, he would never go so far with the father of Don Juan as to prefer the honest, worthy son of a porter to a degenerate prince or patrician, for the notion of a porter being worth consideration would never even occur to him. To his mind, all real merit belonged exclusively to the noble classes ; and for the common people, one and all, he entertained on principle a supreme contempt. His only feeling towards them was that of a boundless and outrageously absurd and unjust disdain. For him they were in fact devoid of all rights, natural as well as political; that he should wish to abolish the recently granted office of tribunes was a small matter,—he went far beyond this, and would not even recognize their right to live, or to eat "even as dogs must," or to be hungry.

> "They said they were an-hungry; sighed forth proverbs,
> That hunger broke stone walls, that dogs must eat,
> That meat was made for mouths, that the gods sent not
> Corn for the rich man only. . . .
> Would the nobility lay aside their ruth,
> And let me use my sword, I'd make a quarry
> With thousands of these quarter'd slaves,
> As high as I could pick my lance."

When the pride of birth reaches such an altitude as this, it simply places the speaker outside the circle of humanity, and inevitably lays him open to the retort of the tribune, Junius Brutus :—

> "You speak o' the people as if you were a god
> To punish; not a man of their infirmity." (Act III., Sc. 1.)

These are the two sides, good and bad, of the aristocratic nature of Coriolanus. True valour could alone win his approbation, and a nobleman unworthy of his birth would never find favour in his sight; but he considered this and every other virtue to be the exclusive possession of the patricians, and the only sentiment excited in him by the poorer classes—called by a saintly King of France, the "common people of our Lord"—was that of a pitiless and inhuman scorn.

This duality of temperament was greatly fostered by the education he had received from his mother, a Roman matron of a lofty but rigid nature, who kindled a warm and generous spirit in him, but also taught him to call the plebeians—

> " Woollen vassals, things created
> To buy and sell with groats; to show bare heads
> In congregations, to yawn, be still, and wonder,
> When one but of my ordinance stood up
> To speak of peace or war."

Having lost his father in infancy, he was brought up entirely by his mother, and though, as Plutarch says—

" the loss of a father is no hindrance to a man's improving himself in virtue, and attaining to a distinguished excellence, yet, on the other hand, Marcius became witness to the truth of that maxim, that if a strong and generous nature be not thoroughly formed by discipline, it will shoot forth many bad qualities along with the good, as the richest soil, if not cultivated, produces the rankest weeds. His undaunted courage and firmness of mind excited him to magnificent actions, and carried him through them with honour. But, at the same time, the violence of his passions, his spirit of contention, and excessive obstinacy rendered him intractable and disagreeable in conversation. So that those very persons who saw with admiration his soul unshaken with pleasures, toils, and riches, and allowed him to be possessed of the virtues of temperance, justice, and fortitude, yet in the councils and affairs of state, could not endure his imperious temper and that savage manner which was too haughty for a republic." *

But this haughtiness of temper arose not merely from aristocratic instincts, in what they have of either good or bad; other elements mingled in it, and no adequate definition of its nature and species can be arrived at, if it is considered merely from a social standpoint, as an intense class-prejudice, nor would it be very easy to understand all his conduct. For the pride of Coriolanus was essentially a *personal* pride, and intensely egoistical. A word that drops from his mouth at the beginning of the play clearly shows that the interests of his party, and even of his country, only hold a secondary place in his heart, and that his own glory and aggrandizement was, and would remain to the end, his primary con-

---

* Langhorne's Translation.

sideration. Speaking of the Volscians, the enemies of
Rome, he says (Act I., Sc. 1) :—

> " They have a leader,
> Tullus Aufidius. . . .
> And were I anything but what I am
> I would wish me only he. . . .
> Were half to half the world by the ears, and he
> Upon my party, I'd revolt, to make
> Only my wars with him."

A striking contrast to these singularly un-romanlike
sentiments may be found in those of Corneille's Hora-
tius :—

> " My country must command against what foe
> I am to fight ; my duty is to obey :
> A soldier's highest glory doth consist
> In full obedience to his country's word,
> And he who lets a single thought intrude
> Of private ends, deserves the name of traitor.
> And now Rome bids me draw my sword, I arm
> And tarry not to reason."

Here we have the true ring of Roman patriotism. But
mark how admirably the exclamation of Shakespeare's
Coriolanus strikes the key-note both of his character
and of his history, and prepares us for the crime against
his country to which his overweening pride will in the
sequel lead him on. The man who is capable of be-
traying his cause simply for the pleasure of fighting with
Aufidius, may one day be driven, out of mere resentment, to seek the alliance of this very enemy in order
to wreak his vengeance upon Rome if it happens to
offend him.

His first action in the tragedy is a grand military
exploit: alone and single-handed, like the colossal hero
of some epic poem, he captures the whole town of Corioli.
He is alone, for the Romans have fled before the Volscians, an act of cowardice which provokes him to a
splendid outburst of rage :—

> " All the contagion of the South light on you,
> You shames of Rome !—you herd of—— Boils and plagues
> Plaster you o'er. . . .
> 　　　　　　　　You souls of geese
> That bear the shapes of men, how have you run
> From slaves that apes would beat ! Pluto and hell !
> All hurt behind ; backs red, and faces pale,
> With flight and agued fear ! Mend, and charge home, ·
> Or, by the fires of heaven, I'll leave the foe,
> And make my wars on you ! " (Act I., Sc. 4.)

The Romans, stopped in their flight and rallied for
the moment by his voice of thunder, again attack the
Volscians, who retire into their town of Corioli. Marcius pursues them to the very gates, and calling upon
his soldiers in vain to follow him, he enters alone, and
the gates are closed upon him. That he is slain is taken
for granted by all his wonder-stricken soldiers outside,
but he shortly reappears covered with blood, on the
threshold of the gates, which he has forced open : whereupon all the rest of the soldiers rush into the town,
where the only work left to be done is that of pillage
and plunder ; a scene still more ignominious in the sight
of the indignant hero than even that of their flight.

> " See here these movers, that do prize their hours
> At a crack'd drachm ! Cushions, leaden spoons,
> Irons of a doit, doublets that hangmen would
> Bury with those that wore them, these base slaves,
> Ere yet the fight be done, pack up :—down with them ! "
> 　　　　　　　　　　　　　(Act I., Sc. 5.)

Marcius, bleeding " as he were flayed," hastens to·
the succour of Cominius, and finding he has withdrawn
in safety, joyfully presses him to his heart as warmly
as he embraced his wife on his wedding-day. He
entreats Cominius to let him set out at once against
Aufidius, and departs in search of him. They soon
meet, and after taunting each other after the fashion of
Homeric heroes, the combat begins ; several Volscians

come to the rescue and save the life of Aufidius, though
they are unable to repulse Marcius, who finally forces
the Volscian army to beat a retreat, and succeeds in
making the Roman arms everywhere victorious.

Great and signal services like these call for praise
and reward, but Marcius will accept neither the one
nor the other. "Pray now, no more," he says to Titus
Lartius :—

> "My mother,
> Who has a charter to extol her blood,
> When she does praise me, grieves me."

To all the compliments and proffered wealth heaped
upon him by Cominius he returns a persistent refusal,
and vehemently deprecates the acclamations of the
crowd. "Too modest, are you!" exclaims the general;
but it was in reality the very reverse of modesty.
Honest Cominius is here the dupe of the "pride that
apes humility." In point of fact, the conduct and language of Coriolanus bear so plainly all the marks of an
inordinate pride, that they might serve as an illustration
of this first of the seven deadly sins. Pride should
never be confused with vanity; not only is there a
distinct difference between the two, but they are even
contrary and incompatible.

"To be vain," remarks Dean Swift, "is rather a mark of humility
than pride. Vain men delight in telling what honours have been
done them, what great company they have kept, and the like, by
which they plainly confess that these honours were more than their
due, and such as their friends would not believe if they had not been
told : whereas, a man truly proud thinks the greatest honours below
his merit, and consequently scorns to boast. I therefore deliver it as
a maxim, that whoever desires the character of a proud man, ought to
conceal his vanity." ("Thoughts on Various Subjects.")

When Marcius speaks of "his little," and further on
of "his nothings," he must not of course be taken at
his word : no one was more deeply convinced of his
surpassing, unparalleled merit than he was himself, but

2 F

he was perfectly sincere in his refusal of eulogy and reward, his very pride making the bare thought of them intolerable to him.   So exalted an opinion had he of himself, that he held the highest honour that could possibly be conferred upon him as infinitely beneath him, —what Antony says of his love for Cleopatra, might justly be applied to his unbounded self-esteem.

> " *Ant.* There is beggary in the love that can be reckoned.
> *Cleo.* I'll set a bourn, how far to be beloved.
> *Ant.* Then must thou needs find out new heaven, new earth."

To accept the tenth part of the booty and the flattering murmurs of the chiefs and the acclamations of the whole army, in recompense for his services, would have been an admission on his part that his deeds were in some sort within the limits of human measurement, and this was a concession that his unbounded pride forbade him to make.

The single favour he begs of the general is not for himself, but for a poor Volscian who had used him kindly, and for whose liberty he now asks.   It would be easy to ascribe a personal and self-interested motive to this apparently generous request, if any such were needed for the sake of consistency in his character,— Coriolanus might for instance deem his honour directly engaged in the protection of the rites of hospitality; but all such suggestions have been rendered quite superfluous by Shakespeare himself, who having found the incident in Plutarch, accepted it and rounded it off, bringing it into perfect harmony with the blunt and imperious nature of the man by adding a touch of his own : when Lartius inquires the name of the poor Volscian, in order to set him at liberty, Coriolanus replies :—

> " By Jupiter, forgot !—
> I am weary; yea, my memory is tired.
> Have we no wine here ? "

Coriolanus can be kind and gentle, he is capable of warm friendship and of sincere and generous sympathies; but only within the restricted circle of aristocratic tradition. He shows the utmost deference to those above him in command; he is respectful towards old age, and almost gallant towards noble ladies; he greets his wife with a gracious little speech, and tenderly embraces her; and he bows his knee before his mother. It is his mother who exercises the greatest influence over him:—

"The only thing that made him to love honour," says Plutarch, "was the joy he saw his mother did take of him. For he thought nothing made him so happy and honourable, as that his mother might hear everybody praise and commend him."

Shakespeare prepares us for the final catastrophe by a hint given by a citizen (Act I., Sc. 1): "Though soft-conscienced men can be content to say it was for his country, he did it to please his mother and to be partly proud."

Volumnia like most mothers, was ambitious for her son, even more so than he was for himself. It was she who urged him to stand for the consulship, a step which for many reasons was extremely repugnant to Coriolanus, and he only yielded to her wish after strenuous resistance:—

> "Know, good mother,
> I had rather be their servant in my way,
> Than sway with them in theirs."

Words profoundly true, significative of the fact that independence shuns the highest places and is only to be found in midway and intermediary positions. It was this law of independence that prevented Coriolanus from desiring the position of commander-in-chief in the war against the Volscians, and induced him gladly to accept a post of subordinate importance under Cominius. He was willing to obey that he might be the freer. The true motive of his conduct was divined by the acuteness of the tribune, Junius Brutus. "Fame," he says—

> " Cannot
> Better be held, nor more attain'd, than by
> A place below the first : for what miscarries
> Shall be the general's fault, though he perform
> To the utmost of a man ; and giddy censure
> Will then cry out of Marcius, ' O, if he
> Had borne the business ! ' " (Act I., Sc. 1.)

Coriolanus is nominated consul by the senate without any difficulty, but it still remains for him to get elected by the people. In Plutarch, Coriolanus fulfilled all the requirements of the law, but Shakespeare has taken good care not to make his Coriolanus so docile a candidate.

> "I do beseech you,
> Let me o'erleap that custom; for I cannot
> Put on the gown, stand naked, and entreat them,
> For my wounds' sake, to give their suffrage; please you
> That I may pass this doing. . . .
> What must I say?—
> I pray, sir,—Plague upon't! I cannot bring
> My tongue to such a pace :—Look, sir;—my wounds ;—
> I got them in my country's service, when
> Some certain of your brethren roar'd, and ran
> From the noise of our own drums."

There is however, no help for it, and the usual formalities must be submitted to,—Coriolanus bravely making up his mind, proceeds to the Forum, but here, on coming in contact with the plebeians, the feelings of an aristocrat of the deepest dye rush over him,—of an aristocrat, be it noted, after the English fashion : unwashen faces and black teeth fill him with the same disgust that we have already noticed in Casca and Cleopatra. When good old Menenius, in his anxiety that Coriolanus should bear himself well before the citizens, beseeches him to speak to them in wholesome manner, Coriolanus grimly asks whether he shall—

> " Bid them wash their faces,
> And keep their teeth clean ? "

In one of Euripides' tragedies, Menelaus reminds Agamemnon of the electoral campaign he had to go through
to get chosen as general of the army :—

> " Remember the time when thou desiredst to be elected chief of
> the Greeks, ready to start for Ilion, without seeming openly to wish
> for it, but fervently. longing for it in thy heart. How humble thou
> wast then! Taking every man by the hand, thy house was open to all;
> thou gavest free access to whomsoever would, whether friendly or not,
> seeking by such lowliness to purchase from the people the object of thy
> ambition."

Nothing of all this was demanded from Coriolanus : with
their habitual rectitude of feeling, the people recognized
his claims, and approving in principle the choice made by
the senators, they only asked that he should conform to
the invariable custom in a polite and good-tempered
fashion, and make his request in the Forum with ordinary
civility. But for the aristocrat, whose inveterate hatred
of the people was as unreasoning as his pride was im-
measurable, this simple matter was far too difficult; his
mode of canvassing is more than imperious, and takes
the form of a lion's roar. His intense irony is directed
against himself as well as against the people, and he is
evidently annoyed at having stooped to place himself
in so humiliating a position. As one of the characters
remarks, " he seeks the hate of the people with greater
devotion than they can render it him." He despises
their meanness, but at the same time he rejoices in it, on
account of the hatred he feels towards them, which
derives its liveliest pleasure from his being able to justify
his instinctive contempt for them by averring everywhere, in peace and in war, in the camp and in the
market-place, that low as their social condition might be,
it was fully equalled by the baseness of their moral
nature. Never could his pride forgive him the advances

he had condescended to make to such a set of electors, unless in the very act of gaining their voices he had mocked and insulted them.

And yet he succeeds! The people are good-hearted and simple enough to promise him their votes. "He has done nobly," they say, "and cannot go without any honest man's voice.—Therefore let him be consul; the gods give him joy, and make him good friend to the people.— Amen, Amen. God save thee, noble consul!"

With these words and a parting mockery from Coriolanus, the mob quietly disperses, reflecting on the strange proceedings and the not very re-assuring political programme of the newly elected consul. "An 'twere to give again — but 'tis no matter." It costs the demagogues little trouble to make these wiseacres see that they have been laughed at, and to make them repent the promises they have given. Fickle as the wave, the crowd, at the voice of the tribunes and ex-asperated by a sense of the folly they have committed, turn like one man against Coriolanus. The news of this sudden change is brought to him by the tribunes themselves, who stop him on his way to the market-place. Coriolanus is naturally indignant at such treat-ment, and waxes hotter and hotter, while the patricians who foresee an outburst, try in vain to calm him. He raves against the "mutable, rank-scented many," and against their possession of any power in public matters, and beseeches the senators to—

> "At once pluck out
> The multitudinous tongue; let them not lick
> The sweet which is their poison : your dishonour
> Mangles true judgment, and bereaves the state
> Of that integrity which should become it ;
> Not having the power to do the good it would,
> For the ill which doth control it."

Coriolanus was conservative, much in the same sense

that various ministers of the French Republic have been
so within the last few years; he wished to destroy the
constitution of his country for the purpose of establishing
what he conceived to be the right form of government.
Not indeed that he was a stranger to liberal doctrines,
or had any tendency towards a spirit of routine or of
inaction, against which he utters a splendid protest
(Act II., Sc. 3); but the only species of liberty he would
hear of was a right and proper liberty, which is merely
another expression for signifying liberty as interpreted
by himself. He looked upon the liberal and democratic
institution of Tribunes for the people as constituting one
of the great perils of society, and accordingly proposed to
the senators to "throw their power i' the dust." But
the persons of the tribunes having been declared by law
inviolate and sacred, this proposition was a positive
crime. They had been granted to the people, when the
intolerable tyranny of the patricians had provoked a
general emigration of the plebeians to the Sacred Mount,
where they remained for four months, and from whence
they only consented to return upon obtaining the establishment of the office of tribunes, who were to be chosen
from amongst their own order, and to be invested with
power to defend their rights against the patricians. As
a matter of history, it may be noted in passing that
Coriolanus' violent outburst of anger could not possibly
have been excited by his meeting with any obstacle,
while standing for the consulship, since the election was
in the hands of the nobles, the consuls being named by
centuries and not by tribes, and was quite independent
of either the people or their tribunes. Matters, therefore,
took a somewhat different course. The cultivation of
the land having been stopped by the withdrawal of the
plebeians to the Sacred Mount, at the time of year
when the crops should have been sown, the ædiles were
obliged to buy corn from Etruria, and this Coriolanus

proposed to distribute to the people only upon condition of their giving up the rights they had so lately won on the Sacred Mount.*

But in whatever manner the suggestion of abolishing the tribuneship may have originated, it was equally a crime. A frightful tumult ensued; the tribunes raised the cry of treason, and the people quickly gathered round them: Junius Brutus declared Coriolanus worthy of death, and Sicinius Velutus without further ceremony called to the ædiles to lay hold of him and cast him down from the Tarpeian rock. The patricians succeeded in rescuing him provisionally from the fury of the populace, but were obliged to consent to his being tried in full assembly of the people, which was a new right wrung by the tribunes from the weakness of their political antagonists by means of the tumult, for in thus citing Coriolanus to the tribunal of popular justice they were overstepping their legal powers.

Plutarch relates that Marcius asked the tribunes what they accused him of:—

" The tribunes answered him, ' that they would show how he did aspire to be king, and would prove that all his actions tended to usurp tyrannical power over Rome?' Marcius with that, rising upon his feet, said: ' that thereupon he did willingly offer himself to the people, to be tried upon that accusation.'"

The absurdity of such an accusation is necessary to explain how Coriolanus could submit to the preposterous demand made by the tribunes for a patrician to be tried by an assembly of the people. The mode of voting by centuries, in which the nobles and wealthiest of the citizens formed the majority, was on this occasion to be replaced by voting by tribes, " whereby," as Plutarch

---

* Niebuhr concludes, says Dr. Schmitz in his "History of Rome," that the story of Coriolanus belongs to a much later date, and has been inserted here by mistake.

says, "the indigent and factious rabble would be sure to carry it at the poll." It was in fact, the substitution of manhood-suffrage for one of which the qualification was the possession of property. Twelve out of twenty-one tribes condemned Coriolanus to exile.

In Shakespeare's tragedy it is Volumnia—who was a woman of expedients rather than of principles, and who had not yet lost all hope of setting things straight and of seeing her son made consul—who induces him to appear before his new judges, that he may retract what he has said, and obtain pardon. Coriolanus is amazed at such advice coming from his mother, but though inwardly chafing at it he yields to her wishes, thus affording a new and most surprising proof of the ascendency his mother has over him.

Cominius and Menenius press upon him the paramount necessity of answering mildly, and he goes off with them, exclaiming impatiently—

"Well, *mildly* be it then; *mildly!*"

but we feel sure beforehand that he will forget all about their injunctions at the critical moment. In the next scene we see him before the assembly of the people; at the moment that the tribunes are about to interrogate him, he cuts them short with—

> "First, hear me speak. . . .
> Shall I be charged no further than this present?
> Must all determine here?
>   *Sic.*   Answer to us.
> We charge you, that you have contrived to take
> From Rome all season'd office, and to wind
> Yourself into a power tyrannical;
> For which you are a traitor to the people.
>   *Cor.* How! traitor? . . .
> The fires in the lowest hell fold in the people!
> Call me their traitor!" (Act III., Sc. 3.)

With Coriolanus the violence of his temper was even

greater than his pride; had he simply been haughty,
he would have met the insults of the tribune with a
calm and cold disdain; but the least word of even
unmerited abuse threw him into a frenzy, and worked
him up into a rage like that of a passionate woman or
child. In the final scene of the tragedy, the epithet of
traitor, added to that of "boy of tears," causes another
frantic outburst, and precipitates him on the daggers of
the Volscians. This excessive sensitiveness to personal
affronts, it may be noted in passing, is a purely modern
quality, far removed from the more self-contained, grave
and manly Coriolanus of antiquity.

But it is when the sentence of perpetual banishment
is pronounced upon him by the people, that he rises to
the full height of his stature. This is the climax and
culminating point of the drama, the moment that would
be chosen by a great painter to represent in all his greatness this embodiment of passion and of pride :—

> " You common cry of curs! whose breath I hate
> As reek o' the rotten fens, whose loves I prize
> As the dead carcases of unburied men
> That do corrupt my air. I banish you. . . .
>   Despising,
> For you, the city, thus I turn my back:
> There is a world elsewhere."

The attitude of Coriolanus is simply sublime—standing forth alone, greater by himself than all Rome, hurling
back on his judges their sentence of exile, and opposing
to the city that thrusts him out, his own colossal personality.

From this moment a strange alteration takes place in
Coriolanus, and he becomes calm; a change which is the
effect of his very violence, and due to the extreme gravity
of his position. Plutarch mentions it as only the cloak
under which he hid his intense indignation and thirst
for vengeance, but it went deeper than this. From the

moment that he conceived the plan of his revenge, a decadence both mental and moral took place within him,
the consciousness of which must have well-nigh begun
his expiation. To approach the Volscians disguised in
mean apparel, to inquire civilly from a passer-by where
Audifius dwelt, to say to the servants who gave him but
a rough reception, "Let me but stand; I will not hurt
your hearth," and to present himself as an ally and guest
before the master of the house, his mortal enemy, must
have been so many bitter trials to his haughty nature.
Shakespeare has inflicted upon him the supreme humiliation of brawling like a common porter with the lackeys
of Aufidius, at whose insolence he finally loses all
patience. This is the only modification introduced by
Shakespeare into Plutarch's account; with the exception
only of Aufidius' answer to Coriolanus, all the rest of
the tragedy,—Coriolanus' speech to Aufidius, the march
of the two chiefs against Rome, the vain embassy of the
patricians, generals and friends of Marcius, and lastly
the procession of Roman ladies led by Volumnia, her
words and complete victory over her son—is all to be
found in Plutarch, whom Shakespeare follows more
closely here than he has in any other part of his Roman
tragedies, not only paraphrasing or imitating him, but
adopting his very words.

That Coriolanus should listen to his mother, and
yield at her intercession, is perfectly in keeping with his
character: even the tribune, Sicinius, allowed himself to
hope that Volumnia, whom as he says Coriolanus "loved
dearly," would prevail with her son to forego his vengeance upon Rome. The very violence of his character
enables him in the supreme moment, when under the
sway of his mother's eloquence, to grant fully and
thoroughly all her desire, undeterred by any thought of
evil consequences to himself:—

"O mother, mother!
What have you done? . . .
O my mother, mother! O!
You have won a happy victory to Rome :
But, for your son,—believe it, O, believe it,
Most dangerously you have with him prevail'd,
If not most mortal to him."

According to Livy and to Fabius Pictor, Coriolanus lived on in exile to an advanced age, regretting indeed his country and given up to remorse, but still enjoying the light of the sun ; but the stern moralist of Chæronea has no such tradition : the man of violence must die a violent death, and he chooses Aufidius and his Volscians as the instruments of a divine vengeance that tarrieth not.

This tragic history may fittingly conclude with a moral reflection furnished by Plutarch, whose remark in speaking of the obstinacy of Coriolanus is full of " sweetness and light," and one which every politician may lay to heart with advantage, as although men have for the most part neither the power nor the will to push things to the same lengths that Coriolanus did, still in every extreme party, in other countries besides Rome, men of violent and narrow views are unfortunately to be found :—

" Marcius was wanting in a due mixture of gravity and gentleness, which are the chief political virtues, and the fruits of reason and education. He did not consider that the man who undertakes to manage public business and to converse with men, should above all things avoid that overbearing austerity, which, as Plato says, is always the companion of solitude ; that is to say, that those who are obstinately wedded to their own opinions and will never accommodate themselves to others, find themselves at last left alone, for he who would live in the world must needs have patience."

CHAPTER XXIII.

"CORIOLANUS" (*continued*). MENENIUS AGRIPPA.
VIRGILIA AND VOLUMNIA.

WHEN the plebeians "encamped themselves," as North
expresses it, "upon a hill, called at that day the Holy
Hill," the senate selected the "pleasantest old men and
the most acceptable to the people," and sent them to treat
with them. Menenius Agrippa was the spokesman, and
concluded his harangue with the celebrated fable of the
mutiny of the members of the body against the belly, a
fable which had been related before Plutarch's time by
Dionysius of Halicarnassus, and by Livy, and which is
included in the collection of fables ascribed to Æsop, and
which after having been mentioned by numerous other
writers in ancient and in modern times, has been used
both by Shakespeare and by La Fontaine. By means of
this allegory, according to La Fontaine, Menenius succeeded in conciliating the people and leading them back
to their duty; but, in reality, its power was not so efficacious—grievances of as serious a nature as were those of
the plebeians were not to be lulled to sleep by an ingenious
allegory,—and it was only by the concession of the
tribuneship that the people could be prevailed upon to
return to their homes. Shakespeare relates the fable
rather for its sake as a time-honoured tradition, than as

an incident of any weight in the action of the drama, and chiefly uses it as an opportunity for exhibiting the peculiarities of the narrator.

We might expect to find in Menenius Agrippa, as he plays the part of mediator between the patricians and the plebeians, a wise and moderate politician, equally removed from the extreme opinions of either party,—a perfect man in fact, like the *Aristes* and *Cléantes* in Molière, who are always softly and gravely insisting upon moderation in all things, and complain sadly of the unreasonableness of men. But Shakespeare, as has already been noticed in speaking of Enobarbus, is not wont to introduce those well-balanced moralists into his scenes, whose "whole knowledge consists in striking a balance between the false and the true." They are certainly not very entertaining personages; what interest they may possess is not of a dramatic kind, but belongs to them as monuments of Molière's courageous good sense, as the expression of a particular state of society, and of a particular period, in which reason was held in higher esteem than any other of the poetic faculties. A certain interest also attaches to them as being the natural product of the French turn of mind, which, as it can never too often be said, is fundamentally solid and serious under all its light and laughing exterior; but there is nothing comic or amusing in their very excellent sermons, and the outlines of their characters are of necessity drawn in such a general manner as not to admit of any individuality. Shakespeare had a horror of the frightfully tiresome person of the reasonable and ratiocinative type. The laughter-moving diversity of the innumerable fools who play a part in the great human tragi-comedy is the stuff whereof he makes his plays,— we need not therefore expect to meet with a sage philosopher in Menenius Agrippa.

He is, to begin with, almost as uncompromising an

aristocrat as Coriolanus himself, only he shows it in a different manner. Coriolanus flies into a passion, Menenius laughs and jokes. No one takes offence, because he is a recognized wag, whose manners have made him a favourite : he is fond of his glass, and is one of those regular old boon companions, very fat, very jovial and outspoken, who are so accustomed to be treated with indulgence that they think they may do whatever they please. Take as an example of the license he allows his tongue, his conversation with the tribunes (Act II., Sc. 1); it will serve to show that in point of aristocratic insolence there is not much to choose between him and Coriolanus. " Our very priests must become mockers if they shall encounter such ridiculous subjects as you are," etc.

Menenius being what he is, it is easy to divine that he plays the part of mediator out of no feeling of calm conviction, or elevated sense of justice, and in fact the only reason of his setting his wits to work to reconcile the hostile parties is that he is a fat old fellow, who likes to be comfortable and able to empty his bottle in peace and quiet ; and civil dissensions spoil a cup of hot wine even more than many drops of Tiber water. In the quarrel of the other members with the stomach, it was greatly to his interest as part and parcel of the stomach, to re-establish order as soon as possible, and it may be fairly conjectured that the idea of his fable was suggested to him by the hindrances thrown in the way of his ease and good living.

The vanity of Menenius offers a marked contrast to the pride of Coriolanus.* His feelings towards Coriolanus were not so much those of genuine affection as of that species of an extended domestic instinct by which courtiers are attached to their princes. When he receives a letter from Coriolanus during the war against the

---

* See Kreyssig on the character of Menenius Agrippa.

Volscians, he is overjoyed at such an honour, which
makes him feel quite young again.   (Act II., Sc. 1.)

But his character is shown most clearly, with his
vanity, his fund of good humour, his lively inconsequent
sallies, and his fussy airs as a hard-worked patriot, after
the blow has fallen and Coriolanus has turned traitor to
Rome. Half a dozen times he repeats to the tribunes, "You
have made good work;" in the midst of the general consternation he takes a satirical pleasure in their political
humiliation, and though it is not a time for laughter, he
still, like an incorrigible jester, continues to pour out his
jokes. When Cominius returns from his futile embassy
to Coriolanus, and relates how he would answer to no
name till he had forged one for himself in the fire of
burning Rome, Menenius exclaims, almost triumphantly :

> "Why, so; you have made good work :
> A pair of tribunes that have rack'd for Rome,
> To make coals cheap : a noble memory ! "

The tribunes implore Menenius to try his powers of
persuasion with Coriolanus, but he at first declines, as he
could not hope for success where Cominius had failed.
The tribunes attack his weak point and appeal to his
vanity, and in the end after a little humouring, he
agrees to do what he can :—

> " I'll undertake it :
> I think he'll hear me.   Yet, to bite his lip
> And hum at good Cominius, much unhearts me.
> He was not taken well : he had not dined."

This is the great point with Menenius : for him, dinner is
the centre of existence, and dinner shall form the basis of
his strategical operations ; when Coriolanus has dined,
he will approach him.

But Coriolanus is implacable, and Menenius returns
crest-fallen and out of countenance, followed by the jeers
of the Volscian guards ; we have no wish for any greater
misfortune to befall him, for he is neither cruel nor ill-

conditioned, but we cannot help rejoicing a little in our inmost hearts at the wholesome little lesson given to his vanity.

Having been thus repulsed by Coriolanus, he is quite sure that the same ill-success must await all and any who should venture to make a similar attempt; he regards the embassy of Roman ladies with no confidence whatever,—where he had failed, was it likely that any other person in the world, be it even the mother of Coriolanus, should succeed? Nevertheless, when the good news comes that the ladies have prevailed, he suffers no small jealousy to dim his praises and rejoicings :—

> " This is good news :
> I will go meet the ladies. This Volumnia
> Is worth of consuls, senators, patricians,
> A city full; of tribunes such as you
> A sea and land full.

Shakespeare's Menenius Agrippa is a good-hearted man in the main, but of no real worth morally or even intellectually, in spite of his celebrated fable.

VIRGILIA AND VOLUMNIA.

Livy, Dionysius of Halicarnassus, Valerius Maximus, and all ancient writers with the exception of Plutarch, give the name of Veturia to the mother of Coriolanus, and that of Volumnia to his wife. Shakespeare here as always, follows Plutarch, and calls the mother Volumnia, and the wife Virgilia. These two women represent very different types of character : Virgilia is essentially womanly, with all that the word conjures up in our mind of graceful and tender, delicate and sensitive; Volumnia is a Roman matron.

The contrast between them is shown at once in the first scene in which they appear. While Coriolanus is

2 G

away, fighting against the Volscians, the two women stay at home; they are seated on two low stools, and whilst busy with their needlework they talk together of the one subject with which each in her own way is engrossed.

Volumnia's imagination rejoices in the thought of the dangers incurred by Coriolanus, and of the honour that will accrue to him :—

> "Methinks, I see him stamp thus, and call thus,—
> ' Come on, you cowards! you were got in fear,
> Though you were born in Rome;' his bloody brow
> With his mail'd hand then wiping, forth he goes. . . .
> *Vir.* His bloody brow! O, Jupiter, no blood!
> *Vol.* Away, you fool! it more becomes a man
> Than gilt his trophy."

A visitor is announced, and Virgilia whose anxiety renders her little in the mood for company rises to retire, but Volumnia will not hear of it, and detains her. The lady Valeria enters and greets them both. A charming little scene of home-life ensues, to which it can hardly be objected that it is more English than Roman in colour; there seems no reason why it should not be as true of antique as of modern times, it being nature itself, taken in the act, with the utmost simplicity.

At last the much-desired news arrives. There are several letters from Coriolanus, one for his wife, one for his mother, one for Menenius, and one for the State. They are not mere repetitions of the same letter; Marcius adapts his style to the different recipients, confiding to his mother various details which he keeps back from his wife, Volumnia being the best-informed of all his correspondents. When Menenius inquires if he is wounded, Virgilia says, "O, no, no, no!" but Volumnia answers triumphantly :—

"O, he is wounded, I thank the gods for't. . . . I' the shoulder, and i' the left arm : there will be large cicatrices to show the people,

when he shall stand for his place. He received in the repulse of
Tarquin seven hurts i' the body. . . . He had, before this last expedition, twenty-five wounds upon him."

This Roman matron who knows so exactly the number
of her son's wounds, welcomes him back, on his victorious
return, with joyful acclamations. He kneels before her
to receive her congratulations, and then turns to Virgilia,
who speechless with emotion, sheds quiet tears of gladness. He tenderly embraces her, and, smiling at her
tears, says :—

> "My gracious silence, hail!
> Wouldst thou have laugh'd had I come coffin'd home,
> That weep'st to see me triumph?"

Volumnia's patriotism is of a purer nature than that of
Coriolanus ; her pride, too, is of a less personal kind, and
her aristocratic scorn less inflexible than his. There is
no tinge of egotism in her character, and with the self-
abnegation peculiar to a mother, her whole joy and pride
is centred in her son, and his advancement is her sole
ambition. Yet even a greater love than she gives to
Marcius she bears to Rome, or rather, the two affections
are inseparably united in her heart. For her, Coriolanus
is but the first and greatest of the Romans, so that when
he turns traitor to his country, it strikes her as not only
horrible but absurd ; to her it seems a monstrous contradiction that he should make war *against* Rome, when
to fight *for* Rome is the one sole object and end of all
possible warfare. She would undoubtedly have died
with her country, preferring death to the dishonour of
accepting mercy, had Coriolanus offered it, at the hands
of one who was endeavouring to destroy all for which in
her view a Roman should alone care to live.*

With Volumnia, the patriotic instinct outweighed
that of the patrician ; she abhorred the plebeians indeed,

---

* See Hudson's character of Volumnia.

as much as her son could abhor them, but in spite of her
hatred she could admit at need, the qualifying suggestions of reason, and she never made it a point of honour
to maintain her hatred without abating one jot or tittle
of its intensity. In this respect she was a thorough
woman, that is, prudent, adroit and acute, with infinitely
more tact and common sense than her son; but at the
same time, it must be admitted that some of her political
doctrines bear an alarming resemblance to that of the
justification of the means by the end, and that she was
an adept in the art of mental reservation.

In her ardent desire to see Coriolanus made a consul,
she urges him to comply with all the requisite formalities,
and he listens with a good deal of surprise and indignation while she teaches him how he may give his word
without binding himself overmuch. Understanding
nothing of the refinements of sophistry, he utters a vague
exclamation, and Volumnia continues :—

> " If it be honour, in your wars, to seem
> The same you are not (which, for your best ends,
> You adopt your policy), how is it less, or worse,
> That it shall hold companionship in peace
> With honour, as in war; since that to both
> It stands in like request? . . .
> It lies on you to speak
> To the people; not by your own instruction,
> Nor by the matter which your heart prompts you,
> But with such words that are but roted in
> Your tongue, though but bastards, and syllables
> Of no allowance to your bosom's truth."

This whole passage recalls the famous line in " Hip-
polytus " for which Aristophanes so severely blamed
Euripides as for a maxim of more than doubtful morality;
" My mouth has sworn, but not my heart."

When Coriolanus is banished, Volumnia utters a cry
of fury, in which critics have been rather over-hasty in
marking the predominance of maternal feelings over those

of a Roman matron : it calls for no such rigid interpretation, and is merely the expression of a sudden, instan-
taneous flash of passion :—

> " Now the red pestilence strike all trades in Rome,
>   And occupations perish ! " (Act IV., Sc. 1.)

She meets the tribunes with bitter taunts. The gentle
Virgilia does her best to second her, but her strength
soon fails, her grief finding more solace in tears than in
harsh words, and her mother-in-law impatiently says
to her—

> " Leave this faint puling, and lament as I do,
>   In anger, Juno-like."

Menenius, who had tried in vain to stop her torrent of
words, invites the two ladies at this most inauspicious
moment to come home to supper with him, to which
Volumnia loftily replies—

> " Anger's my meat, I sup upon myself,
>   And so shall starve with feeding. . . .
>   I would the gods had nothing else to do,
>   But to confirm my curses." (Act IV., Sc. 2.)

The grandest scene in which Volumnia appears is
when, clothed in the twofold dignity of a mother and of
a Roman, she intercedes with her son for Rome. In the
latter portion of the tragedy, reading Shakespeare is in
many passages, as has already been pointed out in the
chapter on Shakespeare's learning, the same thing as
reading Plutarch, or to speak more accurately, as reading
Sir Thomas North. Volumnia ends her pleading most
splendidly, expressing her determination to die in the
flames of Rome :—

> " I am hush'd until our city be afire,
>   And then I'll speak a little."

The Roman ladies, after having prevailed in their suit,
make a triumphant entry into the city they have saved.
A senator points out Volumnia to the people, saying—

> " Behold our patroness, the life of Rome :
>   Call all your tribes together, praise the gods,
>   And make triumphant fires ; strew flowers before them ; . . .
>   Cry,—Welcome, ladies, welcome ! " (Act V., Sc. 4.)

" Ladies you deserve to have a temple built you," said
Coriolanus, and history tells us that his thought was fulfilled. A temple was built to the " Fortune of Women,"
in which matrons took the place of the customary vestal
virgins as priestesses. This victory gained by Volumnia
over her son greatly contributed to the respect and consideration in which women were held in Rome, in spite
of their inferior position legally. Valerius Maximus
writes that by order of the senate, men were ever afterwards to yield precedence in the street to the women
they met.

There is more unity in the tragedy of " Coriolanus "
than in either of the other Roman plays; yet, grand and
powerful as it is, its tragical interest is less than that of
" Julius Cæsar," and its poetical merit less than that of
" Antony and Cleopatra."   There is something ·hard
about it, both in sentiment and in style. The delineation of social and personal pride is not a subject to
evoke much sympathy or emotion, and although it may
in its course reach sublime heights, its sublimity is
wholly independent of moral greatness. Of all Shakespeare's greater works, this is the most difficult to construe; the unintelligibility of several passages is doubtless due to some corruption of the text, but besides this,
the general style is exceedingly obscure, and overloaded
with metaphorical and elliptical expressions. Even the
great scene between Coriolanus and his mother is not of
uniform excellence. Some of its sentences are bombastic
and declamatory—its chief blemish in point of diction
being that the language of Shakespeare and that of Plutarch are placed side by side rather than blended into

each other, so that we jump without any transition from the comparative simplicity of the historian to the exuberance and passion of the poet. The finest portion of the scene is that which is borrowed word for word from Plutarch, whose value and merit as a painter of character can never be too strongly insisted on, and yet our admiration of him is greatly due to qualities which in reality do not belong to him: Amyot has gained for him a reputation of a certain kindly simplicity, which he would never otherwise have had; for in point of fact, what pre-eminently distinguishes him is his poetic and dramatic imagination, which would have been of the highest order if he had also possessed the ingenuous and simple charms with which he has been invested by another.

CHAPTER XXIV.

THE PART PLAYED BY THE PEOPLE IN THE ROMAN TRAGEDIES.

THERE yet remains one personage to be mentioned in connection with the Roman tragedies, and this personage is the people.

But it may be asked whether the term here used can be applied with propriety to the hydra-headed multitude, and whether that mental and moral unity which is presented by individual beings, such as Brutus, Antony, Coriolanus, and Volumnia, can possibly be found in a crowd of men gathered together. To this we may answer unhesitatingly in the affirmative. The people is truly a personage, as Aristophanes well knew when he brought Demos on the stage as a single individual. Every assembly in which men are united together by a common bond of interest, whether it be that of sentiment or of country, of political or religious faith, etc., presents a true and real entity, possessing its own proper moral unity. The general fund of intelligence obtained in this manner, is not the sum of all the individual intelligences, but the mean, or middle term, and may therefore be above or beneath that of any particular man taken separately; in other words, it must by its very definition be *mediocre*. Fools may gain by speaking and acting in common as members of a popular meeting, but wise men may lose by it, in fact are sure to lose by it. The maxim that "union is strength " cannot be applied with equal truth to mental as to physical strength. I once heard a philosopher maintain, with just that touch of paradox which infuses life and animation into the dry utterances of sober reason, that when fifteen hundred otherwise intelligent men are united together in one assembly, they become so many fools, because a crowd is and must be essentially stupid. It is in fact a mulish animal, irritable, violent, obstinate, ready to shy, with or without cause, and to become cruel or vicious out of anger or fear. " To gather men together is the way to move them," said Cardinal de Retz, and the truth of his saying is a matter of every-day experience, under one form or another. We are, it may be, in the midst of some large assembly, at a debating club, or at a concert, or in the theatre ; to take the most elegant example, I will suppose that we are in a hall consecrated to the fine arts, where a fashionable audience is listening to music. A tiresome piece is begun, people yawn, look at each other and sigh. The piece is long, very long, it threatens to be endless ; people get more and more impatient till their nerves can stand it no longer. All at once a few murmurs break out, which in an instant swell into a unanimous clamour, and the orchestra is obliged to stop. Who is it who has hissed ? Every one: even you yourself, a quiet, gentlemanly man, peaceable and tolerant, and disliking all violence and noise, you too have taken part in the brutal deed, carried away by some strange electrical current which seemed to sweep over the whole room. This mysterious epidemic force, by which at times the best and strongest of us are attacked, is *the soul of the crowd.*

But if persons who, as individuals, are refined and gentle become coarse and harsh when brought together in a mass, if fifteen hundred sensible men collected together are equivalent to fifteen hundred fools, what shall be said of a crowd of fifteen hundred men who are, individually, fools to begin with ? The resultant given by the agglomeration of so many ignorant and foolish minds would be appalling. The hundred-headed beast would be capable of every crime ; capable too of wild enthusiasm and devotion, and in fact of excess of every kind and sort—an inert mass without any will of its own, but easily incited to action by others, it is ready to obey every impulse communicated from without, whether for good, or as it more frequently happens, for evil. This mysterious force, this blind and formidable power, this sickening mediocrity of obscure and nameless individuals, devoid alike of either strength or character, who only exist as the unconscious and unknown atoms of some vague total, has been splendidly described by Victor Hugo, in " Les Châtiments : "—

> " Ils s'appellent vulgus, plebs, la tourbe, la foule,
> Ils sont ce qui murmure, applaudit, siffle, coule,
> Bat des mains, foule aux pieds, bâille, dit oui, dit non,
> N'a jamais de figure, et n'a jamais de non.
> Troupeau qui va, revient, juge, absout, délibère,
> Détruit, prêt à Marat comme prêt à Tibère,
> Foule triste, joyeuse, habits dorés, bras nus,
> Pêle-mêle, et poussée aux gouffres inconnus.
> Ils sont les passants froids, sans but, sans nœud, sans age ;
> Le bas du genre humain qui s'écroule en nuage ;
> Ceux qu'on ne connait pas, ceux qu'on ne compte pas,
> Ceux qui perdent les mots, les volontés, les pas." . . .

The people, who never appear at all in French tragedy, play an important part in Shakespeare's plays, a part which deserves to be studied, not only on account of the interest properly belonging to it, but also for the sake of what light it may throw on the puzzling ques- tion of the poet's own personal sentiments. The scenes in which he makes the people speak and act are gene- rally reckoned, rightly or wrongly, among the small number of passages in which he is supposed to lay aside the superb objectivity which is his highest glory, and to give expression to his personal dislikes and antipathies. It is only by carefully examining the people's part in the Roman tragedies,—and that without any bias one way or the other with regard to the question of Shakespeare's own political leanings, and by comparing the Roman populace with the one depicted in some of his other plays, notably in the English historical dramas, that we can hope to render ourselves competent to discuss the point affecting Shakespeare's personality, and to answer the question whether he has or has not failed in impartiality.

In the opening scene of " Julius Cæsar," which plunges us into a rabble of citizens, whose "basest metal" is " moved " by the speeches of the tribunes, so that " they vanish tongue-tied in their guiltiness," the inconstancy and thoughtlessness of the mob stand confessed; but what equally deserves to be noted is the sensitiveness so readily shown by the people to the reproaches of the tribunes, to the violent invective of Marcellus, and especially to the sadder and more gentle words of Flavius.

The people applaud when Cæsar refuses the crown; when Brutus publicly justifies the murder of Cæsar, they cry out, " Live, Brutus, live. . . . Give him a statue with his ancestors. Let him be Cæsar ! " A people like this is ripe for servitude. It is true they cheered Cæsar for refusing the crown, but it was simply because they had a horror of the *name* of king; the thing itself they could easily accept and submit to, so potent is the influence of words over the mind of the crowd, both to attract and to repel. " When once the people have swallowed the bait of liberty," says Bossuet, " they will follow blindly as long as they only hear the name." To Cæsar's despotism, to the concentration of power in a single hand, the people would have offered no objection whatever, as long as the name of Monarchy was carefully suppressed, and that of a *crowned democracy*, for instance, substituted in its place. Words play a wonderfully active part in politics, and until a different standard in public morality is established, and human nature has undergone a good many modifications, a skilful use of them will always form an essential element in the statesman's art. At present, the man whose love of reality and truth and whose contempt for empty sounds and vain shadows, lead him to neglect this mighty instrument in the guidance of men, gives greater proof of his honesty and sincerity, than of his knowledge of human folly in general, and of the folly of the people in particular.

Antony's strength lay in just this knowledge and this art in using words; he well knew the value of popular logic, and with what sort of reasoning the mouths of fools are to be stopped :—

> "The noble Brutus
> Hath told you Cæsar was ambitious: . . .
> You all did see that on the Lupercal
> I thrice presented him a kingly crown,
> Which he did thrice refuse. Was this ambition ? . . .
> 1 *Cit.* Methinks there is much reason in his sayings.
> 4 *Cit.* . . . . He would not take the crown ;
> Therefore, 'tis certain he was not ambitious."

In this scene between Antony and the people, the two parts are as inseparably united as the song of the singer and the orchestral accompaniment. It is an admirably graduated crescendo, beginning very gently at first and then rising—rising—till it finally bursts out into the thunder-clap of revolt. "We'll mutiny, we'll seek the conspirators, we'll fire the traitors' houses, we'll kill, we'll slay."

The blackest action committed by the people in all Shakespeare's Roman plays is the murder of the poet Cinna, in the midst of the tumult. The incident is given in Plutarch, but in his account the crime as perpetrated by the populace whom Antony's speech had worked up into wild excitement, is of a most ordinary and, so to speak, consistent character. It is a very deplorable occurrence, but it is not an odious or a vile one, outraging all feeling and reason. It is the distressing but natural result of a mistake; the assassins seize hold of the wrong man, and kill Cinna the poet, believing him in all good faith to be Cinna the conspirator. Shakespeare, a bolder and more searching anatomist of the human monster, has added a refinement of cruelty and folly to their crime, knowing well what the mob is capable of in its intoxication on the day of revolution, and he shows us the amazing unreasonableness, and lets us hear the loud bursts of stupid and ferocious laughter of a populace in revolt, who are perfectly aware of what they are doing, and who, without the excuse of a mistake as to the poor wretch's identity, tear him to pieces in a most light-hearted manner, as a punishment for bearing a name grown distasteful to them.

> " 3 *Cit.* Your name, sir, truly.
> *Cin.* Truly, my name is Cinna.
> 1 *Cit.* Tear him to pieces; he's a conspirator.
> *Cin.* I am Cinna the poet, I am Cinna the poet.
> 4 *Cit.* Tear him for his bad verses, tear him for his bad verses.
> *Cin.* I am not Cinna the conspirator.
> 2 *Cit.* It is no matter, his name's Cinna; pluck but his name out of his heart, and turn him going."

In the tragedy of "Antony and Cleopatra" the people play no part at all. The military age has begun, and the life and movement of the background is no longer afforded by the people, but by the army. We may therefore pass on at once to "Coriolanus," in which the people have a larger share in the action than in either of the other Roman plays.

The cardinal point to be noticed first of all, is that Shakespeare makes no distinction between the plebeians of the early Republic, and the populace of imperial and degenerate Rome. For this, Plutarch is certainly not responsible, for although he is not in his heart very favourably disposed towards the " common people," as North calls them, he does justice on various occasions to their military courage and even to their civic virtues, noticeably at the time of their withdrawal to the " Holy Hill," when they offered " no creature any hurt or violence, nor made any show of actual rebellion." Here they remained for four months. Right and reason were on their side, and they dishonoured their cause by no act of violence or excess of any kind. To these oppressed and proud plebeians, opposing a passive and what may be called a conservative resistance to the despotic measures of the patricians, with a moderation derived from a sense of their strength and the rightfulness of their cause, it is impossible to refuse our esteem, nay more, our admiration. Nothing could less resemble a vulgar street riot than this orderly retreat to Mons Sacer of four thousand resolute men, ready to suffer anything rather than submit to tyranny. By the firmness of their attitude they compelled the senate to give way, for the land was lying uncultivated, and the inaction of four thousand valiant defenders, as Plutarch acknowledges them to be, left Rome exposed to the attacks of her foes. The chatter of poor old Menenius, and his wonderful fable, had but slight effect upon the seceders, who were only induced to return to their homes, as mentioned in a former chapter, after obtaining the privilege of appointing tribunes " to defend the poor people from violence and oppression."

This aspect of the plebeians of the Roman Republic in its young days, this grave, political, warlike, and wholly estimable side of their nature, does not appear in " Coriolanus." According to his invariable custom, Shakespeare took no heed of what he considered to be a mere historical peculiarity, a local and temporary

exception; he depicts the plebeians, in the early times
of liberty, in conformity with the general type he had
conceived of the populace, a type belonging to no especial
date or nationality, but eternally and everlastingly true,
and as applicable to ancient Rome as to Paris or London
in modern times,—to the Republic and the Empire, as to
periods of absolute or constitutional monarchy, or as
to our own democratic days. The dominant features of
Shakespeare's plebeians, as of all his sons of the people,
are stupidity, inconstancy, and cowardliness. They are
always blundering, always incapable of any political
idea, and impressionable as wax in the hands of their
demagogues. To these vices must be added their feeble
negative good-qualities, which may be summed up shortly
by saying that they are even sillier than they are wicked.

If " Coriolanus " were an historical or political drama,
and if the struggle between the plebeians and the
patricians were what Shakespeare intended to depict,
as has so often been foolishly said, it must be allowed
that he has scarcely carried out his purpose in a satisfactory manner; for no attempt is made to give to each
of the rival pretensions of the two hostile factions
whatever portion of truth it may contain, or even to
state clearly what they are. This contest between two
political ideas, brought into harmony by a chorus of old
men endowed with rather greater wisdom than Menenius Agrippa, would have furnished a magnificent subject
to the Sophoclean drama. Nor would a poet, who like
Corneille was fond of political dissertations, have failed
to put an eloquent vindication of the rights of the people
into the tribune's mouth. But Shakespeare leaves all this
side of the matter entirely in the shade. The plebeians
would appear to have no solid foundation for their
grievances, nor are we even able to perceive what benefit
they expect from the establishment of the tribuneship,
nor why, when their petition is granted them, it should

throw them into such a 'rapturous state, shouting with joy, and throwing their caps "as they would hang them on the horns o' the moon." *

But the truth is, that the interest of "Coriolanus" is anything but of a political or historical order; it is on the character of the hero, on the development of his nature, that the poet has concentrated all the effort of his genius: he pictures him as a giant of passion and pride, towering over the heads of all who surround him, who, with the single exception of his mother, are utterly insignificant, weak, and contemptible. Without going so far as to say, with Hallam and Gervinus, that there was no other possible treatment of the subject, it is enough to state that this is the manner in which Shakespeare has treated it, and which is fully in accordance with the admiration for great personalities and strongly-marked characters which his writings so often testify. He has sacrificed in one huge holocaust nearly all the other personages of the drama, that he might add to the colossal proportions of the patrician and warrior. To form any notion of the distance that separated Coriolanus from the plebeians, of the remote spot whence he surveyed them and was dismayed, as it were, at their smallness, we must turn to mediæval times, and picture to ourselves a knight equipped for battle giving orders from horseback to his churls and serfs: his intense contempt is simply inconceivable at a time when all citizens were on a footing of military equality. But in fact we are not in Rome at all, we are in the full stream of chivalry, with the warlike nobles on the one side and on the other the peasants that dig the ground.

These flights of fancy in the Shakespearian drama rather interfere with our comprehension of the logical sequence of the facts: it is difficult to understand, if we

---

* Kreyssig, "Vorlesungen über Shakespeare," Vol. I., p. 471.

stop to consider, how such utterly contemptible creatures as the plebeians and their tribunes are represented to be, should all at once become powerful enough to dictate laws to the nobles, and to banish their great enemy. But the vigour of the poetry carries the reader along with it, and leaves no time or space for the cold objections of historical accuracy. " Coriolanus " is, at one and the same time, the play in which Shakespeare has borrowed from the historian the greatest number of details which he reproduces with peculiar exactitude, and also that in which he has most widely departed from the spirit of historical truth.

The part played by the plebeians in " Coriolanus " must therefore be regarded merely as a representation of the populace in general; and it is, moreover, the best portrait of the kind given by Shakespeare, the shadows are not painted in so deep a hue as elsewhere, and one or two redeeming features possible to the picture are pleasantly brought forward.

But, to begin with, the people are stupid. When Coriolanus, their mortal enemy, politically speaking, enters Rome as the conqueror of the Volscians, the dazzled multitude intoxicated with the pomp and grandeur of the sight, welcome him with every token of joy :—

> " All tongues speak of him, and the bleered sights
> Are spectacled to see him. . . .
> > Stalls, bulks, windows,
> Are smother'd up, leads fill'd and ridges horsed
> With variable complexions : all agreeing
> In earnestness to see him." (Act II., Sc. 1.)

The people are utterly wanting in penetration. They let themselves be deceived by the apparent kindliness of Menenius Agrippa, who, as we have seen, was as haughty a patrician as Coriolanus himself. " Worthy Menenius Agrippa," exclaims a delighted citizen, " one that hath always loved the people."

The people are not inherently envious, but they become so. Until perverted by the sophistries of their
leaders, the superior rights conferred by merit and by
birth are instinctively recognized by them, which is the
best point about them in Shakespeare's drama. The
false theory of the natural equality of all men is not
originally an article of their creed, but is a lesson they
learn from their masters, a lesson only too well understood and too quickly accepted. As Saint-Just said to
the Convention after the fall of the Girondins, " You
would have no man either virtuous or famous ; to a free
people and a national assembly it is impossible to admire
any one." That doctrines so flattering to the inherent
vanity of mankind should have a rapid success is inevitable; and when once they have penetrated the masses,
the jealous spirit of democracy imposes its own level
upon all that would soar above it ; and everything that
is mediocre, at times even everything that is shameful,
bids for success by outdoing all rivals in whatever is base
and mean. One of Coriolanus' most stinging taunts
refers to this ignoble tyranny from below :—

> " Your virtue is,
> To make him worthy, whose offence subdues him,
> And curse that justice did it. Who deserves greatness,
> Deserves your hate."

These are striking words, the truth of which may well
in these days make us shudder. But the people of themselves, when not stirred up by agitators, are not really
unjust or given to envy. They consider it quite fair
that Coriolanus should be consul : they weigh his merits
and demerits in the scales, and are even generous enough
to plead extenuating circumstances in his favour, such as
the services he has done for his country, that he cannot
help his nature, and that whether proud or not, at all
events he is not covetous. Nothing can exceed the
patience and good-temper of the plebeians when Corio-

lanus solicits their votes, laughing and sneering at them all the time.

But these kindly natures become warped and twisted under the influence of the demagogues, who are here represented by the tribunes Junius Brutus and Sicinius Velutus.

The people with some embarrassment tell their tale, describing the election of the new consul, and his extraordinary mode of proceeding which turned the whole affair into a regular comedy. In the scene that ensues, the characters of the tribunes are unfolded by themselves, and their roguery laid bare, with infinitely more delicate and exhaustive touches than could ever be laid on by the hand of an enemy. They are complete adepts in the art of shielding themselves and of throwing all the responsibility upon the people, while pretending to take it on their own shoulders; "Lay the fault on us," they say, as if the election of Coriolanus were a fault that could in any way damage their reputation, or make them appear in any other than a favourable light to the friends of the consul; and while leaving to the people all the odium attaching to their retractation, they leave a door open for themselves through which in case of need, they might creep into the good graces of their adversary.

But schemes laid with so much skill could not but prevent any such need arising, and henceforth the two tribunes hold the reins in their own hands and can drive in what direction they please. The great secret of the demagogue is to make use of the people while letting them believe that he is serving them: the well-meaning flock of dupes, deceived by the apparent zeal and devotion to the public good shown by the tribunes, becomes an obedient instrument in their hands, very useful for the furtherance of their design of a social upheaval. When Coriolanus appears before the tribunal of his accusers, everything has been arranged beforehand by the tribunes; the number of votes necessary to procure his condemnation has been secured, the people have been taught their lesson, and are ready at a given signal to support their orators with their cries and shouts :—

> " When they hear me say, ' It shall be so
> I' the right and strength o' the commons,' be it either,
> For death, for fine, or banishment, then let them,
> If I say fine, cry ' Fine ;' if death, cry ' Death.'"

To rouse into fury so impetuous and inflammable a temper as that of Coriolanus was only child's play for such cunning and crafty plotters as the tribunes. He flies into a passion at almost their first words, so that they have no difficulty in carrying out their plan of provoking him to anger to his own hurt.

" I am the State," Louis XIV. was wont to say, and his courtiers flattered him in the notion. " You are the State," say popular agitators in democratic times to the mob, who willingly accept their words. When the senators represent to the tribunes that to kindle the fire of internal dissensions is to ruin and to destroy the city, the tribune promptly asks, " What is the city but the people ? " and all the people cry in chorus, " True, the people are the city."

Shakespeare, with a fine perception of the character of an ordinary demagogue, makes his tribunes violent in nature, and at the same time capable of moderation when their interest requires it. After they have won the victory, they are wise enough not to triumph openly, but to " seem humbler after it is done than when it was a-doing," and they return calm answers to Volumnia's furious indignation,—but they wish to have the messenger whipped who brings the news of the approach of the Volscian army. The natural ferocity of their disposition suddenly breaks out with all the greater vehemence because of their uneasy consciousness of the mischief they have worked.

When doubt becomes a certainty, and the rumour spreads that not only the Volscians are marching against Rome, but Coriolanus himself at their head, the people as a matter of course turn against the tribunes as the authors of the evil, and even threaten their lives. This movement on their part is as regular in its order, as much to be expected, as the ebb and flow of the tide, or the changes of the moon; but the best of it all is, that the multitude now allege that they never wished Coriolanus to be banished; and in this they are not exactly telling a falsehood, so utterly are they without any will of their own, or any sequence of thought.

> "1 *Cit.* For mine own part,
> When I said, banish him, I said 'twas pity.
>
> 2 *Cit.* And so did I.
>
> 3 *Cit.* And so did I; and, to say the truth, so did very many of us. That we did we did for the best, and *though we willingly consented to his banishment, yet it was against our will.*"

On the whole, the people in "Coriolanus" are not very wicked: they may even, in that equivocal form of praise so distasteful to persons of any intellect, be called good-natured fellows. They are not indeed good in the sense in which La Rochefoucauld says "a fool has not stuff enough in him to be good," but in that, which by a deplorable abuse of words has in all civilized languages come to be synonymous with folly.

CHAPTER XXV.

SHAKESPEARE'S POLITICAL VIEWS.

IT can hardly be said that the populace in "Coriolanus"
is painted in very harsh colours, since the worst faults
imputed to it are those of pusillanimity, fickleness, and
stupidity; to these, in "Julius Cæsar" that of ferocity is
added. If with these two we compare the further
picture, drawn by Shakespeare of the people in Part II.
of "Henry VI.," we shall be able to form an adequate
notion of Shakespeare's conception of the "many-headed
multitude."

Turning to the play in question, we find Jack Cade,
in Act IV., Sc. 2, explaining his communistic schemes of
social reform to the gaping crowd.

"There shall be, in England, seven halfpenny loaves sold for a
penny : the three-hooped pot shall have ten hoops, and I will make it
felony to drink small beer. All the realm shall be in common, and in
Cheapside shall my palfrey go to grass. And, when I am king (as
king I will be)—

All. God save your majesty !

Cade. I thank you, good people :—there shall be no money : all
shall eat and drink on my score ; and I will apparel them all in one
livery, that they may agree like brothers, and worship me their lord.

Dick. The first thing we do, let's kill all the lawyers.

Cade. Nay, that I mean to do."

This mode of applying the doctrines of liberty,
equality, and fraternity, is highly approved of by the

people, who have founded great hopes upon their leader, and look forward to the day when the magistrates shall be labouring men, and labouring men shall be magistrates.

To Jack Cade and his followers, all aristocracy, whether of birth, or fortune, or merit, is as a matter of course hateful ; to know how to read and write and cast up accounts is a crime in their eyes deserving of death. " Dost thou use ? " asks Cade of the clerk of Chatham who is brought before him to be tried—

> " Dost thou use to write thy name ? or hast thou a mark to thyself, like an honest plain-dealing man ?
>
> *Clerk.* Sir, I thank God I have been so well brought up that I can write my name.
>
> *All.* He hath confessed : away with him ! he's a villain and a traitor.
>
> *Cade.* Away with him, I say ! hang him with his pen and inkhorn about his neck."

Shakespeare especially delights in showing the grossness of the people's logic. We know how easily Antony made them conclude that, as Cæsar refused the crown, he was not ambitious ; Jack Cade and his band of admirers make the yet more astounding syllogism : the French are our enemies, Lord Say knows French, therefore he is our enemy :—

> " He can speak French, and therefore he is a traitor. . . . Nay, answer if you can :—the Frenchmen are our enemies : go to then. I ask but this,—can he that speaks with the tongue of an enemy be a good counsellor, or no ?
>
> *All.* No, no ; and therefore we'll have his head."

In Act IV., Sc. 7, we have the scene of the trial of Lord Say :—

> " *Cade.* Thou hast most traitorously corrupted the youth of the realm, in erecting a grammar school. . . . It will be proved to thy face, that thou hast men about thee that usually talk of a noun, and a verb ; and such abominable words as no Christian can endure to hear.

Thou hast appointed justices of the peace, to call poor men before them
about matters they were not able to answer. . . .

 Say. You men of Kent,—
 Dick. What say you of Kent?
 Say. Nothing but this,—'tis *bona terra, mala gens.*
 Cade. Away with him, away with him! he speaks Latin."

As none of the other plays add any fresh points of
character to those furnished by " Henry VI.," " Coriolanus," and " Julius Cæsar," we may now turn to the
question affecting the poet's individual sentiments, and
consider whether in his portraiture of the populace he
has remained faithful to his usual impartial justice :
whether in this case, as in that of his other personages, he
has confined himself to holding up the mirror to nature,
or whether he may not have introduced the expression of
some personal bias,—whether he has done his work in
the spirit of an artist, or of a partisan. But indeed
frankly speaking, if the passages already referred to are
all we have to go upon in this little psychological discussion, there can be so little doubt as to the answer, that it
is difficult to understand why the question should ever
have been raised. If it is asked whether the picture
drawn by Shakespeare of the people is true, the only
possible answer is a decided affirmative ; in these days,
in France especially, after '93, and after the Commune, to
allege it to be false or exaggerated would be a palpable
absurdity. No unbiassed critic could ever doubt Shakespeare's impartiality simply from these scenes in which
the people appear in person. It is not, however, to the
great historical scenes, in which the different personages
act and speak in accordance with a given part, that we
must turn in order to decide the question: it is the indirect
passages that we must consult, the incidental phrases in
which Shakespeare would appear to be speaking in his
own name and not from any obligation with regard to
the consistent pourtrayal of character or to the develop-

ment of the plot. It must, obviously, be in these passages—if anywhere—that we may hope to surprise his private opinions.

It is, for instance, very curious to see how many passages occur in the Roman tragedies, in which Casca, Cleopatra, Menenius, and Coriolanus manifest their intense disgust at the odour of the crowd, at their dirty teeth and grimy hands, at their greasy caps, and their breath smelling of garlic and of wine. The same horror of garlic and of those who eat it appears also in " A Midsummer Night's Dream " (Act IV., Sc. 2) and elsewhere. It can hardly be rash to conclude that Shakespeare himself felt what his characters express with so much force and frequency, and that the people were, at all events, offensive to his sense of smell.

In the "Tempest" we see him profiting by the occasion of the shipwreck of Alonzo and his suite on the island, to have a laugh over communistic theories, in a passage which is interesting as throwing some light on the personality of the writer, and also as being a translation from Montaigne. ("Essaies" I., Chap. XXXI., "Des Cannibales.") The old counsellor Gonzales is a reformer of the same type as Jack Cade, but with this difference, that with Jack Cade the enunciation of his social reforms is a necessary fulfilment of his part, while Gonzales seems to point more directly to a satirical intention on Shakespeare's part, from his views being propounded quite by the bye.

> "Had I plantation of this isle, my lord, . . .
> And were the king of it, what would I do ? . . .
> I' the commonwealth I would by contraries
> Execute all things ; for no kind of traffic
> Would I admit ; no name of magistrate ;
> Letters should not be known : riches, poverty,
> And use of service, none ; contract, succession,
> Bourn, bound of land, tilth, vineyard, none :
> No use of metal, corn, or wine, or oil.

No occupation; all men idle, all . . . .
All things in common nature should produce
Without sweat or endeavour : treason, felony,
Sword, pike, knife, gun, or need of any engine,
Would I not have ; but nature should bring forth,
Of its own kind, all foizon, all abundance,
To feed my innocent people."

Shakespeare's irony here is the more remarkable,
because, though Montaigne, from whom he is quoting,
says the same thing, he says it in a wholly different
spirit, honestly admiring the beautiful primitive state
which Shakespeare makes the subject of his mirth. A
national difference is surely plainly visible here, between
the firm practical good sense of the Englishman and the
tendency of French thinkers towards ideal political
schemes, whether of Plato or of J. J. Rousseau. As Professor Dowden remarks, when Shakespeare wrote the
"Tempest" he was about to retire to his Stratford home,
after having amassed a considerable fortune by years of
toil and economy, and he felt no disposition to share his
tenements and lands with his less industrious neighbours.*

In the harangue made by Henry V. to his army
(Act III., Sc. 1), a highly aristocratic distinction is
drawn between the warlike nobility on the one side,
descended from a long line of illustrious forefathers ; and
on the other side, the men of grosser blood who derive
their strength from the soil, and like horses or dogs, are
called upon in the day of battle to show that they are
worth their breeding. A still more noticeable passage
occurs in the same play, where Mountjoy is sent, after
the battle of Agincourt, by the French King to beg
permission to bury the dead (Act IV., Sc. 7) :—

"I come to thee for charitable license,
That we may wander o'er this bloody field,

---

* Page 326.

> To book our dead, and then to bury them;
> To sort our nobles from our common men:
> For many of our princes (woe the while!)
> Lie drown'd and soak'd in mercenary blood;
> So do our vulgar drench their peasant limbs
> In blood of princes."

Shakespeare's plays abound in bitter and contemptuous reflections on the people: not a leader of them, whether he be a rebel, or a dignitary of the Church or State, but complains of their fickleness. "Was ever feather so lightly blown, to and fro, as this multitude?" asks Jack Cade ("Henry VI.," Pt. II., Act IV., Sc. 8), and Richard II. expresses his disgust at the conduct of the mob as vehemently as Casca, Cleopatra, Menenius, or Coriolanus.

These passages have struck various critics as being full of significance; it has been thought, not without some show of likelihood, that in speaking of the people, Shakespeare gave full scope to his personal antipathies. And as nothing rouses men's passions more than social and political questions, critics, according to whether they happened to be tory or whig, aristocrat or democrat, royalist or republican, have either rejoiced over Shakespeare's sentiments or been indignant at them. That he was no courtier of the people, in spite of the attempts made to claim him for the side of democracy and the republic, seems to me to be incontestably clear.

To Dr. Johnson it was a source of sincere pleasure to find the doctrine of the divine right of kings insisted on in "Richard II." (Act III., Sc. 2) by the Bishop of Carlisle, whose orthodox sentiments he unhesitatingly ascribed, in his enthusiasm, to Shakespeare, ignoring the fact that the Bishop's character, and even his words, are borrowed from the chronicles of Holinshed. Johnson also derives great satisfaction from the colours in which the stupidity of the mob and the cunning of the demagogues are painted in "Coriolanus;" while Hazlitt, on the other hand, petulantly writes :—

"The whole dramatic moral of 'Coriolanus' is, that those who have little shall have less, and that those who have much shall take all the others have left. The people are poor, therefore they ought to be starved. They are slaves, therefore they ought to be beaten. They work hard, therefore they ought to be treated like beasts of burden. They are ignorant, therefore they ought not to be allowed to feel that they want food or clothing or rest, that they are enslaved, oppressed, and miserable."

The chief aim of Rümelin—whose work which is well worthy of attention, is written from a realistic standpoint, in direct opposition to the exaggerated conclusions arrived at by Gervinus and his followers who simply deify Shakespeare—is to bring the poet back to human proportions, to place him in the midst of his proper historical conditions, and to search out the most material and commonplace, "earth to earth" explanation of his plays. According to him, all those senseless rhapsodies which would represent Shakespeare as a sort of divine creator, floating with supreme indifference in the empyrean of art, high above all the party questions and interests which agitate and divide the children of men, must be wholly rejected. The author of the historical dramas was, if we may believe this critic of the realistic school, "a royalist of the purest water, and a close adherent to the court party and the nobles ;" a predilection on his part of which the explanation is not far to seek. It was the nobles who favoured the theatre, and defended it from the hostile attacks made upon it by the spirit of puritanism, which was already beginning to press its yoke on men's minds; and as the company to which Shakespeare belonged was under the especial patronage of Her Majesty, there is no occasion to wonder at his being the devoted servant of the Queen. Rümelin has no wish to score it against him as a crime, he only asks that the fact should be recognized. Shakespeare, he says, was a courtier as Virgil, Horace, Calderon, Racine, and so many other poets were, without any damage thereby accruing to their reputation. We learn from contemporary evidence that it was the custom for actors to kneel down and pray on behalf of the Queen at the end of every theatrical performance. "Henry VIII." closes with a hymn in honour of Elizabeth, and although it might be suggested that Elizabeth was dead when this was written, the apology is of no avail, for the dithyramb goes on to address the reigning sovereign, James I., with all the platitudes of court adulation. In order not to stand too utterly aghast at such hyperbolical praises heaped upon so sorry a master as James I., it will be well to remember the essentially insignificant nature of this species of literature, to which no more weight should be attached than to the expressions of sincerity and humility with which we are wont to terminate our letters. "Once more," says Rümelin in conclusion—and we should be careful to give him the full credit he deserves for the persistence with which he reiterates the idea,—"I am far from making the poet's adherence to the court and to the nobles a matter of reproach, I only ask that the fact may not be denied."

Nor will we deny it; we will simply endeavour to reduce it to its true value.

And, indeed, that Shakespeare was a royalist and an aristocrat may easily be conceded by even the most violent radicals among his admirers, when they reflect that the history of his own days and of former times precluded the possibility of his being anything else, and also that in holding these opinions he was but obeying what the very conditions of his art almost necessitated as an æsthetic law. Shakespeare, however vast his genius, was not a prophet that we should require of him to foresee the important part that the people were to play in the future.

"The mediæval attempts to resist oppression," says Professor Dowden, "the risings of peasants or of citizens, inaugurated commonly by the murder of a lord or of a bishop, were for the most part desperate attempts, rash and dangerous, sustained by no sense of adequate moral or material power. . . . In the Tudor period, the people had not yet emerged. The people, like Milton's half-created animals, is still pawing to get free its hinder parts from the mire." (Page 320.)

The facts of history therefore amply justify Shakespeare in his omission to represent the people under a serious aspect, as capable of exhibiting moral dignity or devotion to a cause, and in his not giving them as important a part to act as that which they have now acquired, but which then they were far from possessing, and were only to arrive at after long centuries of deadly struggles. After all, the political sentiments ascribed to him are so completely in harmony with the essential character of his art, that the wiser course is simply to regard them as one of the modes of his poetic thought.

In all poets, as a rule, and in dramatic poets in particular, what may be called the aristocratic instinct is from the very nature of things peculiarly strong. Even Hazlitt himself remarks that the poetic imagination is an exaggerating, exclusive, aristocratic faculty, that the principle of poetry is everywhere an anti-levelling principle, that the lion which attacks a flock of sheep is a far more poetical object than the flock, that we feel far more admiration for the proud arbitrary man than for the humble crowd that bow before him, for the oppressor rather than for the oppressed. Tragedians, whatever their political creed may be, invariably turn to courts and palaces in the selection of their characters, because princes and nobles, by virtue of their position, are ready-made heroes—that is, strong men and free, raised above the ordinary restraints of law. Their figures stand out in solitary grandeur, and easily lend themselves to poetry ; while their subjects, except in times of revolution and revolt when they too become heroic, can never offer attractions like their masters', nor offer as wide a scope to the poet's imagination. And this is the reason why the popular or middle-class drama so soon stops short in the path of tragedy; its wings being cut, it has to confine itself to comedy and to prose. Personal grandeur and power, which it is the chief object of dramatic poetry to represent, can obviously only attain their richest and fullest development in the highest social ranks; as we descend into the lower strata of society, the supreme importance of the individual figure vanishes, and in the place of great and brilliant personalities, we find an obscure mass of nameless and dependent beings. That poets should be fascinated by grandeur and force of character, for the simple reason that it is grandeur and force, and quite apart from all political or even moral considerations, is no rare occurrence: take, for instance, the enthusiastic admiration with which Napoleon has inspired some of the greatest poets of this century, in defiance of every protest on the part of patriotism or humanity, not to mention those of reason or conscience. It is in this predominance of the æsthetic point of view over all others that the true artistic temperament betrays itself, and this temperament Shakespeare possessed in the highest degree. It was his instinct as a poet that led him to make Coriolanus so great, and the people so small, and not any party or political spirit, which would have been at once alien to his habits and degrading to his genius. The interest excited by "Coriolanus" in the true lover of poetry is of a purely æsthetic order. He may indeed, like Goethe, be conscious "throughout the whole play of a feeling of anger at the obstinate refusal of the people to recognize the superiority of those above them," but this superiority is exclusively and wholly due to personal distinction and individual character, or, in other words, to what is inherently poetic. And surely, in the magnificent passage in "Coriolanus," in Act IV., Sc. 5, in which Shakespeare bursts out into a sort of lyrical chant over the greatness of his hero, we can see the immense hold it had upon its imagination :—

> "*Auf.* O Marcius, Marcius!
> Each word thou hast spoke hath weeded from my heart
> A root of ancient envy. If Jupiter
> Should from yon cloud speak divine things,
> And say ' 'Tis true,' I'd not believe them more
> Than thee, all noble Marcius," etc.

Shakespeare had an intense admiration for great personalities, and it was this, and this only, that gave him his aristocratic and I may even add, his royalist predilections. No importance need be attached to the flattering lines at the end of "Henry VIII.," addressed to a weak and imbecile king, and they should be allowed to pass as merely commonplace conventional phrases, for which the speaker is never held responsible, and by which his character is never thought to be compromised, and of which, moreover, the authenticity is regarded as very doubtful. Shakespeare's one political principle seems to have been "the right of the kingliest nature to be king," and Dr. Johnson's admiration, on the strength of the Bishop of Carlisle's speech, of his faith in the divine right of kings was so much waste of energy. In point of fact Shakespeare took no part in the contest between the house of Lancaster and the house of York; and the divine right of Richard II. is hardly as sacred in his eyes as the divine right of the son of the usurping Bolingbroke.* The nature of his royalistic principles, like that of his aristocratic instincts, was of a purely poetic order.

The one great victorious fact which the whole discussion serves to bring out with yet clearer brilliancy is the

---

* Dowden, p. 323.

glorious objectivity of Shakespeare's genius. Though by right of his poet-nature his instincts may have been anti-levelling and anti-democratic, there was no spirit of narrowness in his sympathies, and in his large and simple royalism he seems to retain something of the childlike and patriarchal candour of ancient times. Party spirit may find an exponent in Aristophanes, but Shakespeare, before all, and *after all*, is the grand painter of humanity. He has no petty feelings or resentments, and that the people have good and kindly qualities is easily and frankly recognized by him. In "Coriolanus" the crowd is very well-intentioned; it is the tribunes who do all the mischief. In "Timon of Athens" all the nobles are utterly worthless, and the sentiments more honourable to human nature all proceed from the lower classes, servants and poor people and even thieves; in "Macbeth" Banquo owes his life to the flood of pity that suddenly surges up in the heart of a paid assassin; and in "Richard III." the two ruffians hired by Tyrrel suffer such pangs of remorse after murdering the two little princes in the Tower, that they can scarcely render an account of their bloody deed for weeping. And to return to the play of "Coriolanus," it should be carefully noted that the nobles in it are not depicted in any brighter colours than the populace, no imposing part is taken by the patricians as a class—that is reserved for the hero only, the hero and his mother. And even here, Shakespeare evinces his thorough impartiality, never shrinking from displaying certain features in their characters which, though they leave our admiration intact, greatly diminish our sympathy with them.

Shakespeare is the poet of individual creations, rather than of abstract ideas. He neither teaches nor argues; he never moralizes in a philosophic strain, but he creates living characters. The small amount of political conviction, which by dint of great exertion has been extracted

2 I

from his plays, deserves infinitely less attention than the fact that it is so small; a fact which affords also a fresh argument in support of the conclusion so frequently repeated in these pages, that to Shakespeare all literary or political doctrines were matters of supreme indifference, and that his creative power was of a purely practical character. Strong political feelings were neither unknown nor uncommon among the dramatists who were Shakespeare's contemporaries; but whilst Massinger indulged in republican tendencies, and Beaumont and Fletcher exaggerated the principle of divine right, Shakespeare has nowhere testified his adherence to any fixed political party, and defies any such narrow classification. So little does he trouble himself about abstract political ideas, that he never even makes his characters discuss the subject of the best form of government, as those of Corneille do in the second act of Cinna, although nothing would have been easier than to have introduced such a discussion into "Coriolanus," had the genius of the poet not been concentrated on the character of the hero. In "Julius Cæsar" it is strange and almost inconceivable that no reflections of a political kind should find distinct expression, even in Brutus' soliloquy, in which he finally resolves upon Cæsar's death, not directly in the name of the Republic, but out of regard to the effect the regal condition might have upon the dictator's mind.

We may well tender our grateful praises to Shakespeare for having held himself aloof from the political quarrels of his time; to this complete freedom from all merely local and contemporary pre-occupations, that character of *universality* which makes his plays intelligible and full of interest for all times and places is greatly due. For a poet or a philosopher to become a politician is to descend from his high estate, and to abandon the wide horizons which are his birthright, for a necessarily narrower point of view. Men of action belong to a dis-

tinct race from men of thought : the first see but one
side of a thing at a time, and fortunately so, for the
machinery of the world is only kept going by means of
the limited view of things thus taken, by which alóne
conviction and enthusiasm can be evoked ; the men of
thought see the for and against, and from the moment a
man begins to weigh the pros and cons, as far as public
life is concerned, he is lost.   But what would be the
source of weakness and embarrassment to the man of
action, constitutes the very strength and superiority of
the man of thought.   Rivalling the philosopher in breadth
of intellect, outstripping him in creative genius, the true
poet dwells in those pure realms of art, in which he is
raised high above all kings or people or principalities of
the earth.   From these empyrean heights—with all due
deference to Gustave Rümelin—Shakespeare contemplated
mankind.   His view embraced too wide an area, and he
grasped the secret of comedy too surely, to be very enthusiastic about any of our "great principles," as we call
them ; but the sight of the human puppets in the peep-
show was infinitely amusing to him.   "Man delights not
me," said Hamlet, "no, nor woman neither;" but man did
delight Shakespeare—and woman also.

THE END.